DATE DUE			

School
Public Relations

Courtesy Public Schools, Somerville, New Jersey.

School
Public Relations

Leslie W. Kindred

Professor of Education and Director
of the Department of Educational
Administration, Teachers College,
Temple University.

Prentice-Hall, Inc.

ENGLEWOOD CLIFFS, N. J.

First printing .... *May, 1957*
Second printing .... *March, 1962*

Preface

Evidence that the field of school public relations has grown rapidly in recent years is seen in the literature on the subject, course offerings by colleges and universities, in-service training of teachers, public relations offices in large school systems, school radio and television programs, numerous school publications, and the establishment of citizen advisory committees.

This growth has been stimulated by the urgency of problems confronting school systems and a deepening appreciation by educational leaders of the fact that public education depends for its support upon the will of the people.

Along with the new concern for public relations has come much misunderstanding of what it means, how programs are developed, and toward what ends they should be directed.

This book attempts to clarify the present confusion and chart a course of action for schools that is both practical and consistent with the role of the school as a social institution in a democracy. It recognizes that publicity is inherent in public relations, that informational service is necessary for interpreting the school to the community and the community to the school, and that the heart of a dynamic program lies in citizen cooperation and participation in affairs of the school.

It emphasizes the importance of designing programs around the relationship problems of the school and its special publics. The position is taken that unless these problems are dealt with satisfactorily, there is small likelihood that parent and nonparent taxpayers will take a positive interest in the institution, harbor good will toward the staff, provide adequate support, and feel a sense of responsibility for the progressive improvement of public education.

The treatment of public relations presented here is comprehensive in scope and includes up-to-date findings and conclusions of research workers and practitioners in the field. It contains many more ideas and suggestions than any one system could undertake without devoting entirely too much time, money, and manpower to this aspect of its total enterprise. In this respect, however, it supplies a ready source of reference for the enrichment of local efforts and a guide for the development of sound and defensible programs.

A note of thanks is due to the many graduate students who furnished case illustrations of relationship problems in their own school systems. Special acknowledgement is likewise due professional workers who supplied information on their own practices and furnished photographs from which selections were made for this book. They include Bill Baxter, Director, School-Community Relations, Public Schools, Amarillo, Texas; Sylvia Ciernick, Editor of Publications, Public Schools, Dearborn, Michigan; Martha A. Gable, Director, Radio and Television Education, Public Schools, Philadelphia, Pennsylvania; R. C. Glazier, Director of Public Information, Public Schools, Springfield, Missouri; John M. Hickey, Superintendent, Public Schools, Erie, Pennsylvania; John L. Hunt, Coordinator, School-Community Relations, Public Schools, Wilmington, Delaware; Robert B. Johnson, Director, School-Community Relations, Public Schools, Indianapolis, Indiana; John F. Locke, Director of Community Relations, Public Schools, Cincinnati, Ohio; Dora Mary Macdonald, Director, Public Relations, Public Schools, Duluth, Minnesota; Robert H. Munger, Director, Public Relations, Public Schools, Waukesha, Wisconsin; Margaret W. Parham, Director, Public Interpretation Department, Public Schools, Madison, Wisconsin; Richard Pheatt, Public Relations Director, Public Schools, Toledo, Ohio; Ruth Seward, Assistant to the Superintendent, Public Schools, Roslyn, New York; Edward B. Thiele, Assistant to the Superintendent, Public Schools, Philadelphia, Pennsylvania; and Edmund H. Thorne, Superintendent, Public Schools, West Hartford, Connecticut.

LESLIE W. KINDRED

Table of Contents

vii

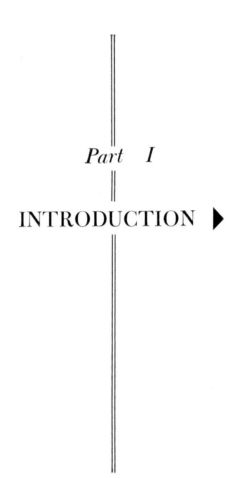

Part   I

INTRODUCTION ▶

1

The School and the Public

Public relations is a comparatively new field in the administration of schools, with possibilities for expansion that have scarcely been explored. It is new in the sense that the importance of this field was not formally recognized until a few years ago and provision made for it in the management of educational institutions. While the idea of public relations has received rather wide attention from boards of education and professional school people, there are still doubts about its place in tax-supported systems and misunderstanding concerning its meaning. Some boards of education and their executive officers seem to feel that they can continue to receive adequate financial support without engaging in planned public relations programs; others question their right to spend public funds for this purpose; and still others, who believe in the need for improving relations between the school and community, are attacking the problem unsoundly. The present situation suggests that American public education has a long way to go before this field of activity becomes an established part of administrative work. However, evidence is available indicating excellent progress in systems where board members and professional personnel understand the nature

3

and place of public relations in education and how public relations may contribute to the improvement of local schools.

In this first chapter, the point of view is stated that public relations is a necessary and natural function of a publicly supported institution. This point of view arises from a consideration of the historical background of the school, the legal framework within which it operates, and the role of public opinion in the shaping of educational policies and practices. While these considerations receive only passing recognition in the chapter, they are nevertheless behind the definition of public relations and the purposes it seeks to accomplish.

THE PUBLIC CHARACTER OF THE SCHOOL

The American public school exists for, belongs to, and is controlled by the people. It derives its public character from the historical background from which it emerged and the legal structure within which it functions.

Historical Background

The public school had its beginning in colonial America where, by the time this country declared its independence of England, public schools supported by taxes, private schools for the wealthy, and pauper schools for those who could not afford to pay for an education were well-established.

That all children should have the benefit of an education was a firm belief among the founders of the new nation. Their conviction was expressed in the Land Ordinance of 1785, which provided that the sixteenth section of each new township, carved out of public lands in the West, should be set aside for the support of schools. Their belief was repeated in the Northwest Ordinance of 1787 with the words "religion, morality, and knowledge being necessary to good government and the happiness of mankind, schools and the means of education shall forever be encouraged." They realized that the government of a free people could not endure without an informed citizenry, and that the constitutional guarantees of civil liberty would be meaningless unless they were understood and exercised intelligently. In their fear of concentrating too much power in the hands of the federal government, they left the right to set up and maintain schools to the states and to the people.

Through the first quarter of the nineteenth century the individual states did little or nothing about the question of establishing systems of schools. They passed responsibility for the education of children back to the local communities and gave each the right to take whatever action the residents wanted. This form of local control first appeared in the New England colonies. It represents the origin of the district or decentralized system which is still found in many states today. Larger towns were often split into a series of districts, for the convenience of the inhabitants who lived too far from the center of the community, and the householders of these districts were made responsible for the operation and maintenance of their own schools.

Town tax money was distributed to the districts, and they were permitted to elect or appoint a committee to spend the funds and supervise the work of the schools. These committees increasingly assumed greater amounts of authority until some became autonomous governmental units. In a few states they were permitted to raise taxes, construct buildings, hire and certify teachers, and perform other tasks of importance.

During the next three decades the story of public education is a story of the small district school and the thousands of young people it educated. But the advantages of the district school were by no means universal in the new nation. A number of states still relied upon private and pauper schools for the education of children. Children from families that could not afford to pay for their schooling or who were too proud to accept charity went without the benefit of a formal education. A good many people in these states, as well as others, were opposed to the idea of taxing themselves for the support of a public school system.

The question of local taxation for the support of free, public education aroused bitter controversy in all sections of the country. Sides were drawn on this issue, and the struggle to resolve it continued for several years. Gradually, people were won over to an acceptance of the principle that all children should be educated at public expense regardless of race, creed, or economic status. One by one the states wrote clauses into their constitutions expressing the popular will, and their legislatures enacted laws making publicly supported schools a reality.

The history of this struggle points up clearly the fact that the public school is a product of the people. They wanted it and created it because they believed in the value of education for both the individual and society.

Legal Structure

The right of the individual states to organize and direct their own school systems grows out of the Tenth Amendment to the United States Constitution. This amendment provides that those powers not delegated by the Constitution to the federal government nor prohibited to the states are state powers. Since no reference of any kind is made in the Constitution to education, the power to establish schools belongs to the states.

Although the states established their own school systems independently of one another, they are remarkably similar in structural design and plan of operation. They placed a state board of education, composed of laymen, at the top of the state system and charged it with responsibility for studying educational needs and conditions, licensing professional personnel, conducting research, and planning for the improvement of public education. General executive oversight of schools was assigned to a state superintendent of public instruction or a commissioner of education, answerable to the state board of education for his conduct in office. He was made head of a state department of education and given the right to select staff specialists for carrying out various duties. His principal functions were made those of seeing that the state minimum program of education was enforced, that opportunities for education were equalized, that services were rendered to local districts, and that leadership was undertaken for the development and improvement of the state school system.

At the same time, the legislatures of the several states created local school districts as subordinate parts of their school systems and freed them from control of other governmental units. The independent local district has been a feature of American education since schools began in the New England colonies. Though changes have occurred in the nature of these districts over the years, nearly one half of them today are in their original form, and their boundaries may or may not coincide with those of local political corporations.

While the organization of local districts differs within states and between states, provision for control of educational effort is much the same throughout the country. Direct authority is delegated to a body of citizens known as a board of education or a board of school directors who are sometimes called trustees. This body is a sovereign governmental agency responsible both to the people of the district and to the state. In this capacity, the local board of education must see that minimum state requirements are carried into effect, and it may develop a supplementary program for meeting the needs of children and respecting the wishes of citizens in the local district. The real strength of American education lies in the measures that local boards have taken to adopt educational offerings to needs and conditions in their own communities.

Because education is a technical process requiring individuals who are trained for the work, administrative responsibility is delegated to a chief executive officer — either a superintendent or a supervising principal — and a professional staff of men and women who function under his direction. Their duties are defined by statute in some states; in others, they are written into the rules and regulations of the local board of education.

It is evident from the legal structure of the state school system and the laws which govern its operation that the power to manage schools resides in the people. On a state-wide basis they have the right to support or oppose suggested legislation affecting the education of children, to work for the repeal and modification of existing laws, and to decide at the polls who shall represent them in the legislature. This right is paralleled at the local level, where they elect fellow citizens to membership on the board of education and expect them to carry out their will. To insure expression of the popular will, the law prescribes that any parent or citizen shall have the privilege of being heard at a regular meeting of the board or to file a written communication setting forth his ideas on matters of educational policy and practice. Regular school board meetings in several states must be open to the public at all times and no vote on school business can be taken by the board in private. The minutes of meetings and records of transactions are public property, and they may be inspected upon request by citizens. The failure of a school board and its members to abide by these and similar regulations may result in dismissal of the board and prosecution of the membership for misconduct in office. The American people conceived the board of education to be a public body, operating with their consent, and they took measures to insure that its character would not change.

THE ROLE OF PUBLIC OPINION

As a social institution, owned and operated by the people, the school depends for its continuance and support upon the status of public opinion. The way citizens think and act in regard to selection of board personnel, tax rates, plant, curricular offerings, salaries, supplies, equipment, special services, and the like, not only establishes the limits of institutional functioning, but also influences the policies and practices by which the work of the institution is done.

It is essential to the effective operation of the school that those who are charged with responsibility for its affairs understand the role of public opinion in a democracy and the way in which it affects the education of children. It is not expected that they be experts on the subject, but they should possess a practical knowledge of what opinion means, why people think as they do, how opinions are formed, and what problems they must deal with in providing leadership for the school.

Public Opinion Defined

No general agreement exists on the meaning of the term "public opinion." Sometimes it is defined as any wide-spread belief or consensus arrived at by members of one or more groups; at other times, as the prevailing customs and traditions handed down by previous generations. The term is frequently associated with the process of developing opinion instead of opinion itself, with fine-line distinctions drawn between judgments reached by logical methods of reasoning and judgments growing out of emotional states of mind. No doubt these and other variations in the meaning of the term have a place in a detailed study and analysis of public opinion, but they are hardly suitable to guide the work of lay and professional school officials. As a working rule, they should think of public opinion as a collection of individual beliefs held more or less in common by the members of a group regarding some person, condition, or proposal.

In this definition, the group may represent one or several of the different publics found in society. A public is any group of persons who are bound together by common beliefs and interests. An individual may be affiliated with a number of publics at the same time. He may, for example, be a member of a political public, a labor public, an art public, a reading public, a sports public, a religious public, and a gardening public. It stands to reason that the members of any given public do not live by themselves in a particular section of the community or even work and play together at one place, yet each public has definite characteristics and patterns of action which set it apart from others. In public relations work, the term "special public" has come into use with reference to particular groups in the community. They are the ones with whom relations are important to the conduct and success of an enterprise. Thus stockholders, employees, suppliers, distributors, retailers, and customers are special publics of the manufacturer; and, by analogy, staff members, pupils, parents, taxpayers, and certain organized groups are special publics of the school.

Determinants of Opinion

The way in which people think about persons, conditions, and proposals is the product of many forces. Not all of these forces are understood, but several have been identified and studied. One of the strongest is custom and tradition. Custom and tradition are decisions made by society in the past which now serve to regulate individual and group conduct without the necessity for bringing the decisions themselves into play. For instance, it is accepted without much question that pupils of different sects shall be dismissed from school for the observance of religious holidays, that the birthdays of famous patriots shall be celebrated annually, and that the cornerstone of a new school building shall be laid by a prominent citizen. Little thought is given to the force of custom and tradition and the influence they exert on attitudes and actions until events arise which threaten or challenge their validity. When this happens, they become live issues which are debated until decisions are reached either to preserve their place in society or to sanction the need for change.

Another force is the system of beliefs and values by which individuals live owing to family rearing, past experiences, economic interests, political outlook, and so forth. This system may be ingrained so deeply that they are unwilling to look at a proposal or study a set of facts about an issue if it in any way runs contrary to their predisposed manner of thought and action. It is difficult to modify the views of these individuals unless the underlying system of beliefs and values is weak enough to yield to a convincing body of factual information.

Public opinion is formed every second of the day by the impact of mass communication media. The more common media are newspapers, magazines, pamphlets, leaflets, motion pictures, radio, television, advertisements, posters, pictures, and cartoons. Because the volume of information poured forth from these sources is too great for any one person to assimilate, much attention has been given to the question of how the average man or woman selects what he wants to see, hear, and read. Some of the findings from studies of this question indicate that information must be reduced to relatively simple forms of thought, feeling, and language in order to hold attention and establish communication; stereotypes, slogans, catch phrases, and similar devices do more to stimulate thought and influence opinion than volumes of reliable information. The average person is swayed more by appeals to emotion than by appeals to reason; now and then, however, emotional tendencies may be overcome by impressive bodies of well-organized information. Information presented to the public is received without much question if it supports the beliefs and opinions of the majority; otherwise the majority may regard it as being idealistic or perhaps radical, and in some instances even socially dangerous.

A number of people prefer to be identified with the majority of their fellow citizens when it comes to taking sides on an issue. They will shelve their own opinions and disregard the known views of experts after it is clear how most members of the group are thinking. They can also be expected to support more willingly the statements of individuals whom they like and admire than the statements of those whom they dislike and to take a stronger interest in arguments involving personalities than those dealing with the merits of an issue.

Face-to-face conversations are a key determinant in the building of public opinion. People like to talk with other people about their views on a controversial matter, to pick up new information, to find out what facts are important, to release pent-up feelings, and to win support for the side they favor. The personal element gives weight and color to information which is exchanged and helps to speed the process of opinion formation. A single conversation, even by telephone, may be more effective in creating attitudes and judgments on an issue than any other form of communication.

Individuals who hold positions of leadership may exert a profound influence on the thinking of those who belong to their group. Often a mere word or suggestion from them is enough to swing sentiment for or against an issue. The facts they present may be accepted without much question and serve as the raw material out of which opinions are fashioned. If necessary, they may resort to clever devices for generating interest and establishing viewpoints along lines of their thinking. While the right to make decisions is an individual matter, the nature of a decision and the action it calls for are, in many instances, the result of leadership.

Real events and happenings enter into the development of public opinion. Events which occur close at hand — in the local community, for example — are usually better understood and have a stronger effect on the feelings and outlook of people than those that take place elsewhere in the county, state, nation, and world. If an event contains dramatic elements and touches human emotions, it may cause a rapid and forceful expression of public opinion. Take for example a newspaper story of a child being seriously injured from corporal punishment received in school for disciplinary reasons. Opinion in the community would be formed within a few hours after the appearance of this story, with the majority of the people probably expressing sympathy for the child and condemning the school. In general, events which stir the thoughts and emotions of people either cause them to view things differently than they did before or tend to strengthen their previous convictions.

This list of determinants would not be complete without making reference to the activities of special interest groups. These are groups of individuals who are joined together for the mutual protection and advancement of their special interests. They represent every social, political, educational, religious, and economic viewpoint in the culture. Some are so well organized and controlled that their members think and act much alike on business, politics, and other matters which lie outside the fields of their special interest. While many are permanent and work for the achievement of a unified and continuing series of objectives, others are temporary and seek the achievement of a single objective. Their methods of operation differ widely. On the one side are those groups who try through legitimate educational means to build public opinion in support of their programs. On the other are those who try to realize their objectives by any means which will produce results, including front organizations, bribery, coercion, and dishonest propaganda. The power of special interest groups and the skillful manner in which their activities are conducted play a significant role in the development of public opinion.

How Opinion Develops

Studies of the process by which public opinion develops show that it moves from one stage to another until a consensus is formed. The stages are discernible but not well marked. Opinion usually begins to develop when an individual is confronted with a problematic situation. The situation may arise from nothing more than an incident reported by the press, a piece of literature received through the mails, or a casual remark of a friend. Often the nature of the situation is not clear — there is a sense of need, a vague feeling, or a cloudy belief about it which the individual tries to express in words but, perhaps, can not do until he has gathered more information.

The concern he feels may be talked over at first with members of the family or a few friends before going any further. If they show interest, display curiosity, and want to know more, the chances are good that they, too, will take up the matter with people they know. As these conversational links continue to increase in number, the problem situation takes on a greater importance and soon becomes a subject of wide attention. It is picked up by the press and radio. Soon the views of prominent citizens are quoted in the newspapers, letters-to-the-editor make their appearance, editorials are written, and popular groups include a consideration of it in their programs.

Once this stage is reached, sides are drawn and efforts are made to win supporters. Ideas, facts, and arguments flow from the newspapers, speeches, debates, public discussions, posters, leaflets, advertisements, motion pictures, and personal conversations. Slogans, myths, stereotypes, symbols, and similar devices help to capture imagination, arouse sentiment, and awaken deep-seated values and prejudices. The extent to which these means are employed to influence public opinion vary with the nature and the importance of the issue.

After a consensus is reached, the final action is an acceptance or rejection of an idea involving a person, a condition, or a proposal. If the issue has been saturated with emotion, the minority may continue to express dissatisfaction and work harder than before to bring about a shift in public opinion.

Problems of the School

School dependence on the status of public opinion brings up problems which require study and solution in order to provide good education for children. One such problem arises from a tendency of the school to lag behind social change and the desires of the people. Those who direct the institution are usually conservative in outlook and hesitant to disturb the established program. If the lag between educational practice and social need becomes too great, the public will take action. It may be in the form of protest meetings, disparaging newspaper publicity, election of new school board members, pressure to replace the superintendent, and refusal to approve tax increase and bond proposals. While these manifestations of discontent may appear to break out rather suddenly, they are more apt to be the product of increasing unrest for some months or even years.

Too rapid a change in educational practice may create a problem which is just as serious. The public always looks with suspicion at any new idea and departure from tradition which is not understood. This has been borne out repeatedly in the history of American education. Many forward-looking plans have died for lack of popular endorsement. The school cannot move too far ahead of the people without inviting their opposition and resentment.

A similar problem arises when professional personnel fail to make a distinction between their own interests and beliefs and those of citizens, or when they confuse the voice of an articulate minority for that of the people. These mistakes inevitably slow down progress and weaken confidence in the school system.

Sometimes the school is a victim of destructive public opinion. People refuse to provide enough support to finance a desirable program and show indifference to the problems which stand in the way of better education. Their attitudes are the product of various causes. These causes may stem from distrust of professional leadership, unpleasant school experiences, ignorance of actual conditions, misinformation, school board policies, and propaganda of special interest groups.

Without doubt the most important problem is that of trying to satisfy the tremendous diversity of opinions and demands held and made by individuals and groups in the state and local community. For example, parents may want a different homework policy; church leaders, a time during the school day for religious instruction; patriotic societies, a stronger emphasis on the teaching of American history; colleges and universities, a high-school curriculum which better meets their admission requirements; tax leagues and real-estate boards, a lower rate of millage; organized teacher groups, a higher salary scale; economic interests, a use of their printed materials in the classroom; labor groups, a more thorough presentation of their views; business concerns, an acceptance of the contests they sponsor; youth groups, a right to solicit members; philanthropic organizations, a drive for funds; and so on. The number is vast. At the same time the more conservative elements of the population bring pressure to preserve traditional values and prevent hasty changes in the educational program, while the more liberal elements try to break down habits of the past and stimulate the rate at which change occurs. No matter what the school tries to do or how it performs daily services, it is always subject to criticism and attack by many individuals and groups in society.

The only defensible answer to this situation is the great principle laid down in the history of democratic peoples. It is the principle of operating in accord with the wishes of the majority. This means that the school must strive constantly to locate on all questions the central tendency of public opinion and to be guided by this tendency in its decisions. However, there are implications attached to this principle which should be examined. (1) Enlightened public opinion cannot be developed unless the people have full access to the facts — know what the school is trying to accomplish, how it is going about the task, how well it is succeeding, and what problems it faces. (2) The people have both the right and the opportunity to an open discussion of this information in order to understand it thoroughly. (3) The people decide in the light of their knowledge and understanding what is best for children and society. Herein lies the crux of sound majority rule.

WHAT IS PUBLIC RELATIONS?

In view of its historical background, legal structure, and dependence on public opinion, the school has a definite responsibility to furnish the tax payers of the community with complete and accurate information concerning its needs and activities and to develop educational policies and practices which are a reflection of their wishes. How to carry out this responsibility efficiently and effectively is the problem of school public relations.

The first formal attack on the problem was made some years ago when the value of newspaper publicity was recognized as a means for keeping the institution before the people and acquainting citizens with the work it was doing. Soon afterwards the realization grew that financial support of education was tied in with the prevailing nature of public opinion. As a consequence, other media of communication were employed to further publicize the school and gain the good will of the electorate. These efforts were followed by the introduction and gradual development of social interpretation, a concept which holds that the school has both a legal and a moral obligation to inform citizens fully and honestly about its purposes, program, needs, and conditions, and that to meet this obligation squarely the community should be interpreted to the school as well as the school to the community. School public relations at present represents an extension of the interpretative point of view, with new discoveries and refinements in communication methods and techniques and a deepening conviction that the school cannot adapt itself to social change nor make the necessary improvements in its program without the intelligent interest and active involvement of citizens.

School public relations, then, is a process of communication between the school and community for the purpose of increasing citizen understanding of educational needs and practices and encouraging intelligent citizen interest and cooperation in the work of improving the school. Stated somewhat differently, school public relations is a combination of the following ideas and practices:

1. A way of life expressed daily by each person on the school staff in his relations with other staff members, pupils, parents, and people in the community—in short, good human relations.

2. A systematic, honest, and continuing series of activities for educating people in the community to the purposes of the school, its program, problems, and accomplishments.

3. A systematic, honest, and continuing series of activities for finding out what people in the community think about their schools and what they want their schools to provide for children.

4. An active partnership between the school and community, in which professional educators and laymen work together for essential modifications and improvements in the educational program.

THE OBJECTIVES OF PUBLIC RELATIONS

The ultimate goal of school public relations is to improve the quality of education for children and youth in a democracy. To realize this goal, some immediate or correlative objectives are necessary in the public relations program. They govern the direction of action and serve as criteria for judging the effectiveness of what is done. These objectives are:

1. To develop intelligent public understanding of the school in all aspects of its operation.

2. To determine how the public feels about the school and what it wishes the school to accomplish.

3. To secure adequate financial support for a sound educational program.

4. To help citizens feel a more direct responsibility for the quality of education the school provides.

5. To earn the good will, respect, and confidence of the public in professional personnel and services of the institution.

6. To bring about public realization of the need for change and what must be done to facilitate essential progress.

7. To involve citizens in the work of the school and the solving of educational problems.

8. To promote a genuine spirit of cooperation between the school and community in sharing leadership for the improvement of community life.

PLANNED PUBLIC RELATIONS

Entirely too many programs in school public relations fail to achieve these or similar objectives. They fall short because they are sporadic in nature, improperly conceived, poorly planned, and crudely executed. A loss of time, effort, and money, some of these programs are actually harmful in their effects upon the public. If a school system wishes to engage in a comprehensive and continuing program of public relations, then it must be willing to plan with care how its character, needs, and services may best be interpreted to the people and how their support and cooperation may best be enlisted in the task of educational improvement.

It will be noted that the organization of the book suggests the steps involved in the successful planning of a school public relations program. The first part establishes the point of view and justification of planned public relations for publicly supported school systems. The second part indicates what information is needed to plan intelligently and what concepts and principles should govern the preparation and operation of the program. The third part takes into account the problems of personal relationships with members of special publics. The fourth part analyzes the problems of institutional relations with organized groups in the community. The fifth part deals with the use of public relations tools for communicating with the school's various publics. The last part treats of organization and administration of the program, including a recapitulation of the steps to follow in planning a program, structural arrangements, responsibilities of personnel, in-service staff training, budget, and methods of determining results.

Montage by Gene Udell.

2

The Need for Public Relations

The public relations point of view has been slow in developing and winning acceptance by boards of education and professional personnel. It was not thought of seriously until the depression years of the 1930's when public clamor grew for a reduction in school expenditures. Educational leaders, seeking to stop the flow of sentiment for lower taxes and limited instructional offerings, wondered why parents and far-sighted taxpayers did not come to the defense and rescue of education. They soon realized, in seeking an answer to their question, that seldom had boards of education and professional personnel taken the public into confidence or asked the people to share responsibility with them for the direction and improvement of their local school systems. The lesson was made clear that public support depends upon intelligent understanding, confidence, and involvement in the affairs of the institution.

Unfortunately, too many school boards and their professional staffs did not profit sufficiently from this lesson and they returned to their old ways after the crisis had passed. The result is apparent today. There are several areas of need replete with public-relations problems that must be solved before satisfactory understanding and effective cooperation between educators and laymen will be achieved.

LEGAL AND MORAL OBLIGATIONS

As discussed in the preceding chapter, education is a function of the state and a responsibility delegated by law to the local school district. Within the local district, statutes specify that the control of schools shall be placed with the board of education or board of trustees who are elected to public office by the citizens and taxpayers of the community. It is their responsibility to place the state foundation program in operation and to develop a supplemental program fitted to conditions and needs of the local district. Because the state foundation program is only a small part of the total educational enterprise, local boards of education and their professional personnel are relatively free to develop almost any kind of education which people in the community want for their children.

In this dual capacity of agents of the state and representatives of the people in the local district, boards of education have far-reaching power and authority over public education. They control the expenditure of funds received from state appropriations and from taxes paid by local residents for support of schools. They have authority over the maintenance and use of school property and the employment of both instructional and noninstructional members of the staff. The decisions which they make regarding curricular offerings, instructional materials, service facilities, and the like have a profound effect on the education and welfare of children who attend the schools. This right to decide what shall and shall not be done is known as the legislative or policy-making function of a board of education.

A board of education also has another function which is just as important as the legislative one. It is appraisal. In the exercise of this function, a board of education decides how efficiently and how effectively its policies have worked out in practice and whether they should be continued, modified, or eliminated. This function is not only implied but is also expressed in the school laws of several states. Its exercise is essential to progress in education.

Both the legislative and appraisal functions of a board of education represent a public trust for which an accounting is due to the people of the state and the local community. Statutes in several states require that school board business shall be public business and that all decisions arrived at by a board of education shall be made in open or public meetings. Some states make it mandatory that the proceedings of the board shall be published in the local press within a specified period of time after each meeting. All records of the board are public property which may be inspected by any citizen upon demand. A number of states have laws calling for the annual audit of financial records and the publication of the audit results. Periodic reports of board actions on certain matters must be supplied to the state department of public instruction, and the tendency is growing to have an annual report of the local system published for the information of taxpayers. The statutes leave no doubt about the public nature of a board of education and the obligations which it has to the people of the state and the local district.

Even if these responsibilities were not expressed or implied in law, boards of education would still have a strong moral obligation to keep the people informed about their actions and the nature of the educational program. They would have this obligation (1) because schools belong to the people, not to school board members or to professional educators; (2) because the cost of maintaining public education is borne directly by citizens of the state and local district; and (3) because those who are paying for the schools have a right to know how children are being educated and whether or not the results are satisfactory.

This is a primary area of need for a carefully organized, continuous informational service to the public.

PUBLIC UNDERSTANDING OF SCHOOLS

The failure of boards of education and their professional employees to interpret the school to the community and the community to the school has brought about a condition which should be corrected in many districts. The people residing in these districts do not understand their own schools, what they are like, the good work they are doing, and what progress they have made in recent years. It is not surprising that they regard their schools as a cause of higher taxes rather than a sound, social investment, and that they view with some suspicion any proposal for their improvement. Until they come into a more accurate and complete understanding of what education their money purchases and how much it is worth to the democratic way of life, they will continue to maintain their present attitudes. The problem of public understanding of public education stands out as a factor that must be studied and met in a public relations program.

Current Confusion

In dealing with this problem, it is well to look at the changes which have taken place in public education since the turn of the century. As the nation has grown, thousands upon thousands of young people have entered the school, swelling its ranks in far greater proportion to the total population than was true before. Compulsory attendance and child labor laws forced many into classrooms who would never have received a formal education or who, if they did enroll, would have left at an early age to enter employment. They brought with them a vast range of individual problems in intelligence, vocational outlook, cultural interests, language usage, and social values, which forced the school to adjust its curricular offerings and provide a host of new services as medical examinations, dental examinations, bus transportation, special classes, cafeterias, guidance clinics, and remedial instruction.

In the absence of accurate information and direct contact with educational institutions, the average person scarcely realizes what this vast population of youngsters has meant in public education. He cannot comprehend with any reasonable degree of understanding why public schools should cost as much as they do, why curricular offerings are different, what standards have been altered, and why high school graduates seem less capable than their predecessors. He still views the school in terms of his own experiences and the comments he hears from others. He would like to judge its work fairly because of his faith in the power of public education, but he does not have the facts to think with or the information for forming sound opinions.

His attitudes toward the school are shaped still more by the disagreements expressed by members of the teaching profession on matters of curriculum and instructional methods. Those who belong to older schools of thought often close their eyes to the necessity of change and are unable to see much that is good in modern practice.

Instead of confining their prejudices to professional circles and threshing out differences in private, the more emotional ones take their grievances to the public. They have been known to denounce colleagues and condemn administrators who stand for ideas and beliefs they are unwilling to accept. The more zealous supporters of modern education sometimes make the same mistake. This type of open conflict between professional personnel is difficult for the public to follow.

But public confusion does not stop here. It is increased by the ideas and opinions of college presidents, professors of education, and prominent laymen. There is scarcely a popular magazine or daily newspaper that does not carry an article or report a speech by a member of one of these groups. Stated in good faith, their views and recommendations range from a return to classical education to ultra-progressive education, with many gradations in between these extremes. It is understandable why interested citizens and parents of school children have trouble trying to decide what to believe and how to appraise their local schools.

Questions and Criticisms

The upshot of these and other forces playing upon the parent, employer, and taxpayer has been a stronger interest in and a more questioning attitude toward the public school program. Studies have revealed that these people are asking many questions for which they would like answers. They want to know what is being taught to children, how they are being taught, and whether or not the results are good. They are concerned as to the place of subject matter in the curriculum, the status of the "3 R's," study habits, discipline, and preparation for life. They ask why the school cafeteria should show a profit, how their schools compare with those of similar size, what records their high school graduates make in college, if so many extracurricular activities are necessary, what provision is made for the gifted child, why employers complain about the pupils they hire, and whether or not they are paying too much for public education.

Their questions are often accompanied by a series of criticisms which strike deeply into the core of the instructional program. The school is accused of practicing "soft" pedagogy, refusing to look at life, neglecting character training, being indifferent to pupil welfare, doing a poor job of citizenship training, contributing to juvenile delinquency, and "watering down" its program.

Whether or not educators take these criticisms seriously and attempt to defend themselves is beside the point for the moment. The fact remains that they represent the beliefs and opinions of a substantial number of people in many communities and pose a problem which must be evaluated in the planning of a public relations program.

INCREASING PUBLIC PARTICIPATION

The historical background of the school and the laws of the state imply a partnership between professionals and laymen in the planning of educational programs and the improvement of educational practices. It is this implication, as much as anything else, which gives rise to the definition of public relations and the purposes of a public relations program. In order for this partnership to become active and vital, situations must be created for the mutual exchange of ideas, discussion of problems, sharing of responsibility, and the formulation of recommendations without denying or infringing upon the legal rights of the board of education.

Although the partnership concept is implicit in the social nature of the school, and although it has been shown by experience that people take more interest, acquire a better understanding, and more willingly support the institution when they participate in its affairs, nevertheless the idea of a working partnership is frowned upon in a good many school districts.

Some superintendents and boards of education have taken this position for a number of reasons: (1) Close cooperation makes it imperative that complete information about the school system be made available to laymen, and the possibility is present that such information may be misinterpreted and work a hardship on the superintendent and his professional associates. (2) Such information in the hands of malcontents and certain special interest groups is often distorted in order to discredit schools and to develop public opinion that is antagonistic to their effective functioning. (3) Experience with lay groups in some communities indicates that their members demand action on important proposals without being willing to assimilate background materials essential to sound thinking, or they use the meetings with educators to air personal bias and further the cause of an organization they represent. (4) The average parent may be strongly interested in sharing responsibility for his child's education, but his contribution to curriculum improvement and instructional methodology is too meagre to compensate for the time involved. And (5) many who participate in instructional programs fail to distinguish between their role as advisers and the authority of principals and teachers; they assume a right to tell school personnel how to run their business and frequently disrupt the normal operation of the institution. "Why", superintendents ask, "should a relationship be encouraged which is fraught with difficulties and uncertain outcomes and one which the public does not demand?"

It is precisely this question which explains why educators have allowed a wide gap to grow between themselves and the public. In doing so they have lost sight of the social character of the institution and the equity of the people. The barriers erected against participation have slowly turned wholesome interest into indifference and a feeling of futility in trying to arouse administrators and teachers to another point of view. This condition has crystallized and is difficult to change. It is unquestionably a major factor behind the loss of popular confidence in various districts and the unwillingness of taxpayers in these districts to support adequately a program they no longer understand. Unless they have a voice in deciding what they want for their children, with the help of educators, and how much should be spent for the purpose, there is little promise for future improvement in the status of schools.

EDUCATIONAL PROGRESS

Making parents and citizens partners in the development of educational programs contributes to the solution of a long-standing problem confronting the school. It is the problem of securing public approval for progressive change in curriculum and methods of teaching. Like other institutions, the school must fit its program to new social conditions and shape its practices in accordance with the findings of research. However, before this can be done, the average man and woman must understand the need for change and see how it will benefit children and society.

The Educational Lag

The strongest influence affecting the instructional program is custom and tradition or the opinions and beliefs that have assumed fixed and definite form in the minds of people. They are the criteria by which institutional effort is appraised, and any departure from them is usually met with sharp resistance. This resistance is sufficiently powerful in American life to prevent change from taking place unless it rests upon a broad, favorable basis of public opinion. Such opinion is usually slow in coming, the exceptions arising in times of outstanding social need.

The prevailing pattern of American education is one with its roots anchored securely in the past. Though some adjustments have been made because of changed political, economic, and social conditions, basic purposes and theories of learning have remained pretty much the same. Great reverence is still shown for the study of organized bodies of subject matter that are often abstract and far removed from contemporary life, and for the power they are assumed to have for the cultural enlightment and economic salvation of the individual who studies them. Tied in with this doctrine is a belief that the study of difficult subjects disciplines the mind and develops the individual into a person who is capable of meeting the problems he will encounter later in life. The process by which learning takes place is that of drill and memorization until mastery of a subject has been attained. Differences between individuals are glossed over lightly in a desire to maintain academic standards, and it matters not whether the information acquired bears any relationship to personal needs of young people or the demands of society.

This formula for education would be an acceptable one if social conditions were not constantly changing. New contributions in the field of science are a daily occurrence; political problems that involve relationships of groups in a world community and affect the way of life of all concerned are constantly arising; democracy is being challenged as never before; and the labor market has undergone radical change in skills required for employment. The adequacy of traditional instruction is doubtful in an environment where the individual must be able to revise or adapt his behavior to different sets of conditions and to cope with problems in a rapidly shifting social scene. Psychological theory and common sense point the way to a type of education that will bring the individual into direct contact with the life around him and, through experience in dealing with actual problems, acquire the knowledge, skills, attitudes, and appreciations essential to successful personal and social living.

The great need for revising traditional education in America has not been recognized nor sufficiently understood by the average person. He continues to hold to his cherished beliefs and convictions; he sanctions a pattern of instruction which lags far behind the demands of the times.

Teacher Attitudes

The failure of the school to adjust to changing social conditions is due not only to the mores of the community but also to the inertia of the teaching profession. The profession is supplied with individuals drawn from the general public who bring into the schools the same attitudes and opinions toward social progress as the people they represent. Likewise, there are teacher training institutions which perpetuate this condition by preparing graduates predominately in the field of traditional education. Moreover, some beginning teachers, inspired with a zeal for progress, often go through discouraging experiences. They find that their colleagues and administrators look with disfavor upon educational concepts and procedures that are different from those of the established program. The discovery is soon made that it is better to leave the real problems of education untouched than to incur the disfavor of colleagues and the possible criticisms of people in the community.

There are, of course, some leaders who have encouraged teachers to approach learning problems from an experimental point of view. They realize that new ideas and the findings of laboratory research must be put to test under practical conditions. Wisely, they have familiarized the public and their professional staff with such proposals before attempting experimentation. Where consent is forthcoming—though securing it is slow in many instances—the results have more than justified their efforts. On the other hand, a graveyard of excellent curricular projects and programs stretches across the country for want of support by the profession and the public. Strangely enough, those who vehemently oppose the application of experimental procedures to learning situations or the creation of special units for educational research in public school systems agree that the scientific and technical testing of theories and ideas has paid big dividends in government and industry.

The lack of progress in public education will not be overcome until the people understand why change must take place and how newer types of instructional programs will affect their children and society. They must be given the information that will enable them to see this problem and to appreciate its implications. The demand must come from the people before the teaching profession as a whole will be willing to assume responsibility or initiate action for instructional improvement.

FINANCIAL SUPPORT

Closely allied with the problem of progress is that of securing greater financial support for schools. Educators believe that most of the difficulties they experience could be met if adequate funds were available. They refer to the loss of excellent teachers, overcrowded classrooms, insufficient supplies, poor equipment, old buildings, and low morale among members of the profession. All are related to the question of finance and must be considered in apprising the public of the needs and conditions of the schools.

The Teacher Crisis

The recent war years witnessed an exodus of men and women from the teaching profession into other fields of employment where salaries were higher and conditions of work better than those in public schools. It was expected that this movement would come to a halt after the close of hostilities and that many former teachers would return to the positions they had left. Some did return, but large numbers were unwilling to accept the salaries offered in education and preferred to remain in the jobs they were doing. This condition has improved, but the profession is still losing hundreds of experienced teachers annually.

Along with the loss of teachers has been the decline in student enrollments in teacher training institutions. The decline started abruptly during the war and has shown only slight gains since that time, notwithstanding the unprecedented rise in college and university enrollments. It reflects the fact that intelligent young people are not entering teaching as a profession when they can enter business and industrial employment for higher wages. Teaching will continue to lose these young people unless stronger financial incentives are offered.

Both the loss of experienced personnel and the insufficient enrollments in teacher training institutions have contributed to the critical teacher shortage now facing the nation. When the shortage first became acute during the early forties, state departments of public instruction tried to meet it by issuing emergency certificates to anyone who had a few qualifications and a willingness to teach. It was thought that emergency certificates would only be needed for the duration of the war and could be recalled shortly afterwards. Unfortunately, supply never caught up with demand and the gap has continued to grow wider.

It is apparent that the public does not understand or appreciate what is involved in directing the learning of a child, otherwise it would sanction the payment of salaries which are high enough to retain experienced teachers and attract competent new ones to the profession.

Physical Condition

Similar indifference to the welfare of pupils is found in the physical conditions under which learning takes place. Owing to national defense requirements, school building construction was halted for nearly five years. The depression period, just before this, cut badly into essential housing for a steadily growing school population. The backlog of construction is tremendous. It has been compounded further by the accumulation of unsafe and outdated structures and the high birth rate of children in the war and post-war years.

The inadequacy of space has forced scores of public schools to enlarge class size and crowd pupils into rooms which were designed to accommodate a limited number. Effective work cannot be done under these conditions. Teachers have difficulty in getting well acquainted with pupils and understanding their needs. Only passing attention can be given to growth in social attitudes, habits of work, critical thinking, healthful living, and the application of principles to life situations. Class size cannot be reduced without increasing costs and raising taxes that must be approved by the public.

Supplies and Equipment

The urgent need for more and better supplies and equipment stands out as a consideration for increased financial support. Schools have been short on these items for several years. During the depression they were required to cut budgets for basic supplies, and then subsequently to abide by war restrictions. The same thing happened in the case of equipment, with the exception of shop machinery which the government furnished for the national defense training program. Most of this equipment was turned over to the schools after the war, but very little has been done since to replace that which was worn out or became obsolete. It is estimated that twice the amount of money now being spent is necessary to bring supplies and equipment up to desirable standards.

Curriculum Improvement

The school curriculum should provide learning experiences which best equip children and youth for life today and tomorrow. To realize this objective, the curriculum must undergo steady revision and improvement. New courses are essential to meet the demands of a changing society. Content must be reviewed and brought up to date, and materials that are no longer useful must be eliminated. Advantage must be taken of discoveries and developments in the fields of education and psychology. The work involved in curriculum improvement is expensive. It calls for the time of trained men and women within the school system and the technical advice of outside specialists. Provision for the cost must be made in current operating budgets. As yet, the public does not understand the need for spending money to meet this cost in their school districts.

Staff Morale

Insufficient funds for salaries and the maintenance of desirable working conditions have affected staff morale in many school systems. This is expected. Teachers cannot feel enthusiastic about their work in an atmosphere of rigid economy and public indifference to the importance of their services. As a group, they do not seek incomes which are unreasonable, but ask instead for the right to enjoy adequate food, clothing, and shelter and freedom from major financial worries. They feel entitled to salaries which are commensurate with the nature and importance of their contributions to society. As matters now stand, the incomes of a high percentage are below those received by skilled and semiskilled labor. The correction of this condition lies in increased financial support of public education.

Local Support

Local taxation is the principal source of revenue for school districts. Taxes are either paid directly to the district or else to the local government. In the latter arrangement, the school budget must be submitted to officers of the political corporation. This type of financial dependence often works a hardship, because funds are diverted from education to other forms of political service. Better support of schools is assured when the local board of education is empowered by law to levy its own taxes and appeal for funds directly to the people.

In either case, however, the amount of tax support depends, in the final analysis, upon the attitudes and opinions of the people. If they do not possess a knowledge of school needs and conditions, they will not approve proposals for increasing the rate of taxes. The failure of school boards and administrators to supply them with accurate and understandable information, to establish communication, or to give them a part in educational and financial planning, has been responsible for the inadequate support of public education.

THE STATUS OF TEACHERS

Raising the status of teachers is an objective which should be included in every public relations program. Compared with the members of other professions, notably law, medicine, dentistry, engineering, and architecture, teachers occupy a secondary place in community life, despite the fact that many have undergone an equal, if not longer, period of preparation for their work. Generally, their services are not held in similar esteem, nor are they accorded much recognition. The public thinks that their work is important, but not as important as that of people in other professions. They have always been regarded as a group apart from the rest of the community and have seldom enjoyed the respect and confidence to which they are entitled. There are reasons why the public feels this way about teachers. Some of these reasons are plausible, others are not. In any case, they should be examined in planning a program to better the status of teachers.

Satirical Treatment

From colonial days to the present the teacher has been the butt of caricature and satire in novels, plays, cartoons, radio programs, television programs, and motion pictures. The early writers of fiction originated the mythical teacher, and their descriptions of him have been accepted as being typical of the whole profession. They pictured the hardships and sorrows of children who were under the stern and unbending discipline of the schoolmaster. Occasionally they made him a rank sentimentalist or a doting crank whose behavior evoked feelings of scorn and contempt. Seldom did he win the respect and admiration of those who followed his career on the printed pages of a book.

The pattern set by these early writers was taken up and perpetuated by cartoonists. With exceptions here and there, they have usually depicted the teacher as a man or woman whose appearance borders on the ludicrous. He is shown in the unpleasant act of reprimanding a pupil or else he is made to appear as a narrow-minded reformer bent on destroying the pleasures of childhood. His caricature has come to symbolize a "species" of individual who comprise the teaching profession. These distortions, though seemingly harmless, continue to damage the reputation of all who are associated with the profession.

A more powerful force in this respect is radio, television, and motion pictures. Through dramatic presentations involving teachers and administrators, feelings of like or dislike may be created in a short period of time. Perhaps those who cast educators in despicable roles do not realize the seriousness of their actions and how this casting has added to popular misconceptions concerning members of the educational profession.

Pupil Reactions

Pupil reactions to teachers are instrumental in molding public opinion. At home and in the community they express their likes and dislikes of teachers and tell of incidents and events that take place in school. Occasionally they exaggerate and distort the facts, but in the main they give a fairly accurate picture of teachers and their relations with pupils. Fortunately, teachers in modern schools are sensitive to the value of good relations with pupils in the learning process. Their understanding and treatment of pupils draws praise and appreciation from discerning parents. However, there are teachers who have not yet realized the importance of friendly and constructive relations with pupils. They continue to embarrass them before classmates, give unreasonable amounts of homework, engage in emotional outbursts, and show their prejudices. These teachers furnish the raw material which lowers respect for themselves in the eyes of the community and casts a murky shadow on the whole profession. The problems they create must be taken up in the public relations program.

Parent Relations

Parent and teacher relations are another area in which the profession continues to pay a price for the short-sightedness of some of its members. Most teachers understand the need for establishing good relations with parents. They see in them a means for furthering the education of children and enlarging upon lay appreciation of the instructional process. But there are some who oppose the idea of joining forces with parents in the pursuit of common purposes. They maintain that parents become trouble-makers if given half a chance, and that their presence means more labor. When occasions arise wherein parents would like to discuss child problems, assist on field trips, provide instructional materials, or make inquiries as to the reasons for certain policies, they are swiftly rebuffed and left with the feeling of not being wanted or welcomed at the school. Many are so incensed by this treatment that they would like to make an issue out of it, but hesitate to do so for fear that teachers will retaliate by taking their spite out on children.

Professional Conduct

Quite often teachers are their own worst enemies in lowering the status of the group to which they belong. They do not keep professional business to themselves, or within their own ranks, but talk about their disputes and disagreements in the community. Usually their complaints are made against the profession itself, colleagues, and the administration under which they are employed. A similar pattern of behavior is carried on by their professional organizations.

The denunciation of the profession of teaching by teachers themselves appears to be paradoxical until the causative aspects of it are considered. It begins with the disillusionment of young people who enter the field with high ideals and a genuine enthusiasm to make teaching an outstanding career. After a year or two on the job they discover that the rewards for superior instruction, material or otherwise, are not much different from those received for an inferior grade of work. The administration appears to be content if they maintain satisfactory discipline, abide by the rules of the board of education, and keep out of trouble. This pattern is fairly typical in traditional schools where established practices repeat themselves year after year and little is offered by way of professional challenge for self-improvement. Laboring under heavy classroom and extra-classroom assignments, seldom receiving recognition for outstanding service or encouragement to experiment with new ideas; harassed daily with financial troubles in trying to make ends meet, they become discouraged and disappointed with their lot in life. No attempt is made to hide these sentiments from the public. As a result, teachers give the impression of being dissatisfied with their own profession and of not having much pride in it.

This impression is intensified at times by the discredit which a small number heap upon their colleagues. They discuss petty differences and personal bias openly with neighbors and friends. Parents are told that lack of pupil success is due to poor instruction in previous classes. Fearful of anything that may threaten their own security, they try to undermine the efforts of supervisors and fellow staff members who wish to make curriculum improvements.

Now and then similar expressions of unethical conduct mark the relationships of teachers and administrators. Each blames the other for undesirable conditions within the system. The unwholesome nature of this relationship soon becomes a matter of common knowledge in the community.

Last, the public has been made a party to disagreement and discord between professional teachers' associations. Seldom do these groups ever present a united front on any issue or keep their conflicts within the family. Their actions on salary, tenure, retirement, sick-leave, and similar matters have created poor impressions. The public has come to think of them as selfish pressure groups that are indifferent to the plight of taxpayers and the welfare of children. While the facts may justify their efforts for economic security and protection, their methods have been damaging to the profession. It is obvious that they are not sensitive to the need for good public relations and that they have created a problem which demands solution.

PRESSURE GROUPS

In all walks of American life people belong to organized groups and associations in which they share common interests and ideals with fellow members. Many of these groups take a direct interest in public education. The reasons for their interests are varied. They may be concerned with keeping down the cost of education; protecting children from un-American ideas; having their views incorporated in the program of studies; advertising products and services; securing competent young people for future employment; rendering needed services, and so forth. Those that seek directly or indirectly to impose their interests on the school are referred to as pressure groups.

Most large pressure groups in this country are organized at national, state, and local levels. They have paid executives and technical specialists for developing and implementing their programs. The methods which they use to influence public education include lobbying, radio programs, motion pictures, visual aid kits, speakers' bureaus, youth movements, printed leaflets and pamphlets, free books and monographs appropriate for classroom use, all sorts of contests, special drives, sponsorship of school activities, membership on boards of education, committees to investigate school costs and practices, newspaper and magazine articles, and direct contact with school officials. Some are handled with such refinement that the public is scarcely aware of them.

As an agency concerned with the wholesome development of children, the school must cooperate fully with all groups exercising an educative function. It is only through such cooperation that educative forces can be marshalled and directed toward the attainment of those goals in community life which make effective growth and development possible. However, a line must be drawn sharply between cooperation and exploitation when working with groups that profess an interest in child welfare. This distinction is important because the American public school is committed by heritage to uphold the principle of being a classless institution, free from bias and prejudice in its teaching. This principle does not preclude the careful study by children of all points of view in our society in a search to discover truth or to understand the social ferment. It means that the moment one viewpoint gains ascendency to the disadvantage or exclusion of another, then the school is no longer fulfilling its obligation to all the people.

The public does not realize the extent to which certain pressure groups have wormed their way into the school. Under the guise of cooperating with educational institutions, they have been active in curriculum development programs and the selection of instructional materials containing propaganda. They have been successful in electing members to boards of education who can exercise authority in shaping school policies. Considerable evidence is available disclosing their legislative activities and the motives behind the measures they have supported. A new high has been reached in contests under their sponsorship. An increase has taken place in front organizations of these groups, known as school development councils and school protective leagues, whose function is that of cutting the tax dollar for education.

Pressure groups stand as a threat to the impartiality of educa-

Part II

PREPARING THE PROGRAM ▶

Courtesy Public Schools, West Hartford, Connecticut.

3

Understanding the Community

The preparation of a school public relations program should start with the collecting, organizing, and analyzing of factual information about the community. The method of obtaining this information on life within the geographical area served by the school is known as a sociological survey. The sociological survey is not new; it has been used by educators, sociologists, and business people to eliminate guesswork in planning various kinds of projects. The survey has been subject to much criticism in recent years because of misuse and wasteful expenditures of time and labor. However, properly conducted surveys have demonstrated their value as tools in the achievement of important objectives.

IMPORTANCE OF THE SURVEY

Effective planning depends upon a thorough understanding of the setting in which the plan will operate. Planning a public relations program is no exception to the rule. It must start with a factual knowledge of people in the community and how they live. The more that is known about them, the better are the chances for establishing successful communication. Some administrators argue that a survey is unnecessary, since they already know their own communities. They may be right. Usually a check on how much they know reveals a limited understanding of the community and a superficial insight into the significant facts that should be known about the life of the people.

The viewpoint of these administrators is reflected in the public relations programs of the school systems for which they are responsible. Copied after the practices of business and industry, they center around the chief executive and his immediate subordinates. With few minor exceptions, the programs consist of several stereotyped activities. They are the publication of an annual report, news releases, special pamphlets and leaflets, membership in civic organizations, identification with charitable and welfare movements, personnel addresses, radio appearances, and cultivation of friendships with members of power groups in the community. Subordinate administrative officers are instructed to handle publicity on extracurricular activities, encourage safe parent-teacher relations, hold open-house programs, and resolve minor conflict situations.

There is no doubt but that these activities have value in promoting goodwill and keeping the taxpayers of the community better informed about their school system. Unfortunately, they seldom get at fundamental public relations problems and fail to establish communication with groups who should be receiving interpretative materials. More particularly, they are not designed with reference to such matters as the reasons for unfriendly attitudes toward the school, the opportunities for working with community groups and agencies, respect for prevailing customs and traditions, avoidance of situations involving a past history of conflict, knowledge of the friends and enemies of public education, educational backgrounds of the population, cultural tensions, and the channels through which public opinion is built in the community. The time has come to eliminate the borrowed program idea and to plan public relations in terms of the known facts about the community.

SCOPE OF THE SURVEY

A comprehensive community survey covers all aspects of land, people, and culture in a geographic area. Such a survey is time-consuming and expensive to make. Most school systems have neither sufficient personnel nor the willingness to spend money that is needed for undertaking this type of survey. If they did, there is still a danger that the staff would not be competent and that the amount of work involved would be too heavy. It is better to limit the survey at the beginning to those aspects of community life which feed most directly into program planning and, after experience has been gained, to increase the scope by continuing study. Accordingly, the survey should concentrate initially upon (1) customs and traditions, (2) population characteristics, (3) communication channels, (4) organized groups, (5) leadership, (6) social tensions, and (7) history of community efforts.

Customs and Traditions

As stated in a preceding chapter, customs and traditions are the common ideas, attitudes, and habits of people which are referred to generally as folkways and mores of groups in the community. They are powerful factors in regulating conduct and shaping social action. The differences found among groups in customs and traditions are due to the influence of race, religion, national origin, economics, politics, and class structure. Thus the way of life followed by the Pennsylvania Amish Mennonites hinges for the most part upon respect for religious principles, while that of the Polish-Americans in Hamtramck, Michigan, owes much to their national origin. For similar reasons, the code of social conduct observed in a wealthy Chicago suburban area would differ widely from the one upheld in the Harlem district of New York City. Saint Patrick's Day is celebrated in this country by the Irish, and ancient dietary regulations are maintained by Hebrews and Catholics because of tradition and religious convictions. Unless the population is fairly homogeneous in race, religion, national origin, or one or two other factors, many different customs and traditions will be found among groups that comprise the community.

The problem in this part of the survey is that of finding out the customs and traditions as well as the patterns of thought and action of groups in the community. The school must have this information to guide its relations with pupils, parents, and others. Nothing evokes

a quicker reaction from parents and citizens than educational policies and practices which run counter to their established attitudes,
beliefs, and habits. This has been evident in the mistakes made in introducing new blocks of subject matter into the curriculum, encouraging pupils to think and act contrary to family customs, retaining
youngsters after school on days for religious instruction in their
churches, and teaching sex education without consulting parents and
religious organizations.

Of equal value is knowing how change takes place in community
group patterns of thought and action. Sociological studies indicate
that safe and rapid change takes place during periods of emergency,
such as a war period; that alterations in the physical characteristics
of a community, like new highways, improved housing, and rezoning
open the way for modifying social habits and customs; and that new
inventions and discoveries have a tremendous impact on conventional
ways of living. Research has also shown that significant changes can
be brought about when members of different groups are brought
together for the solution of problems in which they share a common
interest.

Population Characteristics

Boards of education and administrative officials have learned
the value of making studies of size and growth of population. They
use these studies for estimating enrollments, determining personnel
needs, ordering supplies and equipment, and selecting sites for new
buildings. They have not yet fully learned that there are other characteristics of the population which are worth a great deal in developing educational programs and plans for public relations. These
characteristics concern the educational attainments of the people,
age, sex, gainful occupations, race, color, creed, and nationality backgrounds.

In looking at the educational attainments of the people, attention is fixed on the number of years of formal schooling completed
by adults in the community. The amount of schooling may be classified under elementary, secondary, and college attendance. Finer
distinctions may be drawn. This information has three major uses.
The first is to prepare printed materials which can be understood

Population studies include a systematic check of building permits and new home construction.

without effort by the audiences for whom they are intended. The second is to estimate the best manner of handling ideas and facts so they will command attention and stimulate interest. The third is related to the building of stratified samples for opinion polling, a subject which will be discussed in the next chapter.

Age data should likewise be broken down into three classifications for adults in the population. These classifications are young, middle, and old. The percentage in each classification should be determined. It is possible from this information to make working estimates of community reaction to various kinds of proposals. A population which is skewed more heavily toward the upper age brackets is generally more conservative than one which is skewed in the opposite direction. A high percentage in the upper middle and

43

old age groups means fewer children in school and less interest in the everyday problems of education. The willingness of population to finance an adequate school program is also tied in with age distribution. These data are useful as well in building stratified samples for opinion polling.

Sex distribution is a control factor in building stratified samples for opinion polling.

Occupational information on gainfully employed adults may be treated conveniently under headings used in the United States Census Reports. It is valuable for educational and public relations purposes. Among the educational purposes are the determination of vocational offerings, vocational guidance, and the placement of high school graduates. In public relations planning, the data may be used to check stability of the population, changing occupational opportunities, distribution of occupational classes, and employment outside of the community. Findings on these points may make a significant difference in the selection of program activities and the degree of response expected from members of the community.

The study of population characteristics should be rounded out with data about race, religion, color, and nationality background. These cultural factors are of vital importance in understanding the community and some of the causes underlying social tensions. Sometimes their meaning, however, is not clear until they are correlated with other information. The data should be treated statistically, and summary findings should be prepared for distribution to individual building principals. At the same time, as much of this information as possible should be depicted on social base maps. Separate sections may be blown up for use in respective attendance areas. The statistical summaries and social base maps often provide essential leads in seeking solutions to everyday problems which arise out of relations with pupils, parents, and members of the community.

Communication Channels

Since the development of public opinion takes place through the exchange of ideas and information, it is necessary to know what communication channels are available in the community, how extensively they are used, and which ones are most effective for reaching different groups of people. This phase of the survey might start with an inventory of the homes in which a foreign language is read and spoken. It is reasonable to assume that parents of school children who read and speak a foreign language in the home have difficulty understanding report cards, school notices, and news released to local papers. This problem may be confined to only one or two sections of the city. Positive findings may indicate the need for establishing communication. Possible solutions lie in the employment of bi-lingual home and school visitors, school materials printed in more than one language, and the preparation of news stories for foreign language periodicals and newspapers.

Most attention in the study of communication channels should be directed to the question of where and how people receive a substantial share of their information on local events and happenings. This question is not easy to answer, but it can be worked out by persistent inquiry. It may be found that the general public relies on radio, television, and daily newspapers for most of its current information and that these three channels are significant in the development of public opinion. On the other hand, the investigation may reveal that members of special groups in the community receive their information from a variety of unsuspected sources. These sources may include church pulpits, labor union headquarters, fraternal organizations, volunteer fire companies, tabloid and neighborhood newspapers, and little-known societies. And further, that these sources are by far the most effective means available for reaching members of these groups with interpretative materials. Sound planning requires accurate data on communication channels.

Organized Groups

The American community, large or small, is a composite of groups of people who are organized around special interests. Most groups are easy to join, while a few have a qualifying test for memberships. No community survey is complete without knowing the programs of these groups and estimating their influence on public opinion.

A number of organized groups conduct programs with educational features paralleling welfare and instructional services of the school. They take an interest in public education and stand willing to cooperate with school authorities. This has been true of labor unions which, from their beginning, have maintained a platform on behalf of free, universal education and the enactment of legislation to increase educational opportunities. Luncheon clubs, like the Rotary and Kiwanis, have long sponsored projects for the welfare of school children. At least three national organizations devote a major portion of their program to the teaching of better citizenship and the promotion of American ideals and institutions. There is no end of groups that work on juvenile delinquency, recreation, family life, vocational guidance, museums, libraries, aid for crippled children, and a host of other commendable services. Many offer fine opportunities for the articulation of programs and the strengthening of contributions to school and community.

While cooperation with community groups having an educative function to perform should be encouraged to the fullest, care must be taken to prevent domination and the exploitation of pupils. With some groups, cooperation means the right to insist that the school abide by their dictates and modify its own program to achieve the things they are working for. With others, cooperation is nothing more than a guise for the privilege of disseminating propaganda in the classroom, promoting product sales, and conducting campaigns and contests for the sake of publicity.

It is wise procedure to look for and record on file cards specific types of information on every group in the community. The cards should show the name of the organization, past and present officers, size of membership, purposes, program, methods of operation, accomplishments, and attitudes toward public education. Judgments can then be made respecting cooperation and support for proposals to improve education in the local school system.

The study of organized groups leads into the question of how much power they exercise over social, political, and economic life in the community. The facts may show that power rests in the hands of a relatively small group of individuals and, without their support, nothing of importance can be accomplished in the community. More typically, however, the evidence points to power control by industrial and commercial groups because of the influence they exert over the economic life of the community. Knowing where the power lies and

how the power system operates prevents procedural errors and conflicts that might be harmful to the support of education. The building of informed public opinion is the best antidote for power groups
that are antagonistic to public education.

Also, the question should be raised as to the extent to which individuals and families participate in the activities of organized
groups, and especially those having to do with civic welfare. Amount
of participation is a fairly reliable index of community spirit. The
findings of sociological research show that, when individuals and
families are active in organized group programs, they take a stronger
interest in what happens to their community; and that, when they are
inactive or take part only occasionally, they are indifferent to needed
improvements. Some assistance may be gained in estimating community spirit by using the Chapin Social Participation Scale. Though
it is limited to participation of husband and wife in organized social
groups, nevertheless it is helpful in judging what to expect from the
community. The objectives of a public relations program are harder
to achieve in districts with little community spirit.

Leadership

Group analysis should be followed by research on leadership in
the community. Every group is headed or controlled indirectly by
individuals who are recognized leaders. They have an influence on
the attitudes and opinions of group members. Too much cannot be
known about them. Information should be obtained on their personal backgrounds, family connections, group affiliations, business
interests, fraternal memberships, social and political beliefs, special
competencies, methods of operation, attitudes toward public education, and power in the community. A knowledge of these things is
essential in approaching group leaders on educational problems and
determining what services they may be asked to render for the
schools.

It must be remembered, in working with leaders, that they are
not always free to express their own ideas and to take independent
action. Their behavior is conditioned by the nature of the groups
they lead and by what the members hold to be true. They are particularly sensitive to questions involving patriotism, private property,

economic doctrine, religion, political organization, and conventions, realizing that any radical departure from the feelings and convictions of their followers undermines their own security. However, leadership is a reciprocal arrangement in that groups depend upon them, except in a few highly specialized organizations, to initiate ideas and execute plans of action. People en masse seldom formulate ideas and devise ways to express them in practice. The leaders are the ones who sense what members of the group think or want done, and then they direct thought along lines which meet with acceptance. In this process of directing group discussion and decision, they are a powerful factor in the ultimate determination of the attitudes and opinions held by their followers.

It is an error to think that once community leaders are identified and consulted on school problems they will cooperate with and lend support to the institution. Unless they enjoy the authority to make policy and decision, they will take time to secure the reactions of their followers before making any commitments. What they propose to their groups will likewise be influenced by personal attitudes and beliefs toward public education.

The study of leadership should extend to neighborhoods surrounding elementary and secondary schools in the district. Every neighborhood contains a number of men and women who are sometimes known as block leaders. They are consulted by neighbors and friends whenever questions arise involving the school and its relations with children and parents. Their attitudes and judgments are significant determinants of public opinion. It is well to spot the location of these leaders and to involve them in school activities. They can become excellent interpreters of the school on a neighborhood basis and often do more to win loyalty and support than the heads of major organizations.

As a matter of policy, the school should keep community group leaders informed of its practices and problems and invite their cooperation, when it is deemed advisable, in the development and formulation of educational policies.

Social Tensions

Social tensions and conflicts are found wherever people work and live together. Some are normal manifestations of human behavior, others expressions of weakness in the social structure. They are seen in the refusal of neighbors to speak to one another, sectional struggles over the location of new school buildings, claims that the board of education is favoring the higher residential part of the community, the formation of cliques in parent-teacher associations, open discrimination against certain minorities, and gang warfare.

They arise from numerous causes. The causes may be nothing more than personality clashes, misunderstanding, spite, and petty annoyances, or they may be associated with economic rivalry, social competition, class structure, and racial and religious discrimination. No matter what the causes are, these conflicts leave their mark on the social life of the community.

The school must be fully aware of existing tensions and conflicts in planning the public relations program. It cannot expect people in conflict to work cooperatively for the improvement of educational opportunities. Too many problems which are disruptive of united action arise between them. The solution lies, first of all, in understanding thoroughly the nature of the tensions and conflicts found in the community. Steps can then be taken in classroom instruction to educate children and neutralize the influence of outside pressures. This action can be accompanied by the adoption of means for harmonizing differences between individuals and groups in the community when these differences interfere with the operation of the institution and the attainment of its objectives. It takes competent leadership to make this process work successfully.

History of Community Efforts

The history of community efforts provides important leads in the planning of future activities. At one time or another, every community has undertaken various types of civic projects. How successful they have been is the question which must be answered. Evidence that people can work together successfully means a favorable climate for launching new ventures, while evidence of numerous failures makes the problem of cooperative undertakings more difficult. Disappointments color attitudes and feelings and cause people to hesitate about becoming involved in projects which may repeat their past experiences.

CONDUCTING THE SURVEY

Who shall be responsible for planning and conducting the community survey? A community survey which is made for public relations purposes is an executive activity. Responsibility for it should be located in the chief administrative officer of the school system. He may be aided in the work by his immediate administrative associates and call upon instructional staff personnel for assistance. Or he may see fit to delegate the entire responsibility for planning to a central committee which cuts across the school system and includes representatives from administrative, instructional, and noninstructional groups. Decision on how best to handle the planning of the survey should be guided by present organizational arrangements in the school system; the normal channels through which other administrative activity takes place should be followed.

This same observation holds with reference to allocation of responsibility for conducting the survey. Those who have engaged in this work emphasize the value of having all personnel, and especially teachers, assume responsibility for collecting and tabulating sociological information. Unquestionably, there is merit in this suggestion. Participants become more fully acquainted with the community and feel that they have a share in the success of the public relations program which is subsequently developed. But this is not always a realistic and practical method of operation. Wide staff participation may be so slow and cumbersome as to defeat the purpose of the survey. Nor can teachers be asked to take on additional work when many of them are carrying heavy instructional loads and lack the time and energy to perform the required services. More may be gained by having the survey completed as quickly as possible and then summarizing essential findings in booklet form and reviewing them at staff meetings.

Where the central administrative staff is too small to take on responsibility for conducting the entire survey, provision can be made for releasing competent teachers from classroom duties and assigning them to full-time work on the survey. They should be given a brief period of training on sources of information, methods of operation, and tabulation of findings. With an adequate staff, the survey should be completed in less than a semester. A survey that is completed promptly acts as a stimulant to the planning of the public relations program.

The survey methods consist principally of reviewing available school records, holding interviews, collecting information from outside sources, and administering questionnaires to staff personnel and pupils. Once the methods have been worked out in detail and the forms standardized for recording data, the survey can be placed on a continuing basis and information brought up to date annually.

The careful organization and treatment of survey findings facilitates the process of planning the school public relations program. Specially qualified members of the survey staff should be made responsible for organizing, analyzing, and interpreting the data. This is a technical operation calling for services by those who know most about it. Their work should be summarized in written, tabular, and graphic forms. The summaries should cover data for the entire community as well as separate sections and be carried beyond that, if necessary, to individual school attendance areas. The work sheets these summaries are based on should be available when more detailed information is needed during the course of planning.

SOURCES OF INFORMATION

There is no difficulty in finding an adequate supply of information on the points outlined in a study of the community. The most accessible source is school records. The entry blanks which children fill out when they first enroll in school contain information on family backgrounds. This information usually covers name, address, names of parents or guardians, occupations of parents, size of family, place of birth, religious affiliation, languages spoken in the home, and nationality background of parents. These records are kept up to date when new forms are filled out periodically thereafter. When an annual or biennial census is taken in the district, the returns may supply similar information and other items not contained in the previous records. If supplemental data is wanted, it can easily be obtained by means of questionnaires administered to pupils. These sources furnish a rather good picture of home and family conditions in the community.

There are numerous sources of printed materials which cover

practically all aspects of the survey. City directories and telephone books contain the names of organized groups in the community. United States Census tracts give detailed information on population. If the community is too small for inclusion in the printed tracts, the information can be secured by writing to the Bureau of Census. Most social agencies maintain records that are useful on a number of points. Excellent data is available at the local Chamber of Commerce. City, county, and state historical societies have documentary materials which throw light on the growth of the community. A review of newspaper files tells an interesting story of events, happenings, traditional observances, community efforts, group tensions and conflicts, and outstanding leaders. The *Market Data Handbook* of the Department of Commerce is helpful in understanding the economic life of the community, while the publications of governmental planning boards often prove to be highly valuable sources of broad information. Encyclopedias may be used for biographical information, religious customs, traditional observances, and related items under investigation. The minutes of board of education meetings are sometimes a rich source of data on leaders, group programs, tensions, sectional conflicts, and relations with the community.

Unprinted information may be gathered through interviews with prominent residents of the community. They know a good many of the intimate details of social life which are seldom publicized. Though the reliability of their statements may be open to question, they can be cross-checked when a sufficient amount of information has been collected by this method. The success of these interviews will depend upon how well they are planned and conducted.

An inventory should be made of the knowledge possessed by instructional and noninstructional staff members. Those who have lived for some years in the community may prove to be valuable sources of information. This can be done by asking them to fill out one or more questionnaires designed especially for the survey. Comparison of tabulated replies may be used to test the accuracy and completeness of their information.

PRECAUTIONS

A few practical precautions should be exercised in conducting the survey and in interpreting the results: (1) The general nature of the survey should be explained to the community in order to prevent distrust or suspicion concerning the motives of the school system; (2) printed materials should be examined carefully for evidence of bias that may distort the survey findings; (3) steps should be taken to prevent the careless use of information by members of the survey staff; (4) requests that material be held in confidence should be respected; and (5) a strictly objective point of view should be maintained in the organization and treatment of survey findings.

4

Measuring Public Opinion

No community survey is complete without measuring the attitudes and opinions of taxpayers, parents, teachers, and pupils toward education and the operation of the local school system. Whereas the community survey provides essential information regarding the sociological framework within which the public relations program will function, the measurement of attitudes and opinions tells how people think and feel about the educational enterprise and points up what must be done to increase their understanding, participation, and support. The two are complementary and should be considered as a whole in developing policies and planning means for interpreting the school and involving citizens in its activities.

THE VALUE OF OPINION RESEARCH

The measurement of public opinion is a relatively new development in social science research. Starting in the field of marketing, it is now used in many walks of life. The reliability of opinion measurement has been demonstrated over and over again in discovering useful information, predicting elections, ascertaining consumer wants, and forecasting trends in public thought and action. Despite these results, school people have hesitated to apply opinion measurement to their own problems. They have been reluctant to do so either because of the costs involved or because they have retained a skepticism that surrounded the introduction of opinion polling. Although there are still technical problems to be worked out, enough progress has been made to justify the use of opinion research and to profit from the results.

What is the value of opinion research in planning the school public relations program? Primarily, opinion research supplies information on what the public thinks, feels, and wants the school to do. It enables the planners to determine approximately how well the public understands the educational program, points of satisfaction and dissatisfaction, problems which must be solved before increased support and cooperation may be expected, reading and listening habits of the population, acceptability of plans for instructional improvements, and shifts taking place in public opinion.

Applied to pupils and professional and nonprofessional staff members, opinion research discloses the nature of their attitudes toward the institution and their beliefs in the worth of its policies and practices. The capable administrator is able to use this information to improve internal relationships and make constructive changes in the management of the school.

RESEARCH METHODS

Five different methods of measuring public opinion in the field of education are employed today. They are the open forum, advisory committee, panel, questionnaire, and direct interview methods. A brief description of each will be presented to acquaint prospective research workers with their possibilities. Any one wishing to employ these methods should consult standard references for an enlargement and refinement of the techniques involved.

The Open Forum

The open forum method consists of frank discussions by a selected group of persons on some educational topic of current

interest to taxpayers, parents, teachers, or pupils. Each member of
the discussion group is asked to state his views on the topic under
consideration and the reasons for them. After a definite period of
time, the audience is invited to direct questions to members of the
forum or to express their own opinions on the topic. An attempt is
then made to summarize the entire discussion and to estimate where
the majority of people stand. Sometimes this estimate is based upon
the judgment of the chairman, a show of hands on specific questions
raised by the chairman, and by oral and written comments that are
made after the forum has been concluded.

This method lends itself readily to radio presentation and
usually evokes wide public interest, if sufficient publicity is built up
in advance and the participants are carefully chosen. It is used commonly in parent-teacher association meetings, and occasionally in
high school assemblies with students in charge.

The open forum is difficult to defend scientifically for appraising
public opinion, yet it enables school officials to get a rough measure
of how people feel and where their satisfactions and dissatisfactions
are located. It has the added advantage of releasing tensions and
giving all who are interested an opportunity to express themselves
freely.

The Advisory Committee

The advisory committee concept turns on the idea that a selected
group of laymen, representing a balanced cross-section of organized,
interest groups, can express the needs and reflect the opinions of the
community. Meeting with school officials, they are asked to suggest
what should be done in solving the educational problems which are
presented to them. Their recommendations are in no way binding
and can be accepted or rejected.

From the discussion that takes places and the recommendations
made, each group can be evaluated in terms of its respective attitudes,
opinions, and scale of values. There is always a danger of misinter-
preting personal opinions of committee members as those of the
group they represent, but this danger lessens as experience is gained
in working with the method and personalities are better understood.

While this method is subject to criticism, it does afford educators a practical means for familiarizing people with their problems and getting their reactions before making decisions. It should be noted that the use of an advisory committee is not restricted to this purpose alone, but has potentialities for the improvement of education in ways which will be discussed in a later chapter.

The Panel

The panel method represents another approach to the measurement of public opinion. This procedure involves the selection of a permanent jury of laymen who are interviewed periodically by trained members of the staff. The panel is selected to include representatives from all organized interest groups, or it may be chosen in accordance with criteria for a stratified sample of the community.

Interviews are held with panel members individually in order to elicit their opinions on a scheduled series of questions and to estimate the intensity of the attitudes or feelings attached to their comments and answers. Conducted informally without reference to any printed set of questions, the length of the interview is left to the discretion of the parties. When the interview is over, conversational highlights are recorded on prepared forms.

Research on the panel method indicates that repeated interviews with members not only give a statistically reliable measure of opinion but also reveal causes for shifts in opinion. However, repeated interviews with the same persons over a long period of time may produce mental sets which, consciously or unconsciously, bias their replies.

Questionnaires

The use of questionnaires appears to be favored more by educators than the previous methods of measuring public opinion. They are used for getting at the viewpoints of pupils in the upper elementary, junior, and senior high schools, employees of the school system, parents, and nonparent residents. The cost of using questionnaires is reasonable. The procedure followed is that of deciding what to measure, preparing the questions, administering the instrument, and interpreting the replies. The skills involved can be acquired with a fair amount of study and practice.

A number of considerations must be respected in measuring the opinions of pupils, teachers, and noninstructional personnel. The questionnaires should be administered during the school day with the least interruption of regular routines. The purposes should be explained fully. No pupil or employee should be asked to sign his or her name, as identification tends to bias the replies. This is doubly important when a comment sheet is attached to a questionnaire and respondents are asked to state what they think are the best and poorest practices of the institution.

The tabulation of replies can be done speedily where machine scoring is available, and questionnaires have been designed for this accommodation. Otherwise the task is arduous. A breakdown of the replies should be made in order to locate areas within which problems exist. For pupils, this breakdown includes age, grade, sex, and particular schools, with the addition of curriculums and departments of instruction in the senior high school. For school employees, it covers occupational classes, departments, length of service, sex, age, and location.

Light can be shed on the intensity of feelings and the factors underlying replies and comments through follow-up interviews. Interviews do not need to be held with more than a third or a fourth of the group to get this information. But it is important that interviewers be trained in the art of encouraging individuals to speak freely and to talk about the things which disturb and please them most. Notes should be made after the interviews and then pieced together for the patterns they disclose. Interviews, like questionnaires, should be anonymous, and every assurance given that confidences will not be betrayed.

In a small school system, there is no reason why every pupil and employee should not be included in the opinion survey. Where numbers are large, a random selection may be used. Hand, in his book entitled *What People Think About Their Schools,* suggests that the random selection of pupils be made by going down the alphabetical roster of the school and checking the name of every second or fifth pupil, or in any other fixed sequence that will give the approximate number desired.[1] The same principle holds for the selection of employees in a large system, though a better sample will

---

[1] Harold C. Hand, *What People Think About Their Schools* (Yonkers-on-Hudson: World Book Co., 1948), p. 73.

be drawn if they are divided into occupational classes and a proportional selection made within each class.

Conditions which obtain for administering questionnaires to pupils and school employees are not the same for parents. They are not located conveniently within the system, nor can they be called together and asked to fill out a questionnaire under favorable circumstances. Furthermore, they do not have the benefit of clear directions from the person administering the inventory, and there is no assurance that they will complete and return the form. The questionnaires must be mailed or sent home by pupils.

The question is often raised of how many parents should be included in the opinion survey? On this point, Hand maintains that if fewer than approximately 1,000 sets of parents with children at any given school level are involved, then all should be included in the survey.[2] Where the number is larger, a sample of approximately 1,000 sets of parents should be selected for the elementary, junior, and senior high schools respectively. His figures are partly conditioned by the methods employed in analyzing parents' replies. Statistically, a sample of this size is not necessary to get a representative group of parents even though conditions may be strikingly dissimilar in different sections of the community. A smaller sample, drawn in proportion to the size of a school, should yield equally reliable data.

It is doubtful that a parent inventory conducted by mail gives an accurate measure of public opinion. Many parents are unwilling to take time to fill out a lengthy questionnaire, while some feel that what they think will not make a difference anyway. These attitudes are borne out repeatedly in communities where surveys have been tried by mail. The returns show that individuals at higher educational and income levels are likely to respond, and conversely, those at lower educational and income levels are less likely to respond. Sometimes returns are heaviest from individuals who have grievances and want to air their complaints; and sometimes from groups trying to exploit the school for selfish purposes. Under these conditions mail questionnaire returns may give a distorted picture of what the people think about the schools.

However, the parent inventory should not be discounted too lightly. It has value in stimulating wider community interest and

2 *Ibid.*, pp. 86-88.

causing parents to feel that school officials are actually concerned with their opinions. Even though the returns are small and subject to bias, they furnish the school with sounder information than it otherwise would have. If the findings are published and corrective measures taken to remedy unsatisfactory conditions, the outcomes more than justify the effort in terms of parental good will and confidence in the institution.

Some business and industrial concerns supplement wide opinion surveys with brief questionnaires of postcard size. These are distributed at meetings of stockholders, employees, distributors, and customers with the request that they be filled out and deposited in conveniently located boxes at the close of the meeting. Concerns using this technique are convinced that it has merit in getting quick snap-shots of prevailing attitudes on current issues and shifts in opinion in which they are interested. A similar technique could be adopted and used freely at meetings of pupils, employees, and parents throughout the year.

Direct Interviews

The method of direct interview is one whereby a respondent, in a face-to-face situation, answers a schedule of questions put to him by another person. This method operates on the assumption that the opinions of a large group may be estimated accurately by securing the opinions of a properly selected sample of individuals within the group. There are different ways of selecting the sample, but the one that appears to be used more widely today is known as stratified random sampling. This simply means that people are selected so that the sample in certain respects is a small scale model of the population it is designed to represent. Thus, if one-half of the adult population of a community is above forty years of age, then one-half of the total sample must contain individuals above forty years of age. If men and women occur in equal numbers in the population, they must occur in equal numbers in the sample. This principle of correspondence is followed with exactness and applied usually to age, sex, and economic status. Certain other factors, such as education, race, nationality background, and political affiliation, may be established in drawing the sample, but their inclusion depends upon the nature of the issues on which opinion is wanted.

After the characteristics of the population have been determined on which the sample is based, then the question arises of how many people must be interviewed. Although it would seem that the number of individuals comprising the sample could be fixed at a certain percentage of the population, actually this cannot be done because sample size is influenced by the heterogeneity of the population, the size of the community, the amount of breakdown to which data will be subjected, the degree of accuracy wanted in the results, and the amount of time and money available. None can be overlooked. The sample must be large enough to represent the group it is supposed to represent and statistically so defensible that every strata of the population under study has an equal chance of being included. As a net result, the size of the sample varies with each survey—a few hundred cases being sufficient in one instance and many more being necessary in another.

The questions put to respondents, such as those used in the opinion studies of the Denver Public Schools, page 62, are an important part of the interview method. Unless they produce the information desired, the method is a failure. In devising the schedule, attention must be given to the types of questions which will best yield facts, knowledge, understanding, attitudes, beliefs, and opinions. Efforts should be made to keep them simple in language and free from bias. Even the order of the questions should receive attention so that the answer to one will not influence the answer to another. Despite the careful construction of the questionnaire, it is hard to avoid weaknesses in the wording and sequence of questions. The only way of knowing whether or not the questions will be understood and result in satisfactory answers is to pretest the ballot with a small, sub-sample of the population. After one of two trial runs, the ballot, as the schedule of questions is called, can then be printed in final form.

The actual work of administering the final ballot to people who comprise the sample is the next step in procedure. It takes less time than either the preparation of the ballot or the treatment of the findings. Uniformity in administration is more or less assured by detailed instructions to interviewers. These instructions should be printed and reviewed before interviewing begins. Interviewers should know how to approach respondents, when to hold interviews, what to record, how to deal with questions they are asked, and who makes up their quota. In a large poll, it is customary for interviewers to select at random the individuals to whom they will administer the ballot, but these individuals must meet the criteria of the sample.

1. Most of us think some of our friends are well educated and some not so well educated . . . but how do you tell whether a person has a good education or not?

2. Looking back, what were some of the valuable things you got out of school and school life?

3. In what ways do you think your schooling and school life did not meet your needs in later life?

4. How about our public schools today in Denver . . . are there any things you do not like about the Denver public schools? (What things?)

5. Are there any things you do like about our Denver public schools as they are today? (What things?)

6. Well, in general, would you say the Denver public schools are doing a good job, just a fair job, or a poor job of educating children these days?

   Good job .... Fair job .... Poor job ....
   _____Qualified

7. What are some of the important things they should teach children in the Denver public schools today?

8. Are there any of them you think the Denver public schools are neglecting or not spending enough time on?

Homemaking 1	Mathematics 4	Business, trade 7
Social studies 2	Health 5	Sciences 8
English 3	Arts 6	Foreign languages .. 9

9. How about public school discipline . . . do you think that today the Denver public schools are much too easy on the children, a little too easy, about right, or too hard on them?

   Much too easy.........1   Little too easy.........2   About right.........3
   Too hard 4

10. Have you paid any attention to the recent arguments about the Denver schools in the newspaper and on the radio? (How much attention . . . a lot, some, or very little?)

    Paid no attention.........1   A little.........2   Some.........2   A lot.........4

Questions from Opinion Studies of the Denver Public Schools.

Thus the instruction sheet might state that an interviewer is to select three individuals over forty years of age who have children in the public schools, and who fall either in the low, average, or upper income group respectively. Usually toward the close of the interview, the respondent is asked to furnish personal data on occupation, education, home ownership, and anything else which is helpful in checking the make-up of the sample.

All ballots should be returned by interviewers within a specified period of time. They should be gone over carefully for any slip-ups

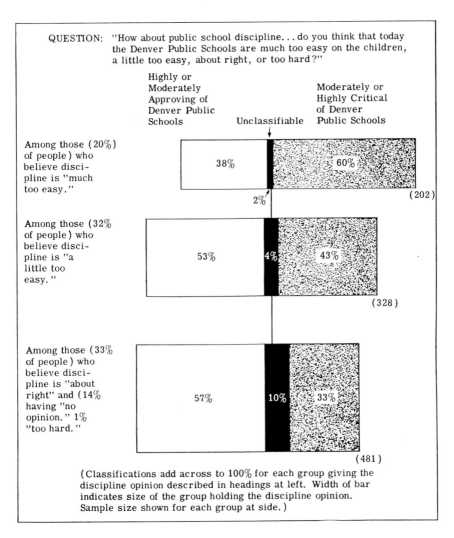

QUESTION: "How about public school discipline...do you think that today the Denver Public Schools are much too easy on the children, a little too easy, about right, or too hard?"

Highly or Moderately Approving of Denver Public Schools

Unclassifiable

Moderately or Highly Critical of Denver Public Schools

Among those (20%) of people) who believe discipline is "much too easy." — 38% — 60% — 2% — (202)

Among those (32% of people) who believe discipline is "a little too easy." — 53% — 4% — 43% — (328)

Among those (33% of people) who believe discipline is "about right" and (14% having "no opinion." 1% "too hard." — 57% — 10% — 33% — (481)

(Classifications add across to 100% for each group giving the discipline opinion described in headings at left. Width of bar indicates size of the group holding the discipline opinion. Sample size shown for each group at side.)

Page from Report on Opinion Studies of Denver Public Schools.

that may have occurred in the interviewing. Incomplete ones should be discarded. Care must be taken to see that the returned ballots are representative of the sample, with no exceptions permitted.

From this point on, planning should include the coding, tabulation, and statistical treatment of the data. The findings should then be summarized in terms of the original questions contained in the ballot. It is good practice in opinion studies of public education to publish the results, such as are shown on the section from the Denver Report and make them available to members of the community.

Modified Direct Interviews

Interest in public opinion polling and its value in school public relations have caused educational research workers to experiment with the method of direct interviews. Their purposes have been to find out whether the method could be simplified and made easier and the cost reduced so it would be used more widely by school administrators. The research done by Hedlund and McCormick is worth reporting.[3]

Hedlund asked high school sophomores in a selected community to preselect a sample of approximately 500 adults whom they knew and to supply information on each one as to name, address, sex, age, race, nativity, and occupation. This information was then used to construct a sample for interviewing. The sample corresponded to a stratification of the community on the factors named to control the sample. Tenth grade pupils were chosen to take part in the study on the assumption that they represented a cross-section of the entire population and were mature enough to follow directions.

These students were given questionnaires, each one being folded in an unsealed envelope, and asked to contact the persons whose names they had submitted and make a request that they fill out the questionnaire. They were instructed to tell these persons to fill out the questionnaire by themselves, seal it in an envelope provided, and that they would call for it in a day or two. They were then to return the sealed envelopes to the school, reporting at the same time

---

[3] The report on both studies is taken from Donald H. Ross, Editor, *Administration and Adaptability* (New York: Metropolitan School Study Council, 1951). The original studies are listed in the chapter bibliography.

the number of persons who refused to fill out the questionnaire and the number who could not be reached.

The findings of this study demonstrated the fact that a good cross-section of public opinion in the community could be polled by students through contacts with acquaintances and by means of a questionnaire which the respondents filled out by themselves.

McCormick employed five methods of polling opinion in the community he selected for study. These methods were (1) using as interviewers interested adults who belonged to the parent-teacher association; (2) using as interviewers high school seniors who volunteered for the service and who were members of a class studying "Problems of Democracy"; (3) using as interviewers high school juniors who were presently taking a course in sociology; (4) using eighth grade pupils as interviewers; and (5) using fifth and sixth grade pupils as interviewers.

The participants were asked to recommend acquaintances for the sample, who met the following conditions: two male and two female adults; two over forty and two under forty years of age; two with children and two without children in the public schools; two living in homes renting for under $60 a month and two in homes renting for more than $60 a month; and, a foreign-born person, if possible.

The findings showed that parent-teacher association members and eighth grade pupils secured the highest percentage of returns on the interviews and that eleventh grade pupils secured the lowest. All methods, however, were efficient in securing a high percentage of completed returns. The methods proved successful in obtaining representative samples of the population with reference to the control factor of sex, but poor with reference to the control factors of rental value and level of educational achievement. Age stratification was weak as a control by the failure of interviewers to secure a sufficient number of returns from persons in the extreme upper age range. In comparing the effectiveness of the five methods, it was evident that sixth grade pupils and eighth grade pupils were superior to the others in obtaining representative samples of the population. From this study McCormick concluded that any one of the five methods will produce samples of the population which accurately and reliably measure understanding of education by adults in the community.

PLANNING FOR OPINION STUDIES

Before detailed plans for making opinion studies are developed, the administrator should answer certain questions to his own satisfaction and to that of the board of education. The questions that need to be answered are the following:

1. *Exactly what is the problem to be studied?* Too often individuals are carried away by their enthusiasm for something they believe is important without taking the time to consider just what the problem is, and what kinds of facts are needed to solve it. This is evident in some of the questionnaires that school systems have devised for appraising the attitudes and opinions of parents and taxpayers.

The administrator who is concerned with the measurement of opinion will strengthen his case and gain board support more readily if he has defined the problem and has outlined the exact points to be studied in connection with it. This is illustrated in the work done by one superintendent who was faced with a steady barrage of criticism about the schools. A preliminary investigation brought out the fact that several individuals were openly declaring that the public had lost confidence in the educational program. With the permission of the board, he undertook a series of interviews with all persons known to be skeptical and antagonistic toward the schools. From these interviews he was able to determine the exact points around which most of the criticism revolved. He then formulated a statement of the problem and the points needing investigation. The board approved his statement in short order and then voted the money for conducting an opinion survey. They wished to find out whether confidence in the schools has been destroyed and, specifically, what practices were under strongest protest. The results of the survey showed conclusively that the large majority of people believed in the worth of the instructional program and had faith in the competency of the administration. They showed further that most of the opposition stemmed from a small but articulate minority who misunderstood many of the practices they were complaining about.

Too much emphasis cannot be placed upon the advisability of formulating the problem for study in writing and attaching to this statement the precise purposes for which information is required to solve the problem. This becomes not only a matter of record, when approved by the board of education, but also serves as a guide to those who are charged with responsibility for making the study.

2. *What is the best method to use for obtaining the information that is wanted?* The choice of method depends upon the problem and its purposes. Leaving financial consideration aside for the moment, the point is that one method or combination of methods is more effective than another for obtaining certain types of data. For example, it would be wasteful to conduct an interview poll if the problem was one of trying to get a broad, general picture of how opinion was developing around a given issue. For this purpose, sufficient information could be collected economically and quickly through the open forum, advisory committee, and panel methods of measuring opinion. By the same token, none of these methods would suffice for obtaining an accurate measure of public understanding, let us say, concerning guidance services in the school. Actually, the method or methods brought into play do not have to be costly and complicated when all that is wanted is a general estimate of opinion.

3. *How much money is required to conduct opinion studies?* The answer to this question varies with the nature of the studies made. Large, city-wide surveys are expensive, ranging from a few to several hundred dollars. Because of costs, many administrators shy away from opinion studies without realizing that limited surveys can be conducted on restricted budgets. A preliminary or pilot study of opinion often yields satisfactory results and costs very little. Some survey organizations make pilot studies regularly before deciding whether or not it is necessary to engage in a large project. The argument on cost falls apart once administrators and school boards understand the need and value of knowing what the public thinks.

4. *How much time is needed to complete a study of public opinion?* The amount will vary with the method employed. It is small for the open forum and advisory committees methods, somewhat larger for the panel method, and considerably larger for questionnaires and direct interviews. The two latter methods, starting with a definition of the problem and ending with the publication of results, may consume several weeks. This can be reduced with experience in polling procedure. Some national polling organizations are now able to conduct a nation-wide survey and report the findings in four or five

days. The significant thing is not how much time is required, but rather learning how to make opinion studies and putting the findings to work in building stronger relations with the community.

5. *Who shall do the research in public opinion measurement?* Typical school administrators do not have the background of training and experience for this research. They can familiarize themselves with the procedures involved and learn to apply the more simple ones in their own communities, but they are not competent to undertake direction of scientific polls. If they wish to undertake scientific polls, they should either employ outside experts or else subsidize the training of staff personnel. While the more convenient alternative is to hire outside experts, it is difficult to sell to boards of education because of the cost. The better choice in the long run is to subsidize the training of staff personnel who are then available to conduct studies whenever they are wanted. Staff personnel who take over this responsibility should be assisted at the beginning by an expert consultant. He can show them short cuts in procedures, eliminate confusion, and prevent serious errors.

6. *How shall the findings be used?* The answers to this question will be governed by the nature of the findings. They may show that the superintendent should act at once to solve a pressing problem. They may suggest that action by the board of education is necessary before anything can be done to clean up an unfavorable situation. They may confirm the soundness of present public relation procedures and the effectiveness of the program. They may point up the need for studying further a practice that is causing trouble. They may reflect a shift in public opinion calling for follow-up studies to chart direction. They may reveal problems for which immediate provision should be made in the public relations program. They may reveal many other things that are important in guiding relations with the community.

In general, the findings should be published in booklet form for distribution to staff personnel and citizens in the community. Such a publication serves to increase interest in and understanding of the educational program. Discussions built around it afford opportunity for citizen participation in the improvement of school policies and practices.

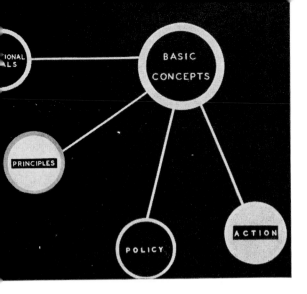

5
Establishing Basic Concepts

Another essential step in preparing the program is to establish the basic concepts by which it will be governed. They are the educational ideals of the school system, the public relations policy, and the principles of interpretation. Their nature and importance will be considered in this chapter.

THE IDEALS OF AMERICAN EDUCATION

The people of this country, through their support of public schools, have shown a strong faith in the power of education. This faith has grown from the beginning of the public school system, because, as Commager has pointed out, "education has had very special and very heavy tasks to perform. Democracy could not work without an enlightened electorate. The various states and regions could not achieve unity without a sentiment of nationalism. The nation could not absorb tens of millions of immigrants from all parts of the globe without rapid and effective Americanization. Economic and social distinctions and privileges, severe enough to corrode democracy itself, had to be fought. To our schools went the momentous responsibility of inspiring a people to pledge and hold allegiance to these historic principles of democracy, nationalism, Americanism, and egalitarianism."[1] They not only met these responsibilities, but met them well.

The faith in public education, thus inspired by meeting successfully the problems of past generations, has been badly shaken through broad and persistent attacks made on schools in recent years. Critics have emphasized the fact that many of the older standards and ideals of education have gradually disappeared and nothing definite has taken their place.

What the critics do not realize is that the school has been going through a difficult period of adjustment in trying to meet a complexity of problems it had to accept. Starting with the turn of the century, a phenomenal rise took place in enrollments. Thousands upon thousands of young people flooded into classrooms at a rate unprecedented in the history of man. They brought with them a host of problems peculiar to their inborn capacities and the cultural conditions under which they were reared. In the matter of intelligence alone, differences were so great that radical alterations had to be made in the instructional program. This can be illustrated most clearly at the secondary level where the nature of the pupil population completely reversed itself during the last three decades. At the outset of this period, at least eighty per cent of all youth attending public high schools were enrolled in the college preparatory curriculum. A carefully selected group, they were able to absorb large amounts of subject matter and deal with problems involving mental skill. The standards of achievement for this group became the standards for judging secondary education in this country.

But what is the situation today?

The high school is predominantly an institution catering to an unselected group, eighty per cent of whom have no intention of going to college. In actual numbers, there are many more pupils enrolled in the college preparatory curriculum than ever before. Without question, their mastery of basic content and skill in performance far outstrips that of their predecessors. But aside from the pupils in the college preparatory program, the remainder, and the largest

---

[1] Henry Steele Commager, "Our Schools Have Kept Us Free," *Life*, 29:46, October 16, 1950.

number, must be taught knowledges and skills, attitudes and appreciations, habits and actions in keeping with their aptitudes, interests, and needs if they are to become decent, self-reliant citizens in a democracy. The academic offerings and sterile experiences of a college preparatory curriculum have had little to offer in satisfying the problems of life adjustment they present. It has been necessary for the school to develop new courses of study, introduce more vocational education, adapt methods and materials to needs and abilities, and place more emphasis upon educative experiences geared to the everyday responsibilities of living now as well as in the future.

This period of adjustment has been accompanied by remarkable progress in educational thought and practice. Developments in philosophy have clarified the ends and means essential to the preparation of young people for active participation in the life of the community. Experimental findings of psychology and studies in child growth and development have opened pathways to a deeper understanding of the learning process and the causative aspects of behavior. Curriculum studies, based upon the analysis of life problems and the nature and needs of young people, have been pursued with intensity. All kinds of experimental work have been undertaken at different grade levels to improve the quality of classroom instruction and to make learning a more dynamic and worthwhile experience.

In spite of the adjustments forced upon the school by the vast influx of pupils of varying needs and abilities or the progress made in educational thought and practice, public education is still evaluated according to the standards and conditions of the past. As a result, seldom has so much blame and so little praise, so much confusion and so little understanding surrounded the school. People are no longer clear in their own thinking as to the purposes of education or the goals toward which its efforts are directed. They are critical and uncertain about the value of the subject offerings and doubtful as to whether or not the methods of teaching are as beneficial as they used to be. They have a feeling that somehow the school is not doing the job they would like to have done, but they are not at all certain what the job should be like. They have been caught in the web of doubt spun by those who have openly disparaged and loudly protested changes made in the program of public education.

A large share of the responsibility for these reactions may be attributed directly to the school itself for failure to keep citizens informed. Instead of taking them into confidence and inviting their aid in the solving of educational problems, school boards and professional personnel have often treated them as strangers. The school now faces the task of restoring faith in the quality of its program.

This task is not an easy one, but it can be accomplished. A first step, and probably the most important one, is defining exactly what the public school stands for in American life, and then standing for it. This means that the ideals, the purposes of American education must be defined and stated with simplicity. They must be understood and identified with the institution. Such a step would go far in clearing the present confusion and paving the way for a restoration of faith in the worth and contribution of the public school system.

The leadership for this task should come from professional educators in the local community. They could bring together representative groups of citizens and thresh out the goals they are striving for and should be striving for in the educational program. True, it would be easier for them to do this job alone, but doing it that way would not build the confidence and understanding that is necessary. The hope for the school depends upon the wide involvement of citizens and the contributions of their thinking to its present and future development.

What are some considerations that enter into a determination of what the school should stand for in American life? Obviously, there are many, and the choice must be limited to those that most directly summarize and reflect the outlook of society. Among others are the need for improving democratic thought and practice, preparation for wise and useful citizenship, instruction in moral values, equal educational opportunity for all, defense against foreign ideologies, the reinforcement of nationalism, the place of internationalism, vocational competency, progressive experimentation, cultural reproduction, healthful living, family life, use of leisure, and service to the community.

Once decisions are made as to what the school stands for, and these decisions are translated into simple, understandable statements, they should then be projected through a public relations program. Every legitimate device should be employed to make the public fully aware of the role of the school and the importance of its contribution to the community.

PUBLIC RELATIONS POLICY

Within the scope of state authority, as expressed and implied in the statutes governing schools, local boards of education have grants of power enabling them to make rules and regulations, define purposes for actions to be taken, hire and assign responsibilities to personnel, raise and allocate monies for supporting their decisions, provide housing, and do many things necessary to the efficient operation of the school system. Boards usually express this power in the form of written policies or measures which describe what they want done and the limits within which personnel can function. Sometimes their policies exist without being stated in written words or spread upon the minutes of their meetings. Such policies represent assumptions which have earned acceptance through usage in much the same way as common law. However, a number of unwritten policies lack the stability of precedence and time and are measures of expediency. They are poorly understood by the staff as a whole and exert little influence on the school system.

It is this latter type of unwritten policy that is generally followed so far as the field of public relations is concerned. Boards of education have left administrators to their own devices in conducting community relations programs. They follow no set policy, but do what they think is necessary for telling the public about the schools. Most activities are limited to news releases and printed publications, with a smattering of speeches and personal contacts. Staff members have little or no part in the program, although they are urged to develop good relations with pupils and parents. Administrators believe that this method of operation is sound because boards are uninterested in public relations and they enjoy the freedom to make their own decisions.

The Need for Policy

While this way of looking at responsibility for public relations is understandable, it does not shut out the necessity for guiding policy. Under any circumstances, good administration depends upon the influence of established policy. It sets the direction for action and furnishes the bases for decision making. It tells professional personnel what is expected of them and, in doing so, enhances their sense of security. Legally adopted policy likewise compels action and eliminates hesitancy about requesting the manpower and materials it calls for. Those who are charged with responsibility for implementing policy find satisfaction in the stability and continuity it gives to their labor.

The Nature of a Policy

The question is raised frequently as to what a policy for public relations should be like? First, a policy for public relations should be in agreement with the state school laws, the philosophy of the institution, and the traditions, beliefs, and opinions of the people. Second, it should stand for a plan of action in which the purposes and means for their attainment are described in written form. Purpose is the crucial element in a policy statement, because it tells why the policy has been developed and sets the goals for all that is done.

An examination of policies in school public relations shows that there are currently four principal purposes in back of efforts to bring school and community closer together. These purposes may be classified as follows: (1) promotion—periodic campaigns for achieving specific ends, such as increases in millage and the floating of bond issues for new buildings; (2) correction—the periodic presentation of facts and opinions selected for offsetting current misunderstandings and dissatisfactions with the school; (3) information—the continuous presentation of information and facts which depict the school in its most favorable terms; and, (4) interpretation—the continuous presentation of carefully organized and explained facts concerning the purpose, needs, and conditions of the school.

Each of these purposes has merit, but the only one that approximates the true function of the school in a democracy is interpretation. In a broad sense, interpretation is a two-way process through which the facts about the school are brought to the people, and the nature and needs of the community are interpreted to the school.

The ultimate objective is to gain intelligent support so the institution may do a more effective job of serving the community.

While still retaining the value of interpretation, the viewpoint taken in school public relations today is that greater emphasis should be placed upon the development of a strong, continuing partnership between the school and community. In the American scheme of government, the right to decide what schools shall do rests with the people. By bringing the people into a dynamic partnership, their needs and wishes can be expressed fully and translated into educational practice. As matters now stand, people may make their wants known through existing legal channels, but they seldom feel a direct responsibility for the improvement of schools. Public relations should aim to create this sense of responsibility by giving opportunities for individuals and community groups to work cooperatively with professional personnel in establishing purposes, planning programs, and making progress. It is this concept that should be underscored in a policy of public relations for education.

A well-defined policy for public relations should likewise include a general description of means to be employed for the achievement of purpose. They should outline the pattern of action, and be flexible enough to allow experimentation in the program. As an illustration, a policy might specify that (1) all institutional personnel shall develop wholesome, friendly relations with pupils, parents, and members of the community, (2) the school shall maintain cooperative, working relations with all institutions and agencies whose interests supplement and strengthen those of the school, (3) parents and citizens shall be encouraged to participate actively in the study of school problems and to make recommendations for their solution, (4) all available media of communication shall be utilized to keep the people of the community accurately and continuously informed of the problems, efforts, and accomplishments of the school.

Policy Development

The first step in developing a public relations policy is the determination of need. This is analogous to saying that some goal must be reached and means found for reaching it. The need at the beginning may be nothing more than a vague feeling of concern which calls for investigation. It may arise quite naturally from the pressures and defects of faulty administration, the complaints of parents, the planning of future programs, or from a variety of other causes. No matter how it arises, the initial step is always to understand and determine the reasons why a policy should be developed.

An understanding of the reasons why a policy should be developed leads to a definition of the purpose to be served by the policy. Sometimes broad purposes will be implied in the study of need, but often an immediate annoyance will set the goal. Unless the immediate situation is analyzed carefully, the resulting policy may be limited in its application to a passing disturbance or to the surface manifestations of a deeper cause. Failure to exercise this caution is evident in some of the "firebucket" measures adopted by school systems to correct misunderstandings, suppress controversy, and promote projects which leave a residue of discontent following their completion.

Once the need for policy has been determined and defined in terms of purpose, the next step is to decide what means or procedures are best suited for achieving the purpose. Their selection will be governed by the nature of the need and considerations of public opinion, finance, personnel, responsibility, organization, and control. All must be explored thoroughly before a general plan of action is outlined. When this has been done, then a written statement of the purpose and procedures should be formulated and submitted to the board of education for adoption. The detailed program is then developed in the light of the adopted policy.

PRINCIPLES OF ACTION

The effective operation of a school public relations program depends upon the application and observance of certain rules of action. Just as in other forms of social effort—play, government, business—experience brings out the wisdom of having a set of regulations to meet problems that come up daily. These rules are called principles and evolve from the critical analysis of experience. Their observance results in a uniform and consistent pattern of action.

Experience in school public relations is rather limited because of the short period of time during which systematic work has been done in this field, yet a sufficient amount of experience has been gained to indicate the necessity of defining rules for governing the program wisely. As more experience is gained, these rules no doubt will undergo modification and new ones will be added.

For the present, the principles of a school public relations program are these:

1. *Integrity*. A successful public relations program holds strictly to the principle of integrity. All factual information presented for public consumption is complete and truthful so far as this is possible. There is nothing to hide in the operation and management of a school system. Any attempt to conceal the truth or suppress unfavorable facts can only lead to suspicion and distrust. The public, by and large, has confidence in the integrity of administrative and instructional personnel and will continue to have confidence unless deception is discovered. If this occurs, it is difficult to regain confidence without a large amount of hard, patient work, or a change in personnel.

It is probable that differences may arise between school officials and members of the community over the interpretation of factual information. Honest differences can usually be reconciled by searching for additional data or by examining openly the exact points at which conflicts in opinion occur. The willingness of school officials to admit these differences and to seek constructive means for adjusting them is, in itself, a process of building public trust and confidence in the institution and its personnel.

It is important in maintaining the principle of integrity that school practices agree with information given to the public. There is a human tendency to put the "best-foot-forward," to make claims that are difficult to substantiate, to overlook less glamorous aspects of the program. For example, a news story may play up the fact that children in the elementary grades are above national norms in spelling, but fail to mention the distribution of scores or the problem of teaching spelling to those in the lower quartile who will subsequently be employed in the community. Or great stress may be placed on citizenship training only to have youngsters repeatedly destroy property on their way to and from school. Of late years much publicity has been given to the teaching of the child and the adjustment of the instructional program to his needs and interests, but the nature and amount of homework he receives suggests to parents that teachers never heard of the doctrine. Such inconsistencies undermine public confidence and lead to doubt and criticism.

2. *Continuity.* The principle of continuity means that there will be a steady program of community education concerning the purposes, efforts, and achievements of the school and a guarantee that citizens will participate regularly in the planning and improving of educational efforts. This principle assumes that the development of understandings and appreciations is an educational process through which individuals will be brought into continuous contact with ideas and facts about the school system. Sometimes administrators become restless because their efforts do not take root at once. They forget that learning is a slow process and that educating citizens to the nature and needs of the system cannot be hurried. In some communities, five to ten years of steady work may be required before a broad, wholesome state of understanding is reached; in others, two to three years of constructive effort will yield satisfactory results. In districts, however, where people are made partners in the planning and improving of school programs, they acquire insight into the school system more rapidly.

The temptation is strong at times to undertake high-pressure, periodic campaigns for influencing public opinion and opening the road to change. Though quick results may be obtained, there is always danger that propaganda will be used, issues emotionalized, controversy incited, and opportunities provided for reactionaries and vested interest groups to attack the school. The injection of these elements, in whole or part, into a program of public relations weakens confidence and lowers support among a large segment of the population.

3. *Coverage.* The public relations program should be comprehensive in coverage, that is, it should include a balanced presentation of factual information pertaining to the entire educational enterprise. As a consequence, no one aspect of the school should receive a disproportionate amount of attention, nor should the more favorable features be emphasized. It is essential that the public be given a complete story of the school in action.

The amount of space assigned in daily and weekly newspapers to student activities, notably athletic events and contests, suggests that the rest of the school program is relatively unimportant by comparison. Only now and then do newspapers carry stories describing or explaining in any detail what is taking place in regular instruction. As studies have shown, parents and citizens are more interested in learning about teaching methods, character training, special services, pupil progress, and similar matters than they are about football games and track meets. This treatment of news is due, in some respects, to poor reporting by the schools, but most of it stems from newspaper people who think that the public is most interested in out-of-class activities. It may take a long time to convince them to change their policy, although there is evidence of better coverage gaining hold in metropolitan papers.

In the meantime, better coverage may be obtained by using many media to reach various individuals and groups in the community. It has been found that well-informed employees of a system do a great deal in this respect. Their personal contacts may be supplemented with bulletins to the home, radio programs, school motion pictures, parent-teacher meetings, lay participation in school affairs, annual reports, and other media. The effective use of several media go far in acquainting the public with the facts about the school and presenting a balanced picture of the institution.

4. *Simplicity.* The problem of educating adults in the community with regard to the purposes, practices, and problems of the school is difficult compared with the problem of teaching pupils a body of facts, skills, and concepts in a classroom situation. The classroom teacher has some control over the learning process and the activities of the learners. These do not exist in adult community education. The best that can be done is to respect those principles that have been discovered in the use of mass communication media. One of the principles is that of simplicity in the presentation of information by oral, written, and graphic means.

When words are symbols for conveying ideas, they must be words which are familiar to people. Unfamiliar words are not understood, nor is time taken to find out what they mean. Imagine the reaction of the average person to a newspaper article from which the following excerpt was taken:

> Because knowledge of the children to be served is essential in developing an educational program for them, we have carried on a study in this county

for several years. It was a cooperative undertaking among teachers, supervisors, and the County Superintendent.

Briefly, our reasons for the study were: 1. We wanted to know what our situation looked like—not what we guessed or hoped it was. 2. We wanted to accumulate reliable data, based on valid findings so that we could intelligently face our problem. 3. We intended to use the knowledge obtained for the betterment of our children.

Our continued study of children guided us in fitting the school program to meet individual needs, instead of exploiting children to meet arbitrary requirements, without consideration of limitations or abilities.

The language of this article does not convey meaning, and it is conceivable that the article might annoy some readers enough to create a feeling of ill-will toward the school.

Besides simplicity of language, the connotations of words are important. A word may be agreeable, disagreeable, or have no emotional effect upon a person. Knowing in advance how individuals react to words helps to better communication. For example, parents are generally pleased when the words attainment, courtesy, desirable, efficient, exceptional, intelligence, notable, and reliable are used in connection with their children. On the other hand, words like alibi, blame, crooked, dispute, flimsy, ignorant, impossible, muddle, and rude leave them with mixed, unpleasant feelings and block communication.

In the absence of research on word usage in school public relations, administrators and teachers can compile lists of common words and phrases they employ. These words and phrases can be checked for positive and negative connotations. Though the method is somewhat crude, it does create a sensitivity to language and the development of a reference guide for preparing various types of communications.

When graphic symbols are used for interpreting factual data, the same rule of simplicity applies. Graphic symbols, such as charts, graphs, pictures, and diagrams, are most valuable in depicting statistical concepts which usually lack appeal. An attractive pie graph can tell more than a two-page printed budget statement in letting people know what educational services their money buys. A drawing of children as symbols for numbers can explain school enrollments more effectively than a column of figures. Like words, graphic symbols hold attention and facilitate understanding when one idea is presented at a time and the idea is plain enough to grasp easily.

5. *Constructiveness.* A public relations program should be constructive in treatment of information presented to the public. People should be told what is good about their schools, where they are weak, what problems exist, and how they can be made better. In telling people what is good about their schools, the accent should be upon pupil accomplishment. How pupils are doing, what benefits they are receiving, and the degree of growth and development they are making —these are the subjects in which people are interested. They are not concerned with information on the personal virtues and achievements of school board members, administrators, and teachers and propaganda to promote their advancement. The pupil and what is being done for him is the theme to be followed.

The public should know the weaknesses of their local system and how they may be corrected. Here an objective presentation and an unemotional discussion of facts, divorced completely from personalities, win respect and confidence in the integrity of the administration. Take for example the weakness of large classes in the beginning grades of an elementary school. It is one thing to complain openly that good instruction cannot be carried on under these conditions and to ask for additional teachers, and another to describe the situation and point out specifically the loss to pupils under these conditions. Constructive explanations appeal to reasonable people and lead to desirable action.

Present and anticipated problems of the school system should be treated in much the same manner. The public should know what the problems are, how they came about, and what alternatives are available for reaching satisfactory solutions. The principle of constructiveness calls for complete and honest information, objective search for truth, positive suggestions, community cooperation, and the child as the center of thought and action.

6. *Adaptability.* A public relations program must be adapted to the community it serves. Adaptability involves the adjustment of activities and informational materials to the cultural composition of the community, understandings and opinions of the people, and factors that help or hinder the growth of good will and citizen participation in the school affairs.

Wide differences are found among individuals in tastes, ideas, mental abilities, educational backgrounds, opinions, attitudes, and values. Ideally, the community relations program should be fitted to these differences in much the same way that classroom teaching is fitted to differences in children. Because this is impossible, the problem must be approached from a group point of view. Through analytical study of the community, certain group characteristics can be determined with reference to racial, religious, social, political, and economic organization; attitudes and opinions toward education; nationality backgrounds; and other significant matters. With this information, public relations personnel can plot activities, prepare materials, avoid controversial issues, and increase community responsiveness. For example, the vocabulary employed in printed or oral media for a neighborhood with a majority of second and third generation foreign born would be more elemental than that intended for an audience of college graduates. Obviously, curricular innovations in a conservative semi-rural district would be handled differently from those in an urbanized industrial area. Public relations work must be adapted to the nature and needs of the local community.

7. *Flexibility.* This principle means that both program and organization for public relations should be kept flexible. Organization is nothing more than a temporary arrangement for aiding in the smooth and efficient operation of the program. It is subject to constant modification in the light of program changes. When organization becomes fixed and permanent, it ceases to serve the purposes for which it was developed. A classic example of this is seen in the departmentalization of secondary schools. This arrangement is perpetuated and protected despite the fact that new developments and improvements in the program of studies render it rather useless. Fortunately, public relations in education is too young to have fixed organizational patterns, though this tendency is beginning to set in among large school systems.

A dynamic program is always undergoing modifications with new needs and conditions. It changes as a result of experience, findings from periodic appraisal of outcomes, and studies of public opinion. Emphases shift with the discovery of new problems and the solution of previous difficulties. Nothing is gained from continuing to interpret the reading program, for example, when parents understand and approve it. Nor can enrollment figures which indicate that the public must be prepared to underwrite the cost of a new building program in six years be ignored. The public relations program must be kept flexible in order to achieve the purposes for which it is intended.

There is a serious danger of narrowness in concept and inflexibility in action associated with the public relations calendar idea which a number of administrators and public relations workers have recommended. According to this idea, public relations activities can be planned for the year and dates assigned for the performance of these activities. This may be a defensible device for taking care of routine announcements and keeping forthcoming events in mind, but it is no substitute for a comprehensive and flexible program adapted to changing needs and conditions in the local community.

Part III

PERSONAL PUBLIC RELATIONS ▶

Courtesy Public Schools, Springfield, Missouri.

6

Staff Relations

A complete program in public relations consists of three separate, but interrelated parts. The first part concerns what might be called personal public relations or the relations which school representatives have, either directly in a face-to-face situation or indirectly through telephone conversations, correspondence, and observations with individuals who are members of different publics. The second involves the relations of the school as a social institution with organized community groups and the opportunities available for cooperative work in strengthening the educational program. The third part covers the more formal and impersonal media through which information is supplied to parents and taxpayers regarding the purposes, program, and problems of the institution.

The present chapter is the first in a series of four dealing with personal public relations. It discusses the causes of good and poor relations among school personnel, their influence on public opinion, and how they can become effective agents in interpreting the school to members of the community.

IMPORTANCE OF INTERNAL RELATIONS

It does not take much imagination to realize that all employees of a school system come into contact daily with many people in the community and, through these contacts, interpret the policies and practices of the institution. If their relations within the system are friendly and cooperative, they manifest interest in and enthusiasm for their work, speak well of colleagues, and discuss the school in positive terms. If they are unfriendly and uncooperative, they manifest little interest in and enthusiasm for their work, speak disparagingly of colleagues, and discuss the school in negative terms.

Too many boards of education and their administrative officers overlook the importance of internal conditions and the influence they have on public opinion. Instead of looking at the quality of relations within the school system, they concentrate their interpretative efforts on costly annual reports, newspaper releases, special pamphlets, report card enclosures, talks before civic groups, radio broadcasts, and open-house exhibits. While these activities help to promote a broader understanding of education and the local school system, their value is soon lost in a district shot through with internal strife and dissension. The ideas and feelings expressed by staff members to pupils, parents, friends, and acquaintances carry more weight in the development of public opinion than tons of literature and hundreds of speeches by school officials. Good public relations demands the presence of a staff in the community who believe in the school system, work well together, and are positive in their approach to a discussion of educational policies, practices, and problems.

SCHOOL BOARD ACTIONS

In analyzing the causes of good and poor conditions within a system that affect the attitudes, feelings, and relations of staff members. it is advisable to start with the board of education. This body sets the climate of the system through the exercise of its authority, the conduct of its business, and the relationships it maintains with administrators and staff members.

Board Authority

A local school board is given broad discretionary powers under state law and the right to manage the school system. Its authority covers the construction and care of school buildings; selection of textbooks; adoption of courses of study; hiring of administrators; hiring of teachers, clerks, and others; levying of property taxes; spending of tax receipts; fixing of salaries; regulations governing pupil and employee conduct; and, anything else that is consistent with the authority it has been granted.

The manner in which the board of education exercises this authority is what matters. If it refuses to listen to the advice of the chief executive officer, shows indifference to the welfare of staff members, usurps the functions of the administrator, rules on matters about which it is ignorant, issues unreasonable orders, makes political appointments, summarily dismisses teachers, listens to parental complaints without consulting principals and teachers, and engages in other undesirable practices, it soon creates unfavorable working conditions and lowers the morale of employees; they no longer feel a loyalty to the system and do not hesitate to say what they think about the board of education and the policies they are forced to comply with in order to make a living.

The Conduct of Board Business

The board of education is legally required to conduct its business in regular meetings and in special meetings called from time to time. All meetings are open, with the exception of executive sessions when problems are taken up which the board thinks should not be discussed in public. In a number of states the decisions reached in executive session are not binding until voted on in open meeting.

The regularly established meetings of the board of education have been created for specific purposes. These purposes are, first to take up the business of the school system; second, to make decisions in accord with the school code and the needs of the community; third, to allow parents and taxpayers to observe their representatives in action; and, fourth, to enable members of the community to present their views on questions under consideration.

Whether or not a board adheres to these purposes in the conduct of its business has an influence on public and employee attitudes. A well-organized meeting in which sincere efforts are made to serve the school and community inspires confidence, respect, and trust, while a poorly managed, perfunctory, and discordant one leaves a residue of discontent with all who are concerned and interested in the school system.

Relations with the Superintendent

School board relations with the superintendent deserve special consideration in any discussion of internal affairs and their influence on his leadership and the morale of staff members. In many systems, the board of education is organized into a series of standing committees. Each committee is made responsible for some area of the school program. There may be committees on personnel, buildings and grounds, transportation, finance, public relations, instruction, and welfare. This system is used to expedite board business and divide the amount of work carried by members. It has, however, definite weaknesses that should be recognized: (1) The executive officer is required to report to committees instead of taking up problems with the whole board of education. (2) These committees become policy-making bodies, because their recommendations are, as a rule, accepted by the board without much question. (3) Members of the board have but slight understanding of the system aside from the areas in which they work on committee assignments. And (4) the tendency is strong for committees to encroach upon the administrative function of the superintendent. This form of board organization can easily produce unfavorable relations with the superintendent and reduce the effectiveness of his leadership in the school system.

Several states permit the local school board to divide executive responsibility between the superintendent, business manager, and other functionaries. This is known as a dual or multiple executive organization. Each executive reports directly to the board and the board coordinates their activities. Again the leadership of the superintendent is reduced in effectiveness when the board shows partiality for another executive and places more value upon business and finance, and plant and equipment than it does upon instruction, pupils, and teachers. A superintendent who fights to maintain balance between instruction and business, to put first things first, and to keep educational objectives in the foreground may find himself at odds with the board of education, especially a board that is made up of politicians and business people who are dollar-minded.

Complaints received by board members from teachers, parents, and people in the community are another cause of poor relationships, if they are handled incorrectly. Sound administration requires that all complaints be referred to the superintendent of schools and cleared through him with members of the staff. If satisfaction is not received by the complaining party, the board can then request the superintendent to report the facts and what he has done before an official decision is made. Instead of following this procedure, or one comparable to it, some board members assume responsibility for settling complaints themselves. Not only do they take over the authority of the superintendent, but also undermine his prestige in the school and community. The incorrect handling of complaints is a fertile breeding place for discord in the relationships of the board and the superintendent.

The interest that board members show in educational problems is another subject that enters into their relations with the superintendent. As the professional adviser of the board and the educational leader of the school system, it is his duty to keep the board informed of conditions and to recommend courses of action for meeting existing needs. Although the superintendent does not expect the board to approve all of his recommendations, he does expect that the members will consider and judge their worth with a fair degree of impartiality. If they are casual or indifferent about his recommendations, or if their decisions are made for personal, business, or political reasons, he is left with the alternatives of either protesting vigorously or else going along with the board for his own security. In the long run, any superintendent who plays the game for his own security may enjoy smoother relations with the board, but his leadership in the school system and the community is forfeited.

Adverse relations may also develop from the methods employed by the superintendent in dealing with the board. For instance, he may withhold vital information to protect himself, or he may initiate

important policies without consulting the board before they are
put into practice. Some superintendents destroy good will by assuming an attitude of intellectual superiority and by insisting upon the
right to decide educational policies. A few may try to bring community pressure to get what they want and, failing this, engage in
a whispering campaign to defeat members who are up for reelection.

Relations With Staff Personnel

Board relations with staff personnel are carried on mostly
through the superintendent and, in systems operating under a dual
executive arrangement, through the business manager. The superintendent is expected to advise the board on staff problems and to
recommend policies pertaining to selection, induction, salary, load,
tenure, sick-leave, and the like. Since members of the board enjoy
relatively few contacts with staff personnel, they do not understand
or appreciate the viewpoints of their own employees. Without this
insight, they are prone to decide matters of policy in terms of finance
instead of human value. Staff members are quick to sense the disposition of a board and feel that it is indifferent to their welfare.
Nothing that a board can do is more detrimental to morale than
to accentuate finance at the expense of human welfare.

Boards engage in other practices that alienate their relations
with the men and women who are working in the school system.
For example: they hire individuals for political reasons without much
regard for their qualifications; they promote a favored few whose
records do not justify advancement; they place on the private lives of
teachers restrictions that they themselves are unwilling to observe;
they bring pressure on employees to patronize selected business firms;
they refuse to support teachers in the face of unfair criticism; they
interfere with classroom instruction; they force teachers to accept
community service jobs after school hours; and they treat them
publicly as social inferiors. It is not to be wondered that teachers
become antagonistic to boards of education and refuse to extend
themselves beyond the minimum requirements of their employment.
No school system can function effectively under such conditions, to
say nothing of trying to undertake a program for better school and
community relations.

It is evident in this enumeration of board practices that resentment could be eliminated by treating employees fairly and by taking advantage of opportunities for developing friendly relations. Boards could raise salaries to meet higher costs of living and win support of teachers by not compelling them to fight for subsistence. When a policy that affects their interest and welfare is under consideration, there is no valid reason why teachers should not be invited to participate in discussions and express their views. Recognition of meritorious service costs the board little or nothing, but it makes a great deal of difference in attitudes of employees when they know that their services are appreciated.

The Education of Board Members

Most board members take office without knowledge of the responsibilities involved in their relationships with the superintendent, staff, and public. They assume that the schools are in fairly good condition, that the superintendent should decide educational policies, and that their work is restricted to the business and financial affairs of the system. This narrow outlook makes it imperative that board members receive training for the position they hold.

All boards of education should develop programs for the orientation and induction of new members through which they may learn their duties and what should be done to operate schools efficiently. This is their responsibility, not that of the superintendent. The idea may originate with the superintendent, but the board should work out its own program.

What should an orientation and induction program for new board members include? Certainly, it should include a manual or handbook describing what is expected of a board of education and the individuals who belong to it. Periodic visits with the superintendent to schools in the district should be a mandatory feature of the program, since there is no better way for board members to become familiar with plant conditions or to gain an understanding of the instructional process. A series of conferences should be scheduled for each new member with the superintendent and president of the board for the purpose of reviewing policies and analyzing problems confronting the schools. Memberships should be provided at public expense in local and state educational organizations, and especially the state school directors' association. Subscriptions should be provided at public expense to three or four leading periodicals on school administration, and each member should be supplied with copies of outstanding books on education. A convenient reference library should be an indispensable part of the program, with every encouragement to use it freely. Some boards have a rotating plan for member-attendance at national educational conventions where they may acquire information related to the solution of their own problems. If possible, new members should be asked to enroll at nearby universities for short, intensive courses which are designed for boards of education. Finally, a code of ethics should be established to govern the actions of members.

ADMINISTRATIVE-STAFF RELATIONS

Relationships between the board of education and the superintendent of schools have a positive or a negative effect upon relationships between the superintendent, his administrative and supervisory assistants, and members of the staff. A superintendent who enjoys good relations with the board is more likely to look upon his job as an opportunity to build a better school system. Staff personnel catch the spirit of the man and welcome the leadership he provides. A different reaction takes place when he is forced to contend with an unpleasant board that is more interested in saving money than in building a good school system.

Primary relations between administration and staff start with the superintendent and flow down a line of authority to the assistant superintendent, directors of special departments, supervisors, and building principals, according to the size of the system. The superintendent is the one who sets the over-all pattern of relationships, owing to his position as the chief executive officer. Under proper administrative conditions, his success or failure is bound up closely with the willingness of the staff to support his policies. In systems where desirable administrative-staff relations are found, the superintendent is usually a capable executive who possesses a dynamic and pleasing personality, a deep respect for human values, and knows how to work democratically with people. His policies follow a clearly defined philosophy of education and management and include recognition of staff achievements, opportunities for growth in service, staff participation in policy and program development, fair treatment, satisfactory working conditions, and a sincere concern for staff welfare. What a school system has by way of organization, administrative procedures, instruction, plant, and *esprit de corps* are due largely to the policies, leadership, courage, and vision of the superintendent.

Except in small school systems, the superintendent must rely upon subordinate administrative and supervisory officers to promote desirable staff relations. Poor subordinates, however, may do much to destroy his leadership and efforts to build a unified school system. They can misinterpret policies and badly manage excellent programs. Their quiet struggles for prestige and power may divide staff loyalties and set up competing factions. Unless a superintendent has capable and reliable subordinates, he may find himself heading a mediocre and strife-torn system.

Aside from the superintendent, perhaps the most important administrative and supervisory officer is the building principal. He is in more intimate contact with the staff than his immediate superiors. His attitudes and actions determine the way in which many teachers and nonteachers think and feel toward the school system. If he lacks character, his personality weakness is met with indifference; if he spends time absorbed in routine matters, the school moves along without much direction; if he interferes with teachers unnecessarily, irritation develops; if he is unwilling to delegate authority, important work does not get done; if he tries to rule with an iron hand, he creates tension and shuts off thinking; if he is concerned with his own advancement, cooperation is difficult to secure; if he is openly critical of the staff, he encourages hostility; if he is indifferent to human welfare, dissatisfaction becomes chronic; if he fails to support teachers, their confidence and respect is lost; if he refuses to recognize meritorious service, he destroys incentives for work; if he keeps policy matters to himself, uncertainty and confusion result.

RELATIONS BETWEEN TEACHERS

Relations between teachers should be evaluated for the effect they have on public opinion. Poor relations have brought on serious

damage to school systems and the status of professional employees
in the community. Teachers have undermined support and respect
by criticizing the work of colleagues to pupils, parents, and the
public. School policies have been openly opposed in newspapers
along with newer educational practices and legislative proposals
aimed at improving their own welfare. Teachers who engage in
these practices are both their own worst enemies and enemies of the
school system. The problems they create must be worked out by
administrators who wish to improve and strengthen relations with
the community.

The reasons for poor relations between teachers can be traced
to a variety of causes. The more typical are lack of administrative
direction, instructional practices, unethical conduct, division of responsibility, and formation of cliques.

Administrative Leadership

Unity among staff personnel is difficult to produce without
strong, administrative leadership. Lack of such leadership diverts attention from problems of teaching and learning and brings into
prominence petty differences and personal irritations common to
any group of people. Their continuance and spread leads to rivalry,
clique formation, destructive criticism, disagreement, and verbal
quarreling. These human weaknesses are less significant and destructive in school situations where the administrative leader brings
teachers together to share ideas, identify instructional problems, pool
resources, define acceptable goals, and coordinate their services.

Instructional Practices

Instructional practices in any good school are guided by a definite statement of the philosophy and objectives of teaching. When
there is no definite agreement on philosophy, objectives, and instructional practices, friction may develop between teachers and
leave parents confused as to the education their children are receiving. One teacher may believe that children grow best in a
democratic institution with as much freedom as they can manage
successfully, while another may believe that children should be kept

under strict control and told exactly what to do. One teacher may give home assignments as an aid to subject-matter mastery, while another may think that home assignments are unnecessary. One teacher may hold to rigid standards of achievement as measured by tests, while another may believe that standards should be broad and varied in terms of educational purposes and the nature of learners. One teacher may wish to follow a syllabus based on a textbook and supplementary readers, while another may wish to discard the textbook and use a wide variety of materials for each topic or problem studied. One may employ a methodology of recitation, drill, and testing, while another may build instruction around problems and projects involving many different types of learning activities. Differences in instructional practices are a serious cause of poor relations among teachers.

Unethical Conduct

Unethical conduct creates friction among teachers. Examples of unethical conduct are numerous. A teacher may attribute the weaknesses of a class in arithmetic to poor instruction by the previous teacher and make this opinion known to pupils and parents. Sometimes parents are told that their children do not read well, thanks to the "progressive" methods used by the second grade teacher, or that their children will pay an educational penalty later on because certain members of the staff are not upholding desirable achievement standards. Teachers who show initiative and imagination, who experiment with newer methods, and who try different curricular arrangements are often ridiculed by colleagues for their efforts. Any teacher who is the target of unfair criticism and abuse by colleagues is bound to feel resentful.

Malicious gossip and rumor are another form of unethical conduct which induces strained relations among faculty members. Illustrations are legion of teachers circulating stories and raising clever questions which throw doubt on the moral character of a fellow worker, thus injuring his or her status in the school and community. They can disrupt harmony among staff members in short order and cause much unnecessary suffering. Teachers cannot work together efficiently and present a solid front to the public when they are beset by malicious gossip and rumor.

Division of Responsibility

Disturbances arise over the division of responsibility among teachers. A heavy classroom schedule will be accepted without too much complaint, provided some teachers do not receive fewer classes, smaller sections, and fewer preparations than others. Sponsorship of extracurricular activities brings vigorous protest from those who are assigned such difficult, time-consuming activities as newspapers, yearbooks, and dramatics, for which no allowance is made in load or in financial compensation. Resentment over unfair division of responsibility becomes acute when there is a reasonable suspicion that favoritism has been shown to some members of the staff. The resentment is directed as much at these members as at the administrative officers who are responsible for staff assignments.

Differences also arise from the failure of teachers to perform the routine duties they receive in school management. For example, indifference to hall-duty during the passing of classes throws an added burden on teachers who take this work seriously. The refusal of a teacher to enforce traffic regulations on stairs and in corridors for fear of hurting his popularity with students likewise makes the work of others more difficult. Though seemingly of slight importance, situations of this character can cut deeply into the maintenance of good faculty relations.

Cliques

Cliques are small, exclusive groups of individuals banned together for their own interest and protection. They keep to themselves as much as possible. In an individual school, members of the foreign language department may remain apart from their colleagues, feeling that they have little in common with the rest of the faculty. Teachers of mathematics and science may set up their own clique because they regard themselves as being intellectually and socially superior, while teachers of college preparatory students may adopt a corresponding attitude toward those who instruct vocational students. It may be necessary for young teachers to remain together in meeting the dominance and abuse of older teachers. Teachers who belong to minority groups are often forced to act as a unit for protection against discrimination.

Cliques thrive mostly in schools where nothing is done to involve the staff in the study of common problems and where administrators remain in the background. Their influence can be modified when the causes are known and suitable measures worked out for diverting attention to instructional improvements.

RELATIONS WITH NONINSTRUCTIONAL PERSONNEL

School administrators and boards of education sometimes forget that noninstructional personnel are also front-line interpreters of the school. Custodians, engineers, secretaries, clerks, bus drivers, cafeteria workers, home visitors, truant officers, dental hygienists, and nurses have many contacts in the community with friends and neighbors and through membership in religious, fraternal, and social groups. Their attitudes toward the institution and its personnel are just as important as those of teachers in influencing the public mind. When they are dissatisfied with their jobs and do not get along well with staff members, the reasons are associated principally with politics, dual administration, job definition, recognition, and economic welfare.

Politics

In quite a number of school systems, custodians, clerks, cafeteria workers, and bus drivers are political appointees. They are employed not because of their ability, but to pay off political favors. Lacking the qualifications required for understanding and performing their duties, they invite criticism and attack by professional personnel who have worked for years to establish high standards of selection.

Unfortunately, citizens are not aware of this condition and much educational work must be done before they will be ready to clean up boards of education that are dominated by political organizations. Teachers associations can assist in educating the public to the facts and in demanding that school boards establish definite qualifications for the employment of noninstructional personnel.

Dual Administration

This arrangement, which was referred to previously, is conducive to conflict in the entire school system. Employees who are hired by the business manager are not responsible to the super-intendent and line officers under his jurisdiction. They take their orders from the business manager and his subordinate officials. Among these employees may be secretaries, engineers, repairmen, stock handlers, clerks, and custodians.

If relations between the superintendent and the business manager are friendly and cooperative, they may form an efficient working team and things will run smoothly in the system. If they are constantly disagreeing and vying with one another for power, the repercussions of this situation may be felt throughout the system. For example, custodians may refuse to take orders from principals; engineers and repairmen may take their time about performing essential services; and classes may be interrupted by window washers; and deliveries of supplies made on irregular schedules. The relationship between different groups of employees may become tense and bitter, reflecting the relationship between the executive heads of the system.

The solution to this problem lies in the adoption of a unit-executive type of organization, with the superintendent as the principal administrative officer to whom the business manager is responsible. Until this change is made in systems now operating under more than one chief executive officer, good staff relations cannot be expected unless those at the top are able to work successfully together and set a commendable example for all employees to follow.

Job Definition

Much of the trouble between instructional and noninstructional personnel could be avoided through the technique of job definition so that each individual understands what is expected of him. In practice this is seldom done with thoroughness, and the result is argument and disagreement over the assumption of various responsibilities. The janitor claims that the teacher should have children pick up pieces of paper on the floor before they are dismissed. The teacher blames the janitor for leaving the window shades uneven or not arranging seats in proper order. Clerks refuse to do mimeograph work needed for classroom instruction and object to teachers using office phones during certain hours. Cafeteria workers maintain that they are not responsible for the conduct of pupils in the lunchroom. The bus driver insists that pupils be supervised by a teacher, and the home visitor denies any obligation to report findings to homeroom advisers.

Recognition

Noninstructional staff personnel want acknowledgment and praise just as much as teachers for outstanding service. They seldom receive any. Instead, they are treated by some teachers as social inferiors and criticized in front of pupils. Conflicts involving noninstructional personnel would be reduced and almost eliminated if friendly attitudes were shown toward them and they were accorded deserved recognition. Better relations have been promoted in schools where these workers are invited to faculty meetings and serve on staff committees dealing with matters in which they have an interest. It does not take too much labor to promote good relations with noninstructional personnel when proper attitudes are taken by other staff members and they are recognized for the worth and contribution of their services.

Economic Welfare

The economic welfare of noninstructional personnel has been notoriously poor with respect to salary, tenure, sick-leave, and retirement. Some improvements have taken place in recent years through collective bargaining, but the condition is still bad in many parts of the country. Their insecurity accounts for a large share of the disloyalty they feel toward the institution and the ill will they hold toward the teaching group whose economic position has undergone steady improvement. As essential workers, they are entitled to higher wages and the protection afforded by sick-leave, tenure, and retirement. If the teaching group took more of a direct interest in the welfare of these workers, their concern would invite friendly and cooperative relations.

IMPROVEMENT OF RELATIONS

The improvement of staff relations starts with the board of education. Through its actions in conducting meetings, showing an intelligent concern for instructional problems, extending fair treatment to administrative and staff personnel, and maintaining a strict division of labor between policy decision and policy execution, the board of education inspires confidence and builds a feeling of security that permeates the entire school system.

Given this condition, the superintendent and those who assist him have an excellent opportunity to foster good staff relations and to make progress toward the achievement of educational goals. The extent to which they succeed depends upon their friendliness, understanding, integrity, and skill in working with people.

In a small school system, the superintendent is the person responsible for establishing cooperative relations with and among members of the staff. This is done largely through leadership in everyday affairs that involve close, personal relations. As a school system increases in size, opportunities for personal relations between the superintendent and the staff become fewer in number. It then becomes the function of the chief executive officer to establish the climate for good relations, with personal contacts being left to intermediary administrative and supervisory assistants. Of this group, none is quite so important as the individual building principal. Unless he seeks to achieve good staff relations, nothing else is likely to produce them.

But more is needed to affect wholesome, internal relations between members of the staff and the administration than a spirit of personal leadership by those in charge of a school system. There must be policies that contribute to the development of good relations. One of these is teacher participation in the formulation of educational plans and programs. Participation means that teachers are free to suggest solutions to problems and to make decisions on how a school system shall be run. It means that legal channels are established through which grievances may be aired, and organizational devices created for pooling the intellectual resources of the staff. Any school system that operates according to a policy of shared responsibility is bound to promote a genuine sense of cooperation between staff and administration.

Another policy of far-reaching importance in building good relations is that of recognizing the outstanding accomplishments of individuals and groups. All individuals, no matter what kind of work they do, are psychologically so constructed that they must know whether or not their labors are being appreciated by those above them in line of authority. They are not willing to do their best or to expend extra effort if what they do is taken for granted. Every morale study of workers in industry has borne out this point, but for some unexplainable reason little has been done about it in the administration of public education.

Continuing attention to the improvement of working conditions represents still another step in the growth of wholesome relations. Improvement of working conditions means more than putting a few easy chairs in the faculty rest room. It involves suitable furniture for pupils and teachers; reasonable work loads; an adequate supply of materials and equipment; classrooms that are painted in pleasant colors and kept clean; a sensible work program for non-instructional personnel; and other considerations.

Sound administration cannot overlook the importance of giving teachers the right to teach within the limits of defined policies. Teachers are highly sensitive to this right and resent petty interruptions and attempts to force the adoption of narrow ideas by those in authority. Not infrequently misguided boards of education and superintendents of schools permit vested interest groups to dictate course content or to insist upon the removal of content that is inimical to their welfare. When teachers are told what or what not to teach they develop feelings of insecurity and become cynical toward the school system and their role in the education of children and youth for life in a democracy.

Finally, good staff relations are achieved when teachers and noninstructional employees are consulted by the board of education and the administration on questions related to their welfare, as salary, load, hours, sick-leave, and tenure. Their recommendations may not always be accepted, but this is less important than the right to make their wants known. School employees are willing to go along with a policy or a program when they understand the facts behind it, even though the policy runs contrary to their opinions. When the facts are concealed and they are not consulted, they become suspicious and take the position that they are not treated fairly.

A school system that follows these policies is its own best source of favorable publicity.

7

Pupil and Alumni Relations

An impressive number of people in every community form their judgments of a school system from the comments that are made about it by pupils. They hear them discuss teachers, talk about homework assignments, express opinions on the value of what they do in classes, evaluate the fairness of rules and regulations, and describe experiences they had with the principal, office secretary, doctor, nurse, cafeteria workers, bus drivers, and other workers employed in the system.

No public school can expect to enjoy the confidence and support of parents and nonparents in the community unless the comments of most pupils are favorable to the system. Much may be done in the name of public relations by the board of education and central administrative officials, but what they do may be neutralized if the primary level of relationships with pupils is unsatisfactory.

An effective public relations program likewise makes provision for continuing contacts with pupils after they have left the secondary school. As alumni, they are in an excellent position to increase community understanding of and faith in the schools they attended.

104

TEACHER PERSONALITY

Teacher personality influences the nature of the thoughts and feelings of pupils toward a school. Analysis of traits in teachers that cause pupils to think and speak favorably are not difficult to determine. Classroom observations and interviews reveal that pupils like to be with teachers who are attractive in appearance, pleasant in voice, and considerate of human dignity; that they respond to teachers who are friendly, fair, and understanding of their personal needs and problems; that they appreciate teachers who possess a sense of humor, yet waste no time in the business of teaching; that they respect those who demand no more in courtesy than they return, and who are able to maintain poise and demonstrate self-control in the face of trying circumstances; and that they cooperate with teachers who give help and offer encouragement when learning difficulties are encountered.

Such teachers are students of children and skilled practitioners in the democratic way of life. They understand the growth patterns of pupils in age groups with whom they are dealing and how to adapt instructional activities to individual differences. They involve pupils in the process of setting up the necessary controls for living together successfully and assuming responsibility for managing their own affairs. They regard organized work as fundamental to learning and insist upon the maintenance of standards attainable by members of the group. Constructive in their own outlook on life, they deflect ideas and expressions away from bias and unreasoned criticism and show pupils how to look for facts and use them in reaching conclusions. These teachers are often firm with pupils but never negative in their criticisms. They do not believe that relationships which promote growth and development can be constructed on a foundation of fault-finding, lack of trust, and domination that leaves little room for pupil initiative and resourcefulness.

TREATMENT OF PUPILS

Allied closely to teacher traits is the use of authority in the classroom. Authority may be used wisely and result in desirable relationships, or it may be used unwisely and destroy the interaction

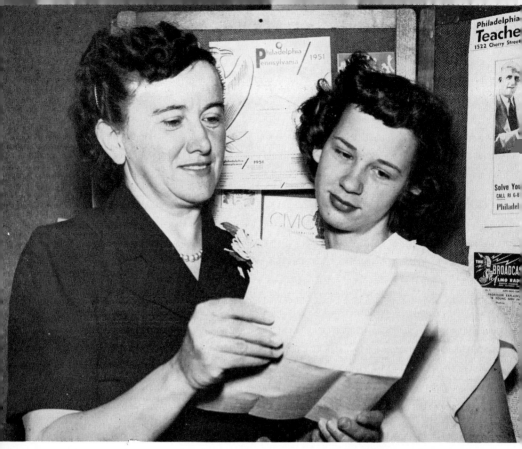

(*Courtesy Public Schools, Philadelphia, Pennsylvania.*)

Pupils respond to teachers who are friendly and helpful.

that is wanted. A few of the critical points on which the use of authority may turn teacher-pupil relationships one way or the other will be described.

Respect for Personality

It has long been an accepted tenet of democracy that respect shall be shown for the worth and dignity of the individual. Effective teachers know that the observance of this tenet leaves its mark on the behavior of pupils and satisfies a human need for security. They uphold it by treating serious breaches of conduct in private and by working quietly with pupils who present problems of social adjustment. Honest mistakes made by pupils are acknowledged pleasantly and suggestions offered for overcoming them in the future. Allowance is provided in the learning process for individual differences and tasks are assigned which can be handled successfully. Conscientious effort is acknowledged in order to encourage continued endeavor. These teachers are not hesitant in helping pupils to understand their own weaknesses and natural limitations, but the help is given without undermining self-confidence or injuring their status in the group. They arrange situations and delegate responsibilities from which youngsters gain a sense of importance. The common amenities of social life are practiced and departures from them are not permitted. Each pupil comes to feel that he is a person in his own right and that he is contributing to the group. Teachers who show respect for personality in these and other ways stimulate better learning and enjoy the cooperation and good will of the learners.

Personal and Professional Problems

Teachers who develop high-quality rapport with pupils seldom, if ever, take advantage of their position to enlist sympathy and aid for their own personal and professional welfare. They maintain that no teacher has the right to involve pupils in discussions of salary, load, staff tensions, administrative policies, family problems, adequacy of supplies, sick leave, or tenure, and that to do so represents a breach of professional ethics and a misuse of authority. They are fully aware that the emotionalizing of their needs may bring pupils closer to them at the time, but that the continuation of this practice can only lead to a loss of respect and the censure of parents and other people in the community.

Elements of Prejudice

Successful teachers guard against possible interpretations of prejudice in their tone of voice, choice of words, physical gestures, and facial expressions. They try to acknowledge the contributions of every pupil, no matter how trivial, so that none may feel slighted. At the same time, they protect members of the group against intolerance and abuse by their peers. Classroom incidents are used for teaching respect for others, intercultural understandings, and the ideals and customs of different groups in society. They make a deliberate effort to treat all alike and to have pupils reach their own conclusions without being influenced. They know that expressed or implied elements of prejudice inhibit responsiveness and produce a dislike of the teacher and the school.

Disciplinary Action

The handling of discipline stands out among the causes of satisfactory and unsatisfactory relations with pupils. Efficient teachers regard good discipline as a condition which is essential to effective instruction. When pupils become restless, inattentive, and annoying, they examine their own practices to find out if they are responsible before anything is done to reprimand the pupils. Experience has taught them that most youngsters do not become restless and disturbing in the classroom when activities move along at brisk pace and when they are being challenged to do their best. Moreover, competent teachers understand the normal behaviors of pupils at different stages of growth and development and make allowances for these in their planning. They are able to prevent situations from arising that would call for disciplinary action. Their knowledge of child growth and development equips them to make distinctions between normal behavior and symptoms of maladjustment and to refer pupils who show these symptoms to trained counselors. The counselors work with physicians, psychologists, psychiatrists, and social workers in seeking the causes of maladjustment and in prescribing remedial treatment. Through their services many pupils, who if the attempted solution to their problems had been based on an indiscriminate use of punishment would have become chronic delinquents, have been restored to their rightful place in society. Pupils recognize that teachers who follow these procedures are firm but fair in the management of the classroom, and that a good state of order is necessary to successful learning.

Less competent teachers make mistakes in disciplinary action, thereby placing a strain on their relations with pupils. One of the mistakes is that of employing punishment freely for slight infractions of rules and failure to meet achievement standards. As examples, they lower academic marks for poor deportment; they prevent participation in extracurricular activities for unfinished homework; they assign copy exercises as a panacea for absence and tardiness; and they detain an entire class for the misdeeds of one or more members. The cumulative effect of their actions is dislike by pupils and criticism by parents.

Another mistake is the sending of pupils to a detention hall for petty reasons. The detention hall is any room in the building to which pupils are assigned after regular dismissal. Under the supervision of a single teacher, it is held for an hour or more daily and pupils must report there until the amount of time called for by the penalty is completed. Penalties are given for such offenses as whispering, loitering, inattention, noise, untidy work, inappropriate remarks, forgetting of books, tardiness, and unexcused absence. This device stands as an open invitation for abuse of authority in the hands of many teachers, and it can scarcely be considered as a satisfactory remedy for the more serious cases of unsocial behavior.

An increasing number of school systems have become concerned with the mass of pupils who receive detention. They have concluded from their studies that the detention hall has two fundamental weaknesses. First, they have discovered that most pupils are sent to detention hall by the least capable members of the faculty, and second, that serious conflicts develop because detention interferes with home duties, medical and dental appointments, after-school employment, and attendance at weekday religious classes. Their solution has been to substitute justifiable detention by individual teachers in their own classrooms and to keep this arrangement flexible enough to avoid conflicts.

A third mistake is the administration of corporal punishment. This may take the form of physical chastisement, pulling of hair, tearing of clothing, and forceful pushing. Although the laws of some states permit the teacher to administer corporal punishment the same as the parent, it is doubtful that the over-all result is ever constructive. A few children may show evidence of better behavior because of rough handling, but the facts do not seem to bear this out with the rank and file of pupils. Instead of trying to abide by rules and regulations, they often make their violation a challenge. Instead of feeling friendly and respectful of teachers, they regard them with suspicion. And instead of entering the school with a sense of enjoyment and enthusiasm, they resent the time that must be spent there.

In addition to these products of corporal punishment, the

school becomes an object of damaging publicity whenever a child is allegedly abused or injured or parents demand action against the cruelty of a teacher. The newspapers always pick up and give full play to stories of this nature. And interestingly enough, no matter how wrong the pupil may have been in his conduct, the chances are far better than even that public opinion will be against the teacher.

Judicious boards of education and superintendents now prohibit any type of physical contact with pupils. They know that corporal punishment is not conducive to the development of wholesome relations with pupils and that it invites destructive complaint and criticism in the community.

INSTRUCTIONAL PRACTICES

Relations with pupils are changed for better or worse by the instructional practices of the teacher. Among the more crucial in this respect are teacher preparation, methods of teaching, controversial issues, marking systems, tests, and policy on failure and promotion.

Teacher Preparation

Other things being equal, pupils hold in high esteem teachers who have a thorough knowledge of subject matter. They work more diligently with these teachers and feel that they are receiving a valuable education. Their opinions of them are transmitted to parents and relayed by parents to other members of the community. A school gains in prestige when the belief is prevalent that faculty personnel are highly qualified in the subject matter of instruction.

Teachers who are inadequately prepared in subject matter background are soon discovered by pupils, especially in junior and senior high schools. Attempts at concealment of this weakness are not successful. As soon as it becomes evident that teachers do not know their subject fields, pupils undergo a change in attitude and suffer a loss of confidence. They are less willing to work hard and to seek the help needed for acquiring mastery of assigned material. It does not take long for their reactions to become known in the school and community.

Methods of Teaching

Teachers who combine knowledge of subject matter with proficiency in teaching methods do more for pupils. They are able to secure attention, maintain interest, and adjust learning to individual needs and differences. Under their direction subject matter takes on life and vitality and the classroom becomes a stimulating and enjoyable challenge to the learner. Pupils respond readily to these teachers and hold them in high regard because of the experiences they are having. No other individual in the school occupies a more strategic position in the cultivation of good, personal public relations than does the teacher who combines mastery of subject matter with skill in the use of teaching procedures.

Controversial Issues

The presentation and treatment of controversial issues affects the relations of teachers and pupils. Teachers who follow a democratic method of problem solving see that all sides of a question are brought out into the open and examined. They show pupils how to gather and appraise information, organize thinking, and draw tentative conclusions from the material available. They are as much concerned with the process of dealing with controversial questions as they are with the knowledge acquired. Ability to divorce their own viewpoints from classroom discussion and to remain impartial commands respect and appreciation by the young people who come under their direction.

Teachers lose status with pupils if they depart from this method of handling controversial issues. Their departures may involve failure to present more than one side of a problem, placement of dogmatic emphasis on personal beliefs and opinions, display of emotion, refusal to evaluate sources of information, injection of propaganda into teaching, and denial of the fact that there is more than one solution for every social problem.

Homework Assignments

Public schools have traditionally followed a policy of giving pupils assignments of homework. They have done so in the belief that the assignments are educationally beneficial to pupils. This policy has been rather generally accepted by young people and their parents. They see in it an opportunity for the development of independent study habits, the study and assimilation of textual materials, the refinement of skills, the making of progress at individual rates of speed, and the worthy use of leisure. Also, it permits the parent to obtain a better understanding of what the child is doing in school and to assist him when necessary.

Continuing support of the homework policy may be lost with the introduction of such questionable practices as requiring so much homework that time is taken from children for rest and relaxation, allowing assignments to pile up unevenly, engaging children in dull and worthless copy exercises, failing to explain clearly what is expected, assigning problems that are too difficult for pupils, and committing the sin of not correcting and returning the assignments turned in by pupils.

Whenever criticisms arise over the nature and amount of work involved in assignments, steps should be taken by school officials to check their validity. They may discover that teachers are beginning to introduce practices that should be corrected before more serious trouble is encountered. This is a far more sensible procedure than resort to time-worn arguments on the value pupils receive from homework assignments. An intelligent parent who takes an interest in homework knows whether or not they are worthwhile and reasonable and does not need to be told so by school officials in defense of poor practices. A better procedure, however, would be that of inviting pupils and parents to meet periodically with faculty members and review the whole question. This is one of the surest means for preventing problems and for bringing pupils and parents closer to teachers.

Marks and Marking Systems

Marks and marking systems should be included in any examination of instructional practices because of the effect they have on pupil attitudes and feelings toward a teacher or teachers in a school. So much importance is attached to marks in connection with promotion, graduation, and college admission that it is natural for pupils to be concerned. Because their welfare is tied up in marks and marking systems, they want to know how teachers evaluate tests, written work, notebooks, and special assignments and whether or not their methods are fair and impartial.

Teachers who establish fine interaction with pupils take full advantage of this interest. They devote as much time as necessary to the enumeration and discussion of factors which enter into the evaluation of tests and work submitted by pupils and the explanation of how these factors are weighed in arriving at the judgments they express in terms of percentage or letter grades. They are receptive to suggestions made by pupils for modifying and improving the marking system, recognizing that pupils will believe more fully in the fairness of the system if they have had a hand in devising it.

These teachers recommend that the whole subject of marking be studied by members of the faculty under the direction of the principal. They are convinced from their conversations with pupils and the remarks they make that some standardization should obtain among the different teachers in the school. There is no justifiable reason why one should allow deportment to influence his marking of a notebook, another penmanship, and a third the matter of form when the assignment called for nothing more than an accurate and organized presentation of factual information on a topic under study. While teachers may never reach complete agreement on what to look for in reading a theme and what is most important, nevertheless they can adopt like methods of scoring examinations and reduce many of the differences that now exist. Consistency among teachers in this respect promotes confidence and faith in the marking system.

Teachers who are concerned about their interaction with pupils try to eliminate the tension and fear which too great a stress on marks inevitably produces. They do not want marks to be regarded as the end products of learning or the principal cause for motivating achievement. They want pupils to look upon marks and marking systems as convenient and helpful tools for understanding their own strength and weakness and for guiding their efforts toward self-improvement. It has been their experience that pupil growth and development take place more rapidly when the progress of the learner rather than the satisfaction of academic standards is made the point of attention.

Examinations

Standardized and teacher-made examinations are accepted by pupils as a necessary part of the learning process. They are challenged by examinations and the opportunity they afford for determining how well they are doing in classwork and where they need to make improvements. Seldom do pupils ever object to the taking of examinations that cover the material they have studied and from which they may receive assistance in understanding their own learning problems. Their attitudes toward examinations only undergo change when certain practices are introduced which they think are unfair and harmful. The more common of these practices are administering examinations for disciplinary purposes, inconsistency among teachers in methods of scoring, test items foreign to the material studied, too much concern for test results instead of their diagnostic value, and criticism for poor outcomes without attempting to discover the causes.

Failure and Promotion

Failure and promotion policies affect the relations of teachers and pupils. It is understandable why pupils dislike the prospect of repeating a grade or a subject and why some parents rebel at the idea and consider it a stigma on themselves as much as on their children. In modern schools the sting of failure is prevented by working with parents. They are notified of unsatisfactory progress at any time during the year and no teacher is permitted to send home a report card with a mark of failure unless they have been contacted previously. Invitations are extended to parents to confer with teachers as soon as notices are received so that they may cooperate in running down the causes of unsatisfactory progress and deciding how they may be treated. If the question of grade or subject repetition must be decided, no action is taken until the parents have had an opportunity to talk with teachers and to review school records. Then the decision is made in terms of what is best for pupils. These and similar procedures have promoted wholesome attitudes in parents which are reflected by pupils in their relations with teachers.

CURRICULUM ADJUSTMENT

A number of state departments of education estimate that one out of three pupils who enter first grade will leave school by the time he reaches the age of seventeen. This is more or less confirmed by figures compiled in many local school districts. Some of the reasons for this heavy mortality lie beyond control of the institution, but many of the others boil down to dissatisfaction with the curriculum. Pupils seem to think that neither the content of required subjects nor the methods by which it is taught are worth much in meeting the everyday problems of living.

Their opinion amounts to a serious indictment of secondary education in this country which is not completely borne out by the facts. The secondary school has made vast strides in recent years in adjusting its programs of studies and course offerings to the life needs of learners. Excellent examples are found in the commercial and vocational programs and the enrichment of subjects like art, music, homemaking, and science. And more is being done every day to adapt the curriculum to the personal and social needs of the learner.

While this is true, it must be admitted that a wide gap does exist between the nature of the curriculum and the needs of youth who drop out of school before graduation. This gap should be closed. It can be done by taking more interest in the growth and development of students and less concern for the achievement of those academic standards that are out of line with reality. It can be done by removing dead material from courses of study and substituting more concepts and problems related to everyday living. It can be done by getting away from routine drill on factual information and questionable skills and emphasizing individual and group methods of solving life problems. A secondary school which does these things increases its holding power and sends forth more students who are loyal to the institution and better equipped to meet life successfully.

RULES AND REGULATIONS

School rules and regulations are indispensable to the efficient operation of the institution and the achievement of educational objectives.

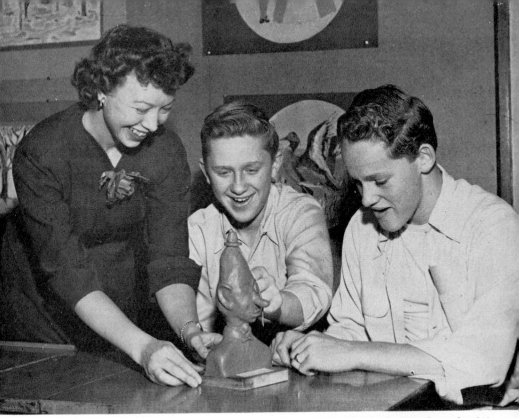

A sense of humor goes a long way in building sound pupil-teacher relationships.

Their function is generally not understood or appreciated by pupils. They are more inclined to look only at the nature of these controls and the methods of administration. The understanding of function may be accomplished successfully when pupils and their parents are involved in the study of need and the drafting of recommendations. This involvement may start in the neighborhood school and extend upward to the board of education when system-wide proposals are under advisement.

Whether or not pupils and their parents are involved in the study of need and the drafting of recommendations, all new school rules and regulations should be publicized fully before they become effective. The school may bring them to public attention through newspaper articles, talks before parent-teacher associations, discussions with members of student councils, and leaflets mailed to

116

parents. Not only the new rules and regulations should be explained but also the reasons for their adoption.

It must be recognized that understanding alone is no guarantee of acceptance. Acceptance is based more upon the nature of the regulation and the extent to which it seems reasonable. For example, pupils accept without much hesitation the small fines levied on the return of overdue books to the library, but should the amount of fines be tripled they would protest vigorously. They may agree to a rule for making up work missed during absence, but not if the rule states that it must be completed in one week no matter how long they have been out for illness. They may accept a schedule fixing the time at which they may be admitted to the building in the morning, yet they can see no reason for being forced to remain out-of-doors in cold and rainy weather simply because the bus arrived earlier than usual.

Their attitudes toward rules and regulations are likewise influenced by methods of administration. Some members of the staff may insist upon a strict observance of every rule and regulation no matter what the circumstances are surrounding a violation. They seldom try to understand the pupil's point of view or make allowance for unusual conditions. To punish pupils for talking in the corridors after an exciting assembly program is an illustration of this kind of enforcement. On the other hand, just as much damage is done by teachers who refuse to call pupils to task for disregarding established rules and regulations. They lose respect and double the work of other teachers in the building. The administration of rules and regulations must be done with firmness and fairness by all staff members in order to achieve the objectives of education and retain the good will of pupils.

In some communities it is essential that attention be given to the cultural background of pupils in the formulation of rules and regulations. It is easy to run counter to deep-seated traditions and customs unless this matter is taken into consideration. Within limits permitted under law, adjustments should be made out of respect for pupils who are required to observe religious holidays, dietary regulations, customs of dress, and the like. They are most appreciative of whatever the school does to make allowance for their particular interests and practices.

RELATIONS OUTSIDE OF THE CLASSROOM

Pupils have numerous contacts with instructional and noninstructional personnel outside of the classroom. These points of contact must be studied for possibilities of increasing friendliness and cooperation between pupils and members of the staff.

Library

The library is one point of contact where pupils form definite opinions of a school. The nature of their opinions varies with the personality of the individual in charge and the services they receive. A librarian who greets pupils with a smile, chats cheerfully, and tries to understand their needs sets an entirely different tone from one who gives short answers, shows impatience, and demands observance of minor regulations.

Good library service calls for (1) a time schedule that allows pupils to borrow and return books both before and after school; (2) instruction—both formal and informal—on how to use the resources that are found there; and (3) special reference shelves where pupils may get books quickly. An efficient library contains interesting bulletin boards, displays of new books, and devices for informing and interesting pupils. When books are overdue or their return is needed for special reasons, courteous notes are sent to pupils by the librarian and her assistants. Pupils like a school library and learn to use it extensively when it is directed by a competent person who gives helpful, considerate, and courteous service.

Medical Centers

The protection of a child's health is now an established part of the school program. School board policies and state laws provide that pupils shall be examined periodically by physicians, nurses, dentists, oral hygienists, and other specialists and receive first aid treatment and care for sudden illness.

How medical personnel handle their contacts with pupils and parents is important in building good public relations. Nothing wins praise more quickly than the tactful and efficient administration of medical services and a high degree of personal interest in children needing corrective and remedial attention. Unless medical personnel are sensitive to their public relations opportunities, they may handle child and parent contacts poorly. A check on complaints received in a number of schools confirms this statement. Both pupils and parents have registered objection against the crude and impersonal practices of some of these workers.

It behooves the administrator to exercise care in selecting medical personnel and then see that they are orientated to the nature of their responsibilities. Too many of these people assume that their duties are limited to a performance of medical services. They are just as much a part of the school as teachers and should be required to respect and uphold institutional policies.

School Office

It is surprising how many times daily, weekly, and monthly pupils have occasion to visit the school office. They go there with messages from teachers, to get information, to see the principal, to use the telephone, and for sundry reasons. Every time they enter the office they have contacts with staff members. If they receive courteous treatment and their business is handled efficiently, the office stands high in their estimation. However, knowing that they are not welcome, that going there may mean several minutes of waiting, and that it may be difficult to see the principal changes their feelings about the office and makes it a liability in public relations.

Cafeteria

School cafeterias exist for the benefit of pupils and the convenience of staff members, not for the accumulation of profits. In this respect, they may be thought of as service agencies having the function of preparing and distributing wholesome meals. The extent to which they fulfill this function determines how they are appraised by pupils. Perhaps no other agency, outside of the classroom, undergoes a more careful scrutiny than does the cafeteria.

In analyzing service features which give rise to positive and negative opinions, it will be found that pupils are keenly observant of food prices, speed of service, cleanliness, attractiveness, seating accommodations, size of portions, quality of food, variations in menus, range of selection, appearance of counter help, and, above all, the understanding and consideration of cafeteria employees.

These points cannot be overlooked, nor a study of them neglected, if the cafeteria is to aid in the development of more satisfactory relationships with pupils.

Physical Plant

Relations between pupils and custodial personnel who are responsible for the physical conditions of the building and grounds should be examined.

Attitudes of pupils toward custodial personnel are conditioned by instruction and personal experience. Administrators and teachers should spend time in classrooms and assemblies explaining the work of custodians and pointing out the need for cooperation in keeping the plant clean and free from defacement. Pupils are generally willing to do their part where good instruction is given and pride is taken in maintaining a clean and attractive school.

The instruction they receive is sometimes off-set by custodians themselves. Though these men and women who perform cleaning and maintenance services have no jurisdiction over pupils, they assume this authority and sometimes treat pupils who disobey their orders with shouts, abusive language, and even rough handling. Resentment against abusive treatment may be expressed by marking walls, plugging lavatory facilities, and scattering paper on floors. This condition is disruptive of the unity sought in a school and should be prevented.

Conflict possibilities between pupils and custodial personnel can be reduced and usually eliminated if thought is given to the problem. The solution starts with the employment of individuals who have more social intelligence than is typically found among the rank and file of this group today. The limits of their authority should be defined clearly and procedures outlined for reporting pupils who violate regulations. They should be made to feel a responsibility for the success of the school and know it is their job to earn the good will and respect of pupils.

Transportation

Pupils who travel by school bus develop an acquaintanceship with the driver that places him in a unique position to influence their thinking. They do not regard him in quite the same way as they do other members of the staff and talk in his presence freely about the school and the teachers they have in classes. In the course of a year he learns a great deal about the school and how pupils appraise it.

A competent bus driver who regards himself as a member of the staff can be exceedingly helpful in correcting false statements of pupils and explaining reasons for policies and practices they do not like. He is in a unique position to listen to their complaints, discuss their problems, and bring out facts they might not consider. His services in interpreting the school to pupils and reporting their attitudes to the principal are invaluable.

These possibilities are never realized in some districts for the reason that the bus driver loses the friendship of pupils. Being responsible for the enforcement of rules on safety and social conduct, he abuses his authority and creates situations which are unpleasant. Pupils dislike abusive language, outbursts of anger, and favoritism. Instead of cooperating with the driver, they try to make his job more difficult by doing annoying things. Their relations may reach a breaking point and become a community issue.

Social Situations

The objective of good relations between pupils and members of the staff may be furthered through informal contacts inside and outside of the building. Within the school, pupils and staff members meet one another during the passing of classes, at the opening and the closing of school, and during recess in the elementary grades. As unimportant as these casual contacts may seem, actually they are an avenue for encouraging and strengthening friendships. This is true because pupils like to be recognized, met with a ready smile, and know that they are wanted. Common everyday expressions of cordiality and good will go a long way in creating a pleasant atmosphere and breaking down barriers.

School functions, such as parties, dances, and contests, provide excellent opportunities for bringing staff members and pupils closer together. Teachers who dance with pupils, teachers who take part in games, teachers who go to pep rallies and cheer lustily are teachers whom pupils like. They are different from teachers who stand on the side and make it their business to see that pupils behave themselves and do nothing irregular or unusual.

Sometimes a few inexperienced teachers confuse friendliness with familiarity in their relations with pupils. They make the mistake of dating high school pupils, spending time talking with them in drug stores and restaurants after school and in the evening, taking pupils of the opposite sex for rides in automobiles, and permitting youngsters to address them by first names. Though their actions may be quite harmless and well-intentioned, they are considered indiscreet and contrary to prevailing codes of behavior. They inevitably invite popular comment and speculation, which lowers their standing with pupils.

Many informal contacts take place outside of the school in stores, on the street, at social affairs, and in churches. Each contact, no matter how brief, has some meaning and influence on pupil opinions. Without much question, pupil opinions are influenced most favorably when teachers and noninstructional staff members extend a friendly hand, engage in pleasant conversation, and accept pupils as they would other persons.

ALUMNI RELATIONS

It is always surprising how many former pupils accept invitations to attend high school alumni dances, homecoming football games, reunions, and similar events. Most of them are young people whose formal education came to a halt either before or at the time of graduation. Their willingness to return suggests that they feel a sentimental attachment to the school. This was apparent during the war years when secondary schools sent out greeting cards, newspapers, and bulletins to former pupils in the armed services. An overwhelming response came back in the form of letters, telephone calls from parents, and school visits by servicemen and women.

The experience of these years reminded secondary school people that they had done little to encourage and maintain contacts with former pupils. It opened the eyes of some to their possibilities for public relations.

School Services

Alumni relations should be founded on a continuing interest in the welfare of former pupils and a desire to provide useful services, such as the following, which alumni understand and appreciate: (1) sponsoring social affairs for the opportunity they afford to meet faculty and pupils; (2) sending congratulatory letters to former pupils on their twenty-first birthdays; (3) mailing an annual inventory card for information concerning their work, marital status, family, and so forth; (4) disseminating this information through publication to former pupils; (5) issuing periodic newsletters concerning individual graduates; (6) providing counseling services for personal problems and vocational placement; (7) publishing honors won by former pupils; (8) mailing the school newspaper to alumni whose addresses are known; and (9) developing any particular services which seem appropriate in the local situation.

Alumni Associations

Practically all of the activities listed previously can be performed without having an alumni association. Those who have worked closely with alumni groups, however, are convinced that better relationships will be developed if these and other activities are channeled through an organization to which the credit can be given.

Initiative for starting an alumni association should come from the school. A faculty sponsor or a principal will find that alumni who have finished school within the last five to six years are interested and even anxious to form an association, but they are uncertain about how to do it. Given direction from a sponsor, they soon learn to develop their own organization and take over activities carried on previously by the school.

Successful alumni associations are managed by elected officers and an executive committee which includes one or more representatives of the high school staff. The executive committee is charged with program planning and appointing committees to perform the group activities. Besides those mentioned, the usual activities are sponsoring an alumni newspaper two to four times a year; giving awards to outstanding pupils for athletics, debating, scholarship, and school contributions; providing financial help for needy pupils; encouraging members of the graduating class to join the alumni association; issuing identification cards to graduates showing their name and date of graduation; maintaining files of information about their members; and sponsoring reunions and social events.

Most alumni associations have not done much work with the school on educational problems. There is no reason why they cannot build a file of resource people who might be called upon to talk in classes, show interesting motion pictures and hobby collections, and serve on curriculum committees. They can be represented in the planning of new school buildings, floating of bond issues, organizing of adult evening programs, planning of recreational centers, and other matters of vital concern to the school and the community.

Courtesy Public Schools, Dearborn, Michigan

8

Parent Relations

Relations between parents and teachers are essential to the operation of good schools and the strengthening of the partnership concept in American education. What these relations are like, how they may be carried on, difficulties that may be encountered, and opportunities that may occur for their improvement are the main topics to be taken up in this chapter.

IMPORTANCE OF PARENT RELATIONS

The partnership concept calls for the free and continuous exchange of information between parents and teachers and the involvement of parents in school affairs. Exchange of information enables teachers to acquire a knowledge of pupils they otherwise would be denied. They come into a direct understanding of growth problems and difficulties experienced by parents, peculiar experiences of children, and influences which have been determinants of behavior. They learn how parents think and act, what their attitudes are toward life, and what they want for their children. They see children differently, as a result

125

of what they learn, and are able to deal more intelligently with their needs.

Parents acquire information that is just as valuable in living with their children at home. So often they are unaware of what their children are like outside of the family and how they act with other people. They know relatively little about their school experiences and what teachers must contend with in directing their growth. They realize from analyses of test results, school records, behavior reports, and classwork how much progress they have made and how much more they could make with help at home. They reach agreements with teachers on common objectives and plans for attaining the objectives.

Out of these conferences parents develop a keener insight into modern education and an appreciation of the teacher's role. They change some of their preconceived ideas and notions of the learning process and the nature of the school. Arrangements for them to observe classes and to take part in pupil activities clear up doubts they may have had on the worth of instruction and the effectiveness of the methods used.

A successful partnership involves more than exchanging information with parents and acquainting them with the school. It includes cooperative work on problems which affect children and advance the cause of public education. Nothing else produces in parents a better understanding of the school and a deeper sense of responsibility for its progress.

In spite of these outcomes, it is usual for some administrators and teachers to oppose the partnership concept. They are, in reality, afraid that parent participation may lead to serious interference with their rights and duties. They do not believe that parents are qualified to decide what education is best for children or to discuss technical matters of curriculum building and instructional procedures. For the most part they are correct in their assumptions. They forget, however, that parents are well-qualified to make contributions for the advancement of education. They can discuss intelligently with administrators and teachers the larger purposes of education and many of the specific outcomes they would like for children. Their knowledge in specialized areas makes them valuable resource persons for committees engaged in curriculum development. They have skills and talents which can be drawn upon for the enrichment of curricular and cocurricular activities. Many are highly competent in problem solving procedures and the formulation of policies that reflect the wishes of the people. They can be of inestimable value in charting the course of education and leaving the technical details to professionally trained educators.

Those who argue against the involvement of parents seem to forget that no other group of citizens in the community exerts a stronger influence on public opinion, and that only through a broad sense of favorable opinion can the school expect to make significant progress.

BARRIERS TO COOPERATION

A genuine partnership between parents and teachers has scarcely been realized in this country. Too many barriers have been erected against it. The public relations problem is to identify these barriers and to reduce and eliminate them as much as possible. As will be shown, they are created by parents as well as educators.

Parent Attitudes

A substantial amount of the resistance against cooperation comes from parents. There are some who will have nothing to do with the school because of earlier experience and the dislike they developed for teachers. They still associate them with feeling of domination, inferiority, police authority, restraint, and unpleasant happenings. They do not realize that much of this is exaggerated and would change if they knew them better.

Other parents refuse to cooperate because they think that teaching is something any well-informed person can do and believe that they can learn little from teachers which they do not already know about education and their own children. Their point of view can be modified if they become parties to discussions and observations of good educational practices.

A third group of parents maintain that education should be divided between the school, church, and home. The school should be responsible for intellectual training, the church for spiritual enlightment, and the home for physical, moral, and social development. Because each has separate functions to perform, there is no common ground for cooperation or benefit to be derived from exchanging information. The problem of educating these parents to a broader concept of a modern school is difficult, yet surprisingly good results may be achieved when they take an interest in the instruction of their children and this interest is exploited carefully.

A fourth group believe that parents have no right to "meddle" in school business. They have been led to believe that teachers are opposed to parent visits because they interfere with their work and take up time that belongs to instruction. They also labor under the impression that if they complain, ask for explanations, and insist upon talking with teachers, their intentions may be misunderstood and work a hardship on their children.

The idea of a partnership with teachers has been held back for another reason. The traditional view is taken that seeing a teacher is a symptom of trouble. There is basis in fact for this opinion. Actual checks in a selected sample of schools on why parents visited teachers revealed that in nine out of ten instances they came in response to a problem concerning their children. This idea is more deeply ingrained than is generally acknowledged. It will not be eliminated until parent visits are placed on a more positive foundation.

Teacher Attitudes

Teacher attitudes are responsible, just as much as those of parents, for blocking a fuller realization of the partnership concept. Many are afraid of parents and the threat they represent to security. They wish to avoid situations in which they must justify their treatment of pupils and defend classroom procedures. They do not like the thought of keeping the more complete and accurate records of pupil performance that parent conferences would make necessary. They visualize possibilities of having to answer searching questions on educational theory and practice and revealing their own lack of knowledge. Even in areas of subject-matter specialization, they face the risk of talking with parents who know more than they do. The poor impressions they might make could undermine their standing in the community.

A number of teachers throw up barriers to cooperation in their treatment of parents. It is common for them to meet parents on days set aside for conferences in elementary and secondary schools and at other times by appointment. Instead of meeting parents half way and extending a cordial welcome, they may become stiff and formal, act annoyed, or assume an air of superiority. Parents are placed on the defensive, as a matter of strategy, and told only what is wrong with their children. If parental complaint is suspected in advance of the conference, other teachers are brought in to counteract possible argument. Parental attempts to establish a working relationship are quickly defeated and advice is given to parents with a note of finality.

Relations are further discouraged by the tactless and cruel manner in which children are discussed and predictions made regarding their future. Parents become bewildered and angered as they listen to their children being described in derogatory words and phrases and blamed for shortcomings in home training. One or two exposures to teachers who engage in these practices is sufficient to sever parental desire for other conferences.

Misunderstanding

Misunderstanding is a fundamental cause for poor relations between teachers and parents. Parents are sometimes quick to blame the school if their children do not make reasonable progress or do as well in classwork as they had expected. They attribute their deficiencies to modern education and the methods employed by teachers without having the slightest knowledge of how instruction is carried on in the local schools. Their conclusions are influenced by popular writings and discussions of "progressive education," the comments of friends, and the dislike of teachers. Their thinking can be straightened out if they visit the school, talk with teachers, and see for themselves how classes are conducted.

Events that take place in school and which are reported by children are another source of misunderstanding. A poor mark received by a child may be interpreted as bias on the part of a teacher. The handling of disciplinary problems is always subject to misinterpretation when children relate the facts incorrectly. Accounts of classroom activities may lead to the conclusion that more work and less play would improve learning. Teachers who have been successful in their relations with parents know that signs of misunderstanding call for action. They may write letters to parents, visit the home, or invite them to school. They have found that time devoted to clearing up misunderstanding of events in school pays dividends in respect, confidence, and cooperation.

A series of misunderstandings arises from cultural differences between parents and teachers. Due to such differences as nationality backgrounds, economic interests, customs, religious outlook, and language usage, they have difficulty in communicating with each other and finding common grounds for discussing behavior and learning problems of children. Sometimes they regard physical manner of dress, language expressions, vocal intonations, and bodily gestures as prejudicial to the welfare of pupils. The inability to understand each other may become a major problem for which there is no easy solution. Patient and persistent effort can make the problem less serious if teachers take leadership in trying to understand and accept parents in terms of their culture patterns.

School Policies

Parents who disagree with school policies and arbitrary methods of administration are not anxious to cooperate with teachers. They become irritated when children are under pressure to contribute to money-raising drives by outside organizations, denied permission to lunch at home when they live a short distance from the building, forced to miss the last bus because of detention, threatened with court action for taking children out of classes for travel, and refused the right to use school facilities in the evening hours. Some object strenuously to the disrobing of children for physical examinations, to the taking of showers after gymnasium classes, to sales of activity tickets, to ability grouping, to ungraded classes, and to conferences in place of report cards. They may be entirely right in protesting against the continuance of some policies and denouncing the methods by which they are administered. However, their opposition can be dissolved in numerous instances when they receive explanations of why policies were adopted and are taken into confidence before new ones are put into practice.

Pupil Welfare Services

The administration of pupil welfare services stands out among the reasons why some fathers and mothers are enthusiastic about a school and others will have nothing to do with it. For example, parents are pleased when the school calls to say that their child's glasses were found in the locker-room and that the building will be open for a half hour if they wish to get them. They look with favor on a courteous note from a teacher stating that the courses their daughter had selected for next year should be reviewed carefully before they are made final. Real appreciation is felt for a principal who advises a boy that he is eligible to apply for scholarships to help himself through college. Human considerations do not pass unnoticed and are genuinely appreciated.

The absence of personal concern for pupil welfare and disregard of family interest sets parents against a school and members of the faculty. For example, a boy who broke his ankle in the gymnasium was confined at home for several days at considerable medical expense to the family. Not once during this time did the school contact the family or inquire about his recovery. The parents took this to mean that school authorities were not interested in his welfare. In another instance, the school bus broke down shortly before the last load of pupils were ready to go home. No one notified the parents that their children would be late. They were put to unnecessary worry and a few called the state police for help. This incident caused the school to receive severe criticism and censure by parents. Principals and teachers sometimes forget that parents are more concerned with the welfare of their children than they are with the amount of subject matter they learn in classes. Schools that demonstrate thoughtfulness and understanding in matters related to pupil welfare and family interest secure the good will and support of parents.

INITIATING CLOSER CONTACTS

Initiating closer contacts with parents in order to break down the barriers to cooperation involves the questions of whether or not staff members are ready and what activities are most appropriate to interest parents in joining the school family.

Staff Readiness

As discussed in a previous chapter, internal conditions have a direct influence on the state of staff readiness to engage in public relations activities. No school system can expect satisfactory results when staff members are indifferent to their responsibilities and dissatisfied with their employment. Before plans are made to encourage better relations with parents, the following questions should be raised:

1. Do administrators and teachers feel secure in their work?
2. Do they derive satisfactions from their work?
3. Do they give evidence of the professional expertness needed for working with parents?
4. Do they have faith in the integrity and ability of parents?
5. Do they possess adequate skill in human relations?
6. Is there enough unity and cohesion among staff members to represent the school system favorably?
7. Have administrators won the respect and loyalty of teachers?
8. Do administrators and teachers believe something may be gained from working with parents?
9. Do the board of education and superintendent back up the work of principals and teachers?
10. Do members of the staff know how to work cooperatively among themselves?
11. Do members of the staff have a sincere and genuine interest in the welfare of pupils?

If the evidence shows that affirmative answers can be given to most of these questions, a school can afford to move into a program for developing closer relations with parents, otherwise it faces the task of putting its own house in order and making it ready to receive visitors. It is far better to postpone moving beyond the walls of the building until conditions inside are satisfactory than to rush into something that may backfire and do serious damage.

Ways of Starting

There are numerous ways of starting a program which appeals to parents and patrons and that brings them into the school so they may become acqainted with teachers and learn to take a more direct interest in various phases of instruction. Parent-grade groups are a commonly accepted means for accomplishing this purpose. Either the principal appoints parents or they elect their own representatives in each grade for the job of promoting good relations with teachers. Periodic meetings are held to discuss school work. The agenda may call for a consideration of pupil difficulties in arithmetic, questions of social development, personal habit formation, and physical health. The agenda is decided by parents, in consultation with teachers, and topics are included of most concern to both parties. Handled adroitly, this plan is highly effective in joining parents and teachers together.

The invitational-visitation technique has produced good results in schools which have used it. It is a technique whereby a certain number of parents — usually five or six — are invited by the principal to spend a half-day visiting classes and observing pupil activities in the school. The parents may be selected at random, named by the parent-teacher association, chosen to represent community interest groups, or drawn from a preferred list. A new group is brought in each week for as many weeks as the principal and teachers decide. Visitors are given a mimeographed evaluation sheet and asked to use it for guiding their observations. It contains such questions as what they think of the way discipline is handled, whether or not they would change the methods of teaching, and how valuable they consider the learning activities to be. Each of these questions is taken up in conference with the principal and one or two teachers at the close of the visitation. The conference provides an excellent opportunity to clarify observations and to further interpret the work of the school.

A variation on this technique is that of inviting committees of parents, from time to time, to sit with the principal and discuss what they like and dislike about the school. There is a danger in this approach that the negative side may be overemphasized at the expense of practices deserving commendation. The technique has some merit when parents are asked what they like most about the school and how they think it could be improved. Concern with improvement is a constructive lead that directs thinking to problems needing solution and offers opportunities for involving and sharing responsibility with parents.

Many parents respond favorably to personal invitations from teachers and pupils asking them to attend some school event. The event may be a room exhibit where they can see their own children's work, a classroom play, an informal tea, an open house pro-

After-school teas promote closer relationships.

gram, a special lecture, a luncheon prepared by pupils, or a discussion on school parties.

The use of check-lists has proven helpful in bringing about closer cooperation between parents and teachers. One type that deserves attention covers the joint responsibilities of home and school. Statements are set forth describing what each can do to further the growth and development of children. Parents are asked to check those which apply to their own practices as well as to those of the school and to confer with teachers on the results. This sort of instrument suggests possibilities they never realized and lets them know that the school wants to work cooperatively. Another type, one that has enjoyed wider use, represents an inventory of contributions parents can make to the educational program. They are invited to check those they are willing to make, such as speaking to a class on a trip to a foreign country; explaining their occupations;

demonstrating their hobbies; lending books, pictures, and objects to the school; and serving as aids on field trips taken by children. The information compiled from these check-lists enables teachers to enrich the learning process and to involve parents voluntarily in the actual work of the school.

A forward step is taken when principals write to parents of new pupils in junior and senior high school inviting them to visit the school at any time and to confer freely with teachers. A similar result is accomplished in elementary schools by brief, friendly phone calls by teachers to parents of children in their rooms. Letters sent to parents of secondary school pupils are sometimes accompanied with a bulletin or handbook containing information parents want on marks, attendance, homework, health requirements, college entrance requirements, cafeteria services, extracurricular activities, and expenses.

Besides these means for promoting closer cooperation with parents, many others have been used successfully. Briefly, some of them are asking mothers to be present at physical health examinations of their children, giving teas for mothers of preschool children, having night sessions so that fathers may attend classes, opening the gymnasium in the evening to parents for recreational purposes, holding individual conferences with the parents of new children, inviting parents to observe their children in activities related to class work, arranging pre-Christmas meetings in the school library for advising parents on books they wish to purchase for their children, and asking them to help with birthday parties and similar events for elementary school pupils.

PARENT VISITS AND CONFERENCES

Schools move closer to a realization of the partnership aim when they adopt policies providing for parent visits and conferences with teachers as a regular part of the educational program. Such policies promote friendly relations and lead to lay-professional cooperation.

Parent Visits

The initial problem of motivating parent visits can be surmounted rather easily when the policy is thoroughly publicized and people learn that they are welcome at the school. Shyness gives way to a natural curiosity to see how their children behave in classroom situations, what the teachers are like, how they handle pupils, whether or not methods of teaching are much different today, and how their own youngsters compare with others of similar age.

An open visitation policy also appeals to the skeptical minority of parents and citizens without children in school who are suspicious of modern education and wonder if subversive elements have crept into the classroom. Nothing will dispel their doubts more quickly than a series of visits and the knowledge that schools are open for all to see.

Sometimes principals claim that an open visitation policy disrupts the smooth running of a school and lowers the efficiency of teaching. They are right, especially when parents are permitted to wander in and out of classrooms, collect in corridors, and engage in noisy conversation which distracts pupils and teachers. However, these annoyances can be met by setting aside one or two afternoons weekly for visits and establishing regulations for parents to observe. A brief period of experimentation will show what regulations are most appropriate for a particular school.

Parent Conferences

There is no reason why the same days designated for visitation cannot be designated for conferences with teachers during free periods and after school hours. A letter to this effect could be mailed to each parent at the beginning of the fall term and to parents of children who are received by transfer during the year. A similar statement could well appear in home and school bulletins and handbooks that are published for informative reasons.

Because parent conferences have turned out to be a valuable method of clearing up sources of misunderstanding and of interpreting the instructional program, several elementary schools have substituted them for the time-honored report card system. Teachers are able to tell their story more accurately and parents are able to get a more complete picture of their child's progress by reviewing marks, reading-test scores, achievement-test scores, interest inventories, participation in extracurricular activities, anecdotal records,

Partners in the business of education.

and samples of class work. Neither teachers nor parents in schools where conferences take the place of report cards would go back to the old system of reporting; they get so much more from conferences and the follow-up opportunities afforded for home and school to work together.

Successful conferences require preparation and skill in the use of a few techniques. By way of preparation, teachers should review and know the information found in cumulative folders for pupils in their rooms or, in a departmentalized arrangement, for pupils in their homerooms or advisory units. They should define not only the problems to be taken up with parents, but also the questions they wish to ask and the ways of asking them. Along this line, thought should be given to methods of putting particular parents at ease and making them feel at home and to avoiding emotional sore spots. Sometimes teachers do not know parents well enough to make this kind of psychological preparation, but they can go far by taking the position that parents, like customers, are always right. This does not call for a surrender of their prerogatives as teachers, but implies instead the concept of service. Attitudes founded on a service concept invite respect and friendly responses.

137

There are times when parents come to school tense and excited after being notified of difficulties involving their children. Conferences under these conditions are naturally strained, with both teachers and parents taking the defensive. As in any conference situation, the burden of being tactful, courteous, considerate, truthful, and friendly must be carried by teachers. Any manifestation of attitudes to the contrary will only be met with more tension and the elimination of chances for harmony.

From this point on, good conference procedure rests on the ability of teachers to listen attentively and understandingly, to sift facts, to determine the nature and limits of any conflict, to correct misunderstandings without engaging in arguments, to use simple language free from ambiguity and emotional coloration, and to objectify issues around which thought should be directed. All conferences should end on a constructive note and culminate, if possible, in a mutual plan of action on behalf of children. A record should be made of each conference on a standardized form and filed for future reference.

HOME VISITATIONS

Teacher visits to the homes of pupils are the subject of divided opinion among school people. Superintendents and principals who favor home visitations claim that they help teachers to understand conditions under which pupils live and that they are an effective means for awakening parent interest in school affairs. Those who oppose home visitations point out that they often do more harm than good, because many teachers do not possess the personality traits and social understandings required and because some parents consider these visits to be an intrusion of their privacy.

Despite arguments on both sides, the fact remains that many school systems have profited from following a home visitation policy, while others have undergone experiences they do not wish to repeat. It is rather common to find that home visits are most successful in junior and senior high school years. This is due probably to a tapering off of parent interests and to opposition from older youngsters; they do not like the idea of teachers coming to their homes and making them the object of conversation.

An analysis of community conditions under which visitations have taken place with good and poor results does not disclose any direct relationship between visitations and factors of nationality backgrounds, race, religion, and occupational and economic status. It seems more likely that results are determined largely by teacher attitudes toward home visits and preparation for them.

Aside from teachers, home visits are made by the school nurse, home and school visitor or attendance officer, and increasingly by the counselor. Each of these agents is an important representative of the school whose services should be evaluated for their public relations value. The nurse can make friends for the school through a sincere concern for child welfare and skill in the handling of parents. Her job requires a pleasant personality, an understanding of home life, and the ability to suggest tactfully and convincingly the health conditions and remedial measures that parents should provide for children. A nurse who displays official authority is a liability to a school system and should be replaced unless she is able to profit from directions laid down by school officials.

The home and school visitor, sometimes known as the visiting teacher, has taken over the work of the traditional truant officer. His or her job consists of calling on new families and explaining the purposes and services of the school and the problems children face in a new environment; following up on cases of illegal absence and trying to find the causes; supplying social background material to teachers for their understanding of children, making recommendations that may be carried out at home and in school, and bringing community welfare services to the attention of families requiring special assistance. To perform these functions efficiently, a home and school visitor should have a training in social case work and possess an equally thorough background in educational theory and practice.

Where the traditional attendance or truant officer is employed for the enforcement of attendance, there is a strong tendency for this individual to achieve his ends through the exercise of police authority. Because he lacks the training and social intelligence needed to perform his duties, he forces children back to school by threatening parents with court action. Often bitterness and antagonism expressed toward schools can be traced to the work of the truant officer. Though he should receive in-service training, not much is given in school districts where he is still employed.

The counselor is coming more into the area of home visitation through studies of pupil adjustment problems and the necessity for working closely with parents. His relationships in this respect are similar to those of the home and school visitor, but his activities are wider in scope and demand a different type of specialized training. A competent counselor is a public relations asset to the school system in effecting wholesome relations with parents and community agencies.

WRITTEN COMMUNICATIONS

Written communications in the form of printed materials, letters, and samples of pupils' work constitute another means for promoting home contacts and keeping parents informed of their children's progress. In many districts they are the only direct link with the home and are a primary factor in shaping parent attitudes toward the school.

Printed Materials

The commonest type of printed material is the report card. It is issued several times a year, to inform parents how their children stand in subject achievement. They are also told how many times they were absent and tardy and their rating in citizenship or deportment.

Advances in educational thought and practice have created dissatisfactions with the traditional report card. Leaders in elementary education believe that a more accurate description should be given of the child's growth and development. They have devised cards which include information on growth in subject-matter mastery, skills, habits, attitudes, appreciations, and social behaviors. The newer card reflects the philosophy of the elementary school and is more descriptive of a child's total progress.

Some elementary schools have dropped the report card as a means of informing parents. They use instead either a personal letter from the teacher to the parent telling of gains made by the child and where help is needed, or they invite the parent to confer in person with the teacher and go over the child's record. These schools claim that letters to parents and personal conferences are superior to the formal report card for acquainting parents with the work of their children.

The idea of home and school cooperation in the educational development of children has been extended in a few instances to reporting by parents a couple of times a year. They are asked to fill out a special form covering information on a child's home membership, use of leisure time, and health habits. This system gives a broader picture of the child to the teacher and enables the school to determine more fully how instruction has affected outside behavior.

Like any departure from convention, newer types of report cards and reporting practices have been opposed by many parents. They neither understand what was wrong with the traditional report card nor why the changes were made. Much of their opposition could have been avoided had proposed changes been discussed with them in advance or had they been made parties to the work of devising improved methods of reporting.

Another publication, used by many schools, is the monthly newsletter or bulletin mailed to parents of school children and to selected community leaders. The purpose of the newsletter or bulletin is to keep citizens informed of instructional practices, outstanding professional activities, and problems facing the school system. An example of a bulletin for parents is shown on page 142. Printed on good stock, $8\frac{1}{2}$ x 11 inches in size and four pages in length, it has an attractive masthead, readable print, and photographic illustrations and drawings to hold reader attention. Though small school systems are reluctant to publish printed bulletins because of criticism from taxpayers on the question of expense, they can nevertheless publish similar information in mimeographed form.

Increasingly, schools are issuing annual handbooks for parents, intended to acquaint them with essential regulations and to provide a ready reference for answering questions they commonly ask. Opening usually with a friendly letter from the principal explaining the purposes of the handbook, they supply information on school hours, entrance requirements, cafeteria services, physical

A BULLETIN FOR PARENTS AND OTHERS IN WILMINGTON

| Vol. 8, No. 5 | Wilmington, Delaware | February 1955 |

MEASURING UP TO STANDARDS

Three Wilmington High Schools Are Evaluated

On February 18 the staff of the Wilmington High School bade farewell to twenty guest educators who had just completed a fine-tooth examination of the school. Since September the central city high school teachers and administrative staff have been preparing for this visit. Hours and hours of committee meetings for fact finding and self-evaluation had been held. At P. S. duPont School and Howard "E-Days" are still to come.

It all started over twenty years ago when six regional associations decided that the time had come to agree on some common standards for good high school education. Colleges were aware that some schools were not doing an adequate job of academic preparation. Guidance counselors discovered that students were dropping out of school in droves because the high school program had little to offer. It was time to act. In 1933 a general committee of educational leaders, representing regional associations of colleges and secondary schools, started a seven year cooperative study of secondary school standards. In 1940 they came out of it with three hundred pages of fine print and the title, "Evaluative Criteria." Ten years later there was a revised issue of the same material. Here, at last, was a yardstick by which any high school in the nation could measure its educational efficiency and plan for improvement. In the words of the committee the main aims were:

1. "To determine the characteristics of a good secondary school.

2. To find practical means and methods to evaluate the effectiveness of a school in terms of its objectives.

3. To determine the the means and processes by which a good school develops into a better one.

4. To devise ways by which regional associations can stimulate and assist secondary schools to continuous growth."

This is no restricting set of standards imposed from above to bring about uniformity in education. Schools that wish to participate in this type of evaluation do so voluntarily. The key to success of the whole plan is in the self-evaluation carried on by the entire professional staff of each school. Some schools include representatives of the student body, parents and lay citizens as observers or participants in this self-analysis.

The three Wilmington academic high schools have been a part of this cooperative study since the first. Wilmington, P. S. duPont and Howard High Schools were evaluated in 1945. Each was unconditionally accredited. The time has come for another look. P. S. duPont and Howard High have both completed the bulk of the self evaluation precedure. A visiting committee comes to P. S. duPont March 15, 16 and 17 and to Howard on March 29, 30 and 31. Wilmington High School now awaits the final report of the committee which has just completed its survey.

In the succeeding pages of this issue of *OUR SCHOOLS* the procedures of self-evaluation, the job of the visiting committee and the outcomes of evaluation will be explained in more detail.

Front page of a bulletin for parents issued monthly by the Public Schools of Wilmington, Delaware.

examinations and health standards, report card periods, conferences with teachers, school calendar, and names of staff members. Those intended for parents of high school pupils also have sections on extracurricular activities, eligibility for interscholastic athletics, curriculum offerings, and college entrance requirements. They are an important publication among communication media designed for the home.

In addition, the practice of enclosing leaflets with report cards is used as a device for helping parents to understand specific aspects of the educational program. Because youngsters frequently remove leaflets from report card envelopes and throw them on the street, a number of school districts are now sending them by mail. Their value is somewhat doubtful unless they are kept intentionally brief, easily understood, interesting to read, and timely.

Letters to Parents

Letters and personal notes from teachers improve relationships between home and school. In the past, too many letters were limited — and still are in some schools — to reports of unsatisfactory work and disciplinary problems of pupils. This one-sided reporting has been balanced in recent years by written communications on things pupils do well and contributions they make to the school. For example, if a pupil has done a fine job as a library assistant, a motion picture operator, a stage hand, a receptionist, a hall monitor, a club president, or a committee chairman, a letter of commendation is sent to parents by the activity sponsor. In the same way, alert classroom teachers note outstanding achievements and significant behavior changes that deserve recognition. Their letters may describe superior class work, improvements in study habits, acts of courtesy, special talents, and fine character traits. Parents who receive these letters feel pleased and grateful for the information.

Teachers object to writing favorable notes and letters to parents because of the work involved. The idea is more acceptable if an experimental period is established to determine how many notes and letters are written on a weekly average and how they are received by parents. Usually, teachers find at the end of the experimental period that the load has not been heavy and that parents are genuinely appreciative of the information they are sent.

Schools find it necessary to publish form letters for general distribution to parents on opening and closing dates of school, control of contagious disease, new policies and regulations, use of plant facilities, bus schedules, parent-teacher meetings, and so forth. These letters are important media for conveying information and creating favorable impressions of the institution. Unless they can be mimeographed exceptionally well, they should be printed in photo-offset or letter press form on regular stationery and blocked out attractively. Close attention should be paid to vocabulary, tone, and simplicity. They should close with a hand-written signature. Good form letters invite better relations with parents.

Samples of Pupil Work

Parents of elementary and junior high school pupils are pleased to receive samples of outstanding classwork done by their children. The samples may be self-explanatory, or they may require a written explanation of their merits. Progress over previous work can be pointed out and encouragement given for future efforts. While much of the work done in classes is too intangible to show to parents, there are opportunities to use themes, compositions, notebook pages, science reports, maps, charts, drawings, models, and the like for this purpose.

OPPORTUNITIES FOR PARTICIPATION

The suggestions made thus far tend to establish closer relations between home and school and to set a foundation for parent participation in school affairs. Leadership for parent participation should come from administrators and teachers. In this section a number of successful projects which schools have used to involve parents are described.

Study and Discussion Groups

Study and discussion groups have grown rapidly in the past few years. They represent an increasing popular concern for childhood education and a desire on the part of laymen to know more about the schools their children attend. Organized at times at the request of parents, they are known by a variety of titles. Some titles are mothers' councils, mothers' clubs, mothers' discussion clubs, grade and homeroom councils, parent study councils, parent workshops, and parent round-tables.

Study and discussion group interests fall into about three broad classes. One is instructional policies and practices of school systems and methods by which parents and teachers can work together. Discussion frequently centers around report cards, homework, school parties, discipline, health, pupil adjustment, and the teaching of fundamental skill subjects. Occasionally, modern teaching methods are treated in detail for parents who wish to know how to help children correctly with homework. Suggestions are drawn up by some groups for prevention of home accidents, purchase of children's books and magazines, selection of desirable radio and television programs, practicing of good health habits, and control of teen-agers' social activities.

Child study is another interest that has attracted wide attention. Guided by competent teachers, parents learn how to interpret behavior patterns of children and what to expect as they progress from one stage of growth to another. They are given appropriate reading materials and assisted in analyzing motives behind unsocial expressions of behavior. They come to understand their own children better and to realize that all children have many common characteristics at different ages.

The attention of study and discussion groups turns now and then into channels that move away from the immediate school situation. For example, the Extension Division of the Philadelphia Public Schools furnishes trained discussion leaders for parent groups wishing to take up problems of local government, international affairs, housing, and so forth. The discussion leaders are paid by the school system and the groups meet in neighborhood schools during the afternoon. In other communities, study groups have requested instruction in canning, dress design, handicrafts, and first aid. These services go a long way in cementing strong relationships with parents.

Curriculum Planning

Work connected with the study and improvement of the curriculum at all levels affords rich opportunities for parent participation. Parents have taken an active and constructive role in helping teachers define the purposes of education and the objectives for specific fields and courses of study. They have served effectively on faculty committees concerned with the adequacy of the curriculum, revision of course offerings, and introduction of changes that could not be attempted without their support. They have served as resource persons, because of their specialities, in the preparation of units and have worked with teachers in the selection of materials and equipment for vitalizing the units. Schools in both industrial and agricultural centers have sought their advice for keeping vocational programs in line with prevailing needs and conditions.

Contributions to Classwork

Parents can make worthwhile contributions to classwork. They can speak on topics about which they possess first-hand information. They can loan rare books, objects, phonograph records, and motion pictures. They can aid on field trips by serving as chaperones, checking attendance, exercising accident safeguards, and taking part in follow-up activities. They can be members of textbook committees, report card committees, and others dealing with improvement of teaching.

Extracurricular Activities

Parents enjoy taking part in extracurricular activities with children and adolescent youngsters. Any number possess talents and technical knowledges that can be used advantageously. Some schools call on them to work with teacher-sponsors of clubs in jewelry making, photography, folk dancing, leathercraft, and glass blowing. Mothers are willing to assist pupils and teachers in designing simple costumes for dramatic productions, and fathers gladly lend a hand in building and painting stage scenery. They respond freely to invitations to take part in plays, musicals, assembly programs, and athletic games, to act as judges for contests, and chaperones for parties and dances.

School Plant and Facilities

Educational literature contains numerous accounts of how parents have participated in the planning of the school plant and its physical facilities. Their advice is good on the selection of plots and the geographical location of buildings. Some school officials consider them indispensable in reviewing plans and in deciding how a plant can best meet the needs of pupils and adult members of the community. They have proven to be far-sighted and courageous in recommending building expenditures that boards of education were afraid to approve. They have been responsible for procuring adequate recreational and playground facilities and essential equipment in cafeterias, health centers, and gymnasiums. Some have undertaken repair of old playground equipment and the construction of pieces which school boards refused to purchase. Parents who take part in activities connected with the plant feel that they are members of the school system.

Advisement Panels

In smaller communities and neighborhood schools, parent advisement panels have been established in recent years. A selected group of parents are called together when their advice is wanted on a particular problem or when school officials wish to obtain a sample public opinion. These panels, while not always satisfactory, have demonstrated nevertheless that laymen have a significant contribution to make to the advancement of education.

Community Improvements

Many worthwhile community improvements have been brought about by the cooperation of pupils, teachers, and parents. They have undertaken projects for new recreational facilities, welfare services, child-guidance centers, health clinics, health councils, traffic regulations, and the reduction of cultural tensions. Their work has included elimination of property destruction on Halloween, periodic cleaning of yards, painting of houses, removal of fire hazards, and raising of funds for youth centers. They have inoculated communities with a new spirit of living.

Courtesy Public Schools, Philadelphia, Pennsylvania.

9
Community Relations

The emphasis in community relations is upon direct and indirect forms of personal contact with the public outside of the school. As pointed out earlier, direct and indirect forms of personal contact arise from meetings, conversations, telephone calls, correspondence, home contacts, observations, and the like. They are important in shaping popular attitudes toward and opinions of the institution and its personnel.

It is a reasonable assumption that no school system can expect to develop and maintain desirable relations with people in the community until it studies the nature and location of its contacts. It should have a practical knowledge of where they occur and how they are handled. An attempt should be made to appraise their effectiveness in creating impressions and conveying ideas which develop public understanding, cooperation, and school support.

In this chapter attention will be given to the more significant types of community contacts which influence public opinion, and suggestions will be made on how they should be handled.

CONTACTS WITH THE BOARD OF EDUCATION

What people think and how they feel about a school system is influenced by the board of education. Because of its central position, the behavior of members and the nature of their decisions are watched carefully by citizens and school employees. No public relations program will achieve satisfactory results unless the board of education sets a laudable example for the school system to follow.

Members of the Board

More than three-quarters of the school board members in this country are elected to office by popular vote, while the remainder are appointed by the chief executive officer or by the legislative unit of local government. Once in office, they are expected to serve the entire community, not a geographical subdivision of it, and to place the education of children and the welfare of society above personal interests. As individuals, they have no right to commit the board or to act on its behalf without expressed authority. These concepts are well established by law in several states and are respected in good school systems.

Except in small districts, board members enjoy relatively few direct contacts with people in the community. No board of seven or nine members could possibly talk with the rank and file of taxpayers. Indirectly, though, many people in the community feel that they know their board members from what they hear and read in newspapers. They are not just names, but personalities whose thoughts and actions receive attention. If the public gains the impression that board members are sincere and honest in directing the schools, they will accept their mistakes without much criticism and support them on controversial issues.

But when board members violate their trust, relations between school and community suffer. A board member who goes about expressing rash opinions on education and denouncing parental concern over educational practices soon incurs the ill-will of people. A board member who is high-handed in dealing with citizens and who dictates to administrators and teachers falls into the same category. As reprehensible as these actions may be, they are less damaging than suspicion or knowledge that members are engaged in partisan politics, serve vested interest groups, or use their position for personal profit.

People react adversely to these conditions. For one thing, they become apathetic toward the school, feeling that the odds are too great to effect desirable change. For another, they allow their discontent to smolder for a long time and then break out into open conflict. Charges are hurled back and forth, names are called, and the community is split into opposing factions. The result is disunity and loss of faith in the administration of the school system.

Board Meetings

School board meetings are public business. When scheduled at known times and places and conducted in accordance with recognized procedures, they are effective instruments in building wholesome relations with the community. Good board meetings move on a planned agenda, with ample opportunity provided for citizens to express their views. In the interest of sound decisions, members avoid partisan politics and petty bickering. They are reluctant to yield to strong pressures and are guided in their judgments by the professional counsel of the superintendent. Aware of their social responsibility, they try to see all sides to a question and abide by the ideals of public education.

Board Decisions

The decisions made by boards of education are often restricted to business and financial matters. They operate on the theory that control of finance is their principal responsibility and that they are incapable of making sound judgments on instructional problems. This theory is being attacked by a growing number of citizens. They maintain that no board of education has the right to relinquish its responsibility for instruction, that instruction is the heart of the school system, and that they should decide in the name of the people what policies and practices will govern the education of children. They point out further that this theory takes the power out of the hands of the people and places it with professional employees.

Besides this fundamental question, the public has shown concern over the methods by which school boards reach decisions. People do not have faith in their school representatives when decisions are guided by expediency, when proposals are seldom studied, when pressure and prejudice dominate, and when indifference is expressed toward recommendations of citizens and school executives. They respect a board which deals fairly with controversial problems, adopts long-range plans, considers human values, and appraises facts and opinions before rendering judgments.

Unquestionably, boards of education would give greater attention to instruction and develop sounder methods of arriving at decisions if they were held more accountable by the public and if they accepted their obligation under law to inform the public.

Public Information

Too much stress cannot be laid upon the importance of keeping the public informed of board business. In communities having good schools which are steadily undergoing improvement, the board of education has shared its problems with the people and educated them to the needs and policies of the system. This has been done by publishing complete and accurate reports of official meetings in local newspapers; by letting the public know what questions must be decided at future meetings; by inviting citizen expression of opinion before policy adoption; by authorizing the superintendent to prepare materials for the information of taxpayers; and by doing business in the open. Every board should develop a plan for informing the people of what it stands for and what it does in the interest of children and the community.

RECEIVING SCHOOL VISITORS

Board of education relations with the public are supplemented widely by face-to-face contacts of school employees with businessmen, salesmen, job applicants, parents, social workers, and others who have occasion to visit schools and school system offices. These contacts are crucial in the formation of impressions which influence public opinion. School employees should be trained to handle them successfully, and the appearance of offices should be considered in terms of the effect it has on school visitors.

Staff Training

Every school employee should know how to meet visitors with whom he has contact. He should understand the meaning of common courtesy and realize the importance of performing services willingly and efficiently. This knowledge should be a part of an orientation and training program. A simple but effective device for the purpose is a manual which outlines in attractive form the major points to consider in receiving school visitors. Such topics as being friendly with people, the need for prompt and efficient service, situations calling for patience and tact, meeting requests for information, where to make referrals, and how to be a good listener should be included. The manual can be used as a basis for small discussion groups in which the content is reviewed and its application illustrated. There is scarcely a school system where administrators, teachers, counselors, home visitors, nurses, physicians, dentists, custodians, and bus drivers could not profit from this training.

A more thorough and specialized program should be developed for office secretarial and clerical personnel. These individuals are in the front line of public relations. Usually they are the first, and sometimes the only, point of contact visitors have with the school system. Besides being oriented in the topics that are taken up in the manual, they should be given a thorough training in the details of their assignments, their responsibility for protecting sources of official and confidential information, and the way in which to distinguish between questions they can answer and those requiring referral to someone in an official capacity. They should be instructed in the philosophy of the school system, its organization, and the duties of administrative, supervisory, and teaching staff members.

Personal Qualifications

The training of secretarial and clerical personnel is accomplished more readily and with better results when the right people are selected for these positions. They should be individuals with a high sense of social intelligence, pleasing in appearance, alert, tactful, and courteous. They should be able to wear clothing that is simple, smart, and conservative in line and color. A good memory for names and faces is an asset, as well as the ability to think and act impersonally. They should know how to meet many different kinds of people with poise and to convey the feeling of wanting to be helpful. An even temper and a sense of calmness are indispensable equipment in dealing with outsiders who are irritable and demanding of attention. Correct pronunciation and use of English have their place in this list of qualifications. For good public relations, the personal requirements of office, secretarial, and clerical personnel should be as exacting as they are important.

Appearance of Offices

The appearance of school offices contributes to the impressions visitors take back into the community. As much as possible, offices should reflect the spirit of the system and the educational ideals it stands for. All rooms where visitors contact office personnel and wait for appointments should be furnished in good taste, painted in attractive colors with pictures on the walls, and have facilities for making visitors feel at home. Modern businesses have recognized the contribution of properly equipped offices and waiting rooms in winning the good will of customers. Many employ receptionists trained to meet visitors and to see that their needs are cared for promptly and graciously. The same technique could be employed by school systems at little or no additional cost by placing qualified secretaries or clerks in this position and scheduling other work for them to do at their reception desks.

In making favorable impressions on visitors, school offices should be kept in good condition and used for the purposes they are intended to fulfill. There is no place for cardboard boxes on the floor, supplies piled on window sills and desks, records scattered on tops of files, and bulletin boards covered with faded and poorly placed notices. Visitors should not get the idea from watching secretaries and clerks, and teachers who come into the office, that it is a center for gossip and personal narrative or that derogatory remarks may be made about them after they have departed. Nor should the office be used to house pupils who have disciplinary troubles; their presence is always an invitation for people to ask what they are doing. They should be sent to some other location in the building and kept away from outside visitors. It would be desirable also to have teachers' mailboxes and bulletin boards located elsewhere to cut down traffic into the office and prevent open discussion of school business in the presence of strangers.

HANDLING TELEPHONE CALLS AND CORRESPONDENCE

The number of direct contacts with school visitors is small compared with the number made through telephone calls and correspondence. Too often the use of these tools is taken as a matter of fact, and their part in a public relations program is not considered. As will be pointed out, they determine the nature of the impressions people gain of a school system.

Telephone Calls

Telephone calls are made and received most commonly by administrators, teachers, office secretaries and clerks, and staff specialists. They are functionaries around whom effort should be concentrated to improve telephone manners and telephone service.

Efficient telephone service begins with the accessibility of the school to people in the community. They should be able to find the telephone number of any building without having to ponder on how it is classified in the telephone directory. Numbers are listed in many communities under remote headings like "city of" and "township of" which give parents and business people trouble. Since the average person thinks of "schools" when he starts to look up the number, the first step in improving telephone service is to see that listings fall under the heading of "schools."

A second point concerns the adequacy of equipment to handle telephone calls. Not infrequently, citizens become impatient when they cannot get through to a school office but must try repeatedly before the busy signal stops. This condition can be changed by installing switch boards with a sufficient number of lines to handle telephone traffic. A specially trained office clerk can be stationed at the switch board and supply the service required for good public relations. There should likewise be an adequate number of telephones located conveniently throughout each building where they are readily accessible to staff personnel. It is a mistake to force staff members to make and receive calls in the school office. Even though they are notified, by an intercommunication system, of a telephone call and are requested to answer it, the time it takes to reach the office forces the caller to sit idly by and to speculate on the efficiency of the schools.

But adequate and mechanically excellent equipment is no guarantee that the telephone will be used effectively as an instrument of communication and good will. Certain rules of courtesy and techniques of service must be observed to assure satisfactory results. Incoming calls should be answered with the proper identification. The identification should be the name of the school or the administrator's office, followed by the name of the person answering the call. Sometimes the identification is accompanied by an offer of service, such as "may I help you?" Variations are possible on this form of identification and care should be taken to see that it does not degenerate into a dull, routine expression. This does not happen, as a rule, when the desire to be of service is reflected in the voice tone used.

After the caller has stated his business, it should be handled at once unless transfer to someone else is necessary. If there is uncertainty as to whom transfer should be made, the caller should be requested courteously to wait for a moment until this is determined. In transferring any call, the contact should be kept open until it is certain that the right person has been reached.

The thoroughness and dispatch with which calls are answered and serviced is a good measure of efficiency in a school. No telephone should be permitted to ring several times before it is answered, nor should the practice be tolerated of taking up the receiver without giving any identification until some time later. Where this is done, it is not difficult to guess the reaction of the caller to the delay and to the weird combination of sounds that come to his attention. When delays are necessary in meeting requests for information, the caller should be notified that it may take a minute or two to get what he wants and be thanked in advance for waiting. If several minutes will be required to obtain information, he should be asked if the secretary or clerk may call him back shortly.

All telephone conversations should be carried on in a natural, pleasing tone of voice. This is important because the speaker does not have the support of facial expressions and physical gestures to communicate his thinking. His voice should be free of fashionable accents and artificialities in pronunciation, and care should be taken to control its volume and the pace of speaking. When pace is too rapid or volume too great, it is difficult to understand the conversation; and when voice is too slow and hard to hear, it can be irritating. School systems would do well to consult the telephone company on these points and ask them to test the voice-quality of staff members who use the telephone most frequently.

A telephone conversation should be terminated with a polite "goodbye" or a "thank you for calling." As a matter of courtesy, the other party should be invited to call again, though there are occasions when this would not be appropriate. He should be permitted to place the receiver on the rest first and never exposed to the loud noise that comes from banging it down in a hurry. His feeling, after completing a call, should be one of friendliness toward the school and appreciation of the thoughtful and efficient way in which his request was handled.

Surprising improvement can be made in telephone manners and techniques when special instruction is given to employees. Simple demonstrations and periodic discussions of the problem are enough to bring about good results. The secret of continued success, however, lies in delegating responsibility to a staff member for supervising telephone service within a single building or for the entire school system.

Correspondence

The letter has some advantages over face-to-face relations and telephone conversations as a form of personal contact. It enables the writer to communicate directly and economically with the other person and to exercise more control over the expression of his ideas. These advantages make the letter an effective instrument in public relations, providing the tone is warm and friendly and mechanical details are correct.

The mechanical features start with the letterhead printed at the top of the letter. Set out in distinctive type related to the character of the institution, the letterhead should contain the name of the school, its location and telephone number, and the title of the office from which it is sent. The paper should be of high quality bond with envelope to match, the latter containing a return address printed in the upper left-hand corner on the front.

A letter gets off to a good start when the correct initials, spelling of the name, and address of the person are placed in the heading. The salutation which follows should be stated as *Dear Mr. Williams.* This is less formal than *My dear Mr. Williams* and more formal than *Dear Williams* or *Dear Donald.* The stilted, impersonal salutation of *Dear Sir* or *Dear Madame* should never be used.

The body of the letter should be laid out carefully for balance on the page and the impression it makes on the reader. It should be typed in clear characters, single-spaced, and read before it is signed. No letter should be permitted to leave a school with errors in punctuation, improper capitalization, abbreviations, spelling, overstrikes, margins, and syllabification. Errors of this kind are a reflection on the institution, and they are out of line with the standards it is expected to uphold.

The closing of the letter should be in harmony with the rest of the mechanical details. Because *Sincerely yours* and *Very sincerely yours* are more personal and round out the tone of the letter, they are preferred over the less animated forms of *Yours truly* and *Yours very truly.* This closing should be followed by the name of the person who wrote the letter. All letters should be signed personally above the typed name of the signer so there can be no mistake about the authorship.

Besides the mechanical features of letter production, there are several other factors which enter into the building of good public relations by means of letters. No letter should be allowed to remain unanswered for several days out of respect for the person who wrote it; common courtesy demands a prompt reply. Where facts must be gathered and opinions sought that will cause a delay, an interim letter should be written explaining the situation and promising complete information in the near future. In general, letters should be brief, concise, and to the point, with thought given to an outline of their contents before they are dictated. If it appears that a letter requires a lengthy reply, a telephone call may make it possible to handle the matter through a personal interview instead.

The tone of a letter plays a prominent part in influencing the reaction of its reader. It should be warm, friendly, conversational, and, above all, written as though it were spoken directly to the person who reads it. It is the ability to capture the personal element that makes a letter effective. The simplest rule to follow is to write the letter just as though you were talking informally to the reader. Usually a letter written from this point of view carries a sense of enthusiasm and sounds as though the writer enjoyed writing it.

The tone-quality of a letter may be lowered through the use of stereotyped business phrases. They tend to make a letter stiff and formal. Examples of such antiquated expressions as: beg to advise, happy to inform you, please be advised, permit me to state, replying to yours, due to the fact that, may I call your attention, wish to acknowledge, kindly advise, beg to assure, regret to inform, and so forth should be scrupulously avoided.

As in every profession, there is a tendency among educators to employ a technical vocabulary in discussing their problems and to use phrases that are foreign to the thinking of other people. Words and phrases should convey ideas easily and understandably—they should not be barriers to communication. Words and phrases like rapport, maladjustment, core curriculum, curriculum constant, experience unit, heterogeneous grouping, and resource materials defeat the purpose of good letter writing.

More important still is the necessity for stating ideas in forms of expression that result in positive rather than negative responses. Hundreds of letters go out of public schools every day that do nothing more than invite ill-will and resentment. They contain words and expressions which people react to in an unfavorable manner. Eventually the time will come when educators can be guided in their correspondence by word lists that have been tested for the reactions they produce in readers. Meanwhile reliance must be put upon experience in judging what is good and bad in language usage. In the two lists given below, one contains words and phrases which are considered to provoke negative responses, while the other suggests ways of expressing the same ideas to elicit positive reactions. Both lists may prove helpful as a start in checking school correspondence and improving future writing.

Negative Expressions	*More Positive Expressions*
Must	Should
Lazy	Can do more when he tries
Trouble maker	Disturbs class
Uncooperative	Should learn to work with others
Cheats	Depends on others to do his work
Stupid	Can do better work with help
Never does the right thing	Can learn to do the right thing
Below average	Working at his own level
Truant	Absent without permission
Impertinent	Discourteous
Steal	Without permission
Unclean	Poor habits
Dumbell	Capable of doing better
Help	Cooperation
Poor	Handicapped
Calamity	Lost opportunity
Disinterested	Complacent
Expense	Investment
Contribute to	Invest in
Stubborn	Extremely self-confident
Insolent	Outspoken
Liar	Tendency to stretch the truth
Wastes time	Could make better use of time
Sloppy	Could do neater work
Incurred failure	Failed to meet requirements
Nasty	Difficulty in getting along with others
Time and again	Usually
Dubious	Uncertain
Poor grade of work	Below his usual standard
Clumsy	Awkward in movements
Profane	Uses unbecoming language
Selfish	Seldom shares with others
Rude	Inconsiderate of others
Bashful	Reserved
Show-off	Tries to get attention
Will fail him	Has a chance of passing, if

The subject of letter writing would not be complete without considering the place of form letters, or those which are duplicated in large numbers for reasons of economy. The duplication is usually done by mimeograph, though many schools employ a gelatin process. Too often these letters are reproduced on cheap paper, laid out poorly, and are difficult to read because of imperfections. Sometimes their physical features are enough to discourage a person from reading them. Unless mimeographing is done exceptionally well, it is better to print, multigraph, or multilith the letters, even though the cost is slightly higher. Trying to save a few pennies on poorly prepared form letters is false economy.

Better yet, the number of form letters should be kept to the barest minimum. People have become accustomed to receiving duplicated materials through the mails and do not take the time to look at them. The problem is one of trying to make the appearance of form letters similar to that of personal correspondence so they will be opened and read. They should be sent by first-class mail.

The preparation of form letters should be done as carefully as regular letters. They should convey a tone of warmth and friendliness and be personalized in style. A human touch can be added when the heading and salutation are typed in and a personal signature is affixed at the end.

ATTENDING TO COMPLAINTS

Complaints are made about almost every phase of school operation and the educational program. In some respects they are the inevitable and normal outcome of institutional functioning. Coming from private citizens and organized groups, they are made to all personnel in a school system, including board members, administrative officials, teachers, and noninstructional staff members. Whether the complaints are justified or not, good public relations requires that they be handled systematically and efficiently.

Importance of Complaints

The proper handling of complaints is important for several reasons. Parents and others who make complaints do so because they have grievances, real or imagined. They want them satisfied. Unless the school welcomes their complaints, extends courteous treatment, and takes positive action within reasonable limits, it destroys good will and breeds resentment. A handful of disgruntled citizens is a potential source of serious damage to the institution.

The roots of dissatisfaction are frequently found in partial understandings and total misunderstandings of educational policies and practices. These misconceptions can be corrected rather quickly when channels are established for receiving complaints and opportunities provided for supplying complete and accurate information.

Failure to receive complaints of this character permits their growth in never-ending circles in the community.

Large business firms look upon complaints as their best source of public relations information. They keep careful records of all complaints, no matter how trivial they may seem, and review them periodically. This material enables them to get a picture of prevailing attitudes toward company policies and shifts taking place in public reactions. Of somewhat greater importance, however, is the knowledge they acquire of weak spots in their organization and services which are failing to meet the criteria of good public relations. There is no real excuse for schools overlooking the value of similar information in strengthening their own policies and practices.

Servicing Complaints

The efficient servicing of complaints depends upon organization and assignment of responsibility. Channels must be established for their flow from all parts of the school system. A simple line arrangement from the superintendent downward will meet this requirement, provided the channels are clearly designated. A diagramatic flow for the handling of complaints can be used to depict organizational arrangements.

Responsibility of personnel may be defined and explained in a brief manual, starting with the superintendent and ending with the teacher. Each functionary should know exactly what types of complaints he is expected to handle and procedures to follow in referring unsettled grievances to those next in higher authority.

A monthly summary sheet from individual building principals and intermediate officers will enable the superintendent to obtain a complete description of the nature of complaints and how they were settled in the entire school system. This information enables him to make comparative studies by months and years. He is able to determine whether or not weaknesses are being corrected and what problems remain unattended.

MEETING EVERYDAY CONTACTS

Every person who is connected with a public school system enjoys innumerable contacts with people in the community while going and coming from the school, after regular working hours, and over week-ends, holidays, and vacations. There is nothing formal about these contacts, since they grow out of chance meetings on the street, in stores and shops, and at social functions. Although small attention is paid to their public relations meaning, nevertheless people get many of their ideas and impressions from them about a school system.

For too many years, school boards and superintendents kept teachers and noninstructional employees in ignorance of the systems which paid their salaries. Believing that teacher and nonteacher interests should be limited to the performance of assigned duties, they did nothing to share their problems, to explain administrative organization and operation, or to take them into confidence on policy decisions. As a result, few employees were able to answer questions people asked about their schools. Even today this condition prevails and is a serious obstacle to good public relations.

Employee ignorance of the local school system is, however, probably less devastating in its effect upon public opinion than the attitudes and feelings expressed by teachers to laymen in the community. Those who are dissatisfied with their work, dislike administrative officers, disagree with instructional policies, and quarrel with colleagues often air their complaints and personal disappointments. Others prejudice the public unfavorably by assuming classroom attitudes of superiority or by stating their views freely on topics about which they do not possess too much information. When confronted by criticism and inquiry on their own educational beliefs and practices, they either become indignant or else apologetic. Poor habits of speech, improper wearing apparel, and indiscreet conduct add further to the impressions they leave on the community.

Boards of education and administrators must recognize that the everyday contacts of employees outside of the school are a part of the public relations program. They should see that teachers and non-teachers understand important facts about the system, learn how to think and talk about their work, feel responsible for representing the school in the best manner possible, keep their disappointments and troubles within the institutional family, and ask the public to look ahead with them at the opportunities for cooperation in improving the educational program.

PARTICIPATION IN COMMUNITY LIFE

The number of contacts increases, and the school and its professional personnel take on new importance, when staff members become identified with the social and civic life of the community. In planning this part of the public relations program, thought must be given to staff preparation, opportunities for and obstacles to participation.

Importance

Four significant gains are made in public relations when staff members become active in the life of the community. First, the attitudes of laymen change as they learn to know the men and women who are responsible for their schools. They no longer think of them as a class more or less separated from the rest of society and made up of individuals who are somewhat snobbish, impractical, unsocial, and disinterested in anything but their own profession. There is no better means for changing these attitudes and opinions than direct contact with laymen and the sharing of common experiences.

Second, participation opens opportunities for social and civic leadership and, consequently, higher status in the community. Groups are constantly searching for individuals who can assume and manage leadership responsibilities. They soon discover that professional school employees possess the educational background, social insight, organizational experience, and human relations skills needed in leadership situations.

Third, participation enables staff members to discuss the schools with many people. Most parents and taxpayers are interested in public education; they welcome the chance to talk freely and frankly with school representatives whom they know. Participation likewise brings invitations from organized groups to speak to their members on topics related to education and the local school program. These occasions are usually very effective in helping the public to understand and appreciate the work of the school.

Fourth, available evidence supports the hypothesis that citizen concern for public education increases as staff personnel become more actively identified with the social and civic life of the community. The one stimulates the other. The evidence of increased citizen concern may be expressed in higher attendance at parent-teacher association meetings and school events which are open to the public; in the growing number of laymen who visit the schools; in less criticism of public education and fewer attacks on schools; in a wider reading of news releases and school publications; and in the willingness of citizens to take part in instructional activities and serve on school improvement committees.

Staff Preparation

School personnel who take part in community life should have an insight and understanding of people and institutions if they are to function successfully either in their capacity as professional employees or as private citizens. They should be familiar with local history, ethnic and religious divisions, customs, prejudices, and social restrictions. They ought to know something of the cultural and economic life of the community, its social agencies, form of government, and channels of communication. Awareness of social organization and community leaders is important.

The bulk of this information should be available from the findings of the sociological survey described in an earlier chapter. With this knowledge, staff members are more likely to be tolerant of local customs, avoid pitfalls and conflict situations, and follow an intelligent course of action in their relations with the public.

Participation Through School Activities

Teachers and pupils have many opportunities to participate in community life through school activities. Every neighborhood and district presents real problems for study and social action. These problems may involve traffic hazards, proper methods of handling trash and garbage, youth recreational needs, fire protection, sewage disposal, clean streets, and hundreds of others. Public contacts growing out of successful study projects by pupils and teachers develop respect for the school and lay the groundwork for future cooperation.

Similar outcomes have been attained in districts where administrators, teachers, and pupils responded to requests for assistance from character-building agencies and service organizations interested in the education and welfare of children. They have appealed for school aid in surveying community recreational needs; locating pupils who would benefit from glasses, special shoes, and diet supplements; organizing little league baseball teams for after-school and vacation periods; taking part in home beautification campaigns; participating in forums and public discussions on local problems; increasing public library facilities; developing summer day camps for young children; and so forth.

Another aspect of participation is that of using community resources for instructional purposes. Any number of competent men and women are available to talk with pupils along lines of their special vocational and avocational interests, to loan objects and visual materials high in instructional value, and to share their knowledge and experience with teachers in curriculum study programs. Classes may be taken on field trips to worthwhile places and interviews scheduled with people in positions of leadership. Much may be done by way of cooperative work-experience and tours of business and industry as means for understanding the economic life of the community and appreciating employment demands. Each time such resources are used, they enrich instruction and create friendship between citizens and representatives of the school.

In sponsoring activities which bring school and community into closer contact, the public is sensitive to teacher and pupil behavior and consideration shown for the rights of others. Courtesy, respect for property, thoughtfulness, and obedience are carefully noted. Even the driving habits of the person who operates the school bus as well as its appearance are subject to appraisal. Seasonal efforts to eliminate vandalism on Halloween, to prevent the throwing of snowballs, and to confine playing of sports to school grounds and parks are appreciated. Public goodwill is earned when teachers and high school pupils are not allowed to park automobiles in front of houses near the school and when measures are taken to stop youngsters from cutting across lawns and backyards on their way to and from school. Also, the fact that administrators and teachers wish to share credit with citizens and members of organized groups for community improvements helps to build community confidence and support.

Participation Through Civic Projects

The school and its personnel, acting either as institutional representatives or as private citizens, have numerous opportunities to assist and render service in community drives, campaigns, and improvement projects. They may aid in developing adult education programs, in supporting charitable and philanthropic campaigns, in working for the improvement of public facilities, in planning and celebrating traditional holidays and events, in accepting membership on community councils and special committees, in encouraging the appreciation of art and music, in entertaining special visitors, and in joining in landscaping and home beautification projects.

Too frequently, participation in social and civic affairs is restricted to administrators and teachers. This is a short-sighted policy. It should be changed to include all employees who have a contribution to make to community life. The school doctor and nurse, for example, have much to offer in community health campaigns; men who work around the school grounds can advise on the planting of flowers and shrubs; school bus drivers have a place in safety and safe-driving programs sponsored by public and private agencies; and, custodians are able to supply information on maintenance problems of buildings. In fact, there is practically no aspect of community life in which some school employee cannot participate or lend assistance.

Participation Through Group Memberships

Instructional and noninstructional employees should be encouraged to take membership in community groups and organizations. Their own living becomes richer through association with people of different occupational backgrounds and interests and by engaging in activities of a challenging and enjoyable nature. At the same time, they are in an excellent position to interpret the school and to acquire a knowledge of how people react toward its program.

Some superintendents believe that school employees should be represented in each important group and organization in the community. They recommend an annual inventory of organizations to which employees belong, including church, fraternal, social, civic, political, and welfare. From this information, they are able to determine how adequately the school is represented and where memberships should be taken by individuals who are otherwise unaffiliated. This procedure appears to have merit, yet it may defeat its own purpose. It is one thing to encourage school employees to belong to outside groups and organizations and another to coerce them into membership. Participation value may be stressed and information supplied for managing contacts, but freedom of choice must be left to the individual.

Obstacles to Participation

The importance of staff participation in promoting lay understanding of the school and better relations with the community will scarcely be accomplished until one or two obstacles are removed. These obstacles are negative staff attitudes toward participation and unfair community demands made on school employees.

There are employees in every system, and particularly in teaching, who are not willing to take part in community life. Among them are young, unmarried women who do not expect to remain in the teaching profession and plan to establish homes elsewhere; ambitious teachers who are looking forward to employment in larger systems where salaries are higher and promotional opportunities better; teachers who are too engrossed in their own work to take an interest in outside activities; teachers who do not see any value or necessity for becoming involved in outside activities; teachers who, because of financial need, are engaged in after-school and week-end employment; and teachers who rebel against the idea because it comes from autocratic school boards and administrators.

Unfair community demands are a second major obstacle. For years, teachers have been treated as second-class citizens in many communities. They have been required to conform to narrow codes of conduct and render civic services without thought of compensation. Their contracts have contained restrictive clauses on personal freedom. Pressure has been brought on them to patronize local merchants. These demands and restrictions have amounted to a denial of the rights and privileges which other citizens took for granted.

The weight of demands and restrictions has been lightened in the last two decades, but it is still too heavy in some communities and sections of the country.

Much can be done to modify the negative attitudes of employees. Improved selection and continuing in-service programs will develop understanding of the need for participation and increase the sense of obligation to become identified with the community. Restrictive clauses can be eliminated from contracts and measures adopted to prevent excessive demands of the free-time of staff members. Involvement in public relations activities, under competent leadership is an excellent means for pointing up the value of wholesome contacts with people in the community.

Teachers and other employees should realize that they are expected to conform to the customs and traditions of the community. They should either accept conformity or else seek employment elsewhere. It is only when they are singled out as a special class that objection is warranted. Through action of the school board, administration, and professional organizations, the community can be educated to making a distinction between the rights of teachers as school-board employees and the rights of teachers as private citizens. Teachers must live in harmony with the community and the community must respect their personal wishes if they are to fulfill their obligation as social agents of the school and active citizens in the community.

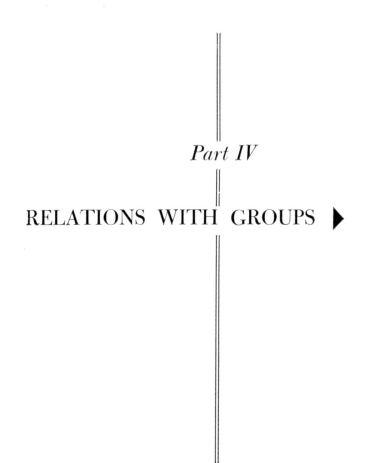

Part IV

RELATIONS WITH GROUPS ▶

Photo by Robert L. Nay. Courtesy Public Schools, West Hartford, Connecticut.

10
Parent-Teacher Associations

Local parent-teacher associations are sponsored by individual elementary and secondary schools and by school systems in villages, towns, and cities in every section of the country. Expressing a recognized need for home-school cooperation in the education of young people from kindergarten through the senior high school, they have grown rapidly since the beginning of the present century and will continue to grow in the future. They are one of the best means available for achieving the partnership concept in public education.

Because of their importance in promoting constructive relationships between the home and school, this discussion will consider the status of local associations, their relationship to the school, their value in public relations, types and activities of associations, their weaknesses and opportunities for improvement, and the place of the National Congress of Parents and Teachers.

LOCAL PARENT-TEACHER ASSOCIATIONS

A local parent-teacher association may be described as a voluntary organization whose membership consists of teachers in an individual school or school system and the parents of children who attend the school or school system they support through public taxation. Devoid of legal authority to make policy decisions or to administer educational programs, the primary purpose of an association is that of promoting child and youth welfare in the home, school, and community. More specifically this purpose may be broken down into the following objectives: (1) to develop parent understanding of the purposes, practices, and problems of the individual school or school system, (2) to see that the home and school work for similar objectives in the education of the young, (3) to facilitate an exchange of information between parents and teachers and thus effect better solutions to the educational problems of individual children, (4) to create public opinion favorable to plans of action for meeting the needs of children and youth in the home, school, and community, and (5) to support any worthy movement for improving public education and social conditions that influence child growth and development.

To accomplish these objectives, or others like them, local associations are usually organized around individual building units and separate divisions of the educational systems, that is, elementary, junior, and senior high schools. Where junior and senior high schools are housed together or the elementary and secondary programs are in the same building, a single association serves the entire school.

Typically, the membership of local associations consists of parents, teachers, and administrative and supervisory officials of the individual school and school system. Invitation to membership is extended by local associations to interested citizens in the community whether or not they have children in school. Of late, a few associations have been experimenting with student membership at the high school level. They have found that parents take more interest in the work of the association when their children belong to it and that high school youth make a valuable contribution to the thinking and activities of the group.

The officers of the association are generally a president, vice-president, secretary, and treasurer. They are elected by members of the association and act as an executive council, along with the principal or faculty members, to plan programs and carry out group decisions. The executive council may appoint standing committees on membership, finance, hospitality, programs, publicity, and the like, or the personnel of committees may be elected at the same time as the officers. Chairmen of standing committes are sometimes members of the executive council.

Each local association is self-supporting, its income being derived from small membership fees and from receipts from such social activities as card parties, dances, and bazaars. There is no restriction on the use of this income other than that set by members of the association. Most of it is spent to support regular programs and to purchase physical equipment and instructional supplies for the school.

City-wide associations are often formed in communities where there are several separate building units. Each unit sends representatives to a central group whose activities are governed by a constitution and set of by-laws. The same idea has been carried out on a county and regional basis in rural and semirural areas. The larger association speaks for the entire membership on important issues that cut across the school system and makes it possible to share experiences and develop better programs.

RELATIONSHIP TO THE SCHOOL

The relationship of a parent-teacher association to an individual school and school system has been a controversial question. It has arisen for various reasons: parental interference in administrative affairs, parental dictation to members of the instructional staff, lack of cooperation, inconsequential achievements over a period of years, political exploitation of the membership, more work for principals and teachers, and the activities of socially ambitious leaders. Usually the fundamental issue behind most expressions of dissatisfaction is where to draw the line between the rights of parents and those of school authorities.

In making a distinction between the rights of parents and those of school authorities, it must be remembered that a parent-teacher association is a voluntary organization which exists solely to protect the interest and advance the welfare of children and youth in the home, school, and community. No board of education is obligated legally to sponsor a parent group or to require that principals and teachers support its work. It exists because school boards and educators recognize that better instruction and guidance will be received by young people when parents and teachers work together, and that cooperation goes a long way in building public confidence and support for the school system.

In keeping with the nature and purposes of the organization, its functions are inquiry, discussion, participation, and recommendation. It may ask for information concerning instructional policies and practices and the reasons on which they are based. It may discuss any matter pertinent to the educational system that falls within the scope of its objectives, and join with the board of education, administrators, and teachers in undertaking projects and studying problems for school improvement. There is nothing to prevent this group from making recommendations, though the recommendations are in no way binding on school authorities. Perhaps its greatest contribution lies in the field of parent and community education regarding child and instructional problems and the formation of public opinion favorable to the school system.

PUBLIC RELATIONS VALUE

Apart from the direct benefits of parent-teacher cooperation received by children and youth in the home, school, and community, several public-relations by-products must be considered in looking at the importance of local associations. Good public relations start when parents and teachers come to know one another and to talk about what they want for young people. Through these conversations, parents soon learn to know the school, to understand what teachers are trying to do for children, and to appreciate instructional conditions and problems. At the same time, teachers and administrators are made aware of the needs, interests, and attitudes of people in the community and the responsibility they have for adjusting the school program to local conditions. This is a two-way process and the backbone, in many respects, of a sound program in school and community relations.

Mutual confidence grows as parents and teachers continue to exchange information and to acquire skill in working together on school and home problems. Suggested changes in instructional policies and practices and proposals to extend the school plant and its facilities are accepted more readily. Parents who understand the individual school and school system, its purposes and limitations, are able to keep the community informed and serve as partners in the advancement of public education.

TYPES OF ASSOCIATIONS

Six principal types of parent-teacher associations are found in school today. They may be classified as individual school associations, home-room and grade councils, room mothers, mothers' and fathers' associations, school and parent councils, and parent study clubs.

Individual School Associations

The most common type of association is organized around the individual school and divisions of the educational system. The popularity of this type is greatest at the elementary level and least at the senior high school level. If there are several individual school associations within the same community, it is customary for them to join together into a federated organization for the entire school district.

All parents of pupils attending a particular school are eligible for membership in the association. Teachers are expected to belong to it and to attend scheduled meetings. The general business of the association is conducted at these meetings, with time set aside at the close for parent-teacher visits and the serving of refreshments. Special committeees may convene between the regular meetings to plan programs, work on projects, or undertake assignments. They make their reports at regular meetings. This pattern is varied somewhat on occasion when open house is held or outstanding programs are presented for the benefit of parents and citizens in the community.

Homeroom and Grade Councils

Even though the parent-teacher association does fine work in developing the partnership concept between home and school, it has weaknesses which parents and educators have tried to overcome by building other forms of organization. One of these is the homeroom and grade council. In this type of organization, the larger group is broken down into small, compact units, each unit being attached to a homeroom or to one or more grades, depending upon the character and size of the school. The smaller units enable parents and teachers to become better acquainted. Time is taken to explain instructional practices and to answer parent questions. The strongest advantage is the opportunity to build programs around the immediate developmental needs of pupils. For example, an eighth-grade homeroom group would be more directly concerned with the needs of children entering adolescence while a second grade group might be more interested in problems of beginning reading.

Under this plan of organization, homeroom and grade units, or core curriculum sections in some schools, are small, semi-independent councils of parents and teachers. Each council may elect its own officers or they may be appointed by the president of the association and the building principal. Teachers act as consultants and co-workers in setting up functional programs within their groups. Occasionally, they assume responsibility for handling discussions that require the guidance of a professional leader. Sometimes pupils are invited to participate and express their views on topics under consideration. Each council reports periodically to the home and school association in order to acquaint the total membership with the work it is doing and to receive suggestions it may wish to incorporate in its program.

The parent-teacher association in high schools seldom reaches a point of popularity found in the elementary grades. In fact, lack of parental response and poor attendance at meetings have been responsible for eliminating some organizations, while others merely go through the motion of existing. Parents have a different attitude toward school affairs when children reach the upper grades. They are not concerned as much with childhood protection and general school practices as they are with social life and vocational preparation for the immediate future. Unless the association in senior high school deals with problems that appeal to parents, they will not attend meetings.

In high schools where the homeroom council idea has been tried, parents respond much better. They seem to enjoy the small group situation and the freedom it provides for expressing opinions. They no longer complain about the nature of the programs. The problems taken up have personal meaning and supply many suggestions applicable in everyday living. The homeroom council plan of organization is by no means a panacea for an ineffective high school parent-teacher association, but it does offer more promise of success than the typical arrangement.

Room Mothers

The room mother system is used rather extensively in elementary schools. A mother is elected by the parents of children in a particular room or grade or else she is appointed to her position by the officers of the parent-teacher association or by the school principal. The purpose of this plan is to have someone act as a liaison between the teacher and the parents. Her duties may be routine in nature and amount to nothing more than contacting parents by telephone and letter to notify them of meetings and urge their attendance. Sometimes she is expected to pass on information about the school and the activities of the association which seem important.

The room mother can be more than just a secretary for the parent-teacher association. By observing classes and helping the teacher she can learn more about the school and its educational practices than any of the other parents. Her presence under friendly conditions provides companionship for the teacher and helps to develop a genuine sense of cooperation between the two. Through reports of her observations and work with children, she supplies information which gives parents a first-hand knowledge of the school. The reactions they express make it possible for her to share their ideas and opinions with the room teacher, and thus complete the circuit of communication.

Principals have discovered that they can get many excellent ideas and learn much about their own schools by holding conferences with room mothers. Room mothers respond to this recognition and feel that they are respected and belong to the school. As a service group, they do not try to dictate to the principal or to compete with the board of education. An efficient room mother system promotes good home-school relations.

Mothers' and Fathers' Clubs

Supplemental to the parent-teacher association, and sometimes independent of it, are mothers' and fathers' clubs. Organized around special school activities, they are more common to the secondary than to the elementary school. A good example is the band mothers' club in junior and senior high schools. This club raises money for the purchase of instruments and uniforms, keeps clothing in repair, and accompanies members of the band on out-of-town trips. Mothers' groups also assist with dramatic productions, build scholarship funds for deserving graduates, aid students needing medical attention, and boost ticket sales for athletic contests. Not infrequently a mothers' chorus is formed by members of the parent-teacher association, and in one large city a mothers' current events discussion club holds regular weekly meetings in elementary schools with the leaders and resource specialists being furnished by the adult division of the school system.

Fathers' clubs operate in much the same way as the mothers' groups. They are formed generally around extracurricular activities for boys like football, basketball, band, and rifle. They raise money for supplies and equipment and perform needed services. Some groups are known as fathers and sons' clubs because both parent and child belong to them. Contests are held for fathers and sons in athletic sports; and they often work together on hobbies as well. Fathers' clubs attract men into the school who would not attend parent-teacher association meetings.

Experience has shown that fathers' and mothers' clubs can be relied upon to support projects and proposals beneficial to an individual school or an entire school system. There are numerous examples of how they have endorsed and worked successfully for the passage of bond issues, increases in tax rates, enactment of essential legislation, development of youth recreational centers, better library facilities, and changes in the program of studies. Once they feel attached to the school and begin to acquire an appreciation of its services, problems, and limitations, they are anxious to help advance the cause of public education.

School and Parent Councils

School and parent councils are advisory bodies of parents and educators created for the purpose of appraising instructional practices and suggesting the nature of school policies. Three principal types of councils have been organized in individual schools. In the first type, the parent-teacher association is asked to send a certain number of representatives to a central council which also includes the principal and selected members of the instructional staff. The group may meet at stated intervals, or it may convene upon call when there is a pressing matter of business. The second type of council is an outgrowth of the homeroom or grade council system, with each unit having one or more representatives on the advisory body. The third type is substituted for the parent-teacher association and is the only medium of formal contact with the home. The members are chosen from a list of parents with children in school and from the roster of staff personnel.

Various uses are made of school and parent councils to justify their existence. A principal may secure a fairly reliable sample of parent opinion on most school matters if the membership represents a balanced cross-section of the parent-teacher association or of people in the surrounding community. He may use the council to find out what parents think of night parties and dances, homework assignments, detention for lateness, medical examinations, and so forth. Sometimes he may ask the council how the school should be improved and take this approach to get at hidden dissatisfactions. He may solicit reactions to possibilities of changing report cards or looking into the merits of a program in general education. When the time seems ripe, he may ask the council to study the need for revising instructional policies and request its recommendations. By working with the council, the principal avoids conflicts and earns the support of parents who share in the actions taken.

Many principals favor the council plan since it is simple to organize and easier to control than the parent-teacher association. But there is also a danger that it may become a rubber stamp for the principal, and lay members will resent his domination and refuse to cooperate.

Parent Study Clubs

While school and parent councils are largely a creation of administrators, parent study clubs are a development of laymen. Given such titles as child study club, neighborhood parent association, mothers' council, and parent study group, they are found mostly in elementary attendance districts where teachers have shown slight interest in cooperation and principals have discouraged the formation of home and school associations.

Organized by parents without assistance from the school, their main objective is the study of children's growth needs and how they may be met in the home, school, and community. Stress is placed upon the nonpartisan character of the organization and the importance of striving for constructive cooperation with school authorities when action must be taken to protect and promote the welfare of children.

Meetings are held in private homes until the membership grows too large, then space is rented or permission is secured to hold meetings in the school auditorium. The public is invited to the meetings. One meeting is given over annually to the election of officers and the appointment of special committees. Usually the officers and committee chairmen constitute the planning and executive committee, which does the major work of the study club.

The value of parent study clubs has been demonstrated in some school districts. Parents have learned a great deal about their own children and have made significant adjustments in family living. They have reminded school boards and administrators of their responsibilities for meeting the educational needs of children. Successful projects have been undertaken to provide play equipment on school grounds, to improve sanitary conditions in school cafeterias, to install better classroom lighting, to organize summer recreation programs for small children, to introduce the teaching of instrumental music in the elementary grades, and others. The most important value has been that of helping administrators and teachers to realize the need for teamwork between home and school.

PROGRAMS OF ASSOCIATIONS

The programs of parent-teacher associations differ from one school to another and among schools within the same system. The range is from the strictly traditional type of meeting to the study-project pattern with its far-reaching effect on school services.

Monthly Meetings

The traditional monthly meeting of parent-teacher associations follows a fixed form. It consists of an opening exercise of prayer or singing, the reading of the minutes of the previous meeting, review of unfinished business, committee reports, and new business. This agenda may be followed by entertainment, and then a speaker, demonstration, or panel discussion. Refreshments are served at the close of the meeting when parents and teachers have an opportunity to talk together. The meetings last from one and one-half to two hours, with eight or nine scheduled during the school year.

Some variation in procedure has been introduced because of American Education Week, open house, and school night programs for parents. All people in the community are invited to visit the school during American Education Week and look at classroom and corridor exhibits of pupils' work, textbooks, and instructional aids used by teachers. The invitation covers any special programs which are staged in the evening instead of the regular monthly meeting. Open house programs are also substituted for monthly meetings and allow parents and taxpayers to see the school in operation. Some schools divide the open house program into two parts. During the first part, parents and interested citizens follow the same daily schedule as children, but with the periods shortened. They receive an explanation from teachers of the material covered in classes and the purposes they are trying to accomplish. The second part consists of either a tour of the building or conferences with teachers, or sometimes a special program is presented in the auditorium. Both American Education Week and open house have brought many people into schools and have increased popular interest in the parent-teacher association.

There are three important aspects of the monthly meetings — committee reports, the speaker or demonstration, and parent visits with teachers. The committee reports are important when they summarize work done by members on significant problems and projects and the group is asked to register opinion before action is taken. Some associations mimeograph and distribute reports beforehand so that parents and teachers may be better prepared to discuss the issues raised. Speakers, panel discussions, and demonstrations interpret the educational program and acquaint parents with conditions and needs of the school. The development of special projects and the formation of study groups may grow out of suggestions made by speakers and panel members. The visits of parents and teachers at the close of the meeting are important, if enough time is available for the discussion of mutual problems involving children. Lack of time has led to the practice of keeping the discussion of individual, child problems out of the meeting and arranging appointments for after-school hours. However, quite a few associations keep their formal meeting brief so that parents and teachers will have time to talk together.

Special Projects and Services

The list of projects and services of parent-teacher associations is long and impressive. Their work can be divided into fund raising activities and concern for educational problems. Fund-raising projects are numerous in communities where the board of education will not purchase the supplies and equipment that teachers need and which parents want for the benefit of their children. Examples are motion-picture projectors, record players, tape recorders, television sets, stage curtains, classroom libraries, and athletic equipment.

Concern for educational problems is an outgrowth of sensitivity to and study of existing needs. Many groups are most careful to define the problems they are concerned with before study-action is taken. Examples of problems dealt with are (1) surveys of parent attitudes toward the instructional program, (2) surveys of college success by high school graduates, (3) revisions of report cards and marking systems, (4) promotion of bond issues, (5) increases in teachers' salaries, (6) establishment of youth recreational centers and canteens, (7) founding of summer day camps for younger children, (8) improvement of school medical and nursing supervision, and (9) the opening of adult evening schools.

Considerable exploration has been done in the field of special services by parent-teacher associations. They have assisted in the school library and with medical and dental examinations, sponsored scout troops, chaperoned field trips and excursions, prepared special informative bulletins for mothers of pre-school children, published a weekly or monthly news-letter for members of the association, helped in the preparation of assembly programs, worked in the cafeteria, supplied glasses and other aids to children, and worked with theatre managers on the selection of films for Saturday afternoon programs.

While these services promote closer relations with the school and should be encouraged, administrators and teachers must be careful that parents do not assume authority which belongs to professional personnel. They must guard against the domination of these services by a few leaders and strive to broaden the base of lay participation. One of their principal tasks is to guide the parent group and, through example, help them to acquire skill in the use of the group process. Under their direction, parents should learn to substitute rational procedures for hasty actions, and recognize that they cannot shift their own responsibilities on to teachers. Sensitivity to these points prevents difficulties and assures the continuance of wholesome relationships.

Study Groups

As a part of the local parent-teacher association program, study groups are excellent for adult education in child growth and development and for the understanding of educational practices. At the elementary school level, study groups may be organized under the direction of teachers for reviewing pertinent literature and discussing the growth needs of children. Their work may be strengthened by the analysis of anecdotal records and the observation of children in classroom situations. Different methods of teaching reading and related tool subjects may be demonstrated and discussed in follow-up conferences. Much may be done through study groups on the question of how parents can provide at home for the continuity of learning experiences.

A similar program may be instituted by junior high school parent-teacher associations because of growth changes which occur at the onset of adolescence. Where parents do not wish to make a thorough study of this subject, they may confine their activities to classroom observations and regular conferences with teachers. Attempts may be made through conferences to share information about young people and to reach agreements on the objectives toward which the home and school should work together. These objectives may be summed up and published in illustrated booklets for distribution to all members of the association.

Outstanding work may be done by study groups in the improvement of the curriculum. The work may start with an invitation from the principal to officers of the association asking that interested parents meet with teachers to review the instructional program and decide whether or not changes in it should be made. Out of the meetings, small study groups of parents and teachers may be formed and given responsibility for revising old courses of study and constructing new ones. Parent members outline what they want for children and serve as resource persons. The technical aspects of building resource and instructional units are left to teachers and curriculum workers. Courses in driver training, work-study programs, first aid, vocational agriculture, fashion design, fine arts, music, extracurricular activities, reading, and the like have been developed by this method in several systems. Study groups may also do a great deal on questions of evaluating pupil progress, selecting appropriate instructional materials, improving health standards, inventorying audio-visual aids, and paving the way for core curriculum.

The study group idea has not been taken up widely by parent-teacher groups because neither parents nor teachers know how to function effectively at this level. No doubt it will gain acceptance as they learn to work together and deal more directly with educational needs and conditions.

Social Affairs

Social affairs have a place in the programs of local associations. Their value lies in the promotion of cordial relations among parents and between parents and teachers. Typical social affairs include parties, dances, bazaars, and entertainments. Some parent-teacher groups give dinners in honor of winning teams; others award prizes to pupils for meritorious service on safety patrol, corridor supervision, and aid to librarians. Teas for new faculty members at the opening of school are popular.

Too much emphasis is given to social affairs by many parent-teacher associations. Their programs, in fact, are more social than educational in nature. There appears to be three reasons for this: (1) social events attract membership; (2) attention is diverted from weaknesses in the curriculum; and (3) the money raised is used for school purposes.

WEAKNESSES OF ASSOCIATIONS

Notwithstanding the fine work done by parent-teacher associations, it is questionable that the rank and file exert much influence on the home, school, and community. According to reported studies and observations, their ineffectualness is due to: (1) professional attitudes, (2) lack of objectives, (3) poor leadership, (4) unbalanced programs, (5) conduct of meetings, and (6) conflict situations. The nature of each will be considered.

Professional Attitudes

The attitudes of principals and teachers in individual elementary and secondary schools are responsible for the weakness of parent-teacher associations. Principals who are opposed to the idea of parent groups and who do not appreciate their value try to prevent their growth and development. They may recommend, as a matter of policy, that staff members attend regular meetings of the association, but seldom do they urge them to take an active part. They may approve parent-teacher conferences during the school week, but openly discourage any attempt to extend the opportunities for co-operation. They may endorse projects on behalf of the school, but refuse to have teachers participate because they are too busy. They may work with the executive council and program committee of the association, but see that nothing is done which will interfere with the operation of the school. They may suggest speakers for meetings and outline means for raising money to purchase supplies and equipment, but seldom permit parents to get at basic issues and fundamental needs of the institution. They may display enthusiasm for the parent group and the ideals it stands for, but use it merely to put across their own pet interests and to indoctrinate members to their way of thinking. They may solicit suggestions for school improvements, but cancel any which are inherently dangerous to security. They may give thoughtful and detailed answers to parent questions, but never invite parent aid in planning the school program or in exploring ways of working together.

Staff attitudes toward parent-teacher associations usually approximate those of principals. If the building principal lacks en-

thusiasm, it will be reflected in the relations of teachers with parents.
They will stay away from meetings unless compelled to attend them
for the sake of appearance. No effort will be made to share in the
work of the association or to advise with parents on problems which
should receive their attention. Whenever criticisms are implied in
questions raised about the instructional program, they will become
defensive and accuse parents of disloyalty. However, principals who
believe in a strong parent-teacher association may find that staff
members will not go along with them. The teachers dislike night
meetings and the necessity for giving time after school hours. They
prefer to remain apart from parents, believing that too close a
relationship leads to trouble and interference with the work they
are doing. Actually, their objections narrow down either to previous
conditioning against cooperation or to lack of understanding of what
a parent group may mean in the improvement of education.

Although the attitudes of principals and teachers are responsible
for weaknesses of parent-teacher associations, their feelings may be
dictated by the superintendent and board of education. It only takes
the example of those who are in charge of a school system to set the
pattern which they are expected to follow.

Lack of Objectives

A striking weakness of parent-teacher associations is the lack
of well-defined objectives. It is true that practically every association
has a paper statement of its objectives, but the statement, more often
than not, is unrealistic and meaningless. Members seldom know the
objectives, and few references are ever made to them in the planning
of activities. They are generalized ideas borrowed and copied from
standard sources instead of being precise goals which the parents
and teachers have defined and believe should govern the work of the
association. Every parent-teacher association should define its own
objectives in precise, simple language. They should be objectives
which grow out of local needs and conditions, define the limits of
the program, and serve as the directional force behind action taken.

Poor Leadership

Poor leadership is another cause of weakness in parent-teacher
associations. No association will grow strong and vital to the school

program when controlled and directed by selfish and incompetent persons. The signs of poor leadership are domination by the principal, indifference to parent wishes, perpetuation of officers, more concern for social affairs than for educational matters, monotonous programs, and a declining membership.

Unbalanced Programs

The programs of too many associations are out of balance with their objectives. Instead of being planned with these in mind, they consist of speakers, entertainment, and social, fund-raising activities. Speakers are chosen not because they have something to contribute to educational needs and problems of the individual school and the interests of parents, but because they can be secured cheaply, are interesting to listen to, and help to fill out the annual program.

In elementary schools, the practice of having children put on entertainments has been a custom for years. Under the direction of teachers, they sing, dance, play musical instruments, present dramatic skits, and do other things to amuse parents and satisfy their pride. Rarely do pupil entertainment programs portray the true work of the school or interpret its educational offerings.

Social, fund-raising activities constitute a major portion of the total program. Here an effort is made to raise money through bake-goods sales, bazaars, dances, card parties, and the like. The money is used to purchase things needed in the school, such as stage curtains, radio, television sets, motion picture projectors, band uniforms, and so forth. These activities become so numerous in some parent-teacher associations that parents believe they are the primary purpose for coming together at the school. Fortunately, a growing number of PTA's are taking exception to money-raising activities and insisting that the board of education purchase what is needed for good instruction. Where they are to eliminate this feature of their programs, more time is given to basic questions of education.

Conduct of Meetings

Parents lose interest in their local association because of the manner in which meetings are conducted. To start with, often nothing is done to welcome new members and make them feel that they are wanted. Several empty rows in the front of the auditorium separate the audience from the chairman and those who take part in the program. Teachers sit together to the side and rear of the parents giving the impression that they need this arrangement for security. Committee reports are usually stiff and formal, with details included that are not important. Few opportunities are made available for open and critical discussion. The meetings are sometimes late in getting over and no time is left for visiting with teachers.

Conflict Situations

The presence of conflict impairs the effectiveness of an association. It diverts attention from basic objectives and gradually replaces cooperation with disunity. Its continuance may bring about either partial or complete inactivity. There are instances where it has divided a community into opposing factions and weakened popular confidence in and support of the school system.

Conflict situations arise from personal differences and mistaken ideas of authority. Such situations develop when lay and professional members try to seize control and exploit their position for selfish purposes. They develop sometimes out of sharp cultural clashes between members and tensions which flow into the association from the community. Many serious ones originate with mistaken ideas of authority. School officials may believe they have the right to dictate exactly what the group shall do, never allowing the association to deal with matters they do not favor. Or parents may hold the opinion that they can tell the board of education, administrators, and teachers what they must do and have their wishes followed. Failure to define clearly the line of demarcation between school authority and parent rights has probably been responsible for more conflict of a serious nature than any other cause.

SUGGESTIONS FOR IMPROVEMENT

Several suggestions for improving parent-teacher associations were implied in the preceding section. To these can be added a few others which deserve study and application.

1. *Finding out what parents would like to take up in association meetings.* The faculty of one school, for example, asked

parents at the beginning of the year what they would like children to learn in the coming months. Their replies were tabulated and compared with the objectives of the school. A mimeographed report of this comparison was sent to parents and subsequently used to form discussion groups around points of difference. In another school, a parent workshop was organized for those who wanted to learn the latest methods of teaching arithmetic, reading, and spelling so that they could help their children correctly with homework assignments. Perhaps parents would like scheduled visits to classes, tape recordings of typical lessons, panel discussions on various topics, demonstration lessons, bulletins on special phases of instruction, and study groups to probe subjects of genuine interest.

2. *Establishing guiding principles for planning the monthly meetings of the association.* These principles might include the following ideas: (*a*) programs should be consistent with the objectives of the association; (*b*) they should deal with subjects reflecting parent choices as determined by interest inventories and survey questionnaires; (*c*) they should be varied from month to month; (*d*) they should be planned by parents with the cooperation of principals and teachers; (*e*) they should be planned around a definite theme or objective; (*f*) several devices should be employed for presenting ideas, such as lectures, panels, motion pictures, demonstrations, plays, and buzz sessions; (*g*) the large group should be divided at times into small, informal groups for work on definite problems; (*h*) findings and decisions on problems studied should be recorded in writing and distributed to the entire membership; and (*i*) time should be set aside for periodic conferences between parents and teachers.

3. *Involving parents in the educational affairs of the school.* One approach is the talent file. Here a cover letter and questionnaire are sent to parents and leading citizens asking them to indicate their special talents, check services they will perform, and underline the committees they will serve on. A card file, developed from this information, is made available to teachers and officers of the association. Parents who are listed in the file can then be asked to take part in the life of the school, participating in activities for which they are qualified and in which they have an interest.

Another means for involving parents is that of assigning them to different kinds of projects that satisfy their interests. Some may wish to explore the educational program of the school, some may wish to take up the question of how the home can cope better with child needs in literature, music, radio, television, hobbies, and play activities. Some may wish to learn hobbies that can be taught to their own children. And some may wish to center attention on the adequacy of after-school and summer recreational facilities.

The high point of involvement comes when parents and teachers work together for the improvement of instructional programs and the solution of significant educational problems.

NATIONAL CONGRESS OF PARENTS AND TEACHERS

Almost 40,000 local parent-teacher associations are affiliated with the National Congress of Parents and Teachers. First organized in 1897, it has undergone rapid growth and now claims a membership of approximately 10,000,000. Because it is a structural part of the local unit and may be a force in directing the activities of parents and teachers in the individual school, its objectives, policies, organization, and services will be reviewed.

Objectives

The objectives of the National Congress of Parents and Teachers are broader than the activities of most local associations would suggest. As stated in an official publication of the national organization, the objectives are the following:

1. To promote the welfare of children and youth in home, school, church and community.
2. To raise the standards of home life.
3. To secure adequate laws for the care and protection of children and youth.
4. To bring into closer relation the home and the school, that parents and teachers may cooperate intelligently in the training of the child.
5. To develop between educators and the general public such united efforts as will secure for every child the highest advantages in physical, mental, social, and spiritual education.

Each local group is expected to work for the accomplishment of these objectives, but few actually do. Their concern is limited almost exclusively to promoting the welfare of children in school.

Policies

The National Congress of Parents and Teachers is quite specific in stating the policies under which it operates. Being a noncommercial, nonsectarian, and nonpartisan organization, it does not endorse commercial enterprises or candidates for political office or permit the name of the organization to be used in connection with any commercial or partisan interest aside from the regular work of the Congress.

A special point is made in the statement of policies that the Congress does not try to direct the administrative activities of the school but to cooperate instead.

The National Congress does not enter into membership with other organizations unless the action is approved by the Board of Managers, but it stands willing and ready to cooperate with all groups and organizations that are working for similar objectives.

Organization

The local parent-teacher association is the basic unit upon which the National Congress is constructed. Authority to organize a local association or to admit an existing group to membership comes from the national office. Upon joining, the local unit must agree to uphold the by-laws of the National Congress and promote its objectives.

After a specified number of local groups in a state belong to the National Congress, they are organized into a state branch or congress. The state branch then has the right to admit local units and the responsibility for supervising and directing their activities. Each state branch elects its own officers, holds an annual convention, and participates in national meetings.

The National Congress is governed by plans and policies adopted at its annual convention. Included at the convention are the Board of Managers and delegates from each state branch. The number of delegates by states is proportional to the size of their respective memberships.

Responsibility between conventions is vested in the Board of Managers. This group consists of the national officers, national chairmen of standing committees, and presidents of state branches. Because of its size and unwieldly character, the Board of Managers authorizes the national officers to make administrative decisions and supervise the work of the national office. The officers, however, must render an accounting of their activities to the Board of Managers.

Services

The National Congress performs several different types of services consistent with the purposes for which it was founded. The national officers and full-time field workers attend state conventions and special gatherings to interpret the policies and the program of the organization. They likewise give aid to state branches and work closely with state officers on problems of membership, organization, and service to local units.

An informational program is maintained through newspaper releases and the publication of innumerable handbooks, pamphlets, and leaflets. This material is prepared by the national office and distributed to state branches and local units. It is designed to provide inspiration, helpful suggestions, and knowledge of where the National Congress stands on important issues relating to the welfare of children.

A monthly newsletter entitled *National Congress Bulletin* is sent to presidents of parent-teacher associations and acts as a clearing house for the organization. All individual members receive a monthly magazine, *National Parent Teacher,* which contains articles of interest to parents, accounts of projects carried on by local groups, book reviews, a guide to motion pictures for children, and other worthwhile material.

Besides cooperating with many national groups and agencies having programs dealing with child welfare and education, the National Congress sponsors leadership training courses, workshops on parent problems, scholarships for young people planning to enter teaching, and the development of parent-teacher groups in foreign countries. It has given strong support to legislation for the health, welfare, and education of children.

11
Citizen Advisory Committees

A further opportunity to bring the public into closer contact with the school and to involve laymen in the educational program is provided by citizen advisory committees. As the name implies, these committees are composed of laymen who study educational needs and problems and then advise school authorities on whatever action they believe should be taken.

Known by such titles as citizens' committee for the advancement of educational standards, citizens' committee for adequate education, citizens' school study council, public school citizens' committee, educational planning commission, citizens' advisory council, and citizens' committee on education, they have grown rapidly in recent years. A number of professional leaders view them as the most outstanding development in American education during the past quarter century. However, they are not new to public education because small groups of citizens have served in an advisory capacity to administrators and teachers of high school agricultural and vocational programs for years. It is the extension of the advisory principle to whole school systems that commands attention.

In order to appreciate the place and importance of citizen

193

advisory committees in public education, this discussion will consider the general purposes of these committees, how they start, types that exist, selection of members, organization, programs and procedures, accomplishments claimed, and cautions and criticisms. A section will also be given over to the National Citizens' Commission for the Public Schools and the services it performs in promoting popular interest in the improvement of local school systems.

PURPOSES OF COMMITTEES

Resolutions adopted by school boards establishing citizen advisory committees as well as programs of groups formed independently of school systems indicate that their general purposes are as follow:

To assist school officials in the development of sound and adequate educational policies and programs;

To identify educational needs and work for the solution of related problems;

To interpret educational conditions to fellow citizens and enlist their support in seeking improvements;

To bring community information, opinion, and planning into the deliberations of school officials concerned with policy-making;

To influence public attitudes in support of an action program for changes in the school system;

To harmonize differences in educational points of view between school officials and members of the community.

Apart from these general purposes, a good many citizen advisory committees are formed at state and local levels to try and solve a particular problem affecting schools. This is the only purpose for which they are created, and when they have accomplished it or have exhausted their usefulness they are disbanded. Some temporary school-sponsored and independent citizen groups, however, have continued on a permanent basis, broadening, in time, their concept of function.

HOW THEY START

According to available research, the initiative for starting advisory committees may come from private citizens, community groups, and school officials for a variety of different reasons. One of these reasons is the desire of boards of education, sparked by dynamic superintendents, to cooperate as fully as possible with members of the community. They realize that the responsibility of long-range planning for better schools is a public one and that the advisory committee is an excellent means for sharing this responsibility. Through it they can acquaint a representative body of the citizenry with the conditions and problems of public education, pool information, and work for common goals. But in most instances advisory groups are formed by school boards and superintendents to meet a pressing problem or an emergency for which public support is needed. New buildings or the remodeling of existing structures is a prevalent reason for their action. They ask advisory committees to recommend acceptable building sites, promote bond issues and higher tax rates, and review architectural plans. This limited use of advisory committees scarcely approaches the true idea of a continuing partnership between the school and community, though it may be beneficial in getting over a critical situation and establishing a desirable precedent for public participation in educational affairs.

The largest, single cause for the organization of independent citizen advisory committees is dissatisfaction with the school system and the officials in charge of it.[1] These committees are formed without invitation from the board of education and the superintendent of schools. Their purpose is to study the school system and to make recommendations for its improvement. Heavy reliance is placed on the publicizing of factual information and the development of supporting opinion to gain acceptance of recommendations.

Expressions of dissatisfaction which have brought about the formation of independent citizen groups include indignation over the refusal of school officials to act upon specific requests for improvements, high incidence of drop-out among secondary pupils, inadequately trained teachers, divided opinion over core curriculum, failure of elementary youngsters to reach norms on standardized tests in reading and spelling, and a great many others.

The initiative for organizing committees has come from parent-teacher associations in a number of places. They have taken the initiative because it seemed advisable to have a wider representation

---

[1] David L. Cline, *An Analysis of Public School Citizens' Committees* (Philadelphia: Temple University, 1956) Chapter III, Unpublished doctoral dissertation.

of taxpayers involved in the study of a problem, knowing that a broad-base committee would carry more weight with the board of education and the general public. Not infrequently, advisory committees have grown out of meetings called by one or more civic groups for the purpose of discussing means for increasing public interest in the schools. Judging from available evidence, there is no doubt that these independent groups have made valuable contributions to state and local school systems.

Somewhat analogously, other independent groups have sprung into existence when citizens took an interest in a particular educational problem and decided to find out what could be done about it. As examples, a women's club took up the question of how to meet the shortage of qualified elementary school teachers; a veterans' organization became interested in a statistical report concerning juvenile delinquency in the community and felt it should help with the problem; and, a neighborhood businessmen's association listened to a speaker on school finance matters and decided to investigate the local situation.

A significant number of independent groups have been founded in recent years by laymen who saw how advisory committees were operating elsewhere and what they were accomplishing. Wanting better schools in their own communities, they discussed the idea with friends and neighbors, called open meetings to test public sentiment, and took steps required for organizing study councils. Many gained courage for their work from the services of the National Citizens' Commission for the Public Schools and from the unexpected support offered by people who always wanted to know more about local schools but had no way of getting complete and accurate information. They have made important contributions in awakening public interest and in demonstrating the value of school-community cooperation for the improvement of education.

A small number of advisory committees have been organized by and at the request of community councils. Councils have recommended the advisory committee plan to take care of problems which member agencies were not equipped to handle and which fell outside the scope of their programs. Usually their recommendations are made directly to boards of education, although there are instances where council members took the initiative in organizing independent advisory committees. This latter course of action is adopted after efforts have failed to secure school board cooperation. Most advisory groups formed by or at the request of community councils enjoy strong support and are effective in solving educational problems.

Another reason for the organizing of advisory committees — although it is not too prevalent — is their use by school administrators to put across pet ideas or to pave the way for changes they wish to make. Examples of this technique are seen in plans for school-district reorganization and consolidation where there is no immediate demand or necessity for this action in many cases; the introduction of sex hygiene courses in the later elementary and junior high school grades; the enlargement of football stadiums; and, the eventual purchasing of expensive equipment for special classes without regard for needs in the rest of the school.

Finally, advisory committees are formed after a partial or complete evaluation of a school or school system has been made and certain problems stand out. In one community, a medical report on the unsanitary condition of school buildings led directly to

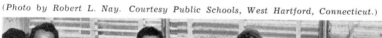

A means for better schools.

(*Photo by Robert L. Nay. Courtesy Public Schools, West Hartford, Connecticut.*)

the organizing of a citizens' committee to make recommendations for improvements. In another, a report of a college accrediting committee aroused strong community reaction and resulted in the appointment of a citizens' group to study and improve the secondary school curriculum.

This analysis of how citizen advisory committees start reveals that the majority have been organized when the schools were confronted with problems and under pressure from taxpayers to do something about them. It also brings out the fact that school boards and school administrators have been remiss in taking leadership for educational improvements and that they have been forced to assume a role which they should take anyway. Although little was said about the effectiveness of advisory committees organized under one set of conditions or another, the data make it clear that stronger, cooperative relationships with the community can be built and more satisfactory results achieved if they are set up when there is no emergency or independent citizens' group prodding the board to action.

TYPES OF ADVISORY COMMITTEES

Citizen advisory committees may be divided according to their sponsorship, duration, and geographic area of service. For purposes of this discussion, they will be referred to as local school district, local independent, and county and state committees, a classification which includes consideration of sponsorship, time, and place.

School-District Committees

Three types of citizen advisory committees are sponsored by local school districts. They are special subject field, individual school, and system-wide committees. They may be temporary or permanent, depending upon the purposes for which they are created. Special subject-field committees are the oldest in point of service, many of them going back several years before the lay advisory plan was popularized and applied to entire school systems. Composed of individuals possessing specialized experience and knowledge in given instructional fields, they act in an advisory capacity to administrators and teachers in the development of new courses of study, in the preparation of instructional outlines, and in the selection of supplies and equipment, and sometimes nominate teaching personnel and place high-school graduates in employment. They have been used

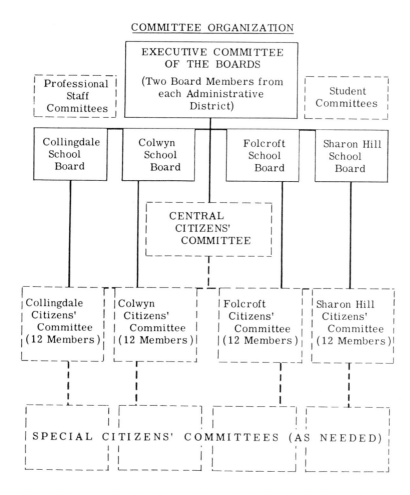

COMMITTEE ORGANIZATION

Committee organization for a joint school district in Pennsylvania.

with remarkable success in all forms of vocational education, adult education, and home economics, and they are now found in such other instructional fields as art, music, health, and science. Most special subject committees are appointed on a continuing basis, with meetings scheduled at stated intervals throughout the year.

Individual school advisory committees are made up of citizens who live in a section of the community served by the school. The members are parents, for the most part, though of late the tendency has been to name an equal number of residents without children in school and to make the committees more representative of the population. It is the function of these committees to report community opinion about individual school programs, study educational problems, and make recommendations to building principals for the improvement of existing policies. Occasionally they confer with their school board and discuss the needs of the entire school system. Although they have proven valuable in many ways, their use has been limited to a few communities.

System-wide advisory committees work with the board of education and superintendent of schools. These officials have found it increasingly helpful to share their problems with lay members of the community. They invite them to investigate educational needs and offer suggestions for improving the instructional program. Care is taken to select laymen who are willing to devote time and thought to the study of school matters and who can express viewpoints of different community groups without being obligated to uphold special interests. Some system-wide advisory committees are appointed for a specific job, as a bond campaign, but many of them are of a general character and serve the school district over an extended period of time. Because single advisory groups must be limited in size to operate efficiently, the practice has been growing of setting up a series of temporary sub-committees, each dealing with one or more problems in clearly-defined areas. In this way central committees can serve as coordinating agencies and, at the same time, increase the opportunities for more citizens to participate in the work of the schools.

Independent Advisory Committees

As described in the previous section, independent advisory committees are launched by private citizens and community groups without sponsorship from local school officials. They generally develop in districts where boards of education and administrators become intrenched and grow indifferent to the public welfare. Their purpose is to stir these officials to action for better schools through a study of educational needs and the building of public opinion to support the recommendations which they make. Although some boards and superintendents refuse to cooperate in meeting their requests for complete and accurate information on problems being studied, the more judicious ones put the resources of the school system at their disposal. They realize the value of getting accurate information into the hands of these committees and what this may mean in the formation of intelligent public opinion. Granted that some independent groups are trouble-makers and fault-finders who are not representative of the community, most of them are sincere in wanting to improve the educational program. School boards have found that cooperation with independent groups is most likely to yield constructive returns.

County and State Committees

Citizen advisory committees, both board sponsored and independent, have been tried successfully at county and state levels. At the county level, they are usually brought into existence at the invitation of the school board and the superintendent. They are found more commonly in states where the county is the basic unit for school control, but many operate in others where the district form of organization is still predominant. In order to increase opportunities for lay participation in the study of schools, county advisory committees are often divided into or supplemented by subgroups to which specific problems are assigned.

On the state level, the structural arrangement for the study and improvement of public education varies rather sharply. In one state, a study commission was established by the state teachers' association and given a grant of money to carry on its work. In another, the committee was appointed by the governor and instructed to make an impartial survey of the school system throughout the commonwealth and to recommend changes in the foundation program. In still a third, the state citizens' council served as a coordinating agency for different groups that were interested in the promotion of better schools. They applied for membership in the council and agreed to undertake any activities which fitted into their respective programs.

Some committees blanket the state with regional and local

subcommittees to which they assign responsibility for making intensive local surveys of schools and reporting their findings to the parent group. The results are brought together in a comprehensive manual that is publicized and used for staking out study areas and making pertinent recommendations. On the other hand, the practice is also followed of encouraging the development of regional and local groups, with the state committee standing by to give assistance, upon request, in organizing and planning continuing programs.

State advisory committees and the combination of state and local groups have been effective in dealing with some of the larger problems of education, as teacher certification, mandated salary schedules, and finance; in coordinating programs for essential changes in state school laws; in enlisting the cooperation of state and national organizations in the fight for better schools; in influencing and bringing about legislative action; and, in creating wide-spread, public interest in education.

The movement to organize citizen advisory committees at the state level has been spear-headed by several different groups, including state departments of public instruction, teachers' associations, state boards of education, state school board members' associations, women's groups, and labor and business organizations.

SELECTION OF MEMBERS

Different methods are used and various factors considered in the selection of citizens for membership on school-sponsored, advisory committees. One method of selection is by the board of education. The board names the individuals whom it would like to have on the advisory committee and asks whether they would be willing to serve. This enables the board to secure competent individuals with whom it can work and fulfills the leadership responsibility the community expects it to take. Those who disagree with this method of selection point out that a weak board of education is likely to appoint only those individuals who will recommend what it wants, thereby destroying the essential value of citizen advice in the development of educational policies. It is conceded, however, that this argument does not hold too strongly in the appointment of temporary advisory committees when influential people are needed to do a particular job.

The most popular method of selecting members is by invitation from the board of education to community interest groups, such as labor, business, medicine, law, banking, religion, and parents, asking them to name one or more representatives to the advisory committee. The method is based on the principle of having a balanced, cross-sectional membership so that all points of view may be represented and channels maintained for a two-way flow of information in the community. Despite its popularity, it has weaknesses which should not be overlooked by boards of education that are planning to establish advisory committees. (1) It is not possible to keep committee size within the bounds of working efficiency and still include all major interest groups. (2) Representation by all major religious sects destroys committee balance. (3) Members should be free to think for themselves, not to uphold organizational interests. (4) Some organizations want representation but are unwilling to accept the responsibility that goes with it. (5) Organizations name representatives without much thought as to their qualifications or fitness for a particular assignment. And (6) if certain representatives are unacceptable, then the board is confronted with a delicate problem in public relations.

A third method, and one gradually gaining acceptance, is asking people in the community to suggest the names of individuals whom they believe would make good advisory committee members. Suggestions come from pupils, teachers, parents, citizens, and organized interest groups. They are turned over to a special committee of citizens, appointed by the board, to screen the list of candidates and develop a preferential register of names from which the board can make its final selections. All invitations to membership on the advisory committee are sent out by the board of education. This method has two advantages: (1) members of the special committee give much more time to the screening of candidates than could be afforded by the board of education; and (2) this process avoids any claims of partisanship by the board which so often creep into the picture.

Whether one or a combination of methods are employed for selecting members, the advisory committee should be as representative of the community as possible. Representativeness can best be assured when population factors are taken into account in drawing up the composition of the committee and criteria determined for the individual qualifications of members. The composition should approximate population distribution with regard to adult age, sex, education, economic status, occupation, and geographic location. These data would be available in systems where opinion polls are conducted, otherwise reference must be made to census tracts. The criteria for the individual qualification of members should include (1) sufficient interest to attend meetings regularly, (2) ability to contribute to discussions of the committee, (3) faith in the democratic process, (4) an open mind, and (5) willingness to carry an equal share of the load.

ADVISORY COMMITTEE ORGANIZATION

In the past, few boards of education considered in detail how an advisory committee should be organized and what authority it should have. They merely approved the superintendent's request to establish such a group or passed an enabling resolution stating that public participation in the educational program should be encouraged. In time, however, they realized the importance of laying down some guiding principles and adopting policies descriptive of the purposes, organization, and activities of citizen advisory committees. The written policies of boards of education today are quite explicit regarding these points and cover much of the information to be discussed in the paragraphs that follow.

Authority

A citizen advisory committee is an agency created by the board of education and is without authority in law. It cannot determine educational policies or direct the activities of professional personnel. Its function is strictly an advisory one within established limits. It expresses this function by studying educational needs, conditions, and problems and deciding what should be done to improve the school system. Its recommendations must come from the committee as a whole and are not binding in any way upon the board of education. The board may accept, reject, or send the recommendations back to the committee for further study. Through agreement, the committee may not appeal to the community for support, nor may it engage in a public controversy with board members. Any individual on the committee is privileged to resign in the face of conflict and carry the fight for his own ideas to the people of the district. The board reserves the right to approve all publicity releases and the distribution of reports. These regulations, of course, do not apply to groups that operate independently of the school system. They have no more authority than a school-sponsored committee, but are free to carry their findings and conclusions to citizens and taxpayers.

Size

An advisory committee should be large enough to represent the community adequately and small enough to encourage informal, efficient working relations between the members. Though size may be affected by the nature of the school district and responsibilities assigned to the committee, the majority of advisory groups have fewer than 5 members. The optimum size appears to fall somewhere between 15 and 25. Where a large committee is organized to increase citizen participation, then an executive body of 10 to 15 members may be established to plan and coordinate the activities of the several subcommittees into which the advisory group is broken. Each subcommittee undertakes a particular problem and reports its findings and recommendations to the executive body.

Term of Office

The term of office for advisory committee members should be stated in the policy of the board of education. Because many of these groups have been formed somewhat hastily, not all of them have decided on a specific term of office. Some members have indefinite tenure, others hold office as long as they are interested or their organizations return them to the committee, and still others remain in membership only until a specific job has been completed. Where the term is specified, it runs from six months to five years. The prevailing practice suggests that three years is a desirable length of time for service, and that one-third of the members change annually so that new personalities and new stimulation are brought into the committee.

Officers and Meetings

During the initial meetings of a new advisory group, the president of the board of education should act as chairman until he is satisfied that the members have learned to know one another well enough to elect their own officers. The officers should be a chairman, vice-chairman, and secretary, and each should hold office for a period of one year. They constitute an executive committee, responsible for handling details between meetings.

Meetings should be held monthly during the school year, more often if necessary, and last no longer than two hours. Longer meetings discourage attendance. Special subcommittees may meet more frequently than once a month if they have definite assignments to finish within fixed time limits.

Subcommittees

An intelligent use of subcommittees makes it possible to widen the scope of the advisory committee program and to tap the talents and interests of many citizens. The number of subcommittees depends upon the amount of work brought before the advisory group and the number of people who are involved. Generally, it seems wise to have subcommittees operate on a temporary basis and make them responsible to the central group. They should be assigned a definite problem for study and given instructions in writing as to procedure, limits of authority, use of school resources, and methods of reporting. Their reports should be sent to the central advisory committee for discussion and approval before being transmitted to the board of education.

Staff Relations

According to reported studies, administrators and teachers constitute 10 to 20 per cent of the members of school-sponsored advisory committees, but seldom belong to independent groups. They have ex officio status with no voting power. They attend all meetings, provide leadership in planning study projects, keep the board informed of activities and developments, and assist in numerous ways. Unfortunately, they have a tendency to dominate because of their superior knowledge of the school system and to assume more responsibility than they should. Experience indicates that their presence may retard the free exchange of ideas and often sets up psychological barriers against the expression of critical judgments. Advisory committees are likely to function better when they are not members.

Lack of membership does not prevent their service as consultants to advisory committees. They should be placed on call and made available to committees for types of service they are best qualified to perform. These might include knowledge of research procedures, specialization in particular aspects of the educational program, command of statistical methods, familiarity with legal requirements, editing skill, and so forth. They should be kept out of meetings, even as observers, unless asked to appear before the group for one reason or another. Recommendations for the improvement of educational programs should be the product of citizen study and discussion and should not be colored by the viewpoints of professional educators. A citizen advisory committee should operate in accord with the title it has been given.

Procedures

The business of most advisory groups is taken up in a sequence fixed by the officers. It is believed that an agenda promotes orderly procedure. This may be true, but it is doubtful that a fixed order of business is needed in small committees and subgroups studying single problems. It is more important to retain a sense of informality and cohesiveness, and likewise to reach decisions by consensus instead of voting. Voting is apt to split the group into rival factions. Sometimes it is difficult to reach a consensus on various issues. As a rule, the restudy of facts and the procurement of additional information encourages harmony. If disagreements persist thereafter, it means that either the evidence is inconclusive or bias is present which only time and patience can eradicate. It is advisable to keep minutes of meetings and supply copies to participants as well as board members and the superintendent of schools.

Joint meetings of the board of education and the advisory committee should be held from time to time for settling questions of expense, clerical service, study procedures, relations with professional personnel, employment of consultants, and other matters. Aside from these questions, joint meetings furnish assurance that board members have a vital and continuing interest in the work of the advisory committee, an element which plays a strong part in its success.

A brief, written report should be filed with the school board immediately after the advisory committee has completed a study. It should contain a list of recommendations and some of the more pertinent findings and conclusions on which they are based. The report should be kept brief, otherwise a heavy burden of writing is imposed on the committee. A joint meeting should then be held after board members have had an opportunity to review the report. Details can be filled in orally and points of understanding cleared up at this meeting. Subsequently, the board's reactions to the report should be sent to the committee along with an expression of appreciation for the work that was done. Committee members should realize that not all of their recommendations may fit into the viewpoints of the board and the superintendent, and that, in any case, they have influenced the board to make better decisions when action is taken.

ADVISORY COMMITTEE PROGRAMS

A new advisory committee faces during its first year the tasks of defining purposes, developing organization, establishing relations with board and staff personnel, and planning its program. Program planning begins with a broad survey of the school system — its policies, organization, staff, physical facilities, finance, and instructional practices. Out of this survey, advisory committee members gain an understanding of existing conditions and acquire an appreciation of the setting for problems they will study. This is a time-consuming but necessary process in the orientation of a committee to its work.

Study problems may be proposed by the board of education or by the advisory committee. Each problem that is brought up should be discussed and its significance explained. This should be done until a sufficient number of problems have been identified thereby enabling the committee to make its own selections and determine the order in which they shall be studied. It is advisable to select initial problems which are readily comprehended and permit the committee to achieve tangible results within a reasonable period of time. Many groups start with problems of the school plant and its facilities, then gradually move toward more difficult ones in curriculum and instruction.

The study of a problem begins with a simple, fact-finding procedure in which each committee member takes responsibility for collecting information on some aspect of the matter being investigated. He may work alone or as a member of a team. He may secure information from school officials or gather it elsewhere, depending upon the problem. For example, in a study of school building needs, the superintendent and staff may furnish data on population trends, family size, number of families per dwelling, and nonpublic school enrollments, while a variety of outside sources may be used for determining vital statistics on births and deaths, population movement, zoning restrictions, and land use.

Fact-finding is followed by the organizing, classifying, and analyzing of data. At this stage of the study, errors can be prevented if the committee works closely with the board of education and professional staff in the weighing of facts and the interpreting of their meaning. But it is advisable for the committee to work by itself in drawing conclusions and formulating recommendations so that its judgments are those of citizens.

The membership, activities, findings, and recommendations of the advisory committee should be publicized. There should not be any secrecy about the membership, the purposes, and work of the committee. Publicity for a school-sponsored group should be handled by the board of education through the superintendent's office. He should have the right to approve, modify, and reject all releases to newspapers as well as other means used for keeping the people informed.

The situation is different with an independent advisory committee, because it is under no obligation to clear publicity with school officials. However, a publicity campaign will be better if it is planned jointly and carries the endorsement of both parties. Should disagreements arise over the means for meeting an issue or solving a problem, then the independent advisory group should carry the facts to the people and ask them to make the decision. Sometimes disagreements are serious enough to result in either a new set of school officials or a new advisory group. Whatever the outcome may be, this is one of the most valuable services which an independent group can perform—people must know the facts and understand the alternatives in deciding questions of public policy. Publicity campaigns are usually carried on through newspaper and radio announcements, public meetings, speeches before civic organizations, pamphlets and posters, and door-to-door calls for explaining the facts to citizens first hand.

An examination of the programs conducted by school-sponsored and independent advisory committees in recent years indicates that they have covered almost the whole range of problems confronting public schools. They have taken up questions of finance, new buildings, teacher tenure, salary schedules, taxation, nursery schools, instructional methods, curriculum development, budgets, report cards, health, subject offerings, social hygiene, schoolwork programs, transportation, cafeteria services, and adult education. Seldom, if ever, have these committees shunned problems which they felt should be studied in their own communities.

ACCOMPLISHMENTS CLAIMED

While the accomplishments claimed by advisory committees are impressive, it should be emphasized that these groups are not a cure-all for the ills of public education. They are only another means for bringing citizens and taxpayers into a working partnership with the school in determining policies and improving programs. Two main types of accomplishments are claimed—those which indirectly have a wholesome influence on public attitudes toward the schools, and those which directly result in specific improvements of benefit to children, youth, and adults. Both are consistent with the purposes for which advisory committees are created.

The claim is repeated many times that the by-products of advisory committee studies and projects are just as important, if not more important, than the products themselves. By way of example, a board of education may be persuaded to install new lighting, provide moveable furniture, correct faulty ventilation, and improve cafeteria services, all because of findings and recommendations made by an advisory group; at the same time, their activities may be significant in awakening citizen interest in schools and giving a long-needed boost to faculty morale. The indirect achievements of advisory committees are summarized in the following statements:

Keener public insight into the educational needs of the community.
Improved citizen attitudes toward schools.
Increased citizen acceptance of responsibility for schools.
Closer working relations between community groups and school officials.
Less friction between the board of education and professional staff.
Renewal of staff faith in the democratic process.
Adaptation of school programs to community needs and interests.
Discussion of issues before they become serious.
More cooperation between various community groups.
Public willingness to support an adequate school program.
Neutralizing of pressures exerted by special interest groups.

The direct accomplishments claimed by advisory committees are too numerous to list completely. A few examples will suffice to sketch their nature and scope. These include the passage of bond issues, erection of new buildings, replacement of school board members, budget increases, improvement of teachers in service, better working conditions, better salary schedules, smaller classes, changes in school laws, new formulas for distributing state aid, consolidation of school districts, plans for sick-leave and retirement, adult education programs, more vocational offerings, nursery schools, and more community use of the school plant and its facilities.

CAUTIONS AND CRITICISMS

Certain cautions and criticisms have emerged from the experience of educators in working with lay advisory groups. They should be examined by boards and administrators who are contemplating the use of advisory committees. Existing groups may find them valuable in determining reasons why their programs have not been too successful.

Cautions to Observe

No lay advisory committee should be formed to emulate the example of surrounding communities or with the thought that this is a good gesture in public relations. Board members and administrators must be convinced, first of all, that the advice of citizens is needed to improve the schools. They should then begin to acquire a thorough knowledge and understanding of how advisory groups are started, who belongs to them, what they do, how they operate, and what they achieve. Unless this is done, there is always a danger of creating nothing more than another pressure group to contend with in the future.

An advisory committee should be organized, if possible, at a time when the schools are free from serious criticism. It is better to start under favorable circumstances than to give the impression that citizens are used for emergencies only. Some old-line boards and superintendents are reluctant to bother with lay groups when things are running smoothly, holding to the adage that there is no use in stirring up trouble. Actually, they would have fewer difficulties if citizens knew about school needs and limitations and were aware of problems that had to be faced.

Experience has shown the wisdom of outlining and discussing the rights and responsibilities of an advisory group soon after it comes into existence. The members should know the nature and amount of authority they have been granted by the board of education, their relations to members of the school staff, the need for acting as a committee of the whole, how publicity will be handled, and why the board is privileged to accept or reject their recommendations. Agreement on these points prevents possible conflict later on.

Committee size should be limited for the sake of efficiency, yet a committee should be large enough to assure satisfactory representation of people in the community. The committee should deal with significant problems and be given free reign in finding facts and making recommendations. Occasionally, boards and administrators forget that laymen are new to the business of education and need encouragement and guidance during the early stages of their work. It is up to them to provide essential leadership and steer the committee until it has enough strength to stand on its own feet. With some beginning groups, the major work should be done within the school system and the committee invited to share in the study of findings and conclusions and assist in the drafting of recommendations. This approach enables a weak group to gain experience and acquire skills required for assuming full responsibility.

As a final caution, boards and administrators should realize that nothing is gained by keeping an advisory committee for which they have no use. Better feelings will result from dismissing the committee with a note of appreciation and an explanation that it has performed a valuable service for the school system and the people of the community.

Criticisms Offered

A surprising number of criticisms have been offered by former members of citizen advisory committees and school officials. The criticisms are serious enough in some instances to caste doubt upon the efficacy of this plan for involving the public in school affairs. However, they suggest that ignorance, dishonesty, and lack of planning are responsible for the dissatisfactions expressed.

Critics point out that advisory committees, if opportunity is present, tend to take over rights and responsibilities of school boards; that boards are placed under pressure to accept recommendations with which they do not agree; that some advisory committees are packed with individuals who will recommend only what boards want; that temporary committees do not provide for continuing contact with the public; and that they are merely a device for meeting problems boards should handle by themselves.

Examples are cited of poor coordination between boards and committees on important problems; of teachers and administrators dominating the thought and action of advisory groups; of administrators setting up committees without authorization from their boards; of boards approving the organization of advisory groups without understanding their relationship to the school system; of committees made up almost entirely of economic leaders concerned with the protection of vested interests; of committees that are less representative of the community than the boards themselves; and of board refusal to appoint representative committees, fearing an upset of power and the defeat of some members at the polls.

As further criticisms, evidence is supplied showing how boards lean on the advice of advisory committees instead of doing their own thinking; how committees bog down after a good start because of board neglect; how a new superintendent may discard an existing

committee or destroy its effectiveness in a short time; how lack of
publicity keeps people from communicating with advisory groups;
how recommendations are unrelated to the entire school system; how
community conflicts and rivalries seep into advisory committees and
obstruct their activities; how committees become agencies for airing
prejudice and complaint; and how a single, continuing committee
is inadequate to cope with the numerous problems of a school system.

NATIONAL CITIZENS COMMISSION
FOR THE PUBLIC SCHOOLS

The development of state and local advisory committees has been
stimulated in recent years by the activities of the National Citizens
Commission for the Public Schools. Organized in 1949, following a
series of exploratory meetings between leading educators and prominent citizens on problems of public education, it was founded as a
nonprofit corporation with two expressed purposes, namely, (1) "to
help Americans realize how important our public schools are to our
expanding democracy," and (2) "to arouse in each community the
intelligence and will to improve our public schools." [2] The Commission went out of existence in January, 1956.

According to published statements, members of the Commission
—who had to be citizens of this country—were drawn from labor, business, social welfare, and other fields of life, but no member could be
identified professionally with education, religion, and politics. Each
was expected to serve in an individual capacity, not as a representative of an organization or group. Starting with 28 members, the
Commission moved toward a membership goal of 60 persons of varied
backgrounds from all parts of the country.

In planning its program, the Commission agreed on a few
fundamental concepts which were respected in the course of its
existence. The position was taken that public education is primarily
a matter of local concern, that people must decide whether or not
schools in their communities are living up to standards they want,
that taxpayers can have better schools if they organize themselves
into study groups at local, county, and state levels and deal realisti-

2 *How Have Our Schools Developed?* Working Guide No. 4, page 2. New York:
National Citizens Commission for the Public Schools, 1954.

cally with existing educational problems, and that efforts for school improvement should be undertaken cooperatively with boards of education and school officials whenever possible.

In keeping with the purposes and basic beliefs of the Commission, three major types of activities were carried on—encouragement of active citizen interest in public schools, assistance to advisory committees concerned with school improvement, and definite studies on significant problems affecting public education. The encouragement of active citizen interest was handled by means of advertising. Popular attention was called to the needs and problems of schools through billboards, car cards, news releases, motion pictures, and radio and television programs. Some of this work was done cooperatively with groups and agencies at the national level, which had the resources, manpower, and experience necessary to arouse strong interest in schools.

The Commission did not believe that public interest alone was sufficient to produce better schools. It went farther in urging citizens to form advisory groups that initiative for better schools might come from people within their own communities. As an impartial agency, it stood ready to assist advisory groups, but assistance never took the form of direct advice. It told the citizens of one group what others had done under similar circumstances. This service was performed by six regional offices maintained by the Commission, whose headquarters were in New York City. It was performed by drawing from files case materials and reports of citizen groups all over the country and sending these to a group requesting information. Each new group that supplied a report of its activities to the Commission enlarged the chances of aiding future citizen committees in the same way.

The direct exchange of information through the Commission clearing house was supplemented by the publication of a monthly newsletter entitled *Citizens and Their Schools* and an annual report, which went to individuals who were interested in the movement for better schools. The newsletter contained accounts of various advisory group programs, regional information, a diary of the Director's activities, case studies, and several miscellaneous items high in reading appeal. Numerous leaflets, pamphlets, and booklets were also published, instructing citizens on what to look for in appraising their local schools and how to go about the job of improving them. An annual meeting and dinner were held to which the Commission invited members of advisory groups, educators, and laymen for the purpose of reviewing its program and charting new developments.

The third part of the Commission's program consisted of intensive studies of educational problems. Problems were selected which cut across the schools of the nation and, it was believed, could best be dealt with by a national group. Teacher education, school boards, finance, and taxation were among the problems staked out for investigation. The studies were conducted by committees of the Commission with the help of specialists.

The annual reports of the Commission indicate that it enjoyed steady success in coming close to the objectives on which it was founded. It admitted that the potential for creating active citizen interest and stimulating action for school improvement had scarcely been touched, but it looked with pride on the achievements it made.

The important work carried on by the Commission will be continued, with some modifications, by the National Citizens' Council for Better Schools. Patterned after the Commission, this new organization, which began in January, 1956, will strive to arouse public interest in school problems and their solution.

12
Organized Community Groups

In every community there are organized groups who maintain programs of an educational character. Some are based upon principles in harmony with the ideals of public education, some are not. The problem in public relations is to cultivate the friendship and cooperation of groups who share mutual interests in the instruction of children and the welfare of society, and to prevent others from exploiting and injuring the public school without creating community conflicts. In considering this problem, attention will be directed to types of groups in most communities, opportunities for cooperation, attempts at exploitation, criticisms of and attacks on schools, and methods for meeting charges brought against local systems.

TYPES OF ORGANIZED GROUPS

Community groups may be divided by types into the following classes: civic, cultural, economic, fraternal, government, patriotic, political, professional, religious, welfare, and youth. This is an optional classification which may be discarded in favor of any other that is more appropriate in the local school situation.

Civic

Among the more prominent civic groups are the American Association of University Women, and the luncheon clubs, namely, Lions, Kiwanis, Exchange, and Optimist. Less well known are the local municipal leagues, city planning commissions, public affairs committees, and community councils. All of these groups concern themselves with problems of education, health, social welfare, better government, delinquency, and recreation. Some operate summer camps for underprivileged children, provide student loans, sponsor civic activities, undertake research, and work closely with community agencies and institutions. Their fundamental purpose is the improvement of social conditions and, through these conditions, the lives of people in the community.

Cultural

Cultural groups are found in the fields of art, music, architecture, horticultural, literature, drama, intercultural education, and race relations. Many are small, self-contained units whose primary purpose is catering to the leisure-time interests of the members. The remainder have broader programs which they direct at a total community audience or, at least, large segments of the population. They try to educate people to their point of view and win support for the causes they sponsor.

Economic

The principal economic groups are labor unions, farm organizations, chambers of commerce, economy leagues, manufacturers' associations, automobile clubs, real estate boards, retail merchants' associations, and others of a specialized character. Organized to increase efficiency, protect their interests, and secure advantages for their members, the majority of local economic groups are branches of powerful state and national associations.

They follow both laudable and doubtful policies regarding

public education. Their policies include support for public schools, opposition to destructive pressures against schools, participation in educational affairs, preservation of democratic ideals and institutions, the extension of educational opportunities, economy in public spending, improvements in vocational training, commercialization of education, and the introduction of propaganda in classroom instruction. Not infrequently an organization which works for the protection of public schools will also work for reductions in educational costs and the use of schools for commercial purposes.

Fraternal

As a rule, groups in this classification are organized to support certain ideals, increase fellowship, and indulge in leisure-time recreational activities. A few have a definite religious interest. Among them are the Masonic Order, Knights of Columbus, Brith Sholom, Knights of Pythias, and a host of lodges bearing the titles of Elk, Moose, Eagle, Beaver, Owl, and Crow. Some have committees on education which take an interest in public education and the welfare of children, and they sometimes join with other groups in worthwhile, community projects.

Governmental

Local, county, state, and national governments maintain agencies that cut across several areas of human activity. They provide services in health, recreation, law enforcement, safety, family life, child care, housing, and so forth. Many of these services complement those of the school and point up the necessity for cooperative relationships.

Patriotic

Groups like the American Legion, Sons and Daughters of the American Revolution, Veterans of Foreign Wars, and United Daughters of the Confederacy have extensive programs for the conservation of real and assumed values pertaining to the American way of life. Stress is placed in their programs on the teaching of government, civic responsibility, health, and patriotism. The school is the medium, they believe, through which most of their work should be done. Evidence of this may be seen in legislation they have sponsored for the teaching of American history and citizenship, the censoring of textbooks, demands for the elimination of alleged subversive activities in public institutions, and the movement for teacher loyalty oaths and tests of patriotism, as well as citizenship awards to pupils, essay contests, flag education, and observance of patriotic holidays. They are vitally interested in the preservation of public schools and have worked with local systems on educational problems.

Political

Political groups include the major political parties, League of Women Voters, and small organizations having a dominant interest in government. For the most part, caution must be exercised in dealing with political groups. The school is a nonpartisan institution which cannot be identified with one political view or another or even permit any suggestion of favoritism. Failure to maintain a nonpartisan position inevitably incurs public disapproval and opens the door to pressure for patronage. The school is limited in its relations with political groups mostly to granting the use of buildings for public meetings and obtaining information for instructional purposes on political activities and voting practices.

Although the League of Women Voters makes politics a subject of strong interest, it is an independent organization without political affiliation. It tries to educate citizens on the issues they must decide at the polls and the qualifications of candidates for public office. It has shown intelligent concern for the problems of schools and other matters affecting the welfare of the community. Some local units of the League do a commendable job in stimulating public interest and getting action on important problems.

Professional

The professional groups in law, medicine, dentistry, pharmacy, architecture, and engineering have consistently supported programs for good schools. They take an interest in the educational program and will cooperate with administrators and teachers on matters related to their special fields. Like many organized groups, their primary motivation is one of enhancing professional interests and protecting their membership.

Religious

The religious groups consist of denominations which maintain churches in the community and secular organizations engaged in religious work. Their purpose is to promote moral and spiritual values. Because of differences in sectarian doctrine, they are divided on issues relating to public education. For example, they have argued both for and against the teaching of religion in the school and the early dismissal of pupils for week-day religious instruction in their own churches. The influence of religious groups is especially strong in small communities and should not be minimized at any time even in the larger ones.

Welfare

Numerous welfare agencies operate in the fields of health, recreation, child care, and family life. Those belonging to the Red Feather Community Chest receive their support from the funds raised by this organization in its annual drive for contributions, while others either conduct their own campaigns for contributions or obtain their support from a parent body. Because welfare agencies are concerned with the alleviation of human suffering and the improvement of social conditions, their activities bring them into contact with the school.

Youth

Among the organizations having a deep-seated interest in young people are the 4-H Clubs, Future Farmers of America, Young Men's Christian Association, Young Women's Christian Association, Boy Scouts and Girl Scouts of America, Junior Red Cross, and Pal. Their activities cover such things as recreation, religion, temperance, social planning, and international relations, safety, health, personal guidance, and conservation.

Organized on local, state, and national levels, many carry on sound educational and character building programs. A few operate within the school as a part of the extracurricular activities program, while several are staffed with teachers and administrators who volunteer their services. With exceptions, these groups are anxious to work closely with the public schools,

OPPORTUNITIES FOR COOPERATION

It is apparent from this description of types of community groups that many hold interests in common with the school. An analysis of their programs shows that interests cluster around problems of individual pupil welfare, special services and events, school improvements, and community social conditions. As a consequence, there are many opportunities for cooperation through which a fine sense of harmony may be developed and worthwhile objectives achieved. Inasmuch as the number of opportunities is too large to take up here, selected examples will be presented to indicate what they are like and how the school may cooperate.

Individual Pupil Welfare

Problems of individual pupils stemming from family life, physical defects, and delinquency invite cooperation. The school becomes concerned with family life when it is detrimental to the health and learning efficiency of pupils. Steps are taken through conferences with parents, visits to the home, and adjustments in the daily program to meet the needs of pupils who are undernourished, tired and listless, unsocial, and emotionally disturbed. Many times improvements are effected by these means, but in difficult cases the school cannot get at the underlying causes or apply remedial measures even if the causes are known, because it has neither the authority nor personnel to undertake deep family studies. Reliance must be placed on family agencies for finding the facts and suggesting the action that should be taken. Assistance can be given to these agencies, and they can reciprocate by pooling information and sharing plans for aiding children and correcting conditions in the home.

Congenital and acquired physical defects are sometimes serious blocks to learning and prevent pupils from becoming useful citizens. Fortunately, several groups and organizations are interested in the physical welfare of children whose parents cannot afford to pay for the services they need. They will furnish them with eyeglasses, hearing aids, and artificial limbs; supply milk and hot lunches; pay for medical treatments and operations; arrange transportation; underwrite the cost of tuition at camps and special schools; and, appropriate funds for the care and treatment of those having tuberculosis, cerebral palsy, infantile paralysis, and diseases of the eyes, ears, and heart.

Cooperation with these groups calls for (1) a definite understanding of the specific types of services they offer, (2) compliance with referral procedures, (3) free exchange of information, (4) an appreciation of the limits within which the school must operate, (5) the implementation of medical recommendations, and (6) a clear-cut division of responsibility in joint plans for assistance.

In the control and prevention of delinquency the school is a natural partner of the juvenile court. It can give valuable help by preparing case histories of children brought before the court and in interpreting their educational experiences and family background. Its records can be placed fully at the disposal of court officials and the information they have collected can be shared with the school. Probation programs may be planned together, with the school taking a leading part in facilitating the adjustment and reporting the progress children are making. Teamwork between attendance and probation officers helps to cut down truancy and prevent other infractions of the law.

Special Services and Events

Excellent opportunities for cooperation are provided through special services and events sponsored by the school and by community groups. On the part of the school, a banking service for children will operate more efficiently if it is planned with the help of representatives from banking institutions. Programs commemorating American Education Week, local traditions, and patriotic holidays will receive strong support when interested groups are asked to take part and to assume responsibility for details regarding speakers, films, exhibits, and publicity.

On the other side, many requests are made of the school to support the programs of community groups. They may wish to confer honors on and make awards to pupils for outstanding achievements in citizenship, American history, agriculture, home management, and so forth. Some are anxious to hold banquets for members of winning teams. They ask the school to supply speakers, entertainment, student panels, and exhibits for their weekly and monthly meetings. Aid is

often solicited for parades, ticket sales, preparation of posters, exhibits
at fairs, and the arrangement of holiday decorations. A surprising
number of groups are interested in furnishing material things, such
as library books, stage equipment, and band instruments, or in
establishing scholarship funds for bright and deserving students who
wish to continue their education beyond the high school. Requests
are numerous to use the school plant and its facilities for meetings,
entertainments, and social affairs. Care, of course, must be exercised
in accepting the requests so that interference with regular instruction
is avoided and hardships to teachers and pupils are prevented.

School Improvements

Worthwhile improvements are made in the educational program when community groups participate in curriculum study and
development, supply instructional materials and services, and share
in administrative problems. In curriculum study and development,
their advice may be sought in building courses of study, preparing
resource units, selecting equipment, and planning learning experiences in subjects corresponding to their special interests. For example,
the county medical association can be asked to render consultant
service in evaluating and revising health instruction just as the
National Office Management Association can be invited to formulate
standards of training for students preparing for clerical and secretarial positions. The possibilities for capitalizing upon the technical
information and practical experience of community groups in the
improvement of the elementary and secondary school curriculums is
almost unlimited.

Allied closely to curriculum study and development is the use
of community resources for instructional purposes. By this is meant
the actual bringing into classroom teaching of free and inexpensive
materials and services furnished by outside groups. These include
books, pamphlets, posters, pictures, slides, films, speakers, demonstrations, exhibits, and field trips to shops, factories, and other places.
Although highly valuable in supplementing textbook information
and bringing the learning process into contact with reality, their use
is conditioned by the attitudes of teachers toward their place in the
curriculum and the willingness of sponsoring groups to abide by the
principles of public education.

Instruction in citizenship affords opportunities for cooperation.

Educational programs undergo other forms of improvement when boards and administrators share their problems with interested groups and individual business firms who are competent to render special services. A better selection of building sites will be made and more support assured when offers of the Chamber of Commerce, let us say, are accepted to work with the school on population and land use studies, traffic surveys, and recommended changes in zoning ordinances. Likewise, the probabilities are greater that a sound tax base will be established to meet future needs if the technical staff of a real estate board is invited to participate in the study of this problem. Comparable services are available in many communities for planning publicity campaigns, analyzing budgetary questions, designing building drafting legislation, and so forth, because of the genuine interest which some groups and individuals have in better schools.

225

Social Conditions

Opportunities are plentiful to join with youth groups, welfare agencies, civic associations, and special committees in programs directed at the improvement of social conditions. The school has a natural interest in programs of this kind because of the beneficial influence they have on the growth and development of pupils. With youth groups, the school can aid in planning worthwhile activities, suggest desirable projects, solicit volunteer leaders from the instructional staff, and turn over its facilities for late afternoon and evening meetings. Such groups can be invited to present assembly programs and to participate in extracurricular activities, among the other forms of cooperation which local circumstances suggest. With groups engaged in major projects, such as slum clearance, traffic control, city planning, housing, recreation, and juvenile delinquency, the school can render valuable assistance by serving as a coordinating center, being represented on study committees, releasing staff members for part-time work on projects, permitting the use of buildings for meetings and conferences, supplying clerical and secretarial help on occasion, preparing resource and teaching units around selected projects, involving pupils in project activities, and supporting recommended courses of action.

ATTEMPTS AT EXPLOITATION

Granting every effort should be made to take full advantage of the opportunities for cooperation, nevertheless administrators and teachers must exercise critical judgment as to the values or dangers inherent in their relationships with community groups. Cumulative experience shows that many groups, both intentionally and unintentionally, try to further their own interests in ways that harm pupils, disrupt the operation of the school, and violate its character as an impartial, nonsectarian, classless social institution. Their attempts at exploitation take the form of demands upon the time and talent of teachers and pupils, clever commercial propositions, and propaganda materials.

Service Demands

The school is deluged every year with requests from philanthropic groups and organizations for help in raising funds to support their work. The requests are made by the Community Chest, Red Cross, Cancer Crusade, March of Dimes, and groups interested in preparing Thanksgiving baskets, selling Christmas and conservation seals, collecting toys, and so on down a long list. Teachers are expected to explain their work to pupils and to get contributions from them. Some groups put pressure on boards of education and administrators to have each employee contribute a suggested percentage of his salary and to solicit funds from door-to-door after school hours. Seldom do schools and school personnel receive much public recognition for what they do.

Even though philanthropic groups perform excellent and needed services, it is questionable that public schools are justified in giving active support to their drives and campaigns. Educationally, any sense of social responsibility that is developed in pupils through a discussion of their work disintegrates after the first few campaigns have been gone through. But more than this, the pressure brought to collect funds takes away any sense of giving and forces pupils to contribute for the sake of conformity, and this, in some instances, imposes a heavy burden on families with several children in school. The strongest objection of educators is the time consumed and the labor imposed on teachers at the expense of the regular instructional program. The problem has grown so acute in recent years that boards of education have found it necessary to eliminate all drives and campaigns or else to lump them into a single one each year.

Similar demands for assistance are made by organizations in their annual membership drives and by other groups for special help on projects. Assistance in membership drives is sought by the Boy Scouts, Girl Scouts, Young Men's and Young Women's Christian Associations, youth forums, dramatic clubs, civic music associations, and the like. They want the right to explain their programs to pupils or have teachers do this work and record the names of those who wish to join or who are undecided and might be persuaded to change their minds. Requests for special help on projects include such things as making posters in art classes, drives for old newspapers, and recruiting pupil volunteer workers for after school and week-ends. No one denies the value of the services these groups perform, but school people question the right of the institution to promote the interests of outside groups at the cost of instructional time.

The problem is complicated further by innumerable invitations for pupil entertainment and programs at meetings of service clubs, women's groups, civic organizations, and other community groups, or their participation in parades, fairs, and festivals which cut into the school day or keep pupils up late at night. There is not much doubt that many of these invitations afford excellent learning experiences and provide opportunities for interpreting the school to the public, but they must be measured against the disruption of class work, the influence of late hours on learning efficiency, and the exploitation of pupils for publicity purposes. Some schools have tried to cope with the demands by setting up criteria for judging each request in terms of educational values and limiting the number which may be accepted during the term.

In addition, outside groups ask for the use of school equipment and physical facilities, including chairs, public address systems, projectors, screens, flags, uniforms, auditoriums, gymnasiums, and play fields. The school should meet their requests to use the facilities of the plant after regular hours, but there is a question with regard to the lending of portable equipment. Its mere physical movement in and out of the building during the school day creates distractions, while delays in the return of equipment defeat the purpose for which it was acquired. The principal criticism, however, is the wear and damage equipment receives in the hands of other people. Many school systems refuse to loan equipment to community groups unless its use is supervised by a representative of the staff. Some systems permit outside groups to use it only on school property, and they supply the operators for delicate and costly pieces of equipment. Any reasonable policy of this kind meets with general approval throughout the community.

Finally, requests that often affect the operation of the school are made by community groups. Local merchants' associations petition for change in the daily schedule so that high school students may be released for part-time employment, or they try to advance the date of Christmas vacation for the same reason. Excluding emergencies, their requests should be appraised strictly in terms of pupil welfare, not economics. Their requests can be denied much more easily without creating ill-will than those of local boosters athletic groups. These groups are frequently composed of influential and powerful members of the community who insist upon outstanding players' taking part in games despite physical condition or scholastic eligibility. Their clamor is loud for the replacement of coaches whose teams fail to build up a winning record. Tact, patience, and parent education on the place of athletics in the school program are required to keep these groups from dominating and controlling interscholastic contests.

Commercial Activities

A considerable number of business firms, industrial organizations, and promotional agencies, under a banner of cooperation, attempt to exploit schools by sponsoring contests, demonstrating products, and distributing materials. They are interested in shaping the present and future buying habits of pupils. A few are on the lookout for youngsters with special talents who can be followed up for future employment. Contests are offered in essay writing, art, music, science, agriculture, forensics, and other fields, with prizes that include college scholarships.

Though important, it is doubtful if the educational value of these contests is worth enough to offset their negative features. The number has grown so large in recent years and the quality so varied that it is no longer possible to coordinate them with instructional activities. The National Association of Secondary School Principals has attempted to meet this problem by screening all national contests and publishing a recommended list for high schools. The published list does not make provision for those sponsored at state and local levels. This list affords to principals a defense for rejecting those which are not included. Second, the complaint is made constantly that contests interrupt the regular school schedule, take teachers away from classes, force students to be absent, and obligate parents to spend money for travel to regional and final tryouts. The strongest objection is registered against commercial motives behind the contests.

The problem can be controlled if boards of education adopt policies and establish criteria by which the number of contests are

limited and judged in terms of the contribution they make to instruction. As an alternative, a contest club may be created in the extracurricular field so that students may enter as many as they wish
without having them forced upon the whole school.

Commercial motives are apparent in offers of household appli-
ance organizations to put on demonstrations in cooking and sewing,
of local automobile dealers to conduct driver training classes, of live-
stock interests to work with pupils in agricultural classes, of book
companies to hold clinics on reading instruction, of typewriter manufacturers to explain short cuts in learning their machines, of farm
implement agencies to explain the use of new equipment, and of
music sales organizations to give free lessons on instruments purchased by the school or by individual pupils. Occasionally, dealers
will request the right to send samples to the entire student body or
suggest schemes for student organizations to make money. The more
blatant attempts at commercialization can be rejected quickly, but
those having educational values must be studied individually. Usually, reputable manufacturing and business concerns will comply with
regulations governing the demonstration of products and keep
commercial elements at a minimum.

Equally serious are the advertising and sales promotion messages
carried in free and inexpensive materials supplied to schools by outside groups. These materials include blotters, calendars, films, slides,
pictures, posters, and displays. Some have no instructional worth,
others are prepared without the faintest knowledge of how teaching
is done or whether or not they are related to specific units under
study. Certain of these materials, however, are educationally sound
and fill a real need. For this reason, administrators and teachers have
tolerated advertising and sales features, but the time is rapidly coming
when their use will no longer be permitted in classes. If business and
industrial firms wish to cooperate with schools in supplying educational materials, they must eliminate advertising and sales promotion
messages.

Propaganda Materials

School people have a grave responsibility to see that pupils
receive an education free from bias, half-truths, and propaganda. In

meeting this responsibility, they are constantly under pressure from organized groups who wish to use the school for implanting their ideas and doctrines in the minds of the young.

In recent years, these groups have spent millions of dollars on printed and visual materials, supplying them to teachers and pupils without cost or at a small fraction of their actual cost. The materials deal with such topics as free enterprise, local business efforts, manufacturing processes, Americanism, American ideals and traditions, labor unions, temperance education, and international affairs. On the surface, they may appear to be excellent sources for the enrichment of classroom teaching, but objective examination discloses the propaganda they contain and the motives behind their publication.

The problem of preventing their use in school is difficult for these reasons: they help to satisfy a need for more instructional materials than boards of education are willing to furnish; they deal with subjects in more thorough and interesting detail than do standard textbooks; the amount available is too large for critical evaluation by a school system; and, it is sometimes difficult to distinguish between propagandist and nonpropagandist materials. Perhaps the solution lies in the establishment of a national clearing house through which all free and inexpensive materials should pass before they are accepted for instructional purposes. Standards could be drawn up, in cooperation with suppliers, which would govern their inclusion in an annual catalogue of approved materials. It should be recognized, on the other hand, that there is a place for books, pamphlets, and audio-visual aids containing propaganda in classes dealing with propaganda analysis and the refutation of ideas and arguments advanced by subversive organizations.

CRITICISMS AND ATTACKS

The problem of trying to develop wholesome relations with community groups is complicated further by unfair criticism of and attacks on schools. Made by misinformed citizens and special interest groups, their condemnations of public education have been responsible for weakening popular confidence in the worth of the instructional program and the competency of professional personnel. Unless checked, they threaten to destroy some of the fundamental principles underlying the free school system in this country. No longer can boards of education, administrators, and teachers ignore the seriousness of the problem and hope that these forces spend themselves in time. Intelligent measures must be taken to counteract their destructive tendencies and to foster friendly relationships. Solutions for this many-sided problem must start with a definite understanding of what the criticisms and attacks are like and how they may be met.

Attacks and Attackers

The principal targets of attack are educational costs, teaching of fundamentals, textbooks, teacher loyalty, social studies instruction, and the secular character of the public school.

Attacks on educational costs are nothing new, but their spread and intensity today are probably greater than at any time since the state system was first written into law. Some who maintain that schools could be operated more economically, and still provide an adequate education for young people, would strip the curriculum of the so-called "fads and frills," such as art, music, and homemaking. Others take the position that compulsory education should be abandoned after the eighth grade so that "unwilling, uninterested, and comparatively less competent students" are not forced to attend high school. The point is often made that equally good, if not better, education was provided in former years without the aid of expensive supplies and equipment and school buildings with gymnasiums, auditoriums, cafeterias, and service units. Despite the low salaries paid to teachers, protests are made against wage adjustments on grounds that real estate is taxed to the limit and that the further expansion of state subsidies to local districts is inherently dangerous. It is not uncommon to hear the comment that vital public works and services are being curtailed because too much tax money is going to schools.

Among the more prominent groups interested in reducing educational costs and real estate boards, businessmen's associations, tax foundations, and state economy leagues. These groups have in many instances been opposed to adequate funds for schools regardless of what happened to the preparation of children. However, they have never really succeeded in saving dollars at the expense of education, though they came dangerously close during the depression years. Unfortunately, they are now in a stronger position inasmuch as their propaganda to cut governmental expenditures appeals to many people who are sincerely concerned with the unprecedented public debt and the amount of personal and corporate income taken by taxes. Their appeal will be stronger in the years that lie ahead when larger budgets are required by school districts to meet increased enrollments, to construct more classrooms, and to set up financial incentives for attracting an adequate supply of qualified men and women to the profession.

A mixture of sincere, disgruntled, and sometimes fanatical parents and citizens constitute another group who are critical of modern education and would prefer a return to the instructional program of former years. Their reactions are due to dissatisfaction with the learning progress of their own children; to unpleasant relations with sharp-spoken principals and teachers; to increases in school-tax rates; to denunciations of modern teaching methods by the older and more conservative members of the profession; to propaganda from organizations interested in weakening and destroying public education; to hearsay that local schools are using progressive methods of teaching; to speakers and writers who decry lack of discipline; and, to the wide-spread belief that the "3R's" are being neglected. Most of these and other reasons seem to point to two main ideas, namely, that people do not understand schools in their own communities, and that they are troubled and uncertain as to what type of education they want for children.

Stimulated by the communist threat to national security and the opportunities to impose their own views on the schools, hypersensitive and self-styled patriotic groups have waged a war on textbooks and their authors. By assuming the right to judge what should or should not be taught in public school classrooms, they have demanded that boards of education remove some textbooks from circulation and delete lines and passages in others. From the nature of their demands, it is evident that they are ready to denounce as subversive any book which disagrees with their viewpoint or which suggests weaknesses in American institutions and the operation of democratic processes. They are strongly opposed to the teaching of controversial issues, to practices "tinged" with progressive education (though they have no idea what progressive education means either in theory or in practice), and to all but bare facts in the teaching of American history. They are quick to question the loyalty of any teacher who defends time-tested textbooks or their authors with whom they disagree. Seldom, if ever, do they offer positive criteria for evaluating textbooks and point out in what way they are undermining allegiance to this nation, its government and institutions. Educators who have witnessed the textbook spectacle and persecution of teachers hesitate to endorse commendable books which have been branded subversive, while teachers are fearful of being brought into the searchlight of distorted publicity. Instead of strengthening the defenses against un-American activities, these patrioteers are actually forcing schools in various communities to conform to a pattern of irresponsible and misguided action.

In like manner, they have accused some teachers in public schools of engaging in subversive activities and of belonging to organizations advocating the overthrow of government by forceful and violent means. Instead of holding their charges in abeyance and cooperating with boards of education in making a thorough and impartial examination of teachers under suspicion, they have resorted to sensational publicity and coercive demands for their dismissal without possessing the facts or trying to find them. Time after time their charges have proven groundless, but only after they have frightened citizens into a distrust of their schools and have injured the reputations of innocent men and women. They cannot seem to understand that boards of education are just as anxious as they to rid the schools of individuals who are disloyal to this government, but that the situation demands respect for human rights and the use of established legal channels for taking action.

A large bloc of criticism revolves around the social studies. Teachers are charged, in this field of instruction, with prejudicing young minds against the American way of life. More specifically, allegations are made that teachers scoff at American institutions, debunk long-held traditions, criticize free enterprise, preach the benefits of a welfare state, advocate increased federal power, and uphold the *United Nations Social, Educational, Cultural Organization.* Critics deplore the fact that some pupils praise old age security, unemployment insurance, wage and hour regulations, price controls, high taxes, and similar social legislation.

To remedy the situation, they would have history, geography, and other social studies taught separately instead of in combination. Their recommendation is based partly on the belief that educators are slighting the teaching of American history, and partly on the desire to remove controversial issues from the classroom. They maintain that social studies instruction should emphasize "the old principles of individualism and idealism," which are regarded as "the real source of spiritual action and economic strength" in this country. They would like to prevent youth from becoming acquainted with existing weaknesses in the social structure and with political and social systems differing from our own. They think that the school should be an instrument for conditioning each generation in what to believe, not for teaching them how to identify social issues and deal with them intelligently.

The attacks on social studies instruction are made by patriotic organizations and reactionary business and industrial interests who reflect a disturbed and distressed state of mind over social legislation and the ideological struggle taking place in the world today. They have made the school a convenient scapegoat for their fears and frustrations.

The secular character of the school has come in for a vast amount of destructive criticism. Historically, this nation subscribed to the principle of separation of church and state because the early founders believed that religion was a matter of personal conscience, the freedom of which would be best guaranteed if the state remained neutral. To assure this guarantee, the Bill of Rights was written into the federal constitution, while state constitutions prohibited the use of public funds for the support of any private or sectarian enterprise. It is under these provisions that the secular public school was organized in the interest of citizens of all creeds and faiths.

Until recent years the wisdom of secular education was regarded as an outstanding example of the democratic ideal. Now well-organized forces are trying to claim that the secular school is a breeding place of atheism and the source of many social ills. Among other things, they charge that juvenile delinquency is attributable to the lack of religious teaching in public schools; that science is being substituted for fundamental truths and virtues; that religious ideals are by-passed in the curriculum; that a new, nonreligious social order is in the making; that the Bible is taught as literature, not a living faith; and that the public school is guilty of neglecting the teaching of moral and spiritual values.

The more crude and narrow charges come from extremists who favor an educational program in which lessons are taught from the Bible and prayer is a normal part of daily living. They recommend that men and women who teach in public schools should qualify on specific religious tests before they are employed. This group is followed by another that maintains that religious instruction would raise the general level of the culture. They recognize, however, the difficulty of trying to break down the principle of separation of church and state; consequently they think that it is more important at this time to increase the number of programs in religious education on released time from public schools. Still another group takes the position that the failure to teach religion builds up negative attitudes in children toward religious organizations. They would like to see a specific body of content put into the curriculum—acceptable to the major religious faiths—emphasizing the contributions of organized religion to society.

Aside from the groups mentioned, some of the more vicious attacks on public schools are the work of a strange coalition of national organizations with strong financial backing. Their motives run from the abolition of tax-supported schools to the elimination of subjects regarded as being costly and unnecessary. As named in the publications of the Defense Commission of the National Education Association, the National Conference of Christians and Jews, and popular magazine articles, these organizations are the Conference of American Small Business Organizations, Committee for Constitutional Government, National Economic Council, Sons of American Revolution, Friends of the Public Schools, American Education Association, National Association for Pro-America, National Council for American Education, and the Employers' Association of Chicago. Details concerning the purposes and activities of these groups may be found in the bibliography for this chapter.

Their Methods

Attacks against public schools are launched through a variety of formal media. A favorite one is an official magazine or newsletter that goes to members of the attacking group. It is used to shape attitudes and lay the groundwork for state and local units to campaign within their respective service areas. Stories based upon the material contained in the magazine or newsletter are released to national wire agencies and handouts are prepared for local newspapers. If an organization's membership is small, a competent writer may be employed to prepare a series of articles for a popular magazine that enjoys wide circulation, thereby enabling the organization to release newspaper stories supporting the ideas and opinions expressed in the articles and giving them greater validity. Other groups confine their initial efforts to the publication of pamphlets and leaflets high in emotional content, with appeal to patriotic and religious motives. These materials are mailed to a selected list of persons in different parts of the country, and they are advertised in magazines and newspapers with the offer that anyone who is interested may receive the publications free upon request or for mailing costs only. Now and then the campaign is started through cleverly devised motion picture films, radio broadcasts, and television programs but, as a rule, these media are held back until the time is right to crystallize public opinion.

In practically all unfair attacks, no attempt is made to support charges and accusations with factual information. As examples, the author of one inflamatory pamphlet states that progressive education is shot through with pragmatism and that this type of education has had a "very deleterious effect" on the character of schools. He defines neither the important terms in this statement nor follows through with reliable evidence to substantiate the charge. In discovering so-called subversive material in textbooks, critics have consistently relied upon distortion, omission, and altering of sentences to set forth their case. A typical trick is to accuse the schools of progressive education and then to make this phrase synonymous with indoctrination for collectivism, socialism, and communism. It is apparent that the parties responsible for attacks know that name calling, emotional words, slogans, appeals to prejudice, half-truths, and other propaganda devices are more effective in arousing suspicion and stirring up discontent than the impartial presentation of facts after careful study and investigation.

When an attack is carried into states and local communities, the attacking group works through its branch units. At the state level, it may bring pressure upon governmental officials to appoint special committees for tracking down alleged subversive activities in state-supported education institutions, a practice employed especially in connection with textbooks and teacher loyalty. The organization may also throw its resources into a legislative campaign for the enactment of restrictive measures conforming to its purposes. Some groups have been responsible for the passage of bills specifying that more time be given to the teaching of American history and government, even though this subject is taught in the elementary, junior, and senior high schools. They have also tried to prescribe the content of American history courses in order to strip them of controversial elements they dislike. They have been behind laws calling for the immediate dismissal of teachers who are disloyal to the government of the United States, despite the fact that the loyalty problem is covered adequately in general state laws on sedition and subversive activities. Through their efforts, now more than one-half of the states require that teachers take loyalty oaths. These are not new, but the present emphasis on the teaching profession weakens public confidence and seldom keeps individuals who have subversive tendencies out of schools.

If there is no local unit of the national organization to handle its campaign, one of three alternatives may be adopted at the community level. First, key people may be selected who feel antagonistic toward the school system. They are aided from behind the scenes to interest others in forming a council or an association to spearhead the attack. Second, a "front" organization may be established or one bearing a different title from the parent group whose real motives are concealed. Paid workers, skilled in getting citizens to assume responsibility for the program, lay out the plan of strategy. Third, offers of cooperation may be extended to existing organizations that are unsympathetic in whole or part to the local school system.

Whether an attack on a local school system is inspired and directed by a national group or whether it represents the hostility of a loosely-organized minority, the pattern of procedures is much the same. Usually rumors are started which cause citizens to believe that serious weaknesses and dangerous influences exist in the school system. Questions are raised about the loyalty and moral fitness of administrators and teachers. After the rumors have circulated for some time, they are brought into the open through a flood of "letters to the editor" of daily and weekly newspapers in the community and surrounding area. A temporary committee may be formed to call on the superintendent or attend a school board meeting where a request is made that something be done to prove or disprove what is being said about the schools. Occasionally, the technique is used of submitting a prepared list of questions to school officials and demanding that correct answers be given. The questions make good news copy, while the answers provide an excellent opportunity to disagree and thereby intensify the conflict. Full advantage is taken of parent-teacher association meetings to plant additional rumors and suggestions that pertinent information is being held back from the public. A high point is reached when citizens throw their support to the organizations leading the campaign or when they fall in line with the idea of forming a citizens' council to conduct a full and impartial investigation of the schools. Thereafter the attack swings into a broad pattern of public meetings, printed literature, newspaper stories, handbills, school board hearings, committee investigations, and the publicizing of charges which the critics demand be satisfied.

MEETING CRITICISMS AND ATTACKS

How shall the individual school system meet the unfair criticisms and attacks of selfish and destructive interest groups? Unfortunately, no single answer or formula can be recommended. Each criticism and attack must be seen against the local setting, studied and appraised, and its development carefully noted. This information is essential to intelligent action, and it will influence the selection of one or more of the following methods for trying to resolve the conflict.

First, the criticism or attack can be ignored completely with the expectation that it will exhaust itself in time. This is often the case with complaints that come from individuals and small groups who seek attention. As a general policy, it implies a lack of courtesy on the part of the school toward the public; it lowers respect for school officials; and it may fan the flames of discontent strongly enough to intensify and spread the criticism.

Second, the critics may be denounced and everything about them revealed to the public. This is an effective method in dealing with some groups, but it is also out of line with the social function of the school. As a creation of society, operating impartially in the public welfare, the school must strive to harmonize cultural differences, not to create them. Denouncements and exposures are almost certain to bring on social conflict within the community and divide citizens into opposing factions. The rejection of this procedure does not prevent professional organizations and teachers' associations from entering into a program for exposing the background of leaders, their motives, sources of finance, and methods of operation. As vested interest groups, independent of public educational institutions, they have every right in a democratic society to defend the ideals of the profession and to protect the welfare of their members.

Third, the school can issue an official denial of the charges and demand that supporting evidence be produced by the accusers without further fanfare. This method works at times, but a denial may get more publicity than a charge that is brought against the school system; few newspapers miss an opportunity to exploit a situation which contains elements of conflict. There is likewise the possibility that a denial may stimulate speculation regarding the truthfulness of school officials or suggest they have something to hide.

Fourth, the charge can be refuted promptly with factual information. No doubt some charges should be handled in this way. On the other hand, there is a chance that educators may find themselves in an embarrassing position or at least one that is difficult to explain. For example, achievement in subject matter may not be as good as they thought it to be, yet they have been preaching for years that smaller classes, better equipment, and newer instructional methods were producing superior results. Granting that this can be explained mostly in terms of a different school population, particularly at the secondary level, still it is an explanation which the public finds hard to accept. Refutation at best gives no assurance, moreover, that the criticisms will not reoccur three or four years later.

Fifth, the local school system can hold fast to what is believed to be right and true. For instance, a vocal minority may claim that most parents of elementary school children are dissatisfied with the newer methods of teaching reading and demand a return to those of the past. The board of education can yield to this pressure and establish an unhealthy precedent, or it can maintain its position until sufficient information has been collected and analyzed showing the way in which most parents feel, whether or not they understand the reading program, and how well children have learned to read. Too many boards of education, in recent years, have given way to pressure groups without having the courage to stand by their convictions and find the facts to verify or refute charges brought against them. When a board displays courage and fairness, it sets an example for the community and for the teachers in the school system.

Sixth, administrative policies and procedures can be adopted for receiving and examining all criticisms, complaints, and suggestions which are filed in writing with the superintendent and signed by the individuals making them. The policies should serve as criteria for evaluating each criticism and complaint and for protecting the civil liberties of teachers and the prerogatives of academic freedom. The procedures should constitute a course of action for expediting the handling of these problems so that full advantage may be taken of situations in which timeliness is an important factor. Quite often the knowledge alone that written complaints and suggestions receive prompt and careful attention paves the way for better public relations and the rejection of unsound proposals. Preferably, this machinery should be planned and organized long before emergencies arise in the local system.

Seventh, invitations can be extended to friendly groups to join with school officials in examining charges and determining whether or not they are borne out by the facts. If these groups believe that it would be better to have the charges investigated by an independent advisory committee, they should be encouraged to form one. It has been found that citizen reports on school investigations exert more influence on public opinion than those of school officials, and that where the charges cannot be substantiated, further attacks are slowed down and reduced immediately.

Eighth, the previous course of action is one aspect of a broad program for interpreting the school to the public and providing for citizen participation in its affairs. Analysis reveals that most attacks flourish in communities where parents and taxpayers possess limited knowledge of their school systems and seldom have occasion to discuss educational problems with teachers and administrators. Conversely, few attacks take root in communities where parents and tax-payers understand the nature and accomplishments of their school systems and take an active part in trying to improve them. Although many educators have been remiss in keeping the public informed and making them partners in the business of schools, they can still do a great deal to meet their difficulties by inaugurating an information service, intensifying parent contacts at all grade levels, and taking advantage of the numerous opportunities at hand for lay-professional cooperation in the performance of services and the solution of im-mediate school problems. This effort, however, should be more than an expedient and clever defense against harmful criticisms and destructive attacks; it should represent a sincere desire to help citizens understand schools and participate in the work of improving them now and in the future.

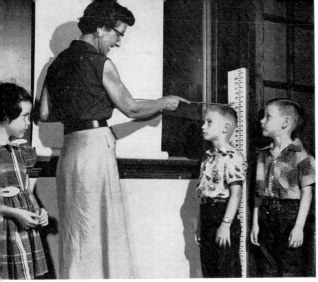

Courtesy Public Information Office, Springfield
Public Schools, Springfield, Missouri.

13
Educational Associations

No program in public relations would be complete without taking into account the problems of the teaching profession and the contributions of educational associations to the improvement of public schools. Instead of looking at these groups from an institutional point of view, emphasis in this chapter will be shifted to the public relations needs of local, state, and national associations and the means available for them to become more effective in promoting the cause of popular education and improving the status of the men and women who belong to the teaching profession.

CHARACTERISTICS OF ASSOCIATIONS

In discussing the public relations activities of educational associations, it is necessary to keep their characteristics in mind. They are voluntary groups composed of individuals who make their living by performing educational services for children, youth, and adults. Since they are voluntary groups, the members join of their own free

243

will. They cannot be coerced into membership by boards of education
and school officials, though it is readily acknowledged that many
boards and superintendents bring strong pressure on teachers to
belong to local, state, and national organizations. This is undemo-
cratic and lies outside the scope of their authority. Teachers must
have the right to determine their own affiliations until such time as
all professional groups are integrated into an organic whole, recognized in law to the same extent as the medical and dental associations,
and authorized to act in the name of the teaching profession.

Educational associations are corporate bodies that enjoy the
privilege of self-government. They may write their own constitutions
and by-laws, elect their own officers, appoint their own committees,
develop their own programs, and disband themselves at any time.

They are likewise special interest groups operating for the protection and welfare of their members. Like any special interest group
in our society, they may express their views publicly on topics and
questions affecting their interests, adopt legitimate means for con-
verting others to support their contentions and beliefs, take whatever
steps are necessary to strengthen their organization, and engage in
political activity of benefit to themselves.

Finally, they are advisory in their relationship to school directors, administrators, and legislative units of government. Their services may be accepted or rejected, since they lie outside the legal
structure of the school system. Increasingly, however, they are being
brought into deliberations on policy matters affecting public education and often take the initiative to inform school officials and legislative bodies of where they stand on issues under consideration.

ACCEPTED PURPOSES

Most educational associations have four major purposes which they
regard as being sufficiently comprehensive for their needs and definite
enough to influence the design of their activities. The primary purpose is that of promoting the cause of popular education in the
United States. It implies that these groups place the welfare of
children and society above their immediate interests, and that they
recognize the necessity for stimulating public awareness and understanding of the aims, shortcomings, and accomplishments of tax-

supported institutions so that citizens will take intelligent action for better schools.

The next outstanding purpose is to elevate the character and advance the interests of the teaching profession. It grew out of a long history of exploitation by dishonest boards of school directors and community pressure groups that lowered the status of the profession and denied its members the right to a private existence.

The third purpose concerns the improvement of professional services by all who are engaged in educational work. It is based upon the assumption that a true profession depends upon the quality of the services which the members perform. The influence of this purpose is seen in the steady rise of certification standards, the adoption of codes of ethical conduct, in-service training programs, incentives for self-improvement, and greater teacher participation in social and civic affairs.

The last purpose points out that the teaching profession should interpret itself to the public. It recognizes that planned action is necessary to bring about popular understanding and appreciation of the role played by the teaching profession in American life. Although constructive steps have been taken toward the achievement of this purpose, they have fallen far short of the goal and will continue to be inadequate until more resources and technical skill are brought to bear on the problem.

EXISTING ORGANIZATIONS

The teaching profession has organized itself extensively for service and mutual protection. Several hundred different associations conduct programs that are national, regional, state, and local in scope. They may be divided roughly into three principal groups. The largest is the National Education Association with its affiliated state and local branches which collectively enroll more than three-quarters of the administrators, teachers, and other professional workers in public schools. The second group, a relatively small one in size of membership, is composed of unions affiliated with the American Federation of Labor-Congress of Industrial Organizations. The third group includes scores of independent organizations serving specialized fields of interest within the teaching profession.

National Education Association

The National Education Association is a voluntary organization of administrators, teachers, and others actively engaged or interested in educational work. It has grown rapidly in the past three decades and now speaks unofficially for the teaching profession on most matters of general concern. There are several departments and different headquarters divisions within the National Education Association which promote the interests of specialized groups and manage the accounts and special services of the Association. Each department is a semi-independent unit that controls its own affairs and charges membership fees. An individual who joins the Association automatically becomes a member of the Department of Classroom Teachers and then has the right to join any of the other departments, such as American Association of School Administrators, Association for Supervision and Curriculum Development, National Association of Secondary School Principals, American Educational Research Association, and the National School Public Relations Association.

In addition to the departments and divisions, the National Education Association has several commissions and committees for undertaking particular aspects of its program. The commissions are mostly deliberative bodies that operate under the supervision of the Executive Committee of the Association. The committees are known as standing, joint, and convention. The standing committees undertake a continuing program of study and activity related to the needs and interests of the teaching profession. For example, there are standing committees on citizenship education, credit unions, tenure and academic freedom, and ethics. The joint committees represent a form of cooperation with national groups that are interested in educational problems and the welfare of children. The convention committees take care of arrangements for meetings sponsored by the Association.

State and Local Branches

Each state and the District of Columbia has an educational association or a state teachers' association which is an affiliated branch of the National Education Association. Although affiliation carries with it an obligation to uphold the objectives and platform of the national group, each state association is autonomous, having its own constitution, by-laws, elected officers, committees and commissions, and program.

The general policies of the state association are determined by a representative assembly composed of delegates from the convention districts into which the state is divided. The number of delegates from a convention district varies with the size of its membership in the state association. A board of directors or an executive committee is responsible for executing policies between the annual meetings of the representative assembly, while a full-time executive secretary and his staff look after the details of administration. The executive secretary exercises strong influence on the character and work of the association and is more responsible for its achievements than any other person. Membership is available to anyone doing educational work in the state upon payment of the annual dues.

State associations provide for the affiliation of district or local teachers' associations. These groups are organized mostly around individual school systems or a combination of systems depending upon their size. As self-governing units, they elect their own officers, appoint their own committees, and develop their own programs to fit local needs and conditions. Major aspects of policy and program are determined by an executive board on which individual school buildings or small school systems are represented. Standing and special committees look after various phases of the program, while some groups in metropolitan centers divide their organization into departments. The departments correspond to the educational interests of the members, such as English, social studies, guidance, and administration. A few local associations are large enough to maintain a central headquarters and employ either a full-time or a part-time executive secretary. Local associations attempt to do for a small community of educators what the other organizations do for the state and nation.

Teachers' Unions

Among the more aggressive of the national teachers' associations is the American Federation of Teachers. Chartered by the American Federation of Labor but affiliated with the American Federation of Labor-Congress of Industrial Organizations since 1955, this associa-

tion maintains several state and local units, the latter being confined
to large industrial centers and smaller areas where labor unions are
prominent in economic and political life. The national organization
and its subsidiary units are self-governing bodies that elect their own
officers, appoint standing and special committees, and develop their
own individual programs. The programs are directed generally at the
improvement of educational facilities for children and better working
conditions for teachers in public schools. Teachers' unions depend
heavily for their success upon the support of organized labor. Membership in the American Federation of Teachers is relatively small,
although its growth has been rather steady over the last twenty-five
years.

The Congress of Industrial Organizations never made a strong
effort to unionize the teachers. Some of its locals claimed a substantial
membership years ago, but the number of locals was small and without much influence in furthering the cause of public education
and advancing the welfare of teachers. At the time of the AFL-CIO
merger practically all of them had gone out of existence except a
handful which were affiliated with the Government and Civic Employee Organizing Committee of the CIO.

Other Educational Associations

Besides the associations mentioned, there are many others which
serve distinct purposes and have an effect on public opinion regarding
public schools. They may be divided according to interests into the
following groups: (1) Accrediting and standardizing associations
whose principal function is the formulation of educational standards
and the accrediting of colleges and secondary schools according to
these standards. The best examples of this type of professional organization are the six regional associations, including the New England,
Middle Atlantic States, Southern, Western, Northwest, and North
Central Association of Colleges and Secondary Schools. (2) Associations which promote interest in the study and teaching of particular
subjects, such as the American Home Economics Association, Music
Teachers' National Association, and the National Council of Teachers of Mathematics. (3) Associations for special phases of education
that include more than the teaching of a single subject. Examples of

this type of association are the American Association for Adult Education, American Child Health Association, National Academy of Visual Instruction, and the National Kindergarten Association. (4) Associations for special types of schools. Here the various associations which make up this group find their membership in institutions rather than in individuals. They try to improve the work of member institutions and encourage constructive cooperation between them. Illustrations are the American Association of Junior Colleges, American Association of Teachers' Colleges, and the American Association of Technical High Schools and Institutes. (5) Associations representing particular employment positions. Among these associations are the American Association of Visiting Teachers, National Association of School Business Officials, National Association of School Secretaries, Council of Chief State School Officers, and the National Association of Personnel and Appointment Officers.

PUBLIC RELATIONS PROBLEMS

A number of associations have public relations programs designed to build good will and create a better understanding of the teaching profession. Some of these programs are effective, but many are not. Those which fail often consist of nothing more than a series of newspaper releases and a collection of printed pamphlets and leaflets on the work of the association, or else the programs are made up of activities for handling issues that arise in connection with legislation. All programs could be strengthened if they were organized around the public relations problems of the teaching profession as well as the peculiar needs of each association. Through the problems approach, there is better assurance that intelligent decisions will be made regarding points of emphasis, appropriate methods, suitable media of communication, finance, and the publics involved. Such problems as the following are illustrative of those which should be considered by professional groups in planning public relations programs.

1. *Eliminating the concept that teachers' associations are selfish pressure groups operating at the taxpayers' expense.* This belief has grown out of the steady demand for higher salaries, retirement plans, tenure legislation, sick leave allowances, and the like, and also from

the failure of educational organizations to show the relationship between their demands and the improvement of instruction.

2. *Changing the opinion that teachers' associations are more interested in economics than in education.* This is a natural corollary of the preceding belief. It emphasizes the fact that too many local and state associations lose sight of their purpose to promote the cause of popular education in the struggle for economic security.

3. *Increasing public respect for members of the teaching profession.* Teachers have seldom received the recognition and respect given to members of other professions, yet they make an equally significant contribution to society. Among other reasons, this difference may be attributed to lack of professional conduct on the part of many teachers, ease of entrance into the profession, low standards of preparation, teacher timidity, and disparagement of the profession by teachers themselves.

4. *Establishing a clear distinction between the rights of teachers as members of vested interest groups and their contract obligations as employees of boards of education.* The public does not realize that teachers have the right to organize and work for their own welfare the same as any other interest groups in our form of society, nor do school boards and administrators always recognize that local teachers' associations are not agencies of the school system which they may control at will.

5. *Establishing a clear distinction between the rights of teachers as private citizens and their contractual obligations as employees of boards of education.* This has been a critical problem in American education for many years, although it was modified somewhat during the war years and in the period since that time. A great deal remains to be done, however, before teachers have the right to live as private citizens without interference from school boards or in accordance with unwritten community codes that set them apart from other people.

6. *Increasing teacher observance of codes of ethics and ideals of service.* Practically all educational groups have adopted codes of ethics outlining professional conduct and advocating ideals of service, but thousands of their members scarcely know them and those that do have only a vague understanding of what they are like. Their influence is negligible. Steps must be taken to increase understanding,

acceptance, and observance of the principles and ideals of the profession.

7. *Developing a united front on professional matters that are brought before the public.* All too frequently educational organizations work at cross purposes and carry their disagreements into the newspapers, school board hearings, legislative contacts, and community groups. They leave the impression that the teaching profession is badly divided within itself and that the members of it don't know what they want. There is much to be learned about the importance of settling disputes within the professional family and presenting a united front in public.

8. *Correcting ignorance and misunderstanding of modern educational theories and practices.* Laymen have been subjected to so many conflicting speeches and articles about modern education that they don't know what to believe. They would like authoritative guidance on what is best for pupils regarding homework, discipline, promotion, core curriculum, methods of teaching, report cards, and so forth. Attempts should be made by professional groups to reach common agreements on these issues and make pronouncements that would clarify public thinking and encourage wider acceptance of modern educational theories and practices.

9. *Helping the public to understand and appreciate the social importance of education in a democracy.* This is especially important in view of the wide-spread criticisms, attacks, and attempts at division going on today. Many people are losing sight of the fact that public schools are the strongest guarantee for the preservation of democratic ideals and institutions and the preparation of young people for their place in society. The teaching profession should keep the positive values of public education before the people and interpret their meaning in American life.

10. *Neutralizing propaganda that public schools are populated with red-tainted teachers.* This propaganda is harmful to the teaching profession. Every known teacher with disloyal tendencies should be expunged from the membership list of educational associations, and this action should be made public. At the same time swift action should be taken to denounce and expose those who bring charges against teachers without evidence to support their claims. Public confidence must not be destroyed in the thousands of loyal men and

women in the teaching profession by the actions of a few or by the irresponsible behavior of organized crackpots and racketeers operating under a banner of patriotism.

11. *Establishing and maintaining wholesome relations with individuals and groups who are sincerely concerned with the improve-ment of public education.* There are many such groups at local, state, and national levels who will join forces with professional organizations in the cause for better schools, providing they receive encouragement and opportunity for constructive cooperation. This aspect of public relations should be developed systematically by educational associations.

12. *Improving public understanding of the reasons for higher educational costs.* Taxpayers realize that it takes more money now than it did in the past to operate schools, but they do not know why the amount keeps on increasing or what they are getting back from their investment. Their lack of understanding is behind some of the skepticism toward schools and the refusal to approve tax increases and bond issues for the construction of new buildings. The changes which have forced educational costs upward must be explained as well as the instructional values being purchased with tax dollars. The time is overdue for an honest and skillful handling of this problem.

13. *Paving the way for desirable changes in school policies and practices.* Social progress in democracy depends upon public understanding and acceptance of the need for change. This state of readiness is not accomplished quickly but often takes a considerable period of time and planned effort in adult education. Professional organizations should lay the groundwork of understanding by bringing significant research findings before the public and by acquainting parents and taxpayers with experimental programs going on throughout the country. This work would pave the way for local school systems to introduce changes without incurring unfavorable reactions from members of the instructional staff and people in the community. Moreover, it would identify the teaching profession with progress in American education and enhance its status in the public mind.

14. *Helping members to become more sensitive to their responsibilities and opportunities for interpreting the teaching profession to the public.* The interpretative task cannot be accomplished suc-

cessfully without the combined efforts of all members of the profession. Educational associations must develop ways and means for keeping their own members more fully informed of the public relations activities in which they are engaging and for stimulating their interest in the meaning and importance of personal opportunities for bringing the profession before the public in a favorable light.

BASIC CONCEPTS

After identifying and defining the public relations problems of the teaching profession and the needs of the individual association, agreements must be reached on concepts to govern the design and operation of the program. The following concepts, though small in number, are basic in the interpretation of the profession to the public.

Proper Balance

The chief function of the teaching profession is promoting the cause of public education. Few people, if any, ever question the validity of this idea. They question only the tendency of teacher groups to make their personal interests paramount to the ideals of service for education. There is nothing in this function which denies to teachers and administrators the right to a legitimate return for their labors and the technical skill involved in performing them. People are willing to pay, and pay well, for services they value, and more so when they are rendered in the interest of children and society. The prevailing stress upon the economic welfare of the teacher must be brought into proper balance with the concept that members of the profession deserve rewards only to the extent that they work for better schools and the continuous improvement of their own services. This means that educational associations must devise and use every means possible for increasing their contributions to the cause of public education while keeping the public fully informed of what they are doing.

Independent Status

While professional organizations should encourage the constructive cooperation of lay individuals and groups who are interested in public education and work with them on projects for the improvement of schools, in no case should they enter into an organic affiliation with other special interest groups. The strength of the teaching profession lies in a strict adherence to its own purposes and the maintenance of a strong program devoted to the ideals for which it stands. It cannot sustain its position successfully if obligated to support the purposes of any special class or group, nor can it retain the respect and confidence of the public if it comes under suspicion of political, economic, and religious partisanship.

Unity of Action

Unity of action is a crying need of the teaching profession. Educational groups should strive constantly to present a solid front to the public. As a working policy, all local, state, and national associations should discuss proposed programs for meeting professional and legislative problems with other professional associations operating at the same level. This is one of the better ways of reaching agreements and taking unified action, even though it may mean conceding certain points of interest. Whatever concessions must be made are less important in the long run than the gains that result from concerted action. The process of striving for unity would be enhanced if professional councils were formed at different levels whereby representatives of various educational groups could meet regularly for the development of programs they would agree to support and the publicity they would release.

Propaganda and Pressure

While the use of propaganda by tax-supported institutions is contrary to their social nature and purpose, special interest groups are justified in using it to influence public opinion. And because educational associations fall into the special interest class, there is a question, therefore, of whether or not they should employ propaganda in promoting the cause of popular education and advancing the welfare of their members and the status of the teaching profession. Sound policy supports the position that professional organizations profit more from a complete and accurate presentation of facts regarding educational and welfare needs than from a concealment and distortion of the truth; and, that the objectives of public understanding, good will, respect, and confidence in the teaching profession will be attained more fully when the presentation of factual information is based on educational methodology instead of high-pressure tactics.

Available Resources

Among the members of professional organizations are many individuals who possess rich backgrounds of special training and experience in psychology, human relations, organization, research, writing, speaking, advertising, and dramatics. These individuals may not know the field of public relations, but under the direction of skillful leaders and paid professional workers their talents have a place in any comprehensive program for interpreting teaching to the public. In fact, no organization could afford to buy the wide range of specialized talents they represent. Educational associations would do well to build resource files of their membership and capitalize upon the wealth of knowledge and technical skill they have available. They are in a stronger position than most interest groups in this respect and should be able to do a more significant job in developing wholesome public opinion.

Planning and Research

The public relations programs of individual associations at each level should be planned thoroughly in terms of meeting both immediate and long range problems of the teaching profession. The planning should be done by competent leaders under the direction of professional consultants or staff specialists attached to the association. They should be responsible for determining the problems, selecting appropriate methods and media of interpretation, and appraising all activities of the association for their public relations value. The actual implementation of the program should be assigned to staff personnel and competent members of the association.

Coupled with planning is the essential work of research in obtaining information needed in developing the program and in preparing materials for popular consumption. This work calls for the employment of research specialists by the larger organizations and their availability upon request by the smaller ones. It is important that research be done carefully so that full and correct information may guide the making of decisions and insure public confidence in reported findings. Planning and research are fundamental to the success of any interpretative program.

PUBLIC RELATIONS ACTIVITIES

Every activity of an educational group influences the opinions of laymen about the group and the profession it represents. The influence may be favorable, unfavorable, or mixed, depending upon the manner in which it is conducted. Concern for this aspect of activity is an essential feature of any comprehensive program in public relations. In a more formal sense, however, a public relations program is usually thought of as a collection of activities for interpreting the work of a group or organization and for developing the understanding, good will, respect, and support of the public that is desired. Some of these activities will now be considered.

Business Contacts

In the daily business management of an association many personal contacts take place between the officers and staff workers and the representatives of various firms, governmental agencies, and special interest groups as well as private citizens and members of the association. The contacts may come about through direct relations or through telephone calls, correspondence, and appearances at outside meetings. Each one is an opportunity for identifying the association with ideals of service and for passing on information and creating wholesome impressions which enter into the formation of public opinion. The importance of these contacts in public relations should be recognized and provision made for handling them with technical proficiency.

Membership Training

The members of an educational association are public relations agents of that association just as much as the officers and staff workers and should be trained to meet their responsibilities. This training should be outlined by national and state associations and carried out for the most part by local branches in their own communities. It should include the preparation and study of handbooks and manuals containing information on the work of professional organizations, problems of the teaching profession, current developments in educational thought and practice, and how individual members can contribute more to the advancement of the teaching profession. Workshops conducted at state and local levels form another part of the program for achieving wider understanding of professional ideals and services and acquiring sensitivities to public relations opportunities. Specific problems in interpretation may be taken up at clinics under the direction of consultants drawn from universities and commercial public relations firms. The entire program would be improved if state associations provided intensive training for local branch leaders in the fundamentals of good public relations and methods of working with their own groups.

Political Action

Most associations have held rather strictly to the belief that member welfare and the cause of education are served best by remaining independent and free of political connections. They have taken this position because they realize that political partisanship would destroy respect and undermine public confidence in the teaching profession. What they do not appreciate, however, is the value of taking intelligent political action on the election of public officials, important social issues, and legislative proposals.

It is a reasonable assumption that better qualified individuals would be nominated and placed in school board, city council, and state legislative offices if professional organizations took a direct interest in their appointment or election. They would not be engaging in party politics by making objective studies of the qualifications and views of candidates on educational questions, nor would they be guilty of departing from their principles by publicly endorsing or opposing candidates and giving reasons for their action. Their standing in the community would even be stronger if teachers went to the polls and backed up these recommendations as testimony to their civic interest and desire to see competent men in office. This is a public service which, in time, could earn an esteem not enjoyed by the profession for some years.

As a special interest group, educational associations have every right to take sides on important social issues and to make known the views of the teaching profession. This is a part of democratic functioning and a means of creating enlightened public opinion. With exceptions, the various associations should confine their work to issues affecting child and youth welfare and public education. The major work of collecting and presenting information on social issues should be done by national and state associations, with local units serving as key points for distributing much of the material through the personal contacts of members, newspaper releases, and open meetings. Whatever danger there may be in taking sides and campaigning is secondary in importance to the defense of social ideals and the adoption of sound public policy.

Lobbying is another form of political action that is justified under our form of government when it is restricted to the dissemination of accurate information and honest forms of persuasion. Educational groups should have trained legislative observers to watch for the introduction of bills which are detrimental to teacher welfare and the educational opportunities of children. They should work to prevent the passage of such bills and to secure the enactment of others without resorting to pressure tactics or taking part in shady political deals. In the final analysis, the best means of influencing favorable legislation is through the continuous development of public opinion and the education of members of the legislature. Observers should know which members have a sincere interest in teacher welfare and public education, and they should work closely with them from the original drafting of a bill to its final passage. They should also petition the right to speak for and against proposed legislation before senate and house committees where specific bills are under consideration. Their influence will be stronger, however, if they work cooperatively with other interest groups, such as school directors, state departments of education, parent-teacher associations, child welfare agencies, and professional associations.

Community Activities

A local teachers' association carries on good public relations when it takes an interest in the community and performs services which establish it in the minds of people as a fine neighbor and a worthy civic agency. How an association may best express this interest and perform services is determined by local conditions and the attitudes of members. The possibilities for being identified constructively with the life of the community are numerous.

In practically all communities the members of teachers' associations can lend support and furnish leadership in drives and campaigns which are conducted by such organizations as the Red Cross, Boy Scouts, March of Dimes, Community Chest, Christmas Seals, and a host of other character building and philanthropic groups. Full advantage has been taken of civic drives and campaigns by business and industrial firms to advance the aims of the community and to associate themselves with the good citizen concept. It is time that teachers' associations took their place alongside of these and other community groups in contributing to the public welfare and bringing attention to themselves.

They should also be represented on civic committees for the study of specific problems affecting the community and for the management of special affairs, such as youth welfare, recreation, housing, slum clearance, civil defense, preservation of historical landmarks, and the celebration of local holidays. Their technical knowledge and skill in a wide range of fields make them valuable members of civic committees.

At the same time, the local organization should make a detailed study of the purposes and programs of organized groups in the community in order to determine which ones are concerned with educational and human welfare problems. They should be invited to discuss their programs with members of the local association and to learn from them what they are trying to accomplish. This exchange of information makes it possible to explore opportunities for cooperation and to develop projects in which there is mutual interest. The more an association works with community groups the stronger its place in the life of the community becomes.

It is advisable further for the local association to match the affiliation of its members with a list of reputable groups and organizations in the community and thus determine where gaps exist. These gaps should be filled on a voluntary basis even if this means paying the expenses of members for joining the groups and organizations in which there is no teacher representation. Wide affiliation with lay organizations ties the association more deeply into the community and enables its members to sound out public opinion, win friends, and take advantage of numerous occasions for interpreting the teaching profession.

The sponsoring of special events and services is another means for the local association to earn prestige and acquire recognition in the community. It can set up a speakers' bureau and furnish a list of speakers to every group and organization. It can entertain civic groups at luncheons and dinners and acknowledge their contributions as well as those of private citizens to the advancement of public education. Community leaders can be brought together for the analysis of educational issues and steps to take for meeting them. Back-to-school drives can be held for youngsters who are beyond compulsory school-age limits. The community can be furnished with unbiased information on school needs and conditions and asked to consider proposals for solving immediate problems.

The community activities of the local association should be supplemented by the state and national associations in their relationships with fraternal, labor, industrial, patriotic, agricultural, child welfare, and nonpartisan political organizations operating on the higher levels. These relationships may take the form of addresses, distribution of literature, participation in conferences, representation on study committees, and the joint sponsoring of projects.

Professional Standards

Steady progress has been made during the past 20 to 30 years in elevating the standards of the teaching profession, but there is still a long way to go before public school teaching will attain a position in society comparable to that of law, medicine, and dentistry. The hope of the future lies in the organic union of educational associations and their power to set the standards of selection, preparation, and public service for members of the profession.

Even though an organic union is not realized for some time to come, one or two national associations, working cooperatively and through state and local branches, could acquire sufficient strength and prestige to control virtually the standards of the profession. They should formulate a definite program and fix a time table for its accomplishment. The program should include standards of admission to teacher training institutions so that only the best qualified young people would be admitted, the number being determined for each state in proportion to present and future demand. It should also include standards for plant facilities, staff personnel, library resources, laboratories, finance, programs of study, and for graduation. Teacher training institutions should be evaluated by these standards and those that fail to meet them should be forced out of business. It was this type of approach that made it possible to effect the reforms in medical education which started that profession up the ladder of public recognition.

Of equal importance is the need to establish uniform patterns of licensure in the several states throughout the nation and the organizing of professional boards under law to administer the issuance of teaching certificates. The certification laws should be written by the national association and their adoption made the work of state associations in cooperation with lay organizations that are interested in the improvement of the teaching profession. Certification requirements should be dovetailed with those maintained for teacher training institutions.

There should be only one code of ethics for the teaching profession, with enforcement left in the hands of state associations. The code should describe the principles of conduct and the ideals of service expected from the members and the procedures for bringing to trial and disbarment those who violate its provisions. Disbarment should carry with it revocation of the right to teach in public schools of the individual state.

Until educational associations develop and maintain high standards for the teaching profession, it will be difficult to secure the amount of public confidence and support required to make teaching a truly outstanding profession.

Research Studies

Research and research findings form another link with the public. Research reports enable people to understand better the problems of schools, and they suggest possible types of solutions for them to consider. They often bring timely and pertinent information to legislative bodies and citizen groups involved in the study and discussion of educational issues. Their planned distribution aids in the formation of public opinion and the development of confidence in professional organizations. Research reports are an excellent tool in a program of public relations.

National and state associations should carry on several different types of research. This research may include surveys of educational needs and problems on national, state, and local levels; studies of current trends in education; experimental projects in special fields; intensive investigations of single problems; historical background of present issues; and comparative studies of educational philosophies. The problems for research emerge from professional meetings, legislative sessions, lay criticism of schools, requests for information, and previous studies undertaken by the association. Some of the more pressing problems for study today are salary schedules, educational costs, teacher retirement systems, sick-leave allowances, methods of teaching, tax systems, controversial materials in textbooks, the teaching of controversial issues, personnel policies and practices, academic freedom, evaluation of learning, and public opinion toward public schools.

The public relations value of research and research reports depends much upon their distribution to consumers. Regular research bulletins should be sent to members of the association and to laymen who have a definite interest in particular problems. The highlights of some studies should be released to the press and radio and to popular magazines with large circulations. Newsletter digests should be sent to lay organizations and outstanding private citizens or special digests should be prepared for similar distribution on studies in which there is general interest. Leaflets and pamphlets summarizing findings and proposing solutions should be placed in the hands of local associations for wide distribution throughout the community.

Publications

Interpretative materials may be presented continuously through the publications of professional organizations. The leading publications for this purpose are the official journals of national and state associations and those of local groups in large communities. They may be supplemented by books, pamphlets, leaflets, newsletters, special bulletins, and reprints of articles appearing in professional and lay magazines.

Distributed primarily for the information of members and their reinterpretation to the public, copies of journals and supplementary publications should be mailed nevertheless to officers of important state and national groups, certain governmental officials, presidents of boards of education, and the principal libraries throughout the country. Local associations should be made responsible for selective distribution within their respective communities, including leaders in social and civic life, newspaper editors, radio commentators, and outstanding private citizens. Planned distribution of professional publications can net excellent results in member and general public understanding, appreciation, and support of the program carried on by educational associations.

Direct Publicity

Coordination between local, state, and national associations is essential to the effective planning of publicity programs. The leadership in outlining the elements of sound publicity and establishing criteria to guide the efforts of state and local branches should be taken by national associations. They should likewise suggest appropriate and timely news stories, furnish mats and publicity tools, produce motion pictures on modern educational practices, sponsor nationwide radio broadcasts and television programs, and prepare publicity materials for affiliated groups.

State branches should follow the general outline of publicity laid down by the national associations in maintaining a continuous flow of news concerning legislation, conventions, school conditions, needs of the profession, and influences affecting public education. Some of the news should be sent out as prepared copy to local units for modification and release to community daily and weekly papers. They should also be supplied with publicity materials and instructed on how to use them. In general, state associations should render service on call to local associations in the planning, executing, and appraising of publicity work.

The real job of publicizing the teaching profession and the

cause of public education belongs to the local association. It is closer to the rank and file of the citizenry and its members enjoy more wide-spread contacts than are possible by state and national groups. Its publicity should be fitted to local needs and conditions, using the services of the larger associations to full advantage. Increasingly, some local associations have carried on effective publicity through regular space in newspapers and by means of radio broadcasts and television programs, while others have placed reliance on an assortment of publicity devices to accomplish their purposes. An inventory of the devices they have employed to gain attention and influence public opinion include photographic literature, articles in lay magazines, articles in house organs of business and industrial firms, window stickers, blotters, letter enclosures, paid newspaper advertising, billboards, car cards, posters, hat bands, milk bottle collars, lapel tags, automobile tire covers, emblems, cartoons, calendars, leaflets, sound trucks, movie trailers, lettergrams, displays, exhibits, and slides, besides newspaper stories, radio broadcasts, and television programs.

Some of the devices appear to be cheap, and these are worse than no publicity at all. Publicity devices should be selected because they serve particular purposes better than some other means of communication, convey worthwhile ideas, uphold the dignity of the profession, and leave the public more fully informed. It is without question much wiser for a local association to do a few things well in publicity than to attempt the promiscuous use of many devices. The present situation can be corrected by improving the planning and coordination of publicity programs between local, state, and national associations.

American Education Week

Special concern should be shown for American Education Week because of the excellent opportunities it provides for interpreting public education and the contributions of the teaching profession. Started shortly after World War I by the National Education Association, in cooperation with the American Legion, National Congress of Parents and Teachers, and the United States Office of Education, to help schools meet critical problems created by the war, it has grown steadily and is now celebrated in every section of the country. Although the general planning and promoting of American Education Week has been retained by the National Education Association with detailed programs carried out by its affiliated branches, this event is of such importance that it should be publicly endorsed and supported strongly by every professional organization.

The value of American Education Week lies in causing people to take stock of the educational assets in this country and in reminding them concretely through open house programs, classroom visits, school assemblies, public forums, and other means of the opportunities young people have to secure sound education and how the schools and the teaching profession are basic to democratic living. Much more could be done to make American Education Week a national event if every educational association cooperated in its celebration and if more community groups were involved in planning and carrying out local programs.

RELATIONS WITH SCHOOL SYSTEMS

The relationship between an individual association and a local school system should be made clear to the public, the board of education, and the superintendent of schools. They should be fully cognizant of the fact that the association is completely independent of the school system and that it has the same rights and privileges as other groups in the community. No question should be left unanswered regarding the purposes and program of the association or its desire to cooperate with school officials and community groups on all matters related to the education of children and the welfare of teachers. Failure to establish clearly the character and position of the association tends to weaken its professional standing and invite the assumption of control by school officials.

Good relations with the local school system are important in achieving the objectives of the association. They develop more quickly when the board of education and the superintendent meet periodically with representatives of the association to discuss mutual interests and to explore opportunities for working on common problems. As the two groups come to know and respect one another, it is easy to reach agreements on the use of school facilities for professional meetings, exchange of information, attendance of members at board meetings, advisement on school needs and conditions, and the immediate and long term problems demanding their attention. School officials are appreciative of the cooperative spirit shown by an association and the value of its services to the schools.

Though every association should strive to promote harmonious and constructive relations with the administration, no association should stand by and permit a local board of education and its officers to exploit the educational system for personal and political gain. It is their duty, as a professional organization, to protest openly against inefficiency, graft, patronage, autocratic administration, injustice, low salaries, incompetent leadership, and other practices detrimental to the welfare of children and staff personnel. They should lay the facts before the people and become a power in the development of public opinion. There are times when this action requires a great deal of courage and strong support from state and national associations. Groups which stand for what is right invariably win popular support and are held in high esteem by the parents and citizens of the community.

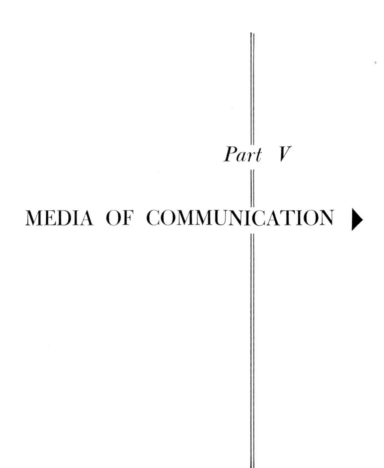

Part V

MEDIA OF COMMUNICATION ▶

Courtesy Public Schools, Dearborn, Michigan.

14
Student Activities

A distinction has been made for years between the learning activities of pupils in regular classroom instruction and those which lie outside the established program of studies, such as athletic sports, dramatics, musical organizations, student publications, and hobby clubs. This latter group has been known commonly as extracurricular, cocurricular, extraclass, and student activities. These titles imply a separation which is no longer recognized in modern elementary and secondary schools, where all activities which contribute to the growth and development of pupils are considered a part of the curriculum. The distinction, however, is retained here because many parents, citizens, and educators still think of student activities as being different from the educational experiences pupils receive in the study of conventional subjects, and also for the reason that their importance in school-community relations can be treated more conveniently.

PUBLIC RELATIONS VALUE

Student activities are an effective medium for publicizing the school and interpreting its work to the community. They are high in public relations value for the following important reasons, among others:

1. They have excellent news potential for dramatizing aspects of school life in which people are interested.

2. They bring parents and patrons into the school where they can see for themselves what pupils are doing and what they are achieving.

3. They assure a continuing interest by parents whose children are participants.

4. They enable skeptics to acquire a first-hand picture of the school at work and the experiences pupils receive under the direction of competent teachers.

5. They permit parents and patrons to decide whether or not pupils are undergoing sound preparation for present and future living.

6. They are the strongest argument against propaganda on "the fads and frills" of modern education.

7. They do more to help parents understand how the school influences the growth and development of pupils than printed literature.

8. They develop local pride in the school system.

9. They develop school spirit among pupils.

10. They offer excellent opportunities for parent and lay participation in the school program.

EDUCATIONAL CONSIDERATIONS

The high potentials of student activities for public relations are seldom realized unless they are based on sound, educational considerations. These considerations are, in reality, the principles which should govern their organization and administration:

1. The program in student activities shall represent at all times an honest and sincere expression of educational purposes and practices. The pupil and his welfare shall take priority over the winning of contests and the publicizing of the institution.

2. Adequate financial support shall be provided by the board of education, and it shall be charged against instruction. No student activity shall be expected to be self-supporting.

3. Student activities shall be carried on by pupils under teacher direction. They shall afford opportunity for the development of initiative, resourcefulness, responsibility, and other traits in character education.

4. Pupils shall be protected from exploitation, their growth and development being primary objectives of the student activity program.

5. Parents and patrons shall be invited to participate when they have a contribution to make to the program. Participation shall be encouraged by membership in policy-making bodies, performance of services, and sharing of special knowledge.

6. The entire program shall be under the supervision of the building principal and staff members to whom responsibility is assigned.

TYPES OF ACTIVITIES

The number and variety of student activities in elementary and secondary schools attest to their place and importance in the education program. Instead of decreasing in number, they have grown steadily until now there is scarcely a school of any size that does not provide for them in the daily schedule. In describing different types of student activities, reference will also be made to their meaning and importance in telling the story of schools and earning the good will and support of the public.

Contests

More interest is taken in contests than in any other type of student activity. Held in sports, music, art, dramatics, home economics, industrial arts, and other fields of learning, they provide a medium for mass attendance at school affairs and receive broad coverage in the press. The average layman in many localities knows more about contests than the rest of the school program. Of the contests held, interscholastic competition in sports heads the list in popularity and attendance. For this reason, it is imperative that these contests accurately reflect educational objectives and be conducted according to rules of decency and fair play. While such contests as debating, extemporaneous speaking, home economics, and art may not attract as many people, they are equally important in the interpretation of the school. Those who attend these contests come to appreciate the knowledge, poise, and skill shown by pupils. More people would be attracted to nonathletic contests if they received better publicity.

Entertainments

Programs in dramatics, forensics, and music attract many parents and friends of pupil participants as well as other people in the community. Plays and pageants are especially popular; they offer opportunities for pupils to show their training in speech, correct use of English, physical posture, and confidence before an audience. Their interpretative value is greater when careful attention is given to details of lighting, staging, scenery, and costuming. Those who attend forensic programs realize what the school is doing to teach public speaking, logical thinking, sensitivity to language, and related objectives. They strongly favor this training because of its value in business and social life throughout adulthood.

Musical programs win many friends, possibly more than any other type of activity. Concerts by a glee club, chorus, *a cappella* choir, band, or orchestra are well attended. Civic associations are constantly extending invitations for musical groups to supply entertainment. Much local pride is felt in an attractively costumed band, and its maneuvers are watched with interest on public occasions. People who attend dramatic productions, baccalaureate and graduation exercises, open house, and assembly programs always have words of praise for the music furnished by the school orchestra. The annual spring concert of combined music groups is rapidly becoming a popular event in school districts.

Social Affairs

Social affairs, such as parties, teas, and dances, are endorsed by parents. They know that these affairs are a necessary part of preparation for the future. Their support is stronger when rules and regulations controlling such affairs are developed cooperatively by the school and home.

Student Publications

Most secondary and some elementary schools publish printed and mimeographed newspapers, annual and semi-annual yearbooks, handbooks, magazines, and special bulletins for pupils. The publication of school newspapers provides experiences for pupils in gathering and writing news, handling production problems, and managing business details. Such newspapers reflect the daily life of the school and keep readers informed of classroom activities, scholastic honors, extracurricular events, school personalities, curricular changes, community events touching the school, alumni news, and pupil opinions on controversial questions.

If school newspapers interpret the institution correctly, they have a definite influence upon the attitudes and ideas of many

Student newspapers should reflect the daily life of the school.

people. Surveys show that they are read by nearly three-quarters of the parents when brought home by pupils, and that parents rely upon them for announcements of parent-teacher association meetings and student events. Also, parents are interested in reports of faculty changes, lists of pupils on the honor roll, what their children are doing in classes, and explanations of special services in guidance, health, and remedial instruction. Many alumni take a corresponding interest in news reported in school newspapers, while school board members, administrators, and teachers read them carefully.

Annual and semi-annual yearbooks are published generally by senior high school graduating classes. These yearbooks contain pictures of those who are graduating, class sponsors, administrative officers, and student organizations. A chronology of events is included highlighting the outstanding experiences of the class during its years in the school. Seniors, for the most part, are required to purchase the yearbooks in order to pay the costs of production. While the yearbooks are valued for sentimental reasons, it is doubtful that they have much public relations worth since their circulation is limited and they are read for only a short period.

Handbooks are usually compiled and edited by student-faculty committees in junior and senior high schools. They supply information on rules of the school, traditions, tardiness and absence procedure, health requirements, student activities, honors and awards, school songs, courses of study, marking systems, marking periods, graduation requirements, and so forth. Both pupils and parents consult handbooks frequently, and they are useful in developing an understanding of the educational program.

Literary magazines are published by a few of the larger high schools in the country. Their purposes are to recognize good literary achievement and to stimulate interest in creative writing. Although literary magazines have small circulation, they do bring their readers into contact with the fine quality of written work which pupils do under teacher direction. Mimeographed magazines containing children's poems and stories in the elementary school are becoming more common. These inexpensive magazines are an effective medium for acquainting parents of elementary pupils with language arts instruction. They enjoy wide circulation among parents and are read with keen interest.

Clubs and Societies

Clubs and societies furnish opportunities for adolescents to satisfy personal and social interests. They are divided into honor societies for those who have demonstrated superior leadership and scholastic attainment; character organizations, such as the scouts, Allied Youth, and Hi Y, which emphasize moral and spiritual values; hobby clubs where pupils may pursue interests in photography, archery, stamp collecting, chess, radio repair, arts and crafts, dancing, and so forth; departmental clubs which grow out of classwork in French, social studies, mathematics, and other subjects; and school service clubs, which are responsible for managing traffic in corridors, collecting attendance slips, safety at street crossings, work in the library, noon-hour recreation, guiding visitors, and managing the student store.

The wide range of interests represented by clubs and societies and the nature of their programs makes it possible to involve parents and laymen from the community. They can take part by demonstrating their own leisure-time activities, supplying technical information, assisting with special projects, and joining with pupils in staging exhibits and demonstrations.

Student Council

Practical training in citizenship is provided by the student council. This body shares in the government of the school, and functions under a constitution and set of bylaws modelled after those of state and national governments. It makes rules and regulations within defined limits of authority, administers many of its own decisions, and performs services for the good of the student group and the school. Typical activities of the student council are (1) planning and conducting school elections, (2) organizing and directing campaigns for school and community improvement, (3) advising with the principal and faculty on matters of educational policy, (4) publishing the student handbook, (5) holding open discussions on questions affecting student welfare, (6) sponsoring social affairs, and (7) creating committees to undertake special assignments.

A good student council is an asset to a school. It stimulates pupils to take a more direct interest in the life of the institution and teaches them lessons in the meaning of social and political action. Its work is viewed favorably by parents and public officials. They are usually anxious to assist the council, upon request, with special undertakings and the installation of new officers. Newspapers give space to reports of council activities, and these are read by the public with interest. Adults who attend student council meetings are impressed with the quality of thinking displayed and the soundness of decisions reached by pupils.

Assembly Programs

Assembly programs are useful in developing school unity, encouraging school spirit, influencing public opinion, and sharing information. They enable pupils to gain experience in self-expression and acquire proper habits of audience behavior. The programs may consist of dramatic skits, student council discussions, demonstrations of class work, hobby exhibits, debates on student problems, musical entertainments, motion pictures, pre-contest rallies, and talks by outside speakers. Their variety permits wide student participation.

The enthusiasm of students for worthwhile assembly programs carries over into the home. Parents are told about the programs, who took part in them, and why they were enjoyed. They learn much about the school from these accounts and come to appreciate what it is doing for the education of their children.

The contribution of the assembly is understood even better when parents are invited to attend at different times during the school year and asked, along with prominent citizens and public officials, to assist with and take part in some of the programs.

Class Organizations

Class organizations are found in secondary schools and to a lesser extent in elementary schools. Each class elects its own officers, appoints committees, and adopts a program. The work is guided by a faculty sponsor who may be elected by members of the class or appointed by the principal. Class organizations undertake such activities as assembly programs, annual trips, drives and contests, intramural sports, dances, plays, parties, special publications, and school services. Kept within reasonable limits, class organization programs aid in the development of school loyalty and pride and make many friends in the community.

Homeroom

The homeroom is more of an administrative unit than a part of the student activities program; however, some schools use the homeroom as the basis for representation in student council and in school-wide committees. Intramural sports are often organized according to homerooms, and each homeroom may be requested to present programs in assembly. Some even draft their own constitutions and conduct activities high in educational value. Outstanding work may be done by homeroom teachers in guidance, recreation, and the development of citizenship. It is not uncommon to find pupils and parents who are more enthusiastic about the homeroom than they are about other features of the student activities program.

Commencement Programs

Commencement programs or graduation exercises are held in junior and senior high schools. They have followed a fairly similar pattern for years. The pattern consists of an invocation by a local clergyman, brief addresses by two or three outstanding members of the graduating class, music, a guest speaker of prominence, remarks by the principal or some other school official, awarding of special honors, and the presentation of diplomas. The main criticism of this arrangement has been the time taken by the guest speaker and the fact that he may not say anything of interest or importance. A number of schools have tried to correct this weakness by dropping the speaker and substituting a series of short talks by pupils on topics related to their educational experiences.

There has been a trend in recent years to get away from the traditional program entirely and to organize commencement around demonstrations, plays, and pageants. Demonstrations may show how classwork is carried on in different subject fields or how extracurricular activities contribute to growth in knowledges, skills, and appreciations, while plays and pageants may depict the history of the school, everyday life in the school, the objectives of public education, or what graduates owe to school and community. Planned, prepared, and presented by pupils, nearly all members of the graduating class participate. Parents like these programs and derive satisfaction from seeing their children in them. Few events offer better possibilities to point out educational accomplishment and interpret school practices than newer types of commencement programs.

HARMFUL PRACTICES

The public relations value of student activities is lessened and may be destroyed by practices which violate educational principles, practices which parents dislike, and practices which taxpayers believe do not belong in a school system. The more harmful of these practices will be described.

Entertainments by Pupils

Heavy demands are made on schools by community groups for entertainments by pupils. They want the glee club, band, orchestra choir, dramatics club, student council, and others to perform during school hours, in the evening, and on holidays. While the experience gained by pupils participating in public engagements is commendable and the motivation they receive stimulates better performance, still this practice is objectionable. It is objectionable because they are taken from classes, use time that should be devoted to home assignments, and are asked to give up holidays with their families.

Parents do not like the interruptions to school work caused by public entertainments and the late hours their children are required to keep for evening performances. They have filed protests in several communities and insisted that school boards interfere to protect children. The outcome has been the adoption of policies controlling the number of invitations which any student group may accept during the year, the establishment of criteria for evaluating invitations, and the securing of permission from parents before pupils are allowed to take part in evening performances.

Neglect of Studies

Besides entertainments in the community, other practices related to extracurricular activities cause pupils to neglect their studies. They are permitted to engage in too many different activities, taken from regular classes for rehearsals, and forced to return to school after dinner for rehearsals and performances. The demands upon their time reduce the amount they would normally give to class work and home preparation.

Parents of children who are enrolled in college preparatory and business skills programs show deep concern over the effect which heavy involvement in student activities has upon the class work. They are disturbed when marks begin to fall and children are too tired to keep up with daily assignments. They believe in the value of student activities, but plead for a sensible balance between these activities and academic instruction.

This balance can be maintained by limiting the number of

activities in which a pupil may participate, by requiring that activity groups meet during the school day at scheduled periods, and by prohibiting faculty sponsors from taking pupils out of regular classes.

Demands for Money

The practice of demanding money from pupils who wish to take part in student activities is a chronic source of irritation to their families. Parents upon whom these demands are made want to know why school newspapers, magazines, and yearbooks must be purchased, considering what they pay in taxes. They cannot appreciate the reasons for admission charges to concerts, plays, noon-hour movies, debates, and informal dances. They are of the opinion that collections and fees for class dues, hobby clubs, supplies, and equipment are unnecessary.

Parents with low incomes are particularly resentful of demands for money because they impose a hardship on the family. They are joined by intelligent laymen who see in this practice a denial of educational opportunities for some children. They further realize that activities are continued which the board of education could not defend if their financial support was provided from the tax budget.

Demands for money have increased remarkably in the past few years, especially in junior and senior high schools. They are so excessive in some systems that the average pupil cannot afford to participate fully in the activities program. Not only is this condition contrary to the ideals of American education, but it is also militant to the concept of a closer working relationship between the school and the home.

Progress has been made to correct this practice where parents have gone to school officials and insisted upon a reduction in demands for money. They have been able to bring about lower costs, fewer charges, and more acceptance of financial responsibility by local boards of education. Most success has been enjoyed in districts where school officials have taken initiative to work with parents, teachers, interested laymen, and pupils on practical solutions to this problem.

Emphasis on Athletics

The popularity of high-school, interscholastic athletic contests has brought with it a succession of undesirable practices. These practices include the erection of costly football stadiums, night football games, high admission charges, exploitation of players, expensive equipment, hiring and firing of coaches, poor sportsmanship among spectators and players, and the favored treatment of pupils belonging to junior and varsity squads.

The influence behind this growing commercialism and loss of educational perspective in interscholastic athletics has originated with persons, both inside and outside of the school, who are obsessed with sports and the idea that championship teams bring honor and recognition to school and community. They are more interested in these ends than they are in educational values, welfare of pupils, and the great lessons of clean sportsmanship that can be taught through athletic contests.

The problem of cleaning up high school interscholastic athletics and restoring them to their proper place in the student activities program is difficult to solve because of their popularity and the support they receive from adults in the community. The solution depends upon the slow education of the public to a different point of view toward athletic contests and the courage of school boards and administrators to stand up and fight for their convictions.

Nonathletic Contests

The championship idea has taken hold almost as strongly in nonathletic contests in which the school is represented both by teams and by individual pupils. These contests, often sponsored by commercial interests, are held in music, journalism, forensics, dramatics, and other fields of learning. Attractive prizes are generally offered to the winners.

The feverish desire to produce champions has destroyed the amateur quality of these contests. Pupils are trained long and thoroughly by faculty sponsors and coaches whose reputations hang on their performance. Time is taken from regular instruction in clubs and classes to get them ready at the expense of other pupils. Educational purposes are secondary in importance to the value placed on winning. Pupils who win and move from regional to state and national eliminations are often forced to pay their own travel expenses and remain for days away from classes. All in all, the emphasis on championships is anything but wholesome; it amounts to a substitution of publicity for education and the exploitation of pupils.

Like interscholastic athletic contests, the public has come to accept these enterprises without realizing fully their implications for teachers and pupils. They can be controlled and their faults corrected when the facts are presented to parents and other laymen and they are asked to help formulate sounder policies.

High Admission Charges

The charges for admission to school athletic contests, plays, pageants, concerts, and similar student programs have aroused public criticism. Since the school is not in the entertainment business or out to make profit, parents cannot understand why high fees are charged for admission to activities in which their children are participants. Some cannot afford the price of admission, while others pay it under protest out of loyalty to their children. The fact that any parent stays away from a student program for this reason defeats one of the principal purposes for having them, that is, to enable parents to experience first hand the quality of instruction provided by the institution.

Whenever the question is brought up of reducing admission charges or eliminating them entirely, it is met with a series of arguments to the effect that admission fees are necessary to finance the student activities program, that total financing by the board of education would increase taxes, and that the public is more appreciative of entertainment that must be paid for. Interestingly enough, these arguments dissolve when parents and taxpayers are given opportunity to discuss the question with school officials; they would rather have the board of education underwrite the complete cost with tax money and make admission to student programs available to all pupils and parents.

In communities where the student activities program is financed by the board of education, and no reliance is placed on income from admission charges, the results are excellent. More people attend

events that are open to the public, they feel a deeper loyalty to the
school system, and they understand better the educational value
of these activities.

Soliciting and Selling

Soliciting advertising and selling merchandise and magazine
subscriptions are common practices in secondary schools. Advertising
is solicited for printed programs which are distributed at plays,
games, and special events, and for student newspapers, magazines,
and yearbooks. The money is used to defray costs of publication.
Merchandise and magazine subscriptions are sold to raise funds for
financing certain activities, notably, the annual spring trip to New
York, Washington, or elsewhere.

These practices may be injurious to good public relations.
Parents regard as a nuisance the constant requests to purchase merchandise and magazine subscriptions, and these requests are even
more of a nuisance to neighbors and friends of pupils. The soliciting
of advertising is resented by shopkeepers, because they are forced to
spend money for space that yields a low economic return rather than
risk the loss of customer goodwill. Soliciting and selling, if strongly
competitive, may provoke conflict with local merchants and business
executives.

Schools which permit soliciting and selling should take measures
to keep down the number of money-raising projects and instruct
pupils in matters of good relations with the public. The best policy
is to prohibit these practices altogether and to confine sales of
products to the school building.

Pupil Conduct

Pupil conduct at school events influences public opinion. Good
conduct seldom draws much attention, while poor conduct is always
noticed. Adults in attendance frown upon rowdiness at interscholastic
contests and discourteous treatment of team visitors. They dislike
talking, movement, and noise from pupils as they watch a play or
listen to a concert. It is their feeling that a school should be able to
control pupil conduct and teach simple rules of courtesy and respect
for the rights of others.

The conduct of pupils on field trips and excursions in the community is observed closely. Shouting from buses, using profanity, and littering streets with paper draws unfavorable comment. Reports of fighting, drinking, and gambling on overnight excursions are almost certain to raise protests from parents and receive unwanted newspaper publicity.

Generally, poor conduct is confined to a handful of pupils. For their own sake and the reputation of the school, they should be denied the privilege of attending student events which are open to the public and membership on trips and excursions until they learn to uphold established rules of conduct.

Social Affairs

School dances and parties are important activities in the student program. They improve school spirit and enable pupils to gain social experiences which balance work in academic studies. Parents endorse school dances and parties so long as their number, hours, and cost are kept reasonable.

Their objection to the number of school parties and dances comes when these affairs begin to interfere with home life, school work, and health in some cases. The question of when they are held receives even more attention. Parents of pupils in elementary and junior high schools approve an occasional affair which is held early in the evening, but they believe that it is better to schedule them during the school day or directly after dismissal. Parents of senior high school pupils realize, however, that their sons and daughters prefer evening affairs in keeping with their new maturity. What they dislike is the fact that these affairs close late in the evening and that children may not arrive home for sometime afterwards. They are also concerned with the cost of social affairs in high schools where formal dress, corsages, and other expenses are common.

These problems trouble many parents. They would like to see uniform rules adopted and enforced by the school and the home concerning the questions of number, hours, and costs of social affairs. As demonstrated in some communities, satisfactory answers to these questions have been worked out through cooperative efforts of teachers, pupils, and parents.

PLANNED PUBLICITY

Citizen awareness and knowledge of student activities depend in large measure upon planned publicity. Planned publicity is the scheduled and continuous flow of announcements and news stories aimed at acquainting the general public with the nature and purposes of the student program, interpreting current needs and accomplishments, and increasing public attendance. It is carried on by means of different devices, some being more appropriate than others for supplying particular types of information about individual activities. The following list suggests those which may be used to publicize student activities:

1. Releases to community newspapers of straight news, photographic, and feature stories on all activities in the program.
2. School newspaper stories prepared according to a definite schedule that makes allowance for seasonal factors and assures complete and balanced coverage.
3. Calendars of events open to the public, either distributed through the mail, enclosed in report cards, listed weekly on the school page of the local newspaper, or printed on the back of school programs.
4. Exhibits in school corridors and other locations for the benefit of visitors to the building.
5. Notices of events on the bulletin boards of other schools in the community.
6. Printed invitations for parents and prominent citizens to attend special programs.
7. Invitations from student leaders to officers of community groups and organizations to attend special programs.
8. Printed leaflets describing the entire program, or special parts of it, distributed to school visitors, parents, and a selected sampling of people in the community.
9. Bulletins prepared by pupils describing their work in different activities.
10. Pupil talks before civic organizations on special aspects of the program.
11. Printed reports to alumni and invitations to attend various events and functions.
12. Printed posters in store windows advertising important programs to which the public are invited.
13. Spot radio announcements of school events which are open to the public.

Montage by Gene Udell.

15
School Publications

Judging from the growing volume of newsletters, leaflets, pamphlets, bulletins, brochures, and reports, greater use is being made by schools of printed materials for interpreting educational needs, policies, and practices to staff personnel and to the public. Administrators have learned from the experiences of business and industrial organizations, and from their own research, that planned and attractive publications are important tools for conveying information and influencing the actions of readers. They can be edited to appeal to particular groups of people and to the general public, issued on schedule and as occasion demands, distributed with a minimum waste of circulation, and made to tell a detailed story on any subject or merely to publicize an idea or a problem, besides having the advantages of ease and timeliness of production.

While these considerations weigh heavily in favor of printed materials, it must be remembered that they are only one type of instrument in the total program of public relations, and that they are not always appropriate for accomplishing particular purposes. As will be pointed out in this chapter, their use and effectiveness depend upon skillful handling and a thorough knowledge of how they should be planned, prepared, designed and distributed.

285

OBJECTIVES OF SCHOOL PUBLICATIONS

The initial step in planning a school publication is that of deciding
exactly what objective or objectives it should accomplish. At present,
too many school publications represent a tremendous waste of time
and money because they have no goal toward which they are pointed
or because they are produced for no better reason than to imitate
practices of other school systems. A written statement of the precise
objective or objectives of a publication is necessary before anything
else is done. Such a statement determines how the publication will
be developed, to whom it will be distributed, and how its effectiveness may be evaluated.

The major objectives of publications addressed to staff personnel
within the school system are to establish communication that is no
longer possible by means of personal contact; to keep staff personnel
informed about educational policies, practices, and problems; to
explain the reasons why particular courses of action must be taken;
to promote efficiency through recognition of outstanding contributions and services to the school system; to improve morale and
stimulate increased loyalty to the school system; to indicate the
importance of each staff member's place in the education of children;
to supply factual information that will enable staff members to
answer questions more intelligently about the school system; to
expose rumors and reports that breed misunderstanding and promote
dissatisfaction; to build good will on the part of staff members'
families; and to help all employees of the school system become
more appreciative of and skilled in their role of interpreters of the
school system.

The major objectives of publications addressed to parents of
children in the schools are to increase their knowledge and understanding of the educational program; to cultivate a partnership
between the home and school; to point out opportunities for constructive cooperation in solving problems affecting the welfare of
children; to supply information about school services that are available to children; to familiarize parents with educational policies and
the reasons on which they are based; to build respect for teachers; to
promote loyalty for the school system; to increase parent participation

in school affairs; to educate parents about specific school problems, including finance, buildings, instructional materials, methods of teaching, treatment of individual differences, guidance, and existing obstacles to progress; and to keep them informed about the progress of their children.

The major objectives of publications addressed to special community groups and to the general public are to keep citizens informed of the policies, practices, and needs of the school system; to cultivate a sense of partnership in advancing the cause of public education; to report on the progress made toward the achievement of educational purposes; to invite increased lay participation; to show what education the tax dollar buys; to dispel misconceptions and neutralize harmful propaganda against the schools; to recognize individuals and groups who have rendered unusual service to the school system; to show how the school contributes to the improvement of the community; to pave the way for important changes in educational practices; to inform and secure the support of governmental officials; to promote better cooperation with special community groups and organizations; to supply information on subjects of interest to people in the community; to develop confidence and arouse a feeling of public ownership in the school system; and to gain goodwill, cooperation, and support of taxpayers and citizens.

STAFF PUBLICATIONS

Staff publications, commonly known as house organs, are any magazine, newspaper, bulletin, or newsletter issued regularly by a school system for its employees. As previously pointed out, staff publications have several definite objectives, the most important being to keep the staff fully informed about school policies and practices. When a system is small, there is no need for a staff publication, since important information is passed back and forth between administrators and employees through personal contacts daily. But as a system grows larger, other means must be found for retaining communication. The three principal organs for bridging the gap in larger systems are (1) the employee handbook, (2) the bulletin or magazine, and (3) the newspaper or newsletter.

The Employee Handbook

The employee handbook is a basic tool for establishing good internal and external relations. It introduces the new employee to his job, the school system, and, in some cases, the community. From it he learns about the history of the local schools, general philosophy and objectives, organization, administrative personnel, routine procedures, instructional and personnel policies, classroom management, finance and financial problems, special services, public relations responsibilities, and community life. The spirit of friendliness in which it is written gives him a sense of being wanted and a feeling of belonging to the organization.

The handbook permits all staff members to answer intelligently the many questions which are asked about the school in the community. They are able to state with accuracy the tax rate, the amount of bonded indebtedness, the ratio of assessed to true valuation of real property, aid received from the state government, current operating costs, costs per pupil in membership, instructional policies, and other facts of interest to people. The depression years made it clear that every employee should be acquainted with this information in order to represent and interpret the school system to the public.

Most employee handbooks are designed either by the administration or by a committee of administrators and staff members. If they are made up attractively, illustrated with pictures and drawings, and revised annually, they stimulate and challenge employees to do their best for the school system.

Magazine or Bulletin

The school magazine or bulletin is regarded by many administrators as an excellent vehicle for achieving a variety of purposes. Copied after industrial house organs, now known as company publications, its chief aims are to keep staff members informed about the policies and practices of the system and to stimulate and secure their cooperation, loyalty, and support.

An analysis of several magazines and bulletins shows that their contents cover the following types of materials: editorials, statements of school board action, book reviews, lists of instructional aids and materials, educational and personnel policies, signed articles by staff members, reports of committees, announcements, personal notes about staff members, and special honors received by the school system. The materials can be classified under four headings: (1) information about the school system, (2) information about staff members, (3) information about teaching methods, techniques, and materials, and, (4) information of general interest to the teaching profession. Only a few devote space to news items and topics of special concern to noninstructional employees.

Circulation is restricted generally to the official school family— board members and staff members on the payroll of the system. The mailing list sometimes contains the names of editors of similar publications, educators who have requested copies, and selected leaders in the community. Their inclusion is valuable in explaining and publicizing the school system, but it should not affect the objectives of the magazine or bulletin unless the publication is definitely planned for both employees and members of the community. A combination publication has merit if the editor is skillful enough to satisfy the divided interests of these groups.

Most employee magazines and bulletins are financed by school boards out of public funds, unless there is a prohibition in state law. The cost is a charge against administration. In some systems, boards either pay part of the cost and rely upon advertising and subscriptions for the difference or they pass it on entirely to the employees, especially teachers.

Newspaper or Newsletter

The newspaper or newsletter has proven to be the most popular style of staff publication in recent years. Having the advantage of speedy and economical production, it can be printed by three general processes, namely, typewriter style by multigraph, multilith, and mimeograph; offset; and letterpress or printing. The typewriter style permits smaller systems to produce an inexpensive newsletter for many different purposes, but the use of illustrations in the newsletter is restricted to simple line sketches and decorations. A more satisfactory product can be made by the offset process. This process not only is more attractive in appearance but also permits the reproduction of photographs and illustrative materials. Some editors, however, believe that the reproductions fall short of desired standards. The majority of editors hold to the opinion that letterpress reproduction is still the best method of putting out an excellent newspaper or newsletter, even though it is the more costly one.

A good example of a newsletter is *The Staff Reporter* published by the Board of Education of Wilmington, Delaware. Issued monthly and distributed to all employees, it is letterpressed on quality paper, 8½ x 11 inches, with a masthead in color. The length varies from four to eight pages. The pages are made up of two and three columns, and the columns are broken with boxed items, photographs, and line drawings.

Comparative study of successful tabloid newspapers and smaller newsletters indicates that they present the following features: (1) announcements, explanations, and interpretations of school policies and practices; (2) discussions of financial structure and operation; (3) sound editorial policy; (4) excellent editorial treatment; (5) modern appearance; (6) attention to employee interests; (7) timely news stories; and (8) a style of writing that breeds goodwill and friendliness in the school system.

HOME CONTACT MATERIALS

The two leading purposes of home contact materials are to increase parental knowledge and understanding of the educational program and to keep parents informed of the progress their children are making in school. Among the materials used to accomplish these and related purposes are handbooks, special publications, pupil progress reports, and report card enclosures.

Handbooks

Parent handbooks provide a ready source of information for facts about the instructional program and requirements of the school. Their contents are selected on the basis of questions that are asked by parents—beginning and closing hours, vacation dates, rules governing absence and tardiness, health requirements, conferences with teachers, and so forth. In addition, the school's philosophy and objectives, methods of teaching, and opportunities for home-school cooperation are given.

Most parent handbooks today are published by elementary schools. Secondary schools rely upon their student handbooks to answer parent questions. The handbooks for parents of elementary school children are written with more personal appeal than student handbooks. They are illustrated to some extent, bound in attractive covers, and revised annually with the help of parents in many communities. Usually mimeographed and typed with double space, they are easier to read than student handbooks and can be produced at a fraction of the cost.

In some systems a single handbook is prepared for distribution to parents of children at all grade levels and in different school buildings. These handbooks are printed on good stock, cleverly illustrated, highly readable, and are just as attractive as many of the better annual reports.

The growing demand for parent handbooks is indicative of increased popular interest in public education and the desire of parents to know more about schools and how they can work to improve them. Every school system should encourage the preparation of handbooks for parents and invite parents to take part in the selection of the contents.

Special Publications

Special publications for parents fall into five classes—bulletins, newsletters, booklets, leaflets, and folders. Bulletins and newsletters are often the joint work of parents and teachers operating through the home and school association. *Affairs,* for example, of the Oak Lane Country Day School of Temple University is a publication of this kind. Printed, well-illustrated, 6 x 9 inches in size, 20 to 30 pages in length, and published monthly, it is paid for out of funds belonging to the association. The editorial board is made up of representatives of the faculty, student body, parent group, and alumni. The contents feature views by the principal, editorials, signed articles by parents, teachers, and pupils, descriptions of classroom activities, new books and records for children, notes on teachers, announcements, and the like. Though publications such as *Affairs* are fairly common, the majority of bulletins and newsletters are put out at public expense by local school systems.

The trend in this type of publication is definitely toward the four-page newsletter. Most of them are monthly periodicals, printed by offset or letterpress on 8½ x 11 inch paper, laid out in three 2¼ inch columns, and bearing a title suggestive of their purpose, such as *Let's Work Together* or *These Are Your Schools*. The newsletter is a first-class tool for getting essential information into the hands of parents when written in a readable, friendly style, with lively text, and attention-getting illustrations.

Bulletins and newsletters are supplemented with booklets, leaflets, and folders. They are planned to give a fuller explanation of the instructional program, each one describing some part of it in detail. They may talk about methods of teaching reading, music instruction, growth problems, report cards, dental hygiene, fundamentals in arithmetic, vocational guidance, citizenship training, and visual aids to instruction. An excellent example is seen in the booklets for parents of children who are about to enter kindergarten or first grade. Bearing titles of *Happy Journey, Now We Go To School, Getting Ready For School,* and *We Come To School,* they tell of the experiences a child will have and offer suggestions on how the parent can cooperate with the teacher and help at home.

These publications are more effective when issued as a continuing series so that parents get a rounded picture of a broad field, though there are situations where they should be directed at weak spots in parent understanding of specific instructional practices. They should be tied together by a special layout, a central theme, or a color arrangement.

Pupil Progress Reports

The conventional type of report card has been a primary form of written contact with parents for a long time. It tells them at six or eight week intervals what their children are achieving in the subjects listed, and it furnishes them with a record of absence, tardiness, and general behavior. Achievement is reported either in terms of percentages or more commonly in terms of numerals or letters of the alphabet arranged on a point scale. Of late, many educators and some parents have expressed strong dissatisfaction with this report card. They maintain that it does not give an accurate or fair picture of a child's growth and development, that it fails to provide for the objectives of modern schools, and that it has other deficiencies which point up the need for revising the reporting system.

Their efforts to meet these weaknesses have resulted in descriptive ratings, letters to parents, and personal conferences. In descriptive ratings, the conventional report card may be modified by the addition of one or more pages containing descriptions of a child's growth in personal and social habits which the teacher checks; or, a new type of card may be used—a card which contains statements describing the specific habits, attitudes, appreciations, and skills the school is trying to develop. The teacher checks each statement on a three-point scale to indicate excellent, satisfactory, and unsatisfactory progress. Parent reaction, especially to this latter form of reporting, is sharply divided between those who favor its diagnostic value and those who claim that they cannot understand it. Most success with descriptive ratings has come in communities where parents and teachers worked together on the new report card and it was explained to the public before being adopted.

Individual letters from the teacher to the parent are a second innovation aimed at the improvement of reporting. They take the place of the report card and are sent home at least four times a year. The teacher tries to draw a word picture of changes in the habits, attitudes, and achievements of the pupil, underscoring his specific needs, accomplishments, and problems. The effectiveness of individual letters depends upon how well the teacher understands the individual pupil, the spirit in which the letters are written, and the written expression. Unfortunately, the continued writing of individual letters tends to produce a formal and stereotyped communication which lacks a diagnostic meaning. The task, moreover, becomes exceedingly heavy for the teacher who meets a large number of pupils daily.

Increasingly, personal conferences between the parent and teacher are being substituted for the report card or they are made supplemental to it. Held mostly with parents of children in the elementary grades, they are scheduled at regular periods during the year. They have the advantage of bringing the parent and teacher together for a friendly and somewhat objective discussion of the child's progress, an examination of class materials, and a review of scores made on different types of tests. More can be done this way to analyze progress and interpret educational practices than is possible by means of descriptive ratings or individual letters. It is essential, however, that teachers receive training in the techniques of conference procedure before this reporting system is started. Without this training, they may place too much emphasis upon negative elements in the child's behavior and arouse antagonisms toward themselves and the school program.

Besides formal reporting, the teacher can send brief, commendatory notes and samples of good classwork home for parents to see what their children are doing and the progress they are making. A clever teacher can also do much to promote understanding and create goodwill by preparing an occasional newsletter for parents telling about the experiences their chlidren are having, naming youngsters who took part in various activities, and evaluating their accomplishments.

Report Card Enclosures

Report card enclosures are still another means for written contact with parents. They are printed leaflets which describe different aspects of the instructional program, such as spelling, arithmetic, penmanship, reading, health, and guidance. Arranged in a series, they are inserted in the report card at each marking period so that the parent receives six or eight in the course of a school term. By planning the distribution in cycles of three years for the early elementary, later elementary, junior high, and senior high school grades, it is possible to supply continuous information on instructional practices from the time a child starts the first grade until he completes the twelfth grade.

Brief and attractive enclosures are read with interest by many parents. The problem is to see that they receive them. A number of systems which experimented with this method of distribution abandoned it after a short trial period. They found that too many pupils removed the enclosures and discarded them on school grounds and adjoining streets; in fact, they created a public nuisance. But they also found that this was less likely to happen with children in the first three grades and that the practice could be continued safely at this level.

THE ANNUAL REPORT

The annual report to the board of education, citizens, and taxpayers of the school district is regarded by some administrators as the corner-stone of a sound program in public relations. Whether or not this is so depends in large measure upon what else is done to interpret the schools and to involve laymen in their affairs. Aside from this consideration, the reported findings of studies bring out the fact that the annual report does make a valuable contribution to public under-standing and support of the local educational effort.

Purposes

The principal purposes of the annual report, as either expressed or implied in the contents, are (1) to highlight the educational accom-plishments of the system during the past year, (2) to account for the use made of public tax monies, and (3) to bring special problems to the attention of the community. There is another purpose which might be added—to provide a historical record of practices and ac-complishments of the local school system.

Contents

The contents of annual reports published by leading school systems cover a wide range of topics or subjects which are consistent with their purposes. Most attention is given to the school curriculum, followed by discussions of educational finance, personnel, enroll-ments, and attendance. Other items receiving attention are special services, citizenship training, building and equipment needs, adult education, teaching methods, extracurricular activities, individual differences, audio-visual aids, supervisory services, democratic admin-istration, vocational education, health, and in-service training of teachers. Several of the reports tie their contents into a central theme, such as education for modern living, free schools in a free land, and purposeful education for tomorrow's citizens. By running the theme through the entire report, unity is given to the presentation.

Types

Three types of annual reports are employed to tell the education story. They may be referred to as general, serial, and concentrated.

The general type covers the entire range of the school program. Each division of the school system prepares an individual report for the superintendent, and these are edited into a single document with an appropriate introduction. The serial type consists of separate parts of the general report which are published in small booklet form and released monthly; they take the place of the general report. The

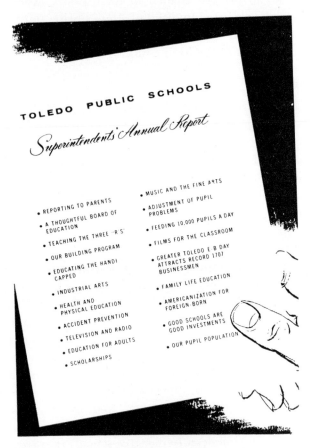

An attractive cover invites attention. Courtesy Public Schools, Toledo, Ohio. (Photo of cover by Gene Udell.)

concentrated type deals exclusively with a single problem or aspect of the total program, such as reading, future building needs, or special class instruction. It affords a more detailed treatment and draws attention to an outstanding need or problem.

Mechanical Features

The mechanical features include size, number of pages, cover, inside stock, illustrative materials, and printing. The most frequent size of the annual report is 8½ x 11 inches, though 6 x 9 and 9 x 12 inch sizes are popular. The length varies from a few pages to more than 100, with the average falling in the interval between 31 and 40 pages. Most reports have attractive covers in two or more colors and a title or theme that appeals to the reader. Printed on good stock, approximately 50 per cent of the total space is given over to illustrative materials—pictures, drawings, and graphs—with suitable headings and captions. The typical report is reproduced by letterpress process. Captions and context are in 6 point type and headings in 12 point type. An increasing number are being put out in 24 point headings, 12 point context, and 6 point captions.

A few districts publish their annual reports in tabloid newspaper form and mail them to all residents. Cities like Toledo, Milwaukee, and Dayton publish their annual reports as rotogravure supplements to Sunday newspaper editions, thus circulating them widely in the community. In smaller districts where printing costs are prohibitive, excellent results have been obtained with mimeographed reports in which pages are broken by line drawings. The possibility of publishing a summary of the annual report, instead of a comprehensive document, should be considered. A summary type of report can be reproduced economically and distributed widely.

SPECIAL REPORTS

A special report is any publication dealing with a single subject or segment of the school program. The purpose is to get information into the hands of the public when it will do the most good. Because local needs and conditions differ, the subjects of special reports differ; nevertheless there are some which should be considered by all districts. These are reports on the budget, building needs, building construction progress, surveys, research studies, and instruction.

Budget

The annual budget statement represents a dollar and cents translation of educational policies and practices. It is one of the most important public documents issued by a school system. Unfortunately, too few laymen understand the technical make-up and vocabulary of the formal budget. Those who do not understand it are likely to base their opinion of the budget on the amount of money it calls for and how this will affect their taxes. They need to have the budget explained and interpreted. One of the best devices for doing this is a special budget report to the people.

This report should be prepared with the average citizen in mind. It should be published in the form of a booklet, bulletin, or leaflet and distributed throughout the community. Technical budgetary terms should be omitted whenever possible or else defined when they are used. Statistical material should be presented in attractive pictographs, colorful charts, and diagrams. The essence of the popular budget should be a brief, clear explanation of services to children in support of each item of expenditure.

Building Needs

There is a place for a special report or a series of special reports, looking ahead to future building needs of the school district. These reports should let parents and taxpayers know how rapidly the district is growing, the influence of this growth upon enrollments, and the anticipated needs for new sites and plant facilities, as well as the age of present structures and when they will need replacement. It is advisable to circulate the reports for three or more years before the public is asked to approve new construction. Unless something is done to educate the community, there is a natural reluctance to increase the rate of millage or support a bond issue, simply because the need is not understood or considered necessary.

Building Construction Progress

Only a small number of school districts publish a special brochure or illustrated booklet on progress being made in the construction of new buildings, yet this type of report is valuable for these reasons: (1) It takes away the feeling which sometimes sets in after a bond or millage campaign that once money is voted the board of education and the administration forget the people; (2) it stimulates a continuing interest in the plant program and the benefits of it to pupils and the community; and (3) it strengthens the concept that citizens are partners in school business. The report should state the name or names of new buildings under construction, tell how far along they are toward completion, approximate dates when they will be opened, describe their features, and list facilities which will be available to the community.

School Survey

The school survey, whether it includes the entire educational program or merely a part of it, is an appropriate subject for planned publicity and a special report which interprets the outcomes to the community. Using all available avenues of communication, citizens should be made acquainted with the reasons for the survey, survey personnel, methods of investigation, scope of the study, possible values for school improvement, and any other points of general interest. The steady flow of this information from the beginning to the completion of the survey allays suspicion and creates a more objective climate for the discussion of findings, conclusions, and recommendations.

The special report which interprets the outcomes of the survey to the community should be prepared after the survey report itself has been presented to the board of education and printed and commented upon in local newspapers. It should take the form of either a concise summary or an accurate digest in which the contents are stated in readable language accompanied by pertinent, visual illustrations. A report of this nature lends itself to general distribution and follow-up through parent-teacher associations and citizens' committees before action is taken on the recommendations.

Research Studies

Research studies and experimental projects are high in publicity and interpretative values. One method for realizing these values is the preparation of special monographs or bulletins reporting specific undertakings and showing how they may apply to the improvement of instruction. Somewhat technical in nature, they can be distributed to staff personnel and capable laymen for their information. Popular interest can be secured more readily through newspaper stories, speakers, and audio-visual devices, although some research monographs should be written for general distribution when the occasion warrants it.

The publicizing of research has several worthwhile advantages. It keeps members of the teaching staff informed of what is taking place within the school system and stimulates interest in the improvement of their own services. It causes parents and people in the community to take notice of another aspect of educational functioning and to reach the conclusion that progress is a fundamental consideration in the school system. Finally, it makes both teachers and the public more amenable to proposals for desirable changes in the curriculum and program of studies.

Instruction

Occasions arise in most school districts when it is important to issue special reports on instruction and instructional practices. The more typical reasons for taking this action are briefly these: (1) to take advantage of a pronounced public interest in some phase of instruction; (2) to meet the need for better citizen understanding of some subject or practice as disclosed by opinion studies or other research; (3) to correct misinformation and rumor that may be detrimental to the school system if allowed to go unchecked; (4) to explain the limitations under which teaching is done and to show how they may be remedied; and, (5) to neutralize the influence of unfair criticism and destructive attacks upon the schools.

The effectiveness of reports depends upon a number of considerations that have been verified by experience. Above all else, they must be accurate, leaving no room for the discovery of errors or grounds on which to question their truthfulness. Moreover, each report should deal exclusively with a single subject, practice, or division of the curriculum in order to produce the understanding that is wanted. As examples, they might bear such titles as the following: *Beginning Steps in Reading, Standards in Business Education, Music for All, Youth Looks at Government, Success in College, Mathematics in Daily Life, Work with Words, No Trouble in Spelling*, and *What Report Cards Say*. Length is not too significant a factor so long as a convincing story is told.

OTHER TYPES OF PUBLICATIONS

Over and above the publications described previously in this chapter are other types which keep the school before the public and help citizens to understand and appreciate more fully the nature of the educational program. They include general information booklets, letter stuffers, miscellaneous publicity devices, diplomas and certificates, instructional guides, and school board proceedings.

General Information Booklets

General information booklets aim to give a broad picture of the school system at work or some division of it. They are prepared for the public at large and represent a means for reaching many taxpayers who may not receive home contact materials and specialized reports.

A few examples of better publications which fall into this class are: *A Vocational School Grows Up* (Philadelphia, Pennsylvania); *Educational Progress in the Chicago Public Schools* (Chicago, Illinois); *Know Your Schools* (Monterey, California); *Public Education in Los Angeles, California* (Los Angeles County, California); *Arlington Schools* (Arlington, Virginia); *Seattle Schools* (Seattle, Washington); *Road Tests* (Dearborn, Michigan); *Connecticut Schools Today* (Hartford, Connecticut); *Distributive Education* (Harrisburg, Pennsylvania); and *Our Children at School* (Allentown, Pennsylvania).

Lacking uniformity in size and shape, these publications take the form of attractive brochures, pictorial pamphlets, illustrated booklets, mimeographed bulletins, and tabloid news sheets. Many are put up in attention-getting covers and have attractive layouts, excellent narrative, and good illustrations. Their physical differences are probably influenced by the imagination of the production team, cost, and the cultural composition of the community.

Letter Stuffers

To increase further public knowledge of the educational program, a few school systems have adopted from business and industry the practice of inserting a printed leaflet or folder in each piece of outgoing, local mail. The leaflets are sometimes planned in a continuous series for a period of two or three years or they are developed in response to immediate needs and conditions. Issued monthly, they are varied in color and design to sustain reader interest. Being light enough in weight, they can be sent postage-free with first-class mail and thereby enjoy a wide distribution in the community.

It is the opinion, in school systems where letter stuffers are used, that they are an excellent means for carrying messages to many individuals who otherwise would have slight contact with the school. However, they must be kept brief, readable, and varied in order to hold the attention of a diversified audience.

Miscellaneous Printed Matter

Several miscellaneous devices for interpreting and publicizing the school are included in the publication program of some systems. One of the devices is that of placing a short statement in each of the printed programs given out at open affairs, like a student musical, a student play, or a school night program. The purpose of printing the statement in the program is to tell something of importance which the public should know about the school system. It could relate to enrollment, building needs, health examinations, attendance laws, and the like. Because members of the audience have time to look through the program before an affair begins, at intermission, and afterwards at home, the statement is read more carefully than most printed matter, including school stories appearing in local newspapers.

A second device consists of using school stationery and blotters to carry a slogan or a factual statement which, through constant repetition, becomes associated in the public mind with the school system. Slogans like "Better Schools Make Better Communities" and "Schools Safeguard Democracy," or the statement, "This School System has Served This Community for 90 Years" are examples. Professional publicity and advertising people state that the schools have not made enough use of slogans and factual statements in the shaping of public opinion. There is no reason why these devices should not be used, providing they are truthful.

Student-made posters for school and community purposes offer further opportunities for constructive publicity when they are labelled plainly with the name of the boy or girl who made them as well as the name of the school. The labelling of posters for community drives, projects, and improvement campaigns gives to the taxpayer the feeling that pupils are being taught to take a direct interest in local affairs and that the school is cooperating with citizens.

In addition, car cards and billboards are considered to be effective means for emphasizing the worth of public education or bringing current needs to public attention. Whether or not they are legitimate publicity devices for a school system to employ is a question presently under debate. It is pointed out by some educators that car cards and billboards take away from the dignity of the school and that it is questionable that boards of education have a legal right to purchase advertising space with public funds. On the other hand, the claim is advanced that such advertising is in the public interest and is, therefore, justifiable.

Diplomas and Certificates

In the earlier, selective high school where the instructional emphasis was almost entirely upon preparation for college, the diploma stood for quality in academic achievement. This is not quite the case today. Many high schools now grant a diploma to every student, regardless of academic achievement, who attends regularly for a period of years, works with reasonable diligence, and behaves as a good citizen. Others grant the diploma to students who receive passing marks in their subjects of study and a certificate to those who meet the requirements of attendance, effort, and citizenship. These departures from the traditional diploma are due to a phenomenal growth in enrollments, the changed nature of the school population, and the vast differences found among students in intellectual, social, and emotional capacities. The high school is for all youth, as it should be, and not just for the few in the upper ranges of scholastic aptitude.

Too many employers of high school graduates assume that the diploma is a guarantee of general, high-level ability. They have scarcely any idea of differences found among students or problems of ministering to their needs. They hire them without looking into their school records or finding out what they are best fitted to do. When graduates fail to measure up to what is expected, the claim is made that students were better prepared in the past than they are today. As inaccurate as this claim is, it raises a serious question of public confidence in the efficiency of the secondary school program.

A number of steps have been taken to off-set this belief by making the diploma and certificate more meaningful to employers. They include (1) reducing the size of the diploma and certificate so they may be carried when graduates apply for employment, (2) designating on the diploma and certificate the name of the curriculum in which the holder was enrolled—college preparatory, general, business, and vocational, (3) issuing different kinds of diplomas for different curriculums, (4) stating on the back of the diploma and certificate the names of the subjects studied, marks received, and a record of student activities, and (5) writing in an appropriate space on the diploma or certificate an estimate of the student's ability or competency in a field of preparation.

While some students and their parents protest against making such information a part of the diploma and certificate, and too few employers make use of either credential in the selection of job applicants, still much criticism has been prevented among professional and business people who insist upon seeing the diploma or certificate and find the information helpful in screening and fitting young people to the jobs they offer. Through continued publicity and personal contacts by school representatives, more employers can be persuaded to include the informative type diploma and certificate in the employment process and to contact schools for supplementary data.

Instructional Guides

Instructional guides are courses of study, outlines of content, resource units, bulletins on methods, and similar publications prepared for use by teachers of particular subjects, grades, or areas of study. Their circulation is restricted to administrators, supervisors, and instructional staff members, with the exception of educators and educational organizations to whom they are sent as a matter of professional courtesy.

It is good public relations practice to place copies of all instructional guides on file in the office of every administrative and supervisory officer where they may be examined freely by any parent or taxpayer who wants to know what pupils are being taught, how they are being taught, and the instructional materials being used for the purpose. The right to see the guides does much to curb possible suspicion of subversive teaching and certainly appeases many individuals who would otherwise be critical of the school. Those who are skeptical about the nature and worth of what is taught can straighten out their own thinking when they have access to an authentic source of information.

School Board Proceedings

Most states require by law that local school boards keep minutes of their official proceedings. The minutes are important for a number of reasons. They furnish a history of the local system and a record of previous decisions. They define the powers and duties of the superintendent of schools and the scope of his authority. They are a ready source of reference in making decisions that are consistent with prior actions. Courts of law admit them in evidence, providing they are properly kept, approved, and signed by a board officer. And finally, they are a significant factor in developing public confidence in the integrity and competency of board members.

A sure way for a school board to undermine confidence and arouse suspicion is to conceal the minutes of its meetings. This is sometimes done by refusing to supply the press with a complete and accurate statement of the proceedings; sometimes by deciding items of business in executive session and then referring to them by a code number when they are voted upon in public meeting. These practices, and others designed to keep the public in ignorance, inevitably bring on the accusation of double dealing and the eventual investigation by newspaper editors and leading groups of citizens.

Copies of board minutes should be kept on file in the office of the superintendent, the board secretary, the individual building principals, and the public library where they may be read by any citizen. It is likewise desirable that they be distributed after each meeting to a selected list of individuals in the community. The press should be asked to cover meetings and assisted in getting accurate reports for publication in local papers. Information should be disseminated concerning deliberations and actions taken by the board of education.

PREPARATION OF PUBLICATIONS

The extent to which informative and interpretative literature is read, understood, and accepted by various audiences depends a good deal upon how well it is written, illustrated, and designed. Writing, illustration, and design are primary factors in telling successfully the school story through the medium of print. Unless these factors are handled skilfully, publications are apt to fall short of their goals.

Writing

The writing should be done by a person or persons who know how to put facts and ideas into simple, readable language which attracts attention and holds interest. Usually, there are one or two staff members in most school systems who have a flair for writing and can learn to produce readable copy. They cannot be expected to do this work along with regular responsibilities; good writing takes time and allowance for it should be made in the daily schedule.

If it is necessary to go outside of the school system, then a local editor or commercial publicist can be engaged from time to time to write the texts of important publications.

The tendency in larger districts is to hire an experienced writer and to place him on the staff of the superintendent, or to hire a director of public relations who is competent enough to supervise the entire publications program. Where these or similar practices have been followed, the results amply justify the cost of the service as measured in terms of increased citizen understanding and support of education.

Every publication should be planned before the text is written. The plan should take into account the purpose of the proposed publication, the audience to whom it will be addressed, their probable interests, and an outline of the contents. The purpose defines need and gives direction to the publication, while the nature and interests of the audience influence the selection and handling of content. In every publication, the audience must be given information in which the members see something of value to themselves or to their children or, at least, they are brought into contact with facts they want to know. The outline guides the writer in his work and tells him how much space should be given to points that are listed. The outline should further describe the length of the text and the illustrations that go with the various parts of it.

Most publications start with a brief but interesting introduction which helps to carry the reader into the main body of the subject. Like the introduction, the body of the subject must be discussed in simple, direct, and precise language that the average person understands. Each word should say what it is supposed to say with just the right shade of meaning. If technical terms and phrases are used occasionally, their meaning should be made clear. This can be done best through realistic examples rather than formal definitions.

Similar concern should be shown for sentence and paragraph construction. Studies in the field of reading indicate that short sentences are easier to read and understand than long sentences, but long sentences may be used now and then to provide variation and prevent choppiness in the style of writing. Brief paragraphs enable the reader to grasp meaning more readily than lengthy ones, besides affording breaks in the solid type to make the page look more interesting.

No copy should be sent to the printer until it has been checked for readability. Readability tests determine whether or not the text can be read with ease and understanding by the general public. A list of the better known tests are cited in the chapter bibliography. They take into consideration such factors as the average length of sentence, number of simple sentences, number of strong verb forms, percentage of familiar words, percentage of abstract words, and the number of personal references. It should be noted that a readability check is made after the text has been written; good writing demands originality and imagination—it cannot be done according to a formula.

Illustration

The effectiveness of publications is increased when the contents are illustrated with photographs, line drawings, cartoons, charts, diagrams, maps, graphs, and pictographs. Because people enjoy looking at illustrations, these visual devices help to dramatize a story and make it more appealing. They are likewise valuable in translating abstract concepts into concrete and meaningful terms, breaking the text into smaller blocks of print, and gaining the attention of people with widely differing interests and educational backgrounds.

The achievement of these values depends, however, upon a series of requirements. (1) Each illustration or visual device must satisfy a particular purpose. A photograph, for example, may be the best medium available for injecting more human interest into a story; a pictograph, for lightening difficult statistical material and making it understandable. (2) The illustration should be excellent in art features. Unless a photograph has a professional touch and line drawings are clean, sharp, and attractive, there is danger that the graphic materials may ruin the impressiveness of the publication. (3) An appropriate caption should be placed either above or below every illustration. A caption is necessary to supply the reader with information about the illustration and draw his attention to the main ideas it contains. (4) The amount of information presented in any one illustration should be limited to essential details. The tendency to include too much information confuses the reader and fails to center his attention on the main ideas. (5) Each illustration should have the same qualities of interest which are demanded of the text—timeliness, simplicity, appeal, and content that says something the reader needs or wants to know.

The question of illustrations may raise a problem in districts where budgets are small and publications are mimeographed. Actually, much can be done with line drawings, maps, charts, graphs, diagrams, and pictographs, but photographs and color cannot be used. Distributors of mimeograph and multilith supplies have tracing patterns for reproducing good drawings, or an art teacher in the system may be enlisted to prepare illustrations. Moreover, shaded effects may be obtained through the use of shading plates to make art work more attractive. It is important that illustrations approximate the requirements stated previously, otherwise they may weaken rather than strengthen the interpretative value of publications.

Design

Scarcely less important than writing and illustration is design or the general appearance of the publication and the arrangement of the materials within it. The principal aim of design is to attract the reader and induce him to become acquainted with the contents of the publication. The achievement of this aim includes considerations of size, length, cover, introductory materials, layout of text and illustrations, headings, color, typography, and paper.

Size and length are determined by purpose, nature of the subject matter, and available funds. In size, school publications range from simple folders suitable for stuffing into report cards and letters to regular newspapers. The more popular sizes are 8½ x 11 and 6 x 9 inches. The larger sizes are better adapted to pictorial presentations, effective typography, and appealing layouts. As to length, they run anywhere from four to one hundred pages. Most of the better booklets and brochures are sixteen to thirty pages in length.

The cover is generally the first thing which a reader looks at when he receives a publication. It may capture his attention and arouse curiosity about the contents or leave him with no feeling at all. In some ways, the cover performs the same function as a headline of a newspaper story or the title of a magazine article. Cover appeal may be achieved with clever drawings and photographs and a subtle use of colors, but there are instances when type alone will do the job.

The doorway to subject matter in a publication is the title page and the table of contents. The reader automatically turns to them for a quick overview or plan of the publication. They should set a pattern for the publication and harmonize with the treatment of the textual material.

The most essential feature of design is layout of the text and illustrations. Every publication presents peculiar problems which call for study, artistic ability, knowledge of type faces, and keen judgment. Weight of color, strength of lettering, location of cuts, balance of white space on sides and at top and bottom, and values assigned to text and illustrations are points of major concern. It is not expected that the author, and the artist who makes line drawings and selects photographic materials, will be responsible for final layout. They should make the preliminary sketches indicating blocks of space, suggested margins, location of headings and captions, and key the text copy and illustrations which an experienced layout man can work from in preparing the final copy for production.

Chapter, section, and subsection headings should be brief, lively, and set in attractive display type. They should give the gist of the story to the person who casually thumbs through a publication and set the stage for the reader who seeks more detailed information. Expressed in color, they lend strength and add interest to a publication.

Design is not complete until the type face or faces have been selected as well as the paper that is appropriate for a specific kind of publication. The selection of type face is something which cannot be left entirely to the person who is responsible for editing school publications. He should be familiar with the more common old style and modern designs of type and their uses, but rely heavily upon the advice of an experienced printer who has originality and imagination. The same is true with regard to the selection of paper.

DISTRIBUTION AND PUBLICITY

Provision should be made in the publication program for the distribution of printed materials to members of selected audiences. Although methods of distribution will differ with different types of publications and the nature of the community, those more commonly employed by school systems may be described as follows:

1. Enclosing leaflets and folders in report cards which children take home for their parents' signatures.

2. Sending booklets and brochures which are too large for enclosure in report cards home with children.

3. Stuffing outgoing, local mail with printed folders which are changed each month throughout the school year.

4. Mailing small and inexpensive publications to occupants at the addresses listed in the city directory or the tax roll for the community.

5. Distributing pertinent publications to persons attending parent-teacher association meetings or else mailing them to members of the association.

6. Distributing packets of published literature to persons attending open house and similar programs held by the school system.

7. Placing important publications in the waiting rooms of physicians, dentists, and other professional persons in the community.

8. Mailing annual reports and special publications to community leaders, officers of various organizations, and a random sample of parents.

9. Sending a definite number of copies of outstanding publications to building principals for redistribution to staff members and parents.

10. Furnishing instructional and noninstructional personnel employed by the board of education with publications containing information they should know about the school system or else publishing concise summaries in their own publications.

11. Developing a classified mailing list of persons who should receive different types of publications and correcting this list periodically for address changes, deaths, and new listings.

Even though publications reach the hands of persons for whom they are intended, there is still a question of whether or not they will be read. It is a safe assumption that a reasonable percentage of the members of any selected audience will either read or scan a publication they receive, but that the percentage will rise or fall with the quality of appeal made by the cover, text, and design. It is also a safe assumption that interest in reading a publication will be much higher when it is called to the attention of people through planned publicity.

Planned publicity should accompany and follow the distribution of publications. Copies of important publications should be sent to newspaper, radio, and telecast news editors whose comments are often helpful in stimulating popular interest. At the same time, straight and feature news stories should be prepared and placed in the hands of these editors with release dates fitted to the distribution and follow-up schedule. Wider circulation and use of annual and special reports may be obtained without additional costs if editors of local newspapers will publish them serially.

Further, notices of important publications may be mailed to parents and announcements printed in student and community newspapers stating that copies are available by writing or telephoning to the office of the superintendent, or that they have been placed in the offices of building principals and in libraries from which they may be borrowed. Attention can likewise be called to publications at parent-teacher meetings, open house and special event programs, and in home contact materials. The possibility should not be overlooked of having board and staff members discuss school reports before community groups and present some of them with the aid of charts, graphs, slides, and film strips.

Montage by Gene Udell.

16

Newspaper Publicity

The newspaper is one of the better mediums for publicizing and interpreting the educational program. Its effective use is contingent upon a thorough and practical understanding of the entire process involved in preparing school news and cultivating wholesome relations with the press.

WHAT IS SCHOOL NEWS?

School news may be defined as information that is of interest to the public. It may be information that people wish to know about the school as well as information they should know in order to judge intelligently the value of the institution and its work.

Since school news must compete daily with material from hundreds of other sources for newspaper space, it must be newsworthy. Newsworthiness means that the information contains elements which make it news—news the press will accept and the public will read. One important element is timeliness, because news is a perishable commodity. What is news in the morning may not be news at night, or what is news today may not be news tomorrow, the next week, or a year from now. The information may concern a new aspect of an

312

old event, an incident or fact connected with interests of the moment, or a forecast or prediction of things to come that make it fresh, alive, and timely.

A story is news when it reports something unusual or something usual done in an unusual way. For example, a proposal that parents and their high school sons and daughters exchange places for a day would be news, because this sort of event seldom, if ever, occurs and many people would be interested in it. If an event contains an element of conflict or if there is a dramatic side to it, the papers will regard it as news. There would be no difficulty in securing space for a story about how secretarial students defeated their prospective employers in a spelling contest and refuted the criticism that schools fail to teach pupils how to spell correctly. Opposition to night football, hearings on the site of a proposed junior high school building, and a parent campaign for higher teacher salaries are further examples of stories in which the elements of conflict and drama are prominent.

The human interest factor stands high in news value because people like to read about other people, and especially children, when the information appeals to sentiment and touches emotions. There is no end to material along this line in the life of a school. Stories can be written describing the care of animals in science laboratories, services of teachers who go to the homes of bed-ridden children, acts of courage and sportsmanship on the playing field, new equipment for guarding health, and the way in which individual pupils succeed despite serious handicaps.

A story that causes the reader to speculate on the consequences of a discovery, action, or decision is news. For example, deep concern would be shown by parents over the news that a case of tuberculosis was discovered in the school, while others might consider what action should be taken to protect the health of children in the future. A similar chain of direct and speculative reaction would be set in motion with the announcement that the board of education voted to eliminate interscholastic athletic contests and to require all pupils to participate in an intramural program at the close of the regular school day.

Anything that happens to a prominent school official, a teacher, or a pupil may have news value. This would be true if they won an award in a nation-wide contest, received appointment to an important civic committee, were invited to visit a foreign government, published an article in a popular magazine, or received a special honor for meritorious service. Even the mentioning of names in the paper is news. Individuals like to read about themselves or see their names in print, and they pass this information on to family and friends. Editors know that the inclusion of names sells newspapers, though the story is nothing more than a brief account of graduation exercises and the listing of pupils who received their diplomas.

Any person who has responsibility for gathering and preparing school news must be sensitive to these and related news elements in the everyday routines and daily life of the institution. Unless this person can distinguish between a story that is worth no more than a paragraph and one that should go on the front page, the chances are slender of being successful in obtaining newspaper publicity.

IMPORTANCE OF PUBLICITY

Healthy newspaper publicity is important to the maintenance of a good school system. Through newspaper publicity, people become better acquainted with institutional activities and take more interest in the program, needs, and objectives of the school system. Handled properly, it increases good will, adds prestige, promotes financial support, prevents the spread of misinformation, points up existing problems, builds intelligent attitudes, develops appreciation of school services, and stimulates individual citizens to accept their responsibilities for the improvement of education. These contributions are consistent with the purposes of the school as a social institution and the objectives of public relations.

PUBLICITY POLICY

A statement of policy should be prepared for the guidance of personnel who are charged with responsibility for newspaper publicity. It should include the following concepts:

The public is entitled to a sincere, honest, and continuous presentation of selected facts and pertinent information on all aspects of the educational program.

Press releases shall qualify as news, say something that is worth saying, and be consistent with the dignity and character of the institution.

The school, rather than the individuals who administer its affairs, shall be the focal point of publicity.

The effectiveness of newspaper publicity shall be judged in terms of popular understanding of the educational program and concern for its improvement, not the amount of space obtained in local newspapers.

Friendly and impartial relations shall be carried on with the press, and at no time shall school officials suppress information or engage in practices which are contrary to the best interests of the institution.

NEWS COVERAGE

As set forth above, citizens and taxpayers are entitled to information on the total school program. Each area of service should be reported and a conscious effort made to keep the reporting in balance so that one area is not favored at the expense of another. The school cannot expect the public to understand and appreciate its work or take constructive action for its improvement unless all the facts are presented for consideration.

Does educational news today represent a broad and balanced picture of the school program? The answer can be obtained readily by running periodic checks on school news appearing in community newspapers. On the average, it will be found that a preponderance of educational news deals with extracurricular activities, mostly sports, and that these stories appear in the back sections of the paper. Judged by column inches of space and number of individual stories, news pertaining to parent-teacher associations and officials and teachers of the local school system will follow in rank order. Thereafter, the inventory will show a wide scatter of items on instructional methods, school board meetings, pupil progress, exhibits, school finance, building needs, adult education, American Education Week, teachers' conventions, scholarships, health of pupils, and so forth. Mentioned from one to six times a year, these topics make up less than one-fourth the total amount of space assigned to educational news.

Despite careful planning, the school may be limited in the scope of its reporting by the newspapers themselves. Many editors believe that educational news does not have much appeal to the reading public. They seem to think that parents and taxpayers prefer stories about extracurricular activities and the material side of the school system rather than instruction and pupil achievement. This point of difference has been made the subject of numerous studies. The results consistently show that parents and taxpayers want information dealing specifically with instructional methods, methods of reporting pupil progress, instructional developments, comparisons of achievement in one school with that of another, promotional practices, guidance programs, special education, classroom techniques and devices, physical examinations, relation of school health to achievement, educational values, discipline, behavior, attendance, and teachers. Actually, editors are supplying their readers with information on topics in which they have the least interest. At the same time, they are preventing the school from meeting its obligation to keep the public fully informed of its aims, activities, and accomplishments.

The coverage may be poor for another and more serious reason —that of bias on the part of the newspaper. While most newspapers respect the canons of journalism and perform a public service, there are some which try to influence their readers against the local school system in the way they handle the news. An inconsequential story may be selected and given a prejudicial headline, for example, "Ex-School Aid Indicted in Theft"; misleading heads may be written which are inconsistent with the body of the story; or the lead paragraphs may be slanted to leave an entirely false impression. Favorable news may be buried on the inside of the paper and critical news placed on the front page. Occasionally, trivial incidents are made the excuse for damaging editorials. In some instances, the story is reported incorrectly or the facts are altered to fit the viewpoint of the paper. Such practices make it difficult for the school to obtain desirable publicity.

But the causes may stem from the school system just as much as from the newspapers. Too few school systems follow definite publicity policies which would help to keep their releases in balance. They have a tendency to seek whatever space is available for the sake of publicity itself, and editors complain openly that much of the copy they receive is loaded with propaganda for advertising the institution and its personnel. Often the responsibility for gathering and preparing educational news is delegated to untrained persons who cannot recognize a good story or sense possibilities for future news developments. Their releases may even be prepared so poorly that they are not suitable for publication. School people could do more in bringing the meaning and news value of reports, programs, and contributions to the attention of reporters and editors.

TYPES OF NEWS STORIES

The types of stories most used to report school news are known as straight news, feature, and photographic stories. They are supplemented at times with editorials and letters-to-the-editor. Each serves a distinctive purpose that will be explained along with other details to show how they can be employed in educational publicity.

Straight News

The straight news story is the backbone of educational publicity. Factual in content, it answers the questions of *who, what, why, when,* and *where* about an event or happening, and sometimes *how.* The style is objective and impersonal, direct and uncolored. Emphasis in the story is placed upon the event or happening. The details are arranged in a decreasing order of their importance.

Here is an example of a simple, straight news story:

NEW TEACHERS DUE WELCOME AT SCHOOLS

Committees from the Duluth Teachers' association and the Principals and Supervisors' association will act as a welcoming committee to new teachers from 8 a.m. to 3 p.m. next Wednesday, Sept. 3. They will be in the administration building of the board of education to help teachers find places in which to live.

The institute for new teachers will open at 8:30 a.m., Thursday, in room 125 of Central high school. Alvin T. Stolen, superintendant of schools, will discuss the philosophy of the Duluth public schools. Following this meeting, and again at 1 p.m., teachers will meet with supervisors.

On Friday, teachers will go to their buildings, where their principals will confer with them on the curriculum, textbooks, supplies, records and reports, and school procedures and facilities.

Duluth, Minnesota, *Duluth Herald*—9/1/53

This story satisfies the questions which a straight news report should answer. But it does more than that. Being an announcement, it sets the stage for the cover and follow-up stories. The cover story will relate in detail what took place at the meetings for new teachers. It will be reported the same day the meetings were held. The follow-up story will summarize and interpret the meetings a day or two later, using the reactions of new teachers to the meetings for a fresh news angle. This sequence of the advance, cover, and follow-up stories assures better publicity for newsworthy events.

Feature Story

The feature story is more than a presentation of factual information. It answers the same questions as a straight news story, but gives the answers in an interesting and lively way. Built around some unique aspect of an event or a personality, it is designed to evoke a smile or a laugh, appeal to the imagination, or stir the emotions of the reader. Perhaps it might concern the predicament of a child who lost his carfare and how he got to school; a comparison of an eighth-grade class today with one twenty years ago; correspondence with children in foreign countries; or unusual projects undertaken by pupils in a general science class. The supply of feature stories is unlimited in every school.

Here are the opening paragraphs of two feature stories written with an appeal to the imagination:

SIXTH GRADERS PLAN A TRIP

By Dora Mary MacDonald

When Miss Dorothy Shaw, sixth grade teacher at Ensign, climbs to the top of the Eiffel tower in Paris this summer, 39 pupils will be with her—in spirit. They became so greatly interested in her European tour that they planned her trip along with her, itinerary, places to see, ways to get there.

From this interest developed a classroom project. Each pupil planned a European trip for himself, gaining information on foreign countries through interviews, travel folders, books, magazines, newspapers, maps and atlases.

Duluth, Minnesota, *Duluth News-Tribune*—5/6/56

STRESS HANDWRITING FOR
EASY READING

"Write so someone else can read it," and "Please print."

These two demands have helped more than anything else to determine the way handwriting is taught today.

Dearborn, Michigan, *The Dearborn Guide*—11/10/55

The feature story offers a better opportunity for talking directly to the reader than any other type of news story. No restrictions are placed on the time element, organization and style of writing. Its literary quality is limited only by the imagination and skill of the reporter. He must, however, respect the facts concerning persons and incidents which are mentioned in the story.

Photographic Story

Increasingly greater use is being made of the photographic story in the reporting of school news. This type of story is made up of an overline, picture, and caption. The overline, which appears above the picture, is a brief statement summarizing the story. The caption, which appears underneath the picture, explains its meaning and points out what is worth noting. In modern journalism, the overline is sometimes eliminated or else it is combined with the caption.

The photographic story almost always draws the highest reader attention. This has been proven in every readership survey conducted in recent years by newspapers and commercial news agencies. It is because people like to look at pictures and prefer them to the printed word. They can grasp the meaning more quickly, besides feeling that what they see is more truthful than what they read.

Editors want picture stories that will measure up to the requirements of their papers. Although the requirements differ somewhat on minor points, there is fairly general agreement on the major ones. First of all, a picture must have photographic excellence. It cannot be too light, too dark, misty or blurred. The details must stand out clearly against a background that is appropriate for a particular story. Second, the composition must be good. Good composition is an arrangement of persons and objects which catches the eye and draws attention to the focal point of the picture. Third, the content of the picture must be important. Content is judged with reference to the person or persons in the picture and the question of whether or not they are prominent enough to arouse reader interest. It is judged further with reference to news value. The picture may say something that is timely—for example, a demolition crew tearing down old houses to make way for a new school and a public playground. It may show something people want to see—perhaps a senior high school student receiving a college scholarship for winning a national science contest. Whatever the picture says or shows, it must be news. And then the content is judged with reference to the amount of action portrayed. Action is what gives life to pictures and determines the impact they have on readers. The action may be subtle and suggestive or it may by direct and moving. Excellent photography and composition, though essential, are secondary to content in any photographic news story.

Whenever possible, pictures should be used to illustrate straight news and feature stories. Unlike pictures in photographic stories, these may not say much by themselves, but combined with text they give meaning to a story. Schools have learned that it pays to maintain a picture file from which acceptable pictures can be pulled at a moment's notice. They keep on hand glossy prints of school officials, teachers, student leaders, new buildings, playfields, laboratories, health units, shops, student organizations, and action photos. They find that more of their stories are published when they are illustrated with pictures.

Editorial

The editorial is a type of story in which opinions are expressed by the newspaper on public questions. As a rule, it is not considered to have a place in publicity releases prepared by the school. This is a mistake for the reason that some local newspapers will accept editorials and print them as a service to their readers. They recognize that educators are more competent to discuss school matters than their own reporters, and that they present the facts without trying to bias the reader. Bond issues, vocational education, reading methods, building sites, parent-teacher associations, athletic contests, and citizenship training are suitable subjects for editorials.

Even though local newspapers discourage the preparation of editorials, the school can influence the nature and quality of those written by editors and special editorial writers. Friendly conferences make it possible to discover what school questions stand out in the thinking of an editor and how receptive he is to suggestions for timely editorials. He may welcome ideas of what should be taken up in editorial columns as well as offers to supply accurate background material. This aspect of educational publicity has been neglected by the majority of school people, yet many excellent editorials have appeared in local papers because of the suggestions from alert administrators and publicity directors.

Letters to the Editor

Letters to the editor are the views expressed by citizens on questions of current interest, published by newspapers under such titles as "Voice of the People," "What People Think," and "Letter to the Editor."

They rank high in reader interest.

Letters to the Editor have several uses in the program of newspaper publicity for schools. When written by board members, administrators, and teachers, they are an effective means for answering some forms of criticism and mischievous errors. For example, suppose the statement was made publicly by a citizen that admission fees from student plays were pocketed by the dramatics coach. In this case it would be well to write a brief letter pointing out the error and explaining the disposition of the money. Under no circumstances, however, should school officials take up serious criticisms or attempt to meet destructive attacks through letters to the editor. There are other and better ways for solving such problems without running the risk of engaging in open conflict.

Letters to the editor provide an excellent opportunity for expressing appreciation for services rendered to the school—help from parents in making costumes for a pageant, interviews granted by city officials to pupils in their study of municipal government, and cooperation of civic groups in the dedication of a new building. Advantage can be taken of this newspaper feature to thank the general public for, let us say, their fine attendance at programs in observance of

American Education Week. The administrator will find that it pays
to write a letter now and then commending the newspaper itself for
fine coverage and accurate reporting of significant school events and
happenings.

A timely letter may inspire parents, taxpayers, and even pupils to
state their ideas and opinions on an important educational question.
Instances are numerous of where an outpouring of letters from a
cross-section of people in the community put across a bond issue,
influenced the school board to improve health facilities, and silenced
a vocal and antagonistic minority. The public should be encouraged
to protect their vested interests in the school and to make their views
known. This is one of the methods by which it can be done.

NEWS SOURCES

News is found everywhere in the school system. There is never a
scarcity of it. For every story published, a dozen more could be
written containing important information. A check list, like the following, indicates sources from which stories may be drawn. If the
check list is developed with the aid of professional reporters, it will
be richer in ideas and practical suggestions, besides having the further
value of familiarizing the reporters with the make-up and operation
of the school system. Daily reference to the check list leads to better
copy and broader coverage.

Check List of News Sources

Administrative Activities
    Board meetings
    Board actions
    Board members
    Board elections
    Board officers
    Speaking engagements
    Programs under consideration
    Addresses made
    Recognition received
    New administrators
    Surveys conducted
    Changes in organization
    Cost of education
    Record systems
Growth in number of employees
Interviews with board members
Interviews with administrators
School calendar
Slogans adopted
Research studies
Educational needs
Long-range problems
Attendance at conferences
Participation in community pro-
    jects
Classroom Activities
    Field trips and excursions
    Methods of teaching
    Curriculum study

Curriculum changes
Testing program
Results of testing
Special study projects
Exhibits
Demonstrations
New instructional materials
Textbook selection
Library references
New equipment
Trends in teaching practices
Promotion policies
New techniques and devices
Work of supervisors
Homework policies
Evaluating pupil progress
Parent participation
Provision for handicapped children
Guidance problems
Course offerings
Educational objectives
Humorous incidents
Unusual happenings
Success stories of individual children
Character development

Community Activities
Services to community
Use of community resources
Citizen participation in school program
Special lay committees
School-community projects
Staff participation in community affairs
Cooperation with community groups
Community surveys and opinion polls

Activities of Graduates
Business success
Special awards and honors
Reunions
Acts of valor
Success in college
Contributions to school
Alumni programs
Marriages and births

Parent Activities
Parent-teacher association programs
Father and son affairs
Mother and daughter affairs
Services to the school
Conferences with parents
Participation in school
Special parent projects
Parent publications
Officers of parent-teacher association
Attendance at educational conferences

Plant Activities
New building construction
New building financing
New building locations
Features of new buildings
Community use of buildings
Special recreation programs for adults
Building maintenance
New installations
Dedicatory exercises
Safety measures
Renovations and extensions

Pupil Activities
Academic achievement
Vocational preparation
Scholarships, awards, and special honors
Hobby interests
Success in special fields
Outstanding talent
School clubs
Musical programs
Athletic events
Various contests
Assembly programs
Student council
Pageants and festivals
Good deeds and acts of heroism
Attendance
Graduation exercises
Special projects
Opening of school
Donations to charity
Speeches

Opinions on school questions
Citizenship activities
Participation in community affairs
Services to community
Vocational outlook
Work after school
Staff Activities
  Scholarships, awards, and special
    honors
  New members
  Exchange teachers
  Summer activities
  Acts of bravery
  Leaves of absence
  Professional interests
  Avocational interests
  Weddings
  Births in family
  In-service education
  Attendance at conferences
  Activities in community
  Retirement
  Deaths
  Speeches
  Donations to charity

Visiting educators
Rewards of teaching
Special talents
Offices in professional organiza-
  tions
Books and articles written
Promotions
Biographical material
Welfare problems
Special Activities
  Open house programs
  Observances—birthdays, holidays,
    special weeks
  Operation of cafeteria
  History of school
  Demonstrations and exhibits
  School bus service
  Visits by celebrities
  Guidance facilities
  Drives and campaigns
  Hobbies
  Research projects
  Health measures
  Teaching homebound pupils
  School camp

Useful suggestions may be obtained from the check list for creating news. By creating news is meant the actual bringing about of an incident or event which has news value. Sometimes this is called manufactured news. Newspapers manufacture news quite commonly in an effort to supply their readers with interesting, informative, and legitimate stories. For instance, an editor might manufacture a story by polling a numeber of parents on the question of whether or not teen-agers have too much freedom. After the story is published, he might then use it as a basis for an editorial, and the editorial might prompt, in turn, a flood of letters to the editor.

Schools have many opportunities for creating their own news. An activity might be initiated because it has news interest, or a scheduled event handled differently to increase its news value. As examples, a good story could be written about a contest that was created to select the boy or girl who had done the most for the school system in the judgment of classmates and teachers, and a citation could be presented at commencement to the winner by the president of the board of education. An assembly to honor outstanding alumni would have more news interest if a large number of former graduates were in the audience. In celebrating the fiftieth birthday of the school, the news value would be higher if responsibility for the celebration was shared with community leaders. Perhaps the parent-teacher association is about to donate a new piece of equipment for testing the hearing of pupils. By making the presentation a public affair, with a prominent hearing specialist present, the story would receive more favorable attention.

NEWS ORGANIZATION

No matter whether a school system is large or small, some form of organization is necessary for news service. In larger systems, prevailing practice holds to a form in which news responsibility is divided between a director of public relations and the individual building principal. The director of public relations may be known by the title of assistant superintendent in charge of public information, co-ordinator of school-community relations, director of planning and public information, or director of public relations. He is responsible for news originating in the board of education and the central administrative departments. Publicity for school-wide events is handled through his office. He discusses potential news stories with reporters and arranges interviews for them with the superintendent and other executives. Some of his time is taken up in periodic meetings with principals and building representatives on questions of sound news practices.

The individual building principal takes charge of publicity in his own school. He usually assigns this activity to a faculty member who is called the publicity chairman or news representative. It becomes his job to collect news items from teachers and write them up for publication. They are cleared by the principal before being sent to neighborhood newspapers. At the same time a carbon copy of every release is forwarded to the director of public relations so that he may know what is being reported, judge its effectiveness, and offer suggestions for improvements.

The organization in medium-size systems may differ somewhat

from that of the larger ones. If there is a director of public relations, he may assume responsibility for preparing all news releases. Material will be supplied by building representatives who either phone in their stories or report the facts on a standard form, such as the one shown here.

NEWS REPORTING FORM

Name of School _____ Date_____
Who _____
What _____
Why _____
When _____
Where _____
How _____
Picture possibilities _____
Remarks _____
Reporter _____Phone _____

It assures coverage of all schools in the system, immediate reports of stories that break, and the professional treatment of releases.

If the director of public relations is employed on a part-time basis, then he may find it expedient to turn the material from building representatives over to a high school English or journalism class, especially where news is compiled weekly for a school page in the local newspaper. Members of the class edit the material and write releases under the guidance of the teacher who is often the person in charge of public relations. Copy is checked for news content and style of presentation, and the better stories are selected for publication. Important news from administrative offices is taken care of by the director of public relations.

It is common in small districts for the superintendent or supervising principal to serve as the news representative for the school system. His success in publicizing and interpreting the educational program depends upon his sense for news, his ability to write interesting copy, and the time he gives to the work. Generally, too few heads of small systems know how to gather and report the news, and most of them are over-burdened with administrative duties. Better publicity would be obtained if news reporting were delegated to an interested teacher and allowance made for it in his instructional load. With encouragement, study, and experience, such a teacher can develop into a fairly competent reporter.

PREPARING NEWS RELEASES

Editors assign more space to school news when releases conform to press standards. The standards take into consideration style of writing, quality of writing, and the mechanical make-up of copy.

Style of Writing

Newspaper articles are written in what is known as reverse pyramid style. The most important elements of the story are told in the first or "lead" paragraph, with each succeeding paragraph somewhat less important than the one before it. The story has no climax, ending, or conclusion like other forms of narrative. The reverse pyramid style is followed by newspapers for two main reasons: first, because many people read nothing more than headlines and lead paragraphs, hence they get the essential facts of the news; and second, it makes it possible for the editor to cut a story at any point below the lead paragraph when he faces space limitations.

The lead paragraph is the most important part of the story. It answers the questions of who, what, why, when, where, and, sometimes, how. In straight news, emphasis is usually placed in this paragraph on a single fact or aspect of the story which is likely to have the strongest reader appeal. In feature stories, the lead varies with the writer and the nature of the material. In either type, the lead paragraph can make or break a story, no matter what information follows it.

The writing of a concise, interesting, and forceful lead is an art in itself, one that requires a sound sense of news and much practice. Most good leads are written in fewer than 40 words, and they never promise more than will be delivered in the rest of the story. Here are three leads that present the facts concisely:

> Penmanship versus printing for children in primary classes was one of the main subjects under discussion at a meeting of the Upper Pottsgrove school board last night.

Home is a pretty good place to be in the opinion of Robert Danford, 16-year-old Clementon lad, who returned there yesterday after a weary week-end of hitchhiking which took him to New York, N. Y.

Aroused by the mounting number of auto accidents, the Johnsville Automobile Club at the monthly meeting last night of the board of directors adopted steps to have safe driving instruction made a part of the curriculum of the Johnsville Senior High School.

Whether the lead features one news element or another depends upon the nature of the story. For example, if the governor declared that school building costs must be reduced, the *who* element would be emphasized because of his prominence. If a similar statement was made by the president of the local school board, the stress might well be placed on reduction in school building costs because of the interest it would have for taxpayers.

Besides featuring a particular news element, the lead paragraph can open with a variety of grammatical forms which bring out essential detail and strengthen reader interest in the story. Among the more popular forms are these:

Direct statement—The Fairmont Civic Association, founded originally to provide a recreational program for youth, has extended its services.

Participial phrase—Speaking before a thousand parents, the superintendent of schools outlined a plan for holding double sessions.

Infinitive phrase—To discuss the nonaccreditation of the Wilson High School, a meeting has been called by the alumni association for 8 o'clock tomorrow night in the school auditorium.

Conditional clause—If the bond issue is approved by the voters, Jamesville will have a new high school in two years.

Substantive clause—That after-school recreational facilities are needed is recognized by the board of education.

Direct quotation—"The schools of this community were never better than they are today," Mayor John Thomas declared this afternoon.

Parody—"A stitch in time saves nine" meant something yesterday to Bill Williams, a senior at Stanton High School,

The lead is followed by the body of the story. The body consists of one or more paragraphs explaining the facts and fulfilling the expectations created in the lead paragraph. The details are arranged in the order of their news importance, a reason why chronological treatment is seldom feasible. This arrangement is evident in the two-column spread given the following story from which material has been omitted to make it shorter:

RATING GROUP AGAIN OKAYS DARBY HIGH SCHOOL

Darby High School has again earned a place on the approved list of secondary schools accredited by the Middle States Association of Colleges and Secondary Schools.

Its qualified students may attend any college or university.

That was the highlight of a verbal report last Thursday by Dr. Herman M. Wessel of Elkins Park, chairman of 13 educators who evaluated Darby High School April 24, 25 and 26 to Superintendent Edward B. Deery, Principal J. Wallace Saner and other school teachers and officials.

After three days of visiting classrooms, observing teaching techniques, examining school records and curricula and scrutinizing every part of the school plant, Dr. Wessel opened the meeting to declare that "we find words inadequate to express our feelings regarding the wholesome attitude of your entire school."

He said that exceptionally high morale was evidenced by the unusual loyalty and respect among administrators, teachers and students for each other plus the stability of the teaching staff and the lack of job turnover.

The committee had found, he declared, the educational philosophy progressive and idealistic, exerting a strong influence on the student body.

The committee's report was not entirely praise. Some improvements were recommended—including an expansion of building facilities and reorganization of the educational program for noncollege preparatory students.

Darby High School was first accredited in 1928 and has since qualified for membership each succeeding year.

Final written report of the committee is expected in about eight weeks.

Upper Darby, Pennsylvania, *Upper Darby News*—5/3/51

Quality of Writing

Another important consideration in preparing releases is the quality of the writing. Newspapers want copy in clear, simple, and concise language. They know that their readers do not understand such technical terms as integration, maladjustment, core curriculum, or life adjustment education; and, that cliches and hackneyed phrases like "last but not least," "breathless silence," "doomed to disappoint-

ment," or "in the last analysis" make for dull and uninteresting reading. They prefer short sentences, and the substitution of periods for
conjunctions. Some editors recommend that paragraphs not exceed
50 words in length.

In straight news reporting, there is no place for stating opinion
unless it is attributed to a person in the story. A direct quotation
should be given, if possible. The use of words that carry emotional
elements or express personal beliefs and feelings should be scrupulously avoided. For example, referring to a meeting as "interesting"
or stating that the superintendent acted "wisely" are opinions which
the reader should decide for himself from the facts presented. It must
be remembered that editorializing is for editors, not reporters.

Mechanics of Copy

Most newspapers have their own style sheet or style book for
reporters to follow in preparing copy. School releases are accepted
more readily when they are written in accord with the style sheet of
the local newspaper. A style sheet can be obtained upon request from
the editor. If none are available, then a check with him can make
the essential rules known. Although newspapers differ somewhat
on technical requirements for spelling, punctuation, abbreviation,
capitalization, and the like, most agree on the following standards
for typed releases:

1. The story should be written on white paper, 8½ x 11 inches in size.
2. The releases should be typed, double or triple spaced, and on one side
of the paper only.
3. The release date should appear in the upper right-hand corner of the
first page.
4. The name of the reporter, school, and telephone number should appear in the upper left-hand corner of the first page.
5. Copy should begin about one-third of the way down the first page
so that enough space is available for the editor to write in the headline.
6. A margin of about one inch should be left on each side and at the
bottom of the page.
7. Pages should be numbered consecutively at the top of the paper.
8. Each paragraph should be ended on one page, with no carry over to
the next page.
9. The word "more" should appear at the bottom of all but the last page
to indicate that the story continues.
10. An end mark of any kind—*****—should be placed at the close of
the story.

By observing these standards the first page of the story would appear like this sample:

W. E. Wells, Reporter   For Release
Merion High School   June 8, 1956
Tel. WE 6-8247

     Superintendent R. S. Williams of the Merion Public Schools startled the board of education last evening at its regular monthly meeting by reporting that enrollments next fall would be 20 per cent higher.

     As surprised as they were, members of the board of education, nevertheless, talked of "holding back for a while" on new buildings to house the growing school population.

     Faced with the possibility that the present anticipated increase in enrollments may go even higher in another two years, the board of education and the superintendent considered how to make better use of the buildings they have before getting into the problem of constructing new ones.

(more)

Directly above the release date, the story may be marked "exclusive to" or "special to" a named newspaper. The words "exclusive to" mean that the story has been sent exclusively to this newspaper. The words "special to" tell the editor that the same story has been sent to other papers but that each release has been written differently. No editor wants to publish copy that will be duplicated in another newspaper; obviously, an exclusive article will receive more attention than a special.

In submitting photographs, a label may be pasted on the back giving the reporter's name, school, telephone number, the release date, and a credit line for a commercial photographer. The caption is glued along the bottom of the picture and may include the identification material. Practice should be guided by the preference of local editors.

NEWS DISTRIBUTION

News distribution takes in more than just the mailing or delivering of releases to the papers. News outlets, editorial arrangements, publication deadlines, and related information must be considered in planning a distribution schedule.

News Outlets

News outlets may be divided into (1) those which serve the general public and (2) those intended for special audiences. The first group consists of daily, semi-weekly, weekly, and Sunday papers, and radio and television news programs. The second consists of foreign language, labor, trade, farm, and professional journals issued daily, weekly, and monthly.

Most newspaper editors and editors of radio and television news programs in large cities receive more material than they can publish. They must necessarily limit their selections to news stories of major importance and occasional items that appeal strongly to popular interest. As a consequence, greater reliance must be placed upon neighborhood newspapers for printing stories and interpretative reports of individual school activities. Outside of metropolitan areas, daily, semi-weekly, and weekly papers are the principal outlets for educational publicity, with radio and television news programs playing a strong role where they originate locally.

Full advantage should be taken of the opportunity to tell the school story in journals published for special audiences. Foreign language newspapers will print a wide range of school stories if they are supplied with copy. This is an outlet which school systems have overlooked almost completely, yet the readers have children in the public schools and pay taxes. The county medical journal will take articles dealing with health programs and health facilities for children, just as trade papers welcome releases on plant construction and maintenance activities, among others that could be written for them especially. School news released through these journals stimulates interest in the work of the school and acquaints people with its program who do not read this type of news in the daily papers.

Editorial Arrangements

Newspapers are divided into departments or sections of news, as sports, science, society, real estate, and general news. Each department is headed by an editor, who is responsible for a special section. General news is under the supervision of the city editor. Of course, on small papers a number of sections must be edited by one person, because the staff is small.

The school publicist should acquaint himself with the departmental organization of the local papers and know the editors of the different sections. He should ascertain, through personal contact, just what types of stories they like to print, how long they should be, what deadlines they set for receiving copy, and similar matters of policy. By holding to their requirements, he can build wholesome relations with the press and increase the likelihood that his releases will receive more attention.

Release Days

A distribution schedule should be drawn up in the public relations office of the school system indicating what day or days of the week are best for sending releases to the papers. Except for perishable news, a school can fix this schedule by analyzing local papers and finding out the days on which most releases are published.

Generally, Sunday is best in communities where a paper is published on that day. Sunday editors will take feature stories, special articles, photographs, and some straight news stories. Some Sunday papers run a section devoted exclusively to school news, and they welcome good copy. Monday and Friday are the next best days, because less space is taken up with paid advertising. Saturday is the worst day of the week according to the experience of public relations directors. As to Tuesday, Wednesday, and Thursday, one day appears to be as good as another, though some differences are found by localities.

Deadlines

The closing deadlines of every local newspaper should be recorded and posted. Unless a release reaches the city editor or a special section editor on time, it may be wasted. It is necessary to note the deadlines separately for morning and evening papers.

Releases for Sunday papers should be received by the city editor at least 24 hours in advance of publication, and sooner if possible. Releases for special editors may require as much as three or four days before Sunday distribution. Some special sections go to press on Thursday and Friday, and therefore copy must reach the editors of these sections even a day earlier.

Memo to Editor

Now and then a memo may be attached to a release telling the editor what the story is about and pointing out its value. The release might be a statement, for example, of an instructional policy in which many parents would be interested and which the editor might pass over unless it was called to his attention. A memo might point up a lead for a follow-up story, and where the facts may be obtained should the editor wish to write the story. If the superintendent is scheduled to make an address to an important group outside the city, the memo might point out that the release is a summary of his talk and that the complete text is available. Used discreetly, memorandums are appreciated by the editor.

THE SCHOOL PAGE

Many daily and weekly newspapers devote a section regularly to educational news in the local community. This section is known as the school page. It varies anywhere from a single column to a full page or more in length. Copy is prepared mostly by pupils in English classes and high school journalism clubs. The news covers announcements, student affairs, contests, class projects, parent-teacher association, school policies, and developments within the system. In some small communities this section takes the place of a student newspaper.

The school page is valuable to the institution and to the newspaper publisher. Pupils have sound learning experiences in collecting and writing news, and they are motivated by the thought of publication to maintain high standards. The assurance of a steady outlet for material makes it possible for administrators and building chairmen to plan ahead and to stress whatever phases of the educational program need most attention. The newspaper publisher receives a wealth of stories with practically no cost to himself, and the fact that educational news is read eagerly by pupils and parents boosts the circulation of the paper.

Several weaknesses that reduce and almost wipe out its value are apparent in the school section of many newspapers. A primary one is the inclusion of poorly written stories replete with glaring errors in word usage and grammar. This happens when teachers fall down on the supervision of pupils and permit inferior copy to get through without careful editing. Not infrequently, the columns of the section are cluttered with petty gossip, personal notes, borrowed humor, and trivial items of no worth in acquainting the adult reader with the real life and activities of the school. Another is the staleness of news and the lack of appeal it has even for pupils. Sometimes the layout of the page is dull and uninteresting, broken here and there with advertisements to further lower its value. These are serious shortcomings. They discredit the institution and leave wrong impressions with parents and others who review the news in this section. It is better to eliminate the school page entirely than to allow such conditions to continue.

It should be remembered that the school page, under any circumstances, is only a supplement to the general newspaper publicity program, not a substitute for it.

BACK-TO-SCHOOL SUPPLEMENT

Somewhat like the school page is the "Back-to-School Supplement." Published annually just before school opens in September, it is usually carried as a separate section of a Sunday newspaper. Pertinent news items of interest to parents and their children are featured. Included also are stories of a general nature on schools and educational happenings as well as stories which help to interpret the local school system.

The Associated Press now prepares a separate 16-page "Back-to-School Supplement" which is distributed to its 1,800 member newspapers throughout the country. These newspapers may use it as a standard-size section, as a tabloid section, or as a source book for their regular pages. It can be developed much more fully through cooperation between the school system and the local newspaper. In some instances, it has been made as large as 72 pages, including a wide array of good photographic news stories to attract and hold reader attention.

PRESS RELATIONS

Establishing good press relations is something which every person who has a responsibility for school newspaper publicity should strive to attain. Good press relations mean developing a feeling of respect and confidence on the part of publishers, editors, special writers, and reporters in the school as a source of sound and essential news. Without their cooperation and support, the publicity program cannot succeed.

Desirable Practices

What should be done to establish and maintain good relations between the school and members of the press? According to experienced publicity directors, the best way to get along with newspaper people is to understand their point of view and to observe the following practices:

1. *Make it a point, in planning the publicity program, to discuss with the editor the types of stories in which he is interested and how the news should be handled.* This responsibility should be assumed either by the superintendent or by the person in charge of school publicity.

2. *Coordinate the news service under one person or group of persons who are available to the newspapers when they are needed.* News is perishable. It must be handled at once. The editor and reporter should know to whom they can turn at any time and get the facts of a story without delay and obstruction.

3. *Establish daily contact with the press, reporting possible news stories and supplying copy that is requested.* A regular time should be set aside for seeing reporters who call at the school.

4. *Treat reporters with the same courtesy that you expect to receive.* Urge that similar treatment be extended to them throughout the system.

5. *Be frank and honest in discussing news stories.* Reporters must have confidence in your integrity and know that the information they receive is complete and accurate.

6. *Take the reporter into confidence when it seems advisable.* Perhaps he should understand the background of a story or know why a release would be more timely at a later date of publication. Speaking "off the record" should never be used as a technique for suppressing unfavorable news—efforts of this kind can boomerang with harmful effects to the school system.

7. *Prepare releases in a style that is recommended by local newspapers.*

8. *Present unbiased news material.* There is no place in school news stories for propaganda or subtle attempts to secure free advertising.

9. *Supply the press with copy that has news value.* Copy must stand on its own news merits.

10. *Keep a directory of city editors, department editors, photographers, and reporters, noting their telephone numbers, office locations, working hours, days off, and special interests.* The school publicity representative should be able to contact them immediately when a story breaks or when the special handling of a release is essential.

11. *Maintain a weekly calendar and future events book that may be shared with the reporter and photographer.* They should know what news stories to look for, how to plan their time, and from whom to obtain detailed information.

12. *Permit the reporter a reasonable amount of freedom to interview professional workers in the system.* He should also be invited to attend official meetings and conferences, visit classrooms, and take part in activities which acquaint him with the aims, practices, and problems of the school system.

13. *Brief the reporter in advance of a board meeting, letting him know what problems and issues will be brought up for discussion.* Give him an opportunity at the close of the meeting to discuss with the superintendent and board members the meaning and importance of the actions taken.

14. *Hold a press conference when something significant happens.* Calling a press conference directs the editor's attention to the story and permits reporters to get the facts correctly. Prepared releases, official statements, and background material may be supplied to increase the accuracy of the reporting.

15. *Treat all papers alike, even when you may feel a dislike for the personnel and policies of a particular paper.* Regardless of attitude, it is still entitled, as a public service agency, to complete information on school news stories.

16. *Compliment editors and reporters for the way they have written and presented a story, but never for publishing the story.*

They are not doing the school a favor in printing a story. This is part of the public responsibility carried by a newspaper.

Common Errors

Good press relations suffer when such common errors as the following are made by school people:

1. *Threatening, denouncing, and bringing pressure on the editor to print or withhold a story.* Nothing produces friction faster and is resented more deeply by the editor.

2. *Complaining when the facts of a story are reported incorrectly, when headlines give the wrong impression, or when individuals are misquoted.* The remedy lies in friendly discussion, accurate copy, and sometimes an objective statement in the section on letters to the editor.

3. *Refusing to release timely information to the press or pretending to be unacquainted with the details of a story.* Such action creates suspicion and reflects unfavorably on the institution. The story will be published anyway without the cooperation of the school and the benefit of complete background material.

4. *Sending out too many releases that do not have news value.* The editor is pressed for time; he cannot waste it reviewing copy that belongs in the waste basket.

5. *Complaining if stories do not get published.* It must be remembered that news selection is a function of the editor. He works under space limitations and publishes whatever he believes will appeal most to readers.

6. *Becoming emotional with reporters and editors over the publication of unfavorable news stories.* School people must learn to accept the good and the bad in the normal flow of publicity.

7. *Being drawn into controversies on a personal basis when the school is criticized or attacked in a news story.* No board member or school official has the right to speak for the system unless he is authorized to do so.

8. *Playing favorites with either the morning or the evening newspapers.* Nothing is gained in the long run through this practice.

9. *Creating the impression that you know more about reader interests than either the reporter or the editor.* The persistence of this attitude is certain to antagonize the reporter and the editor.

10. *Failing to invite the press to special school affairs which should be reported in the paper; or, having invited the press, failing to show the courtesy and hospitality that is expected.*

11. *Causing the reporter to sit in the waiting room for a long time for an interview with a school official.* If an interview must be delayed, word should be sent at once to the reporter. He has a dead-line to meet and cannot afford to lose time under these circumstances.

12. *Always being on the "asking end" in your relations with the press.* The reporter appreciates a news tip and ideas for stories which he can run down and take credit for writing.

Courtesy Public Schools, Springfield, Missouri.

17
Audio-Visual Aids

Without doubt audio-visual aids are the most effective media for mass communication today. They are used extensively by business and industrial organizations to advertise their products and services and to acquaint the public with the ideals they stand for in American life. Schools have used these same media to interpret their programs and to build better relations with parents and other taxpayers, but on a comparatively small scale. They are coming to realize, however, that much more must be done with exhibits, slides, film strip, recordings, motion pictures, radio, and television if they are to create a stronger citizen interest and cooperation in the improvement of education.

SCHOOL EXHIBITS

A school system which lacks experience in using audio-visual aids will do well to start with exhibits. Easy to produce, they provide many experiences of value in working subsequently with the more complex media of sound and sight. Different types of school exhibits will be explained and points considered in their preparation and management.

340

In-School Exhibits

The most common type of school exhibit is that held in a class-room by a single teacher. Its purpose is to let parents and visitors see for themselves what children study and what they accomplish. The work is arranged around the room on wall panels, tables, and window sills. Explanations are given orally and with the help of printed cards and labels. This sort of an exhibit is usually organized in connection with open house programs and special events of public interest. Parents like the classroom exhibit and get a great deal of meaning from it. It should be an established feature of school night and open house programs in elementary and secondary schools.

The corridor exhibit is another type which deserves considera-tion by schools generally. As the name suggests, examples of pupil work are placed on display in the corridors of the school for the benefit of visitors, teachers, and pupils. Illuminated show cases house materials which are changed every three or four weeks. The success of the corridor exhibit is affected by the location of show cases, their construction, and lighting.

The all-school type offers the best opportunity for publicizing and interpreting the educational program through an exhibit. It is usually an annual event held in the spring of the year. Work done by pupils is brought together in a central location from every grade, class, subject, and department. The displays are arranged in a se-quence that follows a pupil's educational progress. Modern teaching methods, instructional materials, and individual and class projects are explained by pupil and teacher attendants. A gymnasium or auditorium is needed to accommodate the displays and to permit the presentation of such student activities as band, orchestra, glee club, dramatics, and so forth. Where these facilities are not available, the school must confine the exhibit to corridors and classrooms in which booths and display tables are erected. The possibilities of this type of exhibit for interpreting education have scarcely been explored.

Out-of-School Exhibits

The out-of-school exhibit is a further opportunity for bringing the public into contact with the work of the school. The out-of-school exhibit may be constructed around any subject or topic, grade or

Exhibits publicize and interpret the educational program.

class which people want to know about or should know about in order to better understand their schools. A little imagination combined with models, specimens, photographs, and technical devices can make such exhibits both interesting and informative.

There are many different places in the community where the exhibits may be shown. A local store is a suitable location, and one that has been used as widely as any. The exhibit may be arranged either in a section of the store or else in the show windows where it can be seen from the street. Another location is the county fair, which schools in rural and semi-rural areas may use to acquaint the public with their work. In addition, exhibits may be shown in public libraries, hotel and bank lobbies, and government buildings.

It is not uncommon for civic groups and organizations to request exhibits from the school which are appropriate for a celebration they are sponsoring. For example, the celebration might be that of marking the first 100 years of the community, the founding of a boys club, or the opening of a new recreation center. These invitations are important in building good will and interpreting education, but precaution must be taken against staging exhibits for affairs that are out of keeping with the character of the school.

While many of the larger exhibits involve much time and labor to prepare and arrange outside of the school, there are occasions when small, portable types could be used to good advantage. They need not be anything more than a series of panels on which pictures, objects, specimens of work, and explanatory cards are fastened. An exhibit can be build around any subject, problem, and practice of the school system of interest to the public. At least one or two such exhibits are valuable to have on hand for meeting community requests and for illustrating talks given by school officials at parent-teacher association meetings, before luncheon clubs, and to faculty groups. Experimentation with the small, portable exhibit soon reveals its potential for sound community relations.

Preparation

Preparation for an exhibit should start with the drafting of a general plan by a committee charged with this responsibility. The committee should be expected to set forth in the plan the purpose of the exhibit; its theme, if any; what will be displayed and demonstrated; who will be responsible for various displays, special events, construction of booths, properties, art work, publicity, and management; and regulations to be observed regarding light, sound, safety, student aids, placards, and other essential matters. The plan in its tentative form should be submitted to the faculty for consideration before final adoption.

Faculty members should be allowed to work out the details of their assignments within the general frame of the plan. As an example, it would be up to social studies teachers to select their own materials for display and to arrange them in an attractive pattern. They would be responsible for having a booth constructed, ordering necessary tables and chairs, instructing student aids, securing advice on color backgrounds, designing placards and explanatory cards, and the like. Their work could be checked by the general committee according to a progress schedule. A check of this sort keeps the work moving forward and helps to integrate the exhibit.

Management

The thoughts and feelings people take from a school exhibit are influenced to a great extent by the way it is managed. A physical layout which allows freedom of movement and time to look at displays without being hurried is important. Readable placards, courteous treatment, attractive displays, and the opportunity to talk with teachers and pupils enter into their general appraisal. Visitors are appreciative of attention shown to their needs—well-placed directional signs and arrows, cloakroom facilities, rest stations, and student guides to answer questions and escort them through the building. A table should be placed either at the entrance or the exit containing printed materials about exhibits and such other publications as visitors care to take along and read at leisure.

SLIDES AND FILM STRIPS

Slides and film strips are visual aids which school systems can employ, regardless of their size, to acquaint the public with education in the local community. They are made from any good series of photographs, either in black and white or in color. They do more than oral discussion alone to help an audience understand facts and to comprehend the realities of a situation.

The $3\frac{1}{4} \times 4$ inch glass slide has been standard equipment in classroom teaching for many years. It is equally effective in public relations work with audiences ranging in size from a few persons to several hundred. The slides can be shown in most rooms and auditoriums without darkening the surroundings. They may be arranged in any order the speaker wishes to present them. They are fairly easy to make from photographs and drawings, and the original cost is not high.

The glass slide has been replaced rather widely by the 2 x 2 inch slide in the presentation of visual material. Made from pictures taken by any camera packing 35 millimeter film, the cost of duplicate copies is low. This slide can be used with small and large audiences.

The newer projection machines are equipped with automatic slide-feeders and other features that make them more desirable. Both the slides and the projector are light enough in weight to be carried conveniently by hand.

The film strip, known also as the film slide, is a series of pictures on a roll of 35 millimeter film having approximately 50 frames. The roll is threaded in the projector and turned by hand. When not in use, it is stored in a metal container one and one-half inches in diameter, small enough to fit into a coat pocket. Like the other slides, the film strip is adaptable to most audiences. Slides and film strip can be combined with sound by recording oral explanations and music on magnetic tape, magnetic wire, and discs. Faint signals, dubbed into a recording, notify the projection operator when the next picture should be shown. This method, although somewhat crude, works out satisfactorily in practice.

Points on Preparation

The visual story should be limited to a specific situation, activity, or subject for every set of slides and roll of film strip. For example, it might be about the physical condition of a building, how spelling is taught, or citizenship education throughout the grades. Whatever the story is, an outline should be developed before any pictures are taken, listing scenes in their logical sequence. Posed pictures give the best photographic results, but they must represent an accurate portrayal of school life. Sometimes enough suitable pictures can be found in a publicity file of the school to supply material for scenes listed in the outline. After pictures have been taken and made into slides or film strip, a script or set of speech notes should be prepared for recording and lecture purposes. It is most important that they be written in a lively and interesting style to hold audience attention and tell the story so that it will be remembered.

Methods of Presentation

Audience reaction to visual materials is affected by the methods of presentation. People want pictures which are easy to look at and can be seen without strain on the eyes. A good projector is necessary to satisfy this requirement as well as pictures which are photographically excellent. The slides should be numbered at the top to maintain a correct sequence and to avoid the risk of being inserted into the projection machine upside down. Though the insertion of a slide upside down is not serious and can be changed quickly, two or three repetitions of this error distract from the main thought of the story.

Whether projection should be accompanied by recorded narrative or by the comments of a lecturer is a point on which there is no definite agreement. Certainly, recorded narrative eliminates the necessity for having a lecturer on hand everytime slides or film strip are shown. Moreover, the narrator can be selected carefully for speaking ability and pleasing voice qualities, and there is a guarantee that explanations of the material will be given accurately and consistently once they are recorded. But it must be admitted that recorded narrative never quite takes the place of a competent lecturer whose personality and enthusiasm is felt by the audience. His presence alone inspires people to greater confidence and encourages the raising of questions in which they are interested. Nor can the public relations value of the personal contacts made in a lecture situation be overlooked in deciding which method to follow.

The double projection technique should be considered whenever statistical data and detailed arrangements of facts are presented. The use of this technique requires two machines and two sets of slides instead of one. The principal data are thrown on the first screen where they remain for constant reference while their meaning is being explained on the second through a series of maps, charts, graphs, and pictures. For example, the first screen might show an entire budget statement or separate divisions of it, and the second screen a translation of the figures into the services which the money buys. This technique is valuable if the relationship of one factor to another must be emphasized.

RECORDINGS

The public relations value of sound recordings of educational activities and special programs is just as high, in many respects, as the value attached to slides and film strip. Recordings can interpret rather vividly and realistically what a school is teaching and how it is taught, the personalities of teachers and pupils, various student activities, special services, and the thinking of administrators on controversial school questions. They further open the door for parents to come closer to the actual instructional process in classroom situations and tend to make the commonplace take on a dramatic quality. Every phase of school life can be captured on recordings so that they serve repeatedly in developing parent and taxpayer understandings and appreciations of the educational program.

The recordings are made either on magnetic tape and wire or else on discs and platters. Fortunately, the cost of recording equipment is low enough that small schools can purchase it. The magnetic recorder is favored in school public relations work because it can be transported by hand and the tape and wire may be used over and over again simply by demagnetizing the signals on them. A recording on tape, furthermore, not wire, can be edited like motion picture film to correct minor errors and to delete material that is not wanted. Though disc and platter recordings are equally good, they cannot be used over again nor edited after they have been cut.

The sources of material for recordings are almost unlimited. Every classroom offers numerous opportunities to illustrate the subject matter of instruction and the methods of teaching it. A typical day in the life of a pupil is rich in examples of what the school does to promote growth and shape character. Interesting and instructive samples of a modern school at work can be drawn from student activities, health services, guidance problems, homeroom meetings, supervisory conferences, and curriculum study groups. The library of recorded materials can be expanded by taking programs directly off the air and by borrowing and purchasing transcriptions and records from commercial companies, other school systems, educational agencies, and governmental bureaus.

Recordings which are presented for public hearing should deal specifically with a problem, subject, or practice that has come up before a group or in which a group has an interest. It would be a mistake, for example, to present excerpts from assembly programs to a group of business men who are more concerned at the moment with the financing of new plant construction; or to spend time on a recorded school board meeting with fathers and mothers who are more interested in modern methods of teaching arithmetic. The selection of appropriate recording is most important in using this medium of communication.

Once selected, the question of how to use a recording effectively must be decided. The mere playing of a recording alone does not produce satisfactory learning. The playing must be accompanied by the skillful use of methods and techniques fitted to the nature of the audience and the goals to be accomplished. In some situations, the record may serve to set the stage for a panel discussion between teachers and parents; in others, to illustrate the points made in a talk by a curriculum specialist. Then again, portions of a record may have to be repeated several times to drive home a significant fact or to clear up an abstraction. A briefing on what to look for may be necessary to alert the members of an audience and to sharpen their sense of discrimination, while a problematic approach may heighten interest and pave the way for follow-up activities.

MOTION PICTURES

With the possible exception of television, the school-made motion picture is the best audio-visual device a school can employ in furnishing information to the public. It permits the showing of actual conditions and practices, and even the technical aspects of plant operation business management, and financial procedures. The material is easily understood and assimilated, and a substantial amount can be presented in a short space of time. The impressions left by motion pictures have a lasting and influential effect upon the formation of attitudes and opinions. The motion picture should have a definite place in the public relations program.

Objectives of Films

The principal objectives of school-made motion pictures may be summarized in a few statements. They should be planned to show citizens what the school is doing and what it is trying to accomplish; to bring the realities of the educational program to community members who have neither the time nor disposition to learn the facts for themselves; to point out problems which require school-community cooperation for their solution; to acquaint parents and other citizens with new educational developments and reasons for changes anticipated in the future; and, to develop a stronger sense of local pride in the school system.

Guiding Principles

The production of school motion pictures should be based upon a set of guiding principles which are consistent with the underlying concepts of the public relations program and the standards of good motion pictures. Every motion picture should (1) carry out a definite objective, (2) fit the type of audience or audiences for whom it is intended, (3) depict school conditions with truth and accuracy, (4) never "sell" personalities or spread propaganda, (5) meet the requirements of excellent photography, (6) tell a well-organized story, (7) cover only one general idea or subject, (8) explain the content in understandable English, and (9) be financed with public funds.

Subjects for Films

Practically every aspect of instruction and operation can be interpreted to the public through the medium of a film. This is evident in a partial list of the films made by school systems in different parts of the country. The list includes films on safety education, laboratory work in science, teaching of reading, teaching of arithmetic, vocational preparation, work in agriculture, maintenance of buildings, health services, teaching of sportsmanship, interscholastic athletics, homeroom programs, business management, student activities, highlights of assemblies, library services, homemaking, practical arts, fine arts, music instruction, business education, school-work experience, guidance, functions of the school office, physical conditions, kindergarten, citizenship education, community improvements, research, and in-service education of teachers.

A school system that is intending to make and use motion pictures in its public relations program should select the subjects with care. Subjects should be chosen which are best adapted to this medium and most in need of being interpreted in the local community. Too much time and money are tied up in production to permit the careless selection of story subjects.

Producing Films

No film is any better than the planning behind it—planning which involves appropriate subject matter, script writing, adequate equipment, competent supervision, expert editing, and excellent sound. An outline should be built of the ideas and facts to be presented in the picture. They should be consistent with the objectives of the film. Only as many should be included as the viewer can understand and retain without difficulty. The tendency of the amateur to crowd too much material into a motion picture is a serious mistake. The completed outline indicates whether or not this tendency is present and what material should be deleted.

The outline also serves as a guide for the script writer after it has been reviewed in a "story conference." It is his task to translate the outline into a series of connected scenes which tell the story in a logical and interesting manner. The script should be reviewed and worked over until these requirements are met. After that, a "shooting breakdown" can be made indicating the approximate length of scenes, close ups, long shots, "prop" shots, and related details.

The actual production at this point of a successful film depends upon the proper kinds of equipment. The minimum equipment a school should own for taking pictures consists of either an 8 mm motion picture camera or a 16 mm one, the 16 mm being more satisfactory for general use; daylight photoflood lamps; reflectors; extension cords; a light meter; a tripod with a revolving head; a splicer; a titler; and, a supply of film. Color film is preferred over the black and white. The initial cost of this equipment may seem rather high, but the real cost does not amount to much considering the life of the equipment.

The taking of pictures should be under the supervision of a competent person. Too often the previous work in planning is wasted because of poor direction and photography. Unless there is a qualified faculty member who can take over this responsibility, a search should be made for someone in the community who knows the motion picture business and is willing to assist with the project. Some of the best school-made motion pictures today have been produced under the direction of interested laymen. If a competent outsider cannot be found, then a contract may be entered into with a commercial agency to furnish professional personnel, but this is an expensive arrangement.

Since children play the lead in a school film, they should know what the story is about and what is expected of them. Moreover, they should be rehearsed before a scene is shot. Rehearsal reduces errors and causes children to act more naturally under the circumstances. They can be rehearsed without injecting a note of artificiality into the picture or altering their mode of behavior in class and extraclass activities. A few authorities frown upon the idea of rehearsals, but the need and value are soon felt in working with children on a picture.

After the shooting is complete, the next step is that of editing the results and photographing the titles. Skillful editing must be done to remove weak spots and to establish sequences which insure sustained audience appeal. With the aid of the script and an accurate record of the scenes taken, the work of editing is made easier. However, editing is a specialized art which should be entrusted only to a person with imagination and a rich background of practical experience.

Titles are important in a film, especially a silent film, because they produce continuity and clarify ideas in need of explanation. They can be created, with slight expense, from line drawings, printed cards, and even book jackets, folders, and magazine covers. Titles should be spliced into the film at the time when sequences are arranged in their final order.

Most commercial motion pictures have sound tracks which are photographed on the film itself to increase their effectiveness. This should be done with school-made motion pictures, but the cost is rather high and the mechanical process is too complex for staff members to handle. The photographing of sound on film is something that should be done by professionals who work with this process for a living. Despite the value which a sound track lends to a picture, it is doubtful that the expense is justified considering the limited market for school-produced pictures.

Instead of spending money for a sound track, the school can substitute a tape or wire recorder. This is not as satisfactory, of course, yet it serves the purpose nearly as well. The problem of using a tape or wire recorder is mostly one of synchronizing sight and sound. The literature on making motion pictures contains many excellent suggestions for dealing with this problem which schools will find helpful.

A third possibility is oral commentary by a staff member with a fine speaking voice and the interspersing of sound, such as music by the school orchestra or from concealed phonograph records. A cleverly-written script in the hands of a competent lecturer is just as good, if not better, than a sound track in explaining the content of a picture and drawing attention to its outstanding features. Many school leaders prefer this method of presenting a motion picture.

Use of Films

Numerous outlets exist in the community for showing school-made motion pictures. Advantage may be taken of parent-teacher association meetings to tell the education story. Films may be presented in connection with open-house programs, graduation exercises, anniversary celebrations, and special events attended by the public. American Education Week is a natural occasion for free distribution of films to local, motion-picture theatres. Notices may be sent to a selected list of clubs, organizations, and civic groups stating that films are available and telling how they may be obtained from school authorities.

Some measure of audience reaction may be gained from short questionnaires which people fill out and deposit in containers or hand to ushers at the close of the picture. Their answers will indicate generally how well the film has achieved its purposes and what else should be done in planning future productions.

RADIO

People spend many hours a week listening to radio broadcasts in this country. They listen at home and in automobiles, stores, barber shops, and places of public assembly. To them, the radio is primarily a source of entertainment, yet it furnishes information on a variety of subjects. Surveys and polls have shown consistently that the information they receive has an influence, and a strong one, on thoughts, feelings, and attitudes toward individuals, products, business concerns, and public affairs.

A few school systems recognized the potential of radio for public relations when it first began. They entered into cooperative arrangements with local stations to broadcast regularly. Their example has been followed by others, and some even acquired their own stations. Though real progress has been made in school-broadcasting over the years, the actual number of schools sending out programs is still relatively small. It will increase in time with the growing need for better community relations and the development of more comprehensive programs in this area.

School systems which employ radio in their public relations work should understand the factors that enter into the planning and presentation of a good program and how this specialized form of communication may be used to best advantage.

Aims

School radio broadcasts may serve one or more of the following aims: (1) to educate the public more fully with regard to the work of the school; (2) to prevent possible misunderstandings of classroom methods and pupil achievements; (3) to lay the foundation for the introduction of new policies and practices; (4) to invite community cooperation in school improvements; (5) to awaken community interest in and concern for public education; (6) to develop a more friendly feeling toward the school system; (7) to point out the contributions of the school to children and society; (8) to explain the need for more adequate financial support; and (9) to present lessons for classroom instructional use.

Advantages

Radio has a number of advantages that are worth noting in school public relations. First of all, most citizens will listen to well-planned school broadcasts because they believe in public education and the role it plays in a democratic society. They also like to know what children are being taught and the quality of instruction their tax dollars buy. Perhaps their strongest interest in listening grows out of a sentimental attachment for the young. Anything which affects the welfare of children and youth, their physical needs and opportunities for learning, is a matter of public concern. No commercial broadcast, despite the money and talent behind it, enjoys this advantage.

Another advantage arises from the fact that radio establishes contact with large numbers of people at one time and acquaints them directly with an event taking place or an activity being por-

trayed. Furthermore, nearly every aspect of the school can be presented authentically over the air and made appealing with voice,
music, and sound effects. Thinly populated sections may be covered
by broadcasts, while people engaged in household duties, driving
automobiles, attending stores, and the like can listen without losing
time from their work.

Last, the doors of the classroom are thrown open to the community when residents can tune in on lessons taught over the air for
in-school listening and the enrichment of instruction. They gain a
first-hand knowledge of a modern school, even to the types of materials used by pupils, the standards of accomplishment maintained,
the points of view expressed, and the subject-matter covered.

Program Requirements

Human interest, timeliness, dramatic suspense, and similar elements must be woven into school radio programs so that they have a
broad, popular appeal. Competition with commercial broadcasts for
listener attention makes this necessary. The appeal should grow out
of the subject matter of the programs and the quality of their presentation. They can be entertaining without becoming entertainment.
Good educational programs leave their listeners with definite impressions and information which help them to understand and appreciate the schools they are supporting.

The script for a school program requires the same amount of
careful attention that goes into a commercially sponsored program.
It starts with a purpose or statement of the effect which the program
should have upon those who listen to it. This might be the acquisi-
tion of selected facts about health examinations, stimulation of public interest in more playground facilities, appreciation of the moral
and spiritual values emphasized in classroom living, or an understanding of the cost-quality factor in instruction. After this decision
is made, attention should then be turned to the content and form of
the script.

A good script is written around a single idea or concept, with
close attention paid to language and human interest. Facts are stated
in familiar words and phrases. Sentences are short and clear. The
tone is informal and the situations natural. Illustrations are drawn

upon from everyday life, and humorous incidents used to clarify meaning and stimulate attention. Personal pronouns and other devices are brought in intentionally to humanize the broadcast. The test of a good script is whether or not it will hold its listeners.

Writing a script which informs and entertains is a task for one or more skillful writers. Staff members with the ability to do creative work and a wholesome sense of imagination can become successful script writers. Unless such individuals are available in the school system, it is wiser to borrow prepared scripts and transcriptions for local broadcasts. They can be borrowed from other school systems and from state and national educational agencies. By adapting them to the needs and conditions of the individual district, an excellent series of programs may be organized and presented. There is so much script and transcription material on hand today that every system can tell its story over the air.

Equally important as the script in securing and holding listener attention are the staging and directing of radio programs. Staging is a technical matter which requires a detailed knowledge of radio production. It can be learned with a fair degree of success by staff personnel working under the direction of professionals connected with the radio station or hired for the purpose. Usually some member of the staff has a background of experience in dramatics and knows the fundamentals of directing the actors. Children and adults who do the acting will get through if the directing is handled well. Schools should hesitate to undertake regular programs if they lack a competent staff or cannot obtain professional services for staging and directing their productions.

Agreements that are entered into with local radio stations for broadcasting school programs should stipulate the exact time and day of the week for going on the air. Having a definite and fixed schedule helps to develop an audience just as regular listening produces a cumulative effect upon those who hear the programs.

Types of Programs

The various types of programs suitable for school radio broadcasting are listed and described below:

1. *Spot Announcements.* These are brief announcements rang-

ing from 75 to 150 words which fit into station breaks before and after the time signal. They are used to fill spots that otherwise would be taken up by "dead" air. Spot announcements should be written in a conversational style and sent to station program directors. An attached memo should explain the purpose of an announcement and the dates on which it should be broadcast. Timely information may be reported in this manner, and the less well-known or misunderstood parts of the school brought out into the open.

2. *Newscasts.* Radio newscasts are another avenue for supplying the public with information on timely events and happenings. Radio news editors will accept releases that have news value. They should be written in the style of a feature story instead of a straight news story and should contain lively and interesting material. The techniques of writing radio news releases can be acquired through consultation with radio news editors of local stations.

Some stations assign time to schools for a weekly round-up of educational news in the public interest. The news writing and casting may be done by students or by faculty members. It is usually a ten or fifteen minute program broadcast on Friday or Saturday in the latter part of the afternoon. The weekly roundup of school news has been received well in communities that have tried it.

3. *Sports Programs.* Interest in sports offers a variety of program possibilities. Local stations may be willing to broadcast a running account of an interschool contest, conduct interviews with high school athletes, or present a dramatic story of an incident that took place on the playing field. News and sportscasters welcome material on participants, build-up stories for forthcoming contests, and final scores. Any special event connected with sports, as a dinner honoring lettermen, receives favorable attention.

4. *Music Programs.* These are as popular as any type presented by the school. The public is always interested in hearing a band, orchestra, glee club, or chorus which demonstrates good musicianship. Music programs are easy to produce compared with many others, and they do a great deal in developing appreciation of the opportunities provided for young people in schools today and the quality of instruction received.

Music, likewise, can contribute to the enrichment of different programs by introducing and closing them, supplying bridges, breaking up dialogue, stimulating interest, and increasing the number of pupils who take part.

5. *Discussion Programs.* These programs take the form of panels, round tables, symposiums, and debates. They permit the exchange of differing viewpoints on educational questions affecting the public interest. Listeners are attracted to discussion programs when they are intelligently planned and directed and the number of participants is limited so that members of the audience can follow their ideas without much difficulty.

6. *Dramatic Programs.* Many aspects of school life are adaptable to dramatic treatment. The script, however, must be written well and the story produced smoothly. Dramatic programs which live up to these requirements can do more to condense and underline a message than a talk or a discussion. Too often the entertainment features of school dramatic programs blot out ideas and impressions that should be left with audiences.

7. *Straight Talks and Interviews.* A straight talk by a school official, board member, leading citizen, or student can make a contribution to public understanding of a timely subject. The talk should be brief and to the point, taking no more than ten or fifteen minutes at most. An interview between a school representative and a prominent member of the community involving a problematic situation can arouse interest. In both the straight talk and the interview the style of delivery and the choice of language become important as well as the rate at which the program moves.

8. *Special Programs.* These programs frequently attract people who seldom listen to school broadcasts. They may include events connected with American Education Week, Arbor Day, Founder's Day, Thanksgiving, Christmas, and patriotic holidays. Or, they may concern the opening and dedication of new buildings, special awards, contests, pageants, demonstrations, and direct broadcasts from classrooms. Here names are news, among other values, and they assure station interest.

9. *Classroom Programs.* This type of program is offered during school hours for classroom use. Various subjects which pupils hear and follow up are taught over the air under teacher direction, with discussion and supplementary reading. The classroom program is not intended for public relations purposes, but the fact that adults tune

into it makes it an excellent device for promoting better insight into the nature of instruction. Some systems maintain that the by-products of classroom programs are worth more than straight public relations broadcasts in securing public goodwill and understanding of the school.

Publicity

When a program has been accepted by a local station, it usually has the qualities needed to attract an audience. However, it is a mistake to assume that many people will listen to the program. They must have their attention drawn to it in advance and their interest stimulated by a continuing series of publicity devices. Even the best commercial programs depend upon publicity and promotional work to win and sustain their audiences.

School systems have many opportunities to publicize programs they send out over the air. A good title for a series of broadcasts draws attention. Spot announcements are effective for advance publicity. Straight news and feature stories, illustrated with photographs, can be released to daily and weekly community papers and published in student newspapers. Posters can be placed on bulletin boards as a further means for informing pupils and encouraging them to listen to the broadcasts. It is advisable to develop mailing lists of parents, alumni, and leading citizens to whom literature may be distributed describing the radio activities of the system. Comments may be invited on the broadcasts and acknowledged promptly after they are received. The radio station may also do a great deal to further publicize school programs.

TELEVISION

Television is more than just the addition of sight to sound. It is an entirely new communication medium combining an array of techniques in the use of color, motion, and sound. It is flexible enough to permit the treatment of any subject in a dramatic and compelling fashion, while local and national events can be shown as they are actually taking place. Television appears to offer exceptional possibilities for the diffusion of knowledge and culture and the molding of public opinion.

School systems have been experimenting with television to supplement classroom teaching, to conduct courses in adult education, and to interpret their activities to the public. As yet, they know very little about the potentialities of this medium, but they have learned enough to appreciate some of its values and the problems involved in telecast productions.

Aims

The public relations aims of television are no different from those of radio. The increased emphasis on programs for in-school viewing and adult education, though intended strictly for educational purposes, contribute indirectly to popular understanding of the curriculum and to goodwill in the community.

Use and Value

The use and value of television in public relations work is much greater than that of radio. The sight factor enables the school to bring its program into a more direct and almost personal relationship with people in the community. They can be shown what a modern school is like and how it functions from the classroom to the business office. They can hear and see the instruction children are receiving under the guidance of skillful teachers. They can be introduced to the problems of public education and acquire a realistic understanding of their importance. They can view school events while they are taking place and occupy front seats at dramatic, athletic, and musical programs. They can listen to talks and hear discussion supported by visual evidence. They can witness demonstrations which are normally available to only small groups of people. They can judge from what they are shown how well a particular policy or change in program is working out in practice. And they can be instructed in the responsibilities of citizens for the preservation and advancement of free, public education.

The value of television in accomplishing these tasks is borne out by experience and survey reports from schools and commercial agencies. It has been found that a good program dealing with a problematic subject is almost as effective in stimulating thought, discussion, and action as a forceful speaker, panel, or round table with a live audience; that information received through a visualized broadcast is understood better and retained longer than through annual reports, home-contact bulletins, newspaper articles, and other forms of printed matter; that people will choose what is best for their children when they are supplied with accurate and complete information; that there is less likelihood of facts being misinterpreted when people can see what they are hearing; that conceptions of the school undergo change with the presentation of telecast programs; that more low-income families are contacted through this medium than any other; that exposure to television programs makes people more conscious of the school and what it is doing; and, that educational, cultural, and informational opportunities afforded by television are appreciated by adult citizens.

Arrangements with Stations

As in radio, television stations are required by law to allocate at least 25 per cent of their time to public service programs. They are willing, for this reason, to discuss what might be done to bring the schools to the people. But they also realize that informative and entertaining programs related to education and children build audiences.

Before the question of school telecasts is taken up with a local station, decisions should be made in the school system on such points as the following: what the system wants to accomplish, the best type of program for the purpose, how long it shall be, how many shall be presented, an appropriate title for the series, the subjects for telecasting, who shall assume various responsibilities, and how much money, if any, will be available to defray production costs. It is recommended that the decisions be reduced to writing as outlined in a brochure for the information of the local station.

Where there is more than one station in the community, the proposed series of telecasts should be made known to all of them. This is necessary in the interest of good public relations, despite the temptation to confine negotiations to the most popular station. The representatives of different stations can be invited to a meeting for reviewing the brochure and deciding whether or not the proposal measures up to their requirements. If it does, they can be requested to work out a plan for distributing the program fairly. The solution to this problem, in instances where it has arisen, is by rotation, mutual agreement, availability of time, and other methods.

The matter of securing time on a station schedule may present some difficulty, even though a program offers excellent promise. Television stations receive more requests for public service programs than they can possibly meet and still remain in business. The evening hours, when most people are in front of the viewing screen, are usually sold out to commercial sponsors on popular stations. If no time is available, the school should be willing to wait until a spot opens and take whatever is offered; it can then prove that it is entitled to a more desirable location on the schedule. Some systems find that Sunday afternoon is a satisfactory substitute for the evening hours to telecast informational types of programs, because children and adults are free to look at them. The situation is somewhat different with regard to telecasts for in-school viewing during the morning and afternoon when classes are in session. Fewer commercial sponsors are interested in time during these periods with the result that the station can accommodate more public service programs.

Once the school has a foot in the station door, it should live up to the arrangements that are made. This means keeping appointments when appointments are scheduled, being on time for rehearsals, controlling the conduct of pupils, submitting advanced copies of scripts when they are due, furnishing necessary properties, and respecting the wishes of the station. Station managers expect this cooperation from the school when they strive to fulfill their part of the bargain.

Planning of Programs

The schedule of public relations telecasts for the year should represent those subjects or topics that are most in need of being interpreted to the public and which cannot be presented as effectively through other media. It should be developed by the person in charge of public relations, assisted by staff members assigned to radio and television work and special committees familiar with the problems of different divisions of the school system. A similar procedure may be followed in building schedules for in-school and adult educational programs.

Practical suggestions may be obtained for planning scheduled programs from the list of "principles in production techniques" drawn up by the radio-television staff of the Philadelphia Public Schools, a system which has done as much as any in the country with educational radio and television. According to the experience of this staff:

1. Simplicity is essential to successful productions. A message can be highlighted and the best camera work done when backgrounds are plain, the number of participants small, and there is a minimum of movement from set to set.

2. A small number of participants facilitates camera work, permits close-ups, and avoids confusion. Close-up enables the viewer to get a better look at the activity or demonstration being presented, while wide-angle shots reduce objects and people on the television screen to a size which is indistinct.

3. Printed materials and charts should be avoided unless they are large enough to be read easily.

4. Detailed scripts are not necessary for television programs. A prepared run-down sheet may be used instead. The run-down sheet should indicate the various people and items to be shown, the order of presentation, and the physical location of persons and items on the set. It should also state the time for each segment of the story.

SCIENCE IS FUN
THE MOSQUITOES ARE COMING

1. Barg introduces show.
2. Barg shows insect project by students in schools.
   Discusses advent of insects in near future.
3. Barg makes model of insect of clay, pipe cleaners and paper explaining parts and characteristics of insect.
4. Barg shows picture illustrating difference between skeleton of man and insect.
5. Barg introduces Dr. Good of Health Department of city.
   Barg and Dr. Good discuss useful and harmful insects.
6. Dr. Good discusses mosquito problem—explains *life history* of mosquito. Shows pictures and specimens.
7. Dr. Good shows how to distinguish "harmful" from other mosquitoes.
8. Dr. Good discusses mosquito control.
   Shows pictures of mosquito trap; control units.
9. Barg and Dr. Good discuss how mosquito pest can be controlled— responsibility of citizens.
10. Barg thanks guest—winds up show.

*   *   *   *

A run-down sheet for a television program of the Philadelphia Public Schools.

5. Interesting content, with a change of pace, helps to produce a good program. Good material is ruined if the pace is too slow or the action does not move fast enough. Smooth transitions enliven the pace of a production.

6. It is not necessary to put make-up on children, but women look better with a medium shade of pancake and dark lipstick, while men need pancake to cover their beards, even after shaving.

7. Contrast in colors is important on black and white television. Pastel colors, for example, look alike and colored maps can be seen better when they are copied in black and white.

8. The integration of pertinent film material adds scope and variety to a program. Short bits of commercial film can be rented for small fees and used at appropriate points with or without recorded sound.

The tendency at present is to omit the formal writing of a script, as suggested above, and substitute a run-down sheet whenever possible. The run-down sheet is preferred because it is easier for the participants and camera crew to follow, besides encouraging greater naturalness in speech and action. Some dialogue may be included, but the amount is kept to a minimum. The preparation of a run-down sheet requires just as much careful planning as a written script.

The success of a televised production may depend a good deal upon the amount of time given to rehearsal. The Philadelphia radio-television staff estimate that it takes from two to four hours to "package" a 15-minute program. Close attention is paid during rehearsals to movement, continuity, exits, entrances, timing, display of exhibits, transitions, film cues, and special effects. Rehearsals are held at school until the cast is ready for a dry camera run at the studio where these points are checked again, and then a final practice takes place just before the program goes on the air. Some television staffs in other school systems believe that too much rehearsing kills spontaneity and believability, and that most programs can be prepared for the cameras in an hour of rehearsal time, including 30 minutes in the television studio in advance of the show.

Examples of Programs

Interesting programs have been developed by different school systems using television to interpret their activities, enrich classroom teaching, and furnish adult education. The public schools of Springfield, Missouri, have presented informative materials through a series of programs entitled "Television Classroom." Broadcast weekly at 6:30 p.m., these programs have helped the public to understand how the schools deal with speech correction, teach arithmetic, use visual aids, and educate for democratic living. A series called "Know Your Schools" has been sponsored by the public schools of Houston, Texas, for the purpose of introducing the staff to the public, showing the scope of the educational program, and demonstrating modern methods of teaching. The series has included programs on arithmetic, geography, school lunchroom, and vocational guidance. In Wilmington, Delaware, the public schools have been presenting a half-hour program on Sunday afternoon known as "School Report." It makes clear what is being done in the schools and the values derived by pupils. The program format includes panels, plays, concerts, exhibits, demonstrations, and interviews.

The public schools of Toledo, Ohio, have used two, half-hour periods weekly over a local television station to explain the curriculum to parents and other citizens, while the schools of Austin, Texas, have demonstrated through a quiz panel of high school students what their youngsters know about geography, history, economics, and government. Interviews with teachers have been a successful feature of "These are Your Schools" in Duluth, Minnesota.

Among other television programs designed to interpret the schools to the community have been "Wisdom's Window" and "Look and Learn," Birmingham, Alabama; "Your Children," Savanah, Georgia; "Touring the Schools," Columbus, Ohio; "Chicago Public Schools in Action," Chicago, Illinois; "Meet Your Schools," Cleveland, Ohio; "Across the Potomac," Arlington, Virginia; "Cavalcade of Choirs," Utica, New York; and "Listen Parents," Philadelphia, Pennsylvania.

Examples of programs for supplementing and enriching classroom instruction have been presented in Ames, Iowa, on a series known as "Iowa TV Schooltime." Programs in the series have included such subjects as adventures in art, exploring science, and planning your future. News events for in-school discussion have been treated on "The News: Places and People" by the Cleveland Public Schools. Three series of programs have been presented by the Philadelphia public schools entitled "Operation Blackboard," "WFIL Studio Schoolhouse," and "Stop, Look, and Listen." Among the weekly programs scheduled in these series have been "R for Rhythm," "Everyone's an Artist," "The World at Your Door," "Museum Piece," "Would You Enter Politics?" "How's Your Social

I.Q.?" "Fit as a Fiddle," "Where But in America," and "Science is Fun." The New York City public schools have offered a unique series of programs known as "Living Blackboard" for the benefit of handicapped children who are unable to attend classes. They receive credit for watching these programs which is applied toward promotion and graduation.

Educational programs for out-of-school viewing by children and adults have been developed by school systems in recent years. A Sunday afternoon series has been offered by the public schools of Salt Lake, Utah, dealing with arts and crafts. In Rochester, New York, the public schools have presented such programs as "French for Travel" and "Spanish Today." Classes in sketching, designing, and hat making have been an educational feature of the public schools of Minneapolis, Minnesota. The Providence, Rhode Island, schools have given a variety of programs for adults under the title, "Let's Go to School." The San Diego public schools of California have given credit courses over their "TV Classroom" in music, art, history, and government for adults who did not finish high school.

Filmed Programs

Motion pictures and kinescopic recordings provide excellent opportunities for broadening the scope of television programming. Many fine films can be secured on a free or rental basis from commercial and noncommercial organizations which are adapted to video. They deal with a wide range of subjects that are valuable for enriching existing courses of study and for supplying educational programs to children and adults for out-of-school viewing.

The motion pictures made by the school of its own activities and the films purchased for instructional purposes may be shown over television, but they do not work out satisfactorily as a rule. Too many long shots and more detail than records well on viewing screens are found in them, while titles and credit lines are often too small for ease of reading. Even with careful editing these and other shortcomings cannot be prevented. The films that are shown should be made for television.

Kine-photography offers real promise for an adequate supply of good public relations films. Kine-photography is a means of making a sound and motion picture record of a television program at the time it is being telecast. The resulting record is known as a kinescope, a term derived from the fact that the pictures are taken directly from the kinescope or picture tube. This process now makes it possible to get a sound-film record of every outstanding educational and public relations program sent out over local stations and to make it available to any school system for telecasting at convenient hours. Already an agency known as The Educational Television and Radio Center has been established to serve as a clearinghouse for the exchange of kinescopic recordings. Without much doubt schools in the future will be able to borrow kinescopes that fit their needs in explaining educational practices to citizens and in stimulating their cooperation in the solution of instructional problems.

Educational TV Stations

Television stations devoted exclusively to educational programs were approved by the Federal Communications Commission in April, 1952. The Commission, acting in response to views of many educators, set aside 242 channels for educational television stations and has since raised the number to 251. A license to operate an educational TV station may be held by an educational or cultural institution or by a group of local citizens organized for the purpose of telecasting programs in the public interest. A station assigned to one of these reserved channels must function on a nonprofit basis and make its facilities available to public schools, colleges, universities, parent-teacher associations, museums, and other educational agencies in the broadcast area.

An educational TV station is different from a station operated by a college or university that holds a license on a regular, commercial channel. A college station may contract to present commercials and sponsored programs at established air-time rates. Or it may present educational programs, the same as a station on a reserved channel. Whether it accepts commercial programs is determined by the financial ability of the institution to support the station.

The money for constructing and equipping an educational TV

station must be raised by the local institution or group applying for a station license. It runs into several thousands of dollars. A review of the practices followed by stations now operating to raise this money shows that they secured grants from local and national foundations, contributions from educational institutions, appropriations from state legislatures, and donations from business firms, civic associations, and private citizens.

Because educational TV stations are prohibited by federal regulations from selling air time, they have no direct means of financing their annual, operating costs. These costs run high. The stations now in operation have attempted to meet this problem by selling subscriptions to a monthly program bulletin, charging membership fees, and conducting an annual community-wide drive for funds. They have been able to raise enough money by these methods to stay in business, but the whole question of long-term financing must be worked out with the cooperation of philanthropic organizations, civic groups, and the general public. Yet despite the uncertainty of financing operational costs, more and more applications for licenses are being filed with the Federal Communications Commission.

Reports of station activities from such cities as Pittsburg, St. Louis, San Francisco, Houston, and Cincinnati indicate that the following categories of programs are being presented on education television: (1) classroom programs viewed by pupils in elementary and secondary schools as a regular part of their instructional work; (2) adult classes under the sponsorship of colleges and universities; (3) late afternoon and Saturday programs for children and youth; and, (4) general interest programs for adults in art, music, literature, homemaking, current events, agriculture, and so forth.

While few programs on educational television at present explain the school or deal directly with its problems, those which are produced for classroom viewing enable citizens who watch them to gain more understanding of present-day instructional practices. Though this is a valuable by-product in building better relations with the community, more should be done to interpret educational policies and to stimulate citizen interest in their schools. Such programs would be in accord with the public service function of educational TV stations. They could be a strong force in developing sound public opinion and intelligent action for school improvements.

Local groups interested in establishing an educational TV station may get pertinent information and assistance from two national organizations. One is the Joint Committee on Educational Television, 1785 Massachusetts Avenue, Washington, D. C.; the other is the National Citizens' Committee for Educational Television, Ring Building, Washington, D. C. The Joint Committee represents seven of the nation's leading educational organizations that are banded together for the purpose of offering engineering and legal services to local, educational TV groups. The National Citizens' Committee, with a field staff for working with local groups, helps to establish, raise funds for, and publicize educational TV. It publishes a semi-monthly *Newsletter,* maintains a speakers bureau, and lends out promotional films and exhibits. Its work is done under the direction of an Advisory Council on which there are representatives from several national organizations that have endorsed educational television.

Courtesy Duluth News-Tribune.

18
Special Events and Services

Special events and services may be defined as activities which a school either provides or takes part in beyond the regular instructional program. While many are entered into without thought of their public relations worth, others are regarded as major mediums for communicating with the public. The nature of special events and services will be reviewed in this chaper, and their value in strengthening ties between school and community will be pointed out.

OPEN HOUSE

Open house is an annual affair to which parents of school children and the general public are invited. It is usually held in the fall of the year, often as a feature of American Education Week, and may be scheduled for a single evening, a day, or as long as a week. The purposes of open house are to acquaint citizens with the nature of the physical plant and members of the staff, to help them understand more fully the work of the school, to allow parents to see concrete evidence of pupil accomplishment, and to build good will and foster pride in the school system.

Open House Programs

The programs presented by the majority of schools during open house are fairly simple in design. A common type is that of an escorted tour, with pupils and teachers serving as guides. Visitors are taken through the building and shown its facilities, introduced to members of the administrative and instructional staffs, told about objects on exhibit and instructional supplies and equipment used in classwork, entertained in various ways, served light refreshments, and presented, perhaps, with a small gift in memory of the occasion. Or the program may consist of a meeting in the auditorium during the first half of the evening at which school officials talk about the educational practices of the institution and pupils furnish musical and other forms of entertainment. This part of the program is followed by visits with teachers in classrooms where pupil work is on display; explanations are made of the curriculum in particular grades and subjects. The program is rounded out with a social period for further visitation and serving of refreshments. It is typical in secondary schools to have parents follow the class schedule of their children on a shortened period basis. By going from class to class they meet teachers, see the physical set-up of classrooms, receive information on what is taught and what is expected of pupils, and ask questions on points of interest. Refreshments may or may not be served at the close of the evening.

Variations from these program designs include a day during the week for observing classes while school is in session, afternoon teas for parents and teachers, discussion forums on school policies, clinics for parents on problems of child development, awards to parents for outstanding contributions to the school, student assemblies which are open to the public, social dancing, and parent-teacher conferences on the progress of individual pupils.

Improving the Programs

Many open house programs may be improved by training teachers to meet their responsibilities and by attending to details which make a favorable impression on the public. Teachers should be trained to greet and talk with visitors in a warm and friendly manner, conveying the feeling that they welcome the opportunity and would like the relationship to continue throughout the school year. They should possess techniques for conducting conferences with parents and be able to discuss children without arousing antagonism. They should know, as a group, exactly what points to cover in explaining the educational program and the facts which are important. Moreover, they should be trained to state these facts with a clarity and simplicity that leaves no question about their meaning in the minds of listeners. These are obligations associated with open house, and failure to meet them satisfactorily injures the standing of the school and lowers respect for the teaching profession.

Good public relations requires further that attention be given to details which make a favorable impression on the public. Well-written invitations to open house should be issued at least three weeks ahead of time and sent to parents and leading citizens. Visitors should be registered as they enter the building, given a name card for identification, and supplied with a printed program listing the schedule of activities, the names and rooms of teachers, and members of the committees responsible for the affair. Provision should be made for the parking of automobiles and the checking of hats and coats. There should be clearly-marked routes to follow, enlarged floor plans of the building hung in corridors, and signs indicating the location of lavatories. The plant should be thoroughly groomed, with interesting displays of materials scattered in different locations of the building. An information booth should be set up and student guides placed at the disposal of visitors. A printed booklet, reviewing the open house program, should be presented to visitors upon leaving the building, together with other printed and pictorial materials interpreting the school system. Cards might be mailed a few days later asking the individuals who registered how they enjoyed open house and requesting their ideas for improving it the next year.

More and more schools are realizing that programs undergo noticeable improvement and enjoy stronger support from the community when parents and pupils are invited to share in their planning. They contribute not only worthwhile ideas and suggestions but also their presence has a stimulating effect upon the thinking and enthusiasm of teachers. Open house can become a dynamic expression of the partnership concept in public education.

AMERICAN EDUCATION WEEK

American Education Week is a national observance in support of public schools. It is held during the week inclusive of November 11 to coincide with Armistice Day. The idea for this observance took root shortly after World War I. Critical problems in education brought on by the war, together with facts disclosed by the 1920 census, drew attention to the importance of education in this nation and the weaknesses of the public schools. A resolution was adopted by the National Education Association, at the request of the American Legion, enunciating the fundamental principles of public education and calling for a week of observance to point out the needs and accomplishments of schools and to secure public support for their improvement. As a result, American Education Week was proclaimed in 1921 under the sponsorship of the American Legion and the National Education Association. Since then the U. S. Office of Education and the National Congress of Parents and Teachers have become sponsors along with the other two organizations.

The most successful observances of American Education Week are planned and carried out cooperatively by the school and community. The leadership is usually taken by the board of education and the superintendent of schools. They invite parents and representatives of civic groups and organizations to plan this celebration with them. After a year or two, the entire project may be turned over to the community. The school then takes its place on committees the same as any other organization. It is expected, however, to furnish ideas, materials, and clerical assistance and to prepare a substantial portion of the week's program. This is logical in view of the nature of the celebration. The school can meet these requests without dominating the situation or in any way destroying the feeling that the project belongs to the whole community.

Each year the national, sponsoring organizations adopt a theme for American Education Week. An example is *Schools—Your Investment in America*. Local groups are urged to build their daily programs for the week around this theme. Their programs may include store window exhibits, posters, a day for visiting schools, speakers, radio and television programs, motion pictures, newspaper stories, open house, paid newspaper advertisements, library and museum displays, special printed materials, a proclamation by the mayor, pageants, and similar activities which illustrate the theme and deepen public understanding and appreciation of what American education has meant to this nation in the past and what it means today.

Much practical aid may be obtained by local groups from the National Education Association in planning their observance programs. It publishes a handbook on planning entitled *American Education Week Primer* and furnishes at a reasonable cost packets of printed materials for distribution in the community, movie trailers, radio scripts and transcriptions, and mats of display advertising that are ready for the signatures of local sponsors, as well as automobile bumper strips, lapel buttons, and similar items for drawing attention to the schools. Examples of successful activities employed by school systems and local groups may be obtained from the National School Public Relations Association.

SPECIAL OBSERVANCES

Besides American Education Week, which every local system should observe, there are numerous special days, weeks, and anniversaries which further serve to publicize the school and link it closer to the community. Among these special observances are Citizenship Day, Arbor Day, Armistice Day, Constitution Day, Navy Day, Army Day, Flag Day, Thanksgiving Day, National Freedom Day, the birthdays of Lincoln and Washington, Fire Prevention Week, National Book Week, National Brotherhood Week, Conservation Week, Bill of Rights Week, National Music Week, and significant dates in state and local history.

It would not be feasible for the school to cooperate in all observances held in this country, worthy as they may be. Its own program would be thrown out of gear and its objectives scarcely realized. Its problem is to choose wisely, deciding which observances fit into the program of studies and how much emphasis they should be given. The whole question should be dealt with through a policy of the board of education, developed with the aid of citizens, and explained fully to the community.

SPECIAL AWARDS

Special awards to employees, board members, school patrons, and public officials provide excellent news copy and win friends for the school system. Employees may be honored for their years of service in the system, service beyond the normal call of duty, acts of valor, and suggestions for school improvements. Awards may be presented to board members and other citizens for their interest in public education, their work on behalf of the local schools, unusual services to children, and their support of the principles of American education. Too few school systems have taken advantage of the opportunity to bestow recognition and express appreciation for the loyalty and contributions of employees and people in the community.

CAREER CONFERENCES

High school students are interested in securing first-hand information on occupations they may wish to enter. They face the prospect of entering employment after graduation from either high school or college, and the problem of making wise choices is an important one. No better sources of information are available than the men and women who work at different occupations in the community.

Many high schools now hold annual career conferences which they organize or plan cooperatively with community groups. Representatives from several different occupational fields are invited to meet with high school students and discuss the nature and requirements of their work. The schedule is so arranged that each student may attend at least two occupational discussion classes.

These career conferences are valuable in relations with the community. They can be evaluated at parent-teacher meetings, publicized in the press, explained in talks before civic groups, and described in literature published by the school. They permit staff members to make many new contacts with business and professional people. Guest speakers are appreciative of the right to serve the school. Most of them are enthusiastic about the career conference idea and surprised at the sincere interest of pupils and the intelligent questions they ask.

VISITS BY LEADERS

The interpreting of education to community leaders who are influential in shaping public attitudes and opinions of the school is a responsibility of administrative officials. They should know who these leaders are and make it easy for them to find out what happens inside of a school while classes are in session. One of the techniques for doing this job is to invite five or six leaders to be guests for lunch in the school cafeteria at two-week or monthly intervals. Each one can be assigned to a pupil and a teacher. After the luncheon period, they can be taken on a tour of the building. The tour should include an inspection of the plant, observation of classes and student activity groups, and visits to special service centers. A short review session should be held before they leave the building, to check observations and answer questions. The suggestion might be made that the visitors should feel free to relate their experiences and impressions to any group in the community, either praising or criticizing the educational program.

This technique enables administrative officials to contact most community leaders in a year or two and supply them with reliable information. A visitation program of this type, planned with the cooperation of teachers and pupils, makes many friends and loyal supporters of public education.

BUSINESS-INDUSTRY-EDUCATION DAY

The visitation idea has been incorporated in a recent and increasingly popular venture known as B-I-E Day. Worked out cooperatively, a day is set aside annually or biennially for teachers to visit different business and industrial firms in the community. Either the same or the next year the school systems play host to business, industrial, and in some instances, labor representatives.

The purpose of this plan is that of having each become better acquainted with the work of the other through first-hand observation and on-the-spot discussion.

Schools reporting their evaluations of B-I-E Day are consistent in saying that they feel, as do business and industry, that it is a most successful enterprise in school-community relations.

INFORMATION BUREAU

Provision should be made in the public relations budget of larger
school systems for the maintenance of an information bureau. This
bureau should be listed in bold-face type in the telephone directory
and referred to in much of the literature distributed by the school
system. It should be a service center for the public. People should
feel free to write, telephone, and call in person, asking for information or inquiring about the names of instructional and noninstructional staff members to whom they should go with their particular
problems. Such a bureau would encourage more inquiry on the
part of the public, increase goodwill, and save a substantial amount
of the time now being spent by administrative and supervisory officers
in answering thousands of requests they receive yearly. The bureau
should be placed in charge of one or two secretaries, trained to
perform this service in a gracious, efficient, and intelligent manner.

SPEAKERS' BUREAU

Another special service for improving public understanding of
schools and increasing their support is a speakers' bureau. Staff
members can be asked to volunteer for this service and to state on
a prescribed form the educational topics and subjects of personal
interest on which they prefer to speak. This information, compiled
in a leaflet containing a request blank, may be mailed annually to
churches, women's clubs, businessmen's organizations, labor unions,
parent-teacher associations, and fraternal groups. The service should
be rendered without charge, but the speakers should be permitted
to accept honorariums that are offered.

It is important in maintaining a speakers' bureau that the persons listed know how to speak and have something to say that
is interesting and worth hearing. It is not necessary that they be
polished speakers, but they should be able to present their subject
without hesitation or embarrassment. A short training program
assures that good impressions will be left with the public. The
speakers' bureau should take a responsibility for collecting and
organizing material for talks dealing with the aims, practices, and

accomplishments of the local school system. It should also supply illustrative materials, such as charts, graphs, slides, and film strip, whenever they are useful.

A follow-up can be made on each speaking engagement by sending a letter, with a reply card enclosed, asking the chairman of the program committee to express audience reactions. Critical replies may indicate the wisdom of cancelling incompetent speakers, changing the subject, or increasing the amount of training. Quite often this procedure helps to secure speaking engagements for another time in the future.

SELECTION OF SITES

The selection of sites for new buildings may have a serious effect upon school-community relations. Examples are numerous of how this problem has torn communities apart, creating conflicts which take years to erase. The task of selecting sites is never easy, but it can be made less difficult and more acceptable by long-range planning for the future.

The local board of education and the school administration can determine through surveys of existing plant facilities and population studies approximately when new buildings will be required and where they should be located. They can draw their plans accordingly and start to acquire sites well in advance of the time they are actually needed. Only those properties should be purchased which best meet the criteria of a good site for the size and type of school to be erected.

Planning should also provide for a full report to the people. They should be given the findings disclosed by surveys and studies and shown how the system is growing, the present condition of school buildings, and what they may expect in the future. Some boards of education invite citizens to review their building plans before any action is taken and to work with them in developing criteria for site selections. They find that long-term planning and the early involvement of citizens eliminates most of the conflicts and pressures experienced commonly in acquiring sites for school buildings.

BOND AND MILLAGE CAMPAIGNS

Eventually the time comes in most communities when school officials must undertake campaigns to win voter approval of bond issues and proposals to increase the amount of millage levied against taxable property. The money may be needed to meet the principal and interest on outstanding debts, purchase property for school sites, build plant extensions, recondition existing structures, erect new buildings, or provide for increases in current operating expenses. The nature and conduct of these campaigns pose many problems in public relations.

Points of View

Three points of view seem to prevail on the question of how to secure taxpayer approval of bond issues and additional millage. One school of thought holds to the belief that no request of this kind should be made to the people by the board of education and its executive officer. In defense of this position, it is argued that since the schools belong to the people, they should decide what they want by way of education for children and raise the money to pay for what they want. Or they may adopt the alternative of deciding how much they wish to spend for education and then fit the school program to this amount. A second school maintains that when a need exists, it is a responsibility of the board of education and its executive officer to present the facts to the community in a quiet and orderly fashion and let the people decide for themselves whether or not the need is justifiable and whether or not they wish to tax themselves more heavily. A third school supports the view that the board of education and its executive officer should launch a vigorous campaign to arouse popular interest and win voter approval of tax proposals by any legitimate means available.

All three points of view have their place in soliciting public support of education. The choice depends upon the type of community and its relations with the school system. For example, practically no campaigning is necessary in a community where people feel a genuine sense of responsibility for their schools and are active partners in the business of education. By contrast, forceful cam-

paigning is necessary in a community where people are indifferent
to their responsibility for schools and seldom share in the solution
of educational problems. However, unusual circumstances sometimes arise—for example, the sudden destruction of under-insured
buildings or a large influx of new residents—which make it imperative to campaign for the support of bond issues and higher tax
levies.

Campaign Methods

A wide range of campaign methods are employed by school
districts in securing voter approval of bond issue and millage proposals. The methods may consist of nothing more in certain communities than press releases by the board of education stating why
more money is needed for school purposes and how they intend
to raise it. This procedure may be coupled with the publication of
an illustrated brochure for public distribution and possibly one
or more parent-teacher meetings at which the facts are reiterated
and the support of parents requested. If more publicity is deemed
advisable, leaflets and folders may be sent through the mails to
resident householders, and members of the parent-teacher association may be asked to telephone their neighbors and friends, explaining why they should support the school tax proposal.

As campaigns grow in size and intensity, any of the following
methods may be used: a scheduled series of releases to community
newspapers, radio and television spot announcements, straw polls
of public sentiment, petitions and resolutions carrying citizen en-
dorsements, a proclamation by the mayor, circular letters to registered
voters, personal interviews with community leaders, radio and television talks and dramatizations, the delivery of bulletins and folders
to home owners, street banners, campaign slogans, bumper strips
on automobiles, billboard and car card advertisements, posters in
store windows, stickers for automobile windshields, paid advertisements in newspapers, distribution of sample ballots, telephone relays
urging people to register and go to the polls on election day, house-
to-house canvassing to explain and urge support of the proposal,
outside poll workers organized by precincts, cartoons, letters-to-the-
editor, contests, lapel tags, and campaign buttons.

Elements of Success

The questions are frequently asked: Why do some bond issue and millage campaigns succeed and others fail? What the are reasons? Is there some formula for success? Unfortunately, no one answer can be given. Each campaign is a unique enterprise adjusted to the local setting. However, the elements which recur in successful campaigns may be noted:

1. The board of education is unanimous in its endorsement and support of the proposal submitted to the voters.

2. Leadership is taken by the board of education in initiating the campaign, and the members work individually and as a team during all phases of it.

3. The superintendent has built a fundamental understanding over the years of school needs and practices in the minds of people. The campaign does not come to them as a surprise, but rather as something they have anticipated.

4. The faculty are taken into the complete confidence of the administration before the campaign and are kept informed during its progress.

5. The faculty are united in their support of the bond issue or tax levy.

6. Complete information is supplied to the public on the need for the proposal.

7. Publicity is planned carefully around the advantages of the proposal for child and community.

8. The public has confidence in the motives of school officials and faith in the quality of instructional services.

9. Personalities are seldom brought into the campaign and respect is shown for the opposition.

10. More reliance is placed on the parent-teacher association for support than any other community group or organization.

11. Campaign contributions are publicized and an accounting rendered of expenditures.

12. Citizens committees, which include a balanced representation of civic groups and organizations, assume a large share of responsibility for planning the campaign and seeing it through to completion.

13. The chances of passing the bond issue or tax levy are greater when the matter is brought before the electorate (a) while schools are in session, (b) during an "off" election year, and (c) if no other bond issue is on the ballot.

14. The timing of the campaign is worked out so that the intensive phase does not exceed six weeks in duration.

Causes of Failure

Just as the elements of successful campaigns may be noted, so may the events and activities which show up repeatedly in those which were failures. These elements are:

1. Responsibility for the whole campaign is carried by the board of education and the superintendent. This mistake is made too often. They forget

that responsibility for schools belongs to the people and that they must understand and feel the need before deciding questions of major policy.

2. Threats to reduce or suspend services if the proposal is defeated, like elimination of kindergartens, half-day sessions, shorter school year, fewer teachers and larger classes, inadequate supplies and equipment, less custodial and maintenance service, curtailment of the health program, and poorer transportation.

3. Too active participation in the campaign by teachers and pupils which arouses suspicion of a selfish motive and permits critics to say that time and energy are being taken from classroom instruction and other duties.

4. Using pupils to distribute literature favoring the bond issue or tax levy and denying a similar privilege to members of the opposition. No literature should ever be sent out of a school system by pupils asking parents and other taxpayers to vote "yes" on a proposal. The school is limited to an impartial statement of facts concerning a need; the right to decision rests with the voters.

5. Levying assessments against teachers to underwrite campaign expenses, in part or whole. Teachers resent this action and work against the proposal. The board of education has a right to spend public funds for disseminating essential information to taxpayers. Other campaign expenses should be met by contributions from individuals and groups in the community.

6. Basing the appeal for community support of a bond issue or tax levy on personal reasons rather than the facts and what an affirmative vote will mean for the education of children.

7. Inaccurate, incomplete, and exaggerated statements of factual information. Nothing will kill a campaign any quicker than the discovery or exposure of such information. One or two incidents are all that are necessary to cast doubt and stir up suspicion in the minds of people.

8. Centering the campaign on parents with children in school and neglecting other taxpayers. A break-down of population data will show that parents with children in school constitute only about a third of the adult population.

9. Too frequent requests for financial support of the school system. Taxpayers grow weary and resentful of being asked to pay more money into public treasuries.

10. Withholding information about schools until something is wanted.

11. Organized opposition from individuals and groups in the community. The chances of a campaign's being successful are greatly reduced if the opposition develops more than token resistance.

12. A history of previous failure on bond issues and tax levies which have come before the voters. The longer this history is, the more likely will be the defeat of the present proposal.

13. Lack of endorsement by the parent-teacher association. When this organization withholds endorsement, the proposal is invariably defeated.

14. Failure to lay a groundwork of understanding some months before the intensive campaign is started.

NEW BUILDING CONSTRUCTION

Too many times taxpayers are forgotten after they have approved a bond issue or tax levy to finance the construction of a new build-

ing. Instead of being forgotten, they should be invited to take part
in conferences for the planning of the building. Though some of
their ideas may be impractical, others may prove valuable. At the

(*Montage by Gene Udell.*)

New building needs must be explained to the people.

same time, these conferences promote an understanding of the
reasons why certain things must be done to have a functional building. Planning conferences may be followed by interim reports in
the form of newspaper articles and illustrated brochures informing

taxpayers of construction progress and pointing out any changes in the plans necessitated by increased costs and shortages of building materials. When the building is completed and ready for occupancy, the public can be invited to dedicatory exercises and to take a guided tour of the plant and see its facilities. Guided tours through a new building present a further opportunity to explain design and facilities and to show how they contribute to instruction, maintenance, and operation. Citizens are less likely to complain about the amount of money spent on new schools when they have a voice in planning and understand their features.

SCHOOL PLANT APPEARANCE

The appearance of the school plant, both outside and inside, has a continuing and cumulative effect on public attitudes toward a school system. An attractive plant, even though the buildings are old and located on sites that fall below modern standards, is generally regarded as an asset to the community and an expression of educational accomplishment. People have a feeling for and a sense of pride in a system which maintains well-kept grounds and buildings. School plant appearance is a factor to be weighed in planning a public relations program.

Outside Appearance

There is no justifiable reason today why new plants cannot be designed attractively and older ones improved in outward appearance. New plants should be designed to harmonize with their surroundings and to create esthetic impressions by mass arrangement, lines and angles, color and texture of building materials, treatment of terrain, and effective landscaping. With older plants, improvements may be achieved by proper maintenance of grounds, excellent building repair, grading of sites, erection of appropriate barriers, renovation of exteriors, expanses of glass panel and glass block, and the planting of grass, flowers, shrubs, and trees. Landscaping and window decoration can be used to introduce seasonal variations and holiday themes—for example, Thanksgiving and Christmas—which lend interest to the appearance of a building, and advantage may be taken of spot-lighting at night to draw attention to beautiful flower beds, shrubs, and window displays.

Inside Appearance

The inside appearance of the plant is influenced, for the most part, by furniture, decoration, and housekeeping standards. A building is always more attractive when it is equipped with good quality furniture, attractively arranged, and kept in excellent repair. Broken, scarred, and worn pieces detract from its appearance and strongly imply to the taxpayer a waste of public money. The design and finish of modern furniture in light stains and colored upholstery has done a great deal to improve the appearance of classrooms and offices, special suites, auditoriums, and cafeterias.

Tasteful decoration can transform the tone of a school almost overnight. New effects may be produced by repainting walls in pastel colors that are varied throughout the building, by improved lighting, and by near-white ceilings. What appear to be shabby rooms

Plant appearance is a factor in public relations.

(*Photo by The Shaws. Courtesy Public Schools, West Hartford, Connecticut.*)

and offices can sometimes be made into pleasant working areas by dressing up windows, hanging good pictures, and replacing furniture. Decorative touches may be added with living plants, mural paintings, exhibit cases, statuary, and a beautiful foyer. The acoustical treatment of floors, walls, and ceilings to reduce noise and the installation of modern sanitary facilities go far in improving the general atmosphere of a building.

Housekeeping standards are of primary importance in the maintenance of a clean, sanitary, and attractive building. Nothing detracts more from its appearance than dirty walls, floors, and windows; unclean lavatories and drinking fountains; paint that is pealing; untidy classrooms and offices; and, corridors reeking with unpleasant odors from shower rooms, cafeteria, and gymnasium. Good housekeeping requires the full cooperation of pupils and faculty members and a knowledge by custodians of the standards they are expected to uphold. It also requires that they have satisfactory equipment and supplies for performing their cleaning duties and enough time to do their work efficiently. Some administrators believe that custodians take more pride in their work and make a better impression on visitors when they are dressed in attractive but practical uniforms.

COMMUNITY USE OF SCHOOL FACILITIES

The policy of permitting individuals, groups, and organizations to use school facilities during evening hours, vacation periods, and at other times which do not conflict with their use in the regular school program has been adopted rather widely. This policy is consistent with the function of the school as a social institution and represents a service in the public interest. Permitted by law in most states, it brings a large number of people into direct contact with the physical plant and develops a finer appreciation of the educational system.

Plant Design

The concept that the school should become more of a center for community life, which this policy implies, is being carried forward in modern plant design. New buildings now provide special rooms for conferences and small meetings, adult libraries, and units in separate wings containing the auditorium, gymnasium, cafeteria, and shops, all of which are readily accessible from the street and parking areas. Buildings are placed on large sites having recreational sections and equipment, playing fields, and parking lots which can be illuminated at night. Care is taken to control the flow of pedestrian and automobile traffic and to prevent the hazards of fire and accident. Modern plant design encourages the community use of school facilities and guarantees, at the same time, an effective learning environment for pupils.

Use of Facilities

Some uses of school facilities by individuals and community groups are as follows: The cafeteria may be used for special dinners and banquets; the gymnasium for dances, basketball, exhibits, and community recreational programs; the auditorium for conferences, forums, lectures, motion pictures, dramatics, and other forms of entertainment; the shops for making and repairing furniture and household equipment and the repairing of automobiles and farm machinery; the library for recreational reading and sources of information on personal and business problems; the homemaking rooms for constructing and repairing clothing, cooking, community canning, and working out schemes for home decoration; the commercial rooms for using office equipment; the science rooms for hobbies and soil testing; the music rooms for community singing and band and orchestra practice; regular classrooms for informal meetings and discussions; and the grounds for community baseball leagues and other recreational activities.

Regulations

The community use of school facilities should be regulated by written rules of the board of education. Adequately publicized, these rules prevent friction and assure all groups of fair treatment. They also reduce much of the administrative work to a routine operation. Generally, the rules should specify when school facilities are available and the purposes for which they may be used; the procedure for making application and securing approval; the fees, if

any, that will be charged; the priority of school functions; the responsibilities of the school district; and the responsibilities of those
who use the facilities.

ORGANIZED RECREATION PROGRAMS

As an extension of the concept that the school should become more
of a center for community life, organized recreation programs have
been developed in many localities. They are usually developed to
satisfy a need for the worthy use of leisure time and to meet the
problem of inadequate public and private recreational facilities. No
age barriers are erected in the programs, because provision is made
for groups ranging from small children to senior citizens. The local
board of education may take the entire responsibility for planning,
financing, and supervising the program, or it may share it with
the community.

The nature of the individual programs, as well as the amount
of time each is given, differs rather widely. Organized team sports
are common in baseball, basketball, softball, and volley ball for
children, youth, and adults. Nights may be set aside for family-group
activities, perhaps father and daughter, father and son, mother and
daughter, or the whole family. Centers for teen-agers to dance, play
ping-pong, and take part in other games under supervision have
been established somewhat widely. The summer day-camp idea for
children has been given prominence in a number of programs. Youth
and adult interests are often served through dramatic groups, bands
and orchestras, choral singing, hobby clubs, and athletic activities.
Swimming is featured wherever pools are available, while social and
folk dancing, handicrafts, and motion pictures are always popular.
Once or twice a week the golden-age group go on picnics and motor
excursions or take part in singing, dances, hobby shows, arts and
craft work, and similar activities adapted to their interests. A few
school systems operate year-round camps and farms for the education
and recreation of high-school youth.

Recreation programs under school sponsorship are usually scheduled for the evening hours, five days a week, and throughout the
summer vacation period. But in congested neighborhoods and in
communities where play areas and other facilities are limited, they

may be offered in late afternoon, following school dismissal, and on Saturday. Here and there, school grounds and buildings are opened for community recreation on Sunday.

ADULT EDUCATION

The extension of educational opportunities into adult life is another service which the school can perform for the community. It can establish programs, both formal and informal, cultural and practical, built around the personal and social desires of adults for self-improvement. The programs may start with the beginning grades of school, as classes for illiterates, and run through the upper years of college.

Determination of Need

An adult education program, to be sufficiently broad and vital, should be more than the offerings which school officials believe adults want or they should take for their own betterment. It should represent the actual needs and interests of the adult population, as closely as they can be determined. They may be determined with a fair degree of reliability by dividing the adult population in different ways—by age, educational achievement, socioeconomic background, family status, and groups affiliations—and then analyzing the needs in each of the divisions. Or a council on adult education may be formed, consisting of men and women drawn from a cross-section of the community. This council can be asked to study the problem and to make recommendations for a suitable program of activities. However, better results are possible when both methods are employed, or others equally beneficial. This combination gives more assurance that the interests of major groups will be considered, that the educational challenge will be brought into sharper focus, and that the programs will be planned to serve a higher percentage of the adult population.

Administrative Control

Three principal patterns of administrative control are common to successful programs in adult education. The first pattern is that of complete control by the local board of education. It plans, organizes, directs, and finances the program. Regular employees are used to supervise and teach the classes. The second is a partial plan of control in that the board of education works cooperatively with community agencies and shares responsibility with them for all phases of the program. The third pattern is one of control by a private, nonprofit group or organization of citizens. The board of education merely supplies the buildings and physical facilities, and it may or may not charge a fee to cover the cost of heat, light, and custodial service.

Program Possibilities

The possibilities are numerous for developing interesting and worthwhile programs suited to the personal and social needs of adults. As examples, creative experiences may be offered in art, music, drama, crafts, and writing; discussion groups for the consideration of local problems in politics, intercultural relations, civic improvements, world affairs, and so forth; special workshops and seminars to train leaders for the parent-teacher association, community service clubs, women's organizations, and business firms and labor unions; forums and debates on pertinent issues with the school supplying moderators, speakers, and perhaps students to present facts that they have found on both sides of an issue; special courses for the foreign born to teach them the American way of living; classes for illiterates who wish to learn the simple fundamentals of reading, writing, arithmetic, and spelling; shops under the guidance of competent instructors where adults may go for aid in making and repairing equipment; a standard evening high school program for men and women who would like to earn a secondary school diploma; clubs for the pursuit of hobbies; informal sewing and cooking classes and classes in other phases of home and family living; and, a wide variety of offerings in subjects to satisfy cultural interests and to increase the competency of adults on their jobs.

Public Relations Outcomes

Community adult education which meets the needs of large numbers of people is bound to have a favorable influence on public opinion. Those who take part in the programs are almost always appreciative of the opportunity provided for continuing their education and satisfying other interests. They become acquainted with regular employees who teach many of the classes and, through these relationships, have more confidence in the school system. Moreover, every class taught by a regular employee serves to demonstrate the advancement made in instructional methods and materials over the years. Many are awakened to a deeper realization of the contribution education makes to their own lives and the lives of others and they become stronger supporters of the school. The public goodwill and understanding thus created is worth much more than the cost of this service alone.

LIBRARY SERVICE

The school library can take care of an unmet need in some localities and perform a service for parents in others. Where there is no community library, it can be opened during the evening and on Saturday for the public. In communities where this need does not exist, a special room or a section of the school library can be set aside for the use of parents. Books, pamphlets, and articles may be brought together on child growth and development, education, and intelligent family living. Parents may be encouraged to borrow these materials for home reading, and they may be supplied to study groups working on parent-teacher association projects and neighborhood councils interested in child problems.

COUNSELING SERVICE

It is likewise possible for the school to furnish counseling service to parents and alumni. Many parents would like the chance to lay child problems before a skilled counselor and discuss what might be done about them. They are free at present to bring these problems before counselors in progressive school systems, but the time is not always convenient and many feel that the school is unwilling to deal with the behavior of children in home and family situations. This could be changed rather easily by fixing evening hours for parent consultations and publicizing the service to the community.

Youth want practical assistance in obtaining suitable employ-ment and in coping with their personal problems after graduation from high school. They have relatively few places, in the average community, to turn to for this type of service. It could be supplied by the school guidance department and coordinated profitably with outside agencies. Such a service would be a contribution to the community, and it would develop in youth a realization that the school maintains a continuing interest in their welfare as individuals.

COMMUNITY IMPROVEMENT

A dynamic school system takes a direct interest in the community and tries to make it a better place in which to live. It regards this as a social obligation. It may work with citizen groups, social agencies, and other institutions on problems of community living, as pointed out in an earlier chapter, or it may work by itself when this approach is practicable. Examples are numerous of how administrators, teach-ers, and pupils have initiated community services that were needed, such as a family bureau, and continued them until they could be taken over by qualified persons or proper agencies; of how they stimulated action for home beautification and urged the removal of rubbish from yards, basements, and attics as fire prevention meas-ures; of how they increased popular awareness of citizenship duties; of how their efforts resulted in improved recreational facilities, greater traffic safety, and better street lighting; of how they in-fluenced local and regional farm economy by soil testing, crop ex-perimentation, and control of erosion; of how they helped to elim-inate malaria and hookworm and secure dental care for children; of how new parking areas were opened, street signs erected, and houses numbered; of how they promoted the laying of sidewalks, installa-tion of traffic signals, rehabilitation of slums, and the building of swimming pools. The net result of these, and other activities like them, has been better communities.

No amount of literature, talk, and publicity can take the place of social usefulness in cultivating good public relations.

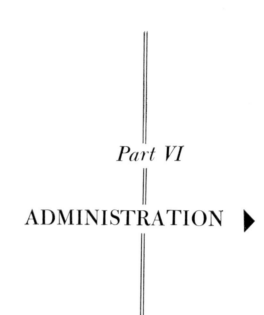

Part VI

ADMINISTRATION ▶

PLANNING
Public Information
Research
Budget
Communication

Photo by Lawrence S. Williams.

19
Organizing and Administering the Program

This chapter has been reserved to last for the reason that it helps to tie together many of the ideas and suggestions made previously. It gives attention to the procedures for developing the program, types of organizational arrangements, responsibilities of personnel, in-service training of staff, budgetary provisions, and appraisal of the program.

DEVELOPING THE PROGRAM

A somewhat logical series of steps is followed in developing a public relations program, although the number and order may vary with the size of the school system and the character of the problems it faces.

Identifying the Publics

The first step recommended is that of identifying the special publics with whom the school has relationships, and then finding out as much as possible about them, their composition and characteristics. They are staff members, pupils, parents, other citizens, and organized groups in the community. Information about these publics may be obtained by means of the community survey, opinion polls, and other methods discussed in earlier chapters. All too frequently this step is omitted or treated casually by school officials; yet it is basic in the development and administration of the program.

Defining Problems

Before an intelligent course of action can be plotted, the school must define the unmet needs and problems of relationship with its publics. It must know, for example, what unmet needs and problems are critical in the improvement of relations with parents, where points of misunderstanding and conflict have arisen in relations between teachers and pupils, and how taxpayers feel about the rising costs of education.

Though all unmet needs and problems cannot be located in a single move because the task of collecting and analyzing data is too large to undertake at one time, a start can be made by asking staff members to define carefully the problems in public relations which they have experienced. This procedure might be supplemented by a review of newspaper files, in search of articles and editorials which would confirm and add to the information they had supplied. Depth interviews might be held with selected staff members, pupils, parents, and interested citizens; or short questionnaires might be devised and administered to a sampling of members belonging to the various publics. Useful data might also be obtained from records of complaints received by the school from parents and other citizens in the community.

Formulating the Objectives

After data has been collected from which the unmet needs and problems of relationships with the school's special publics may be determined, then objectives should be formulated. A school system should know where it is trying to go and what it wishes to accomplish within the framework of the local community. Judging from oral and published statements, the inclination is strong to copy the objectives of business organizations. The statement appears time and again that schools should "sell" themselves to the public, or that the aim of a public relations program is to run a good school system and tell the public about it, or that the real aim is to win friends for the institution. These may be acceptable as final goals in private enterprise, but they are not in a tax-supported institution. The ultimate objective of school public relations is to improve the quality of education for children and youth in a democracy. While there can be no other purpose, it must be recognized that some immediate or corollary objectives may be necessary before the ultimate one can be achieved. The study of unmet needs and problems may bring out such objectives as increasing popular understanding of educational policies and practices, raising staff morale and loyalty to the school system, elevating the status of teachers in the community, neutralizing the influence of unfair criticism and attacks on instructional methods, and establishing channels through which ideas and concepts from the community may flow into the school system.

Selecting the Means

The next step is to select the means for reaching the objectives of the program. Here the principal consideration is what the school system can do, not what it is going to say to the public. It may have to decide, for example, what will be done to improve relations among staff members; how parents can be brought into the life of the school; what improvements are desirable and what things should be done to effect better relations between teachers and pupils, teachers and parents; what items will be included in an in-service training schedule for clerks and secretaries who come into contact with the public; or what specific changes shall be made in the conduct of school board meetings. These decisions are the core of the program. However, it must be remembered that few school systems are able to undertake at the beginning as much as they desire and that they must be satisfied to limit their activities to the staff and material resources which are available. They select only those activities which they can carry out successfully and which staff personnel can understand, contribute to, and accept as part of their responsibility. This changes in no way the fact that the technical phases of the program must be assigned to an experienced administrator or qualified director of public relations.

Drafting the Plan

The final step is to write out the plan of the program, setting it forth as simply as possible. The first part should be a three or four page summary of the objectives, unmet needs and problems, means selected, established limits, and lines of future expansion. Supporting detail should be presented in the body and illustrated with helpful charts and diagrams. Copies should be circulated to staff members for their comments and criticisms before the plan is presented for adoption by the board of education.

FACTORS INFLUENCING ORGANIZATION

When a program has been approved by the board of education, the question arises of what organizational arrangements are needed to carry it out. Inasmuch as planned public relations is a comparatively new undertaking in the field of educational administration, few organizational patterns have been established, and even some of these are of doubtful value. The answer should be worked out locally. In working it out, there are several factors which determine where the program shall be placed in the structure of the system and what machinery will be required to make it operate efficiently.

Size of the system is one of the factors. Formal organization for public relations is seldom necessary in small systems because of close, personal relationships among staff members and between them and the public. Nor is an elaborate plan of organization essential in systems of medium size, so long as communication channels remain open. It is only when systems are large that the more complex forms of organization must be built for retaining contacts and disseminating information to the various publics.

The nature of the program itself will determine to a considerable extent what must be done by way of setting up organization. For instance, if the program is restricted mostly to the improvement of relations with pupils and parents, the details can be developed through teacher committees, but if it calls for the intensive use of specialized communication media, like television, motion pictures, news releases, and printed bulletins, a public relations office may have to be established and staff employed to work with these media.

The internal structure of the system is another factor of some importance. In districts having a unit executive type of organization, the superintendent is the chief administrative officer. He has authority to delegate responsibility to subordinates and to create whatever machinery the program calls for. The scope and flow of authority

changes in districts having a dual or multiple executive type of organization, since the superintendent is but one of two or more administrative officials who answer directly to the board of education. As a
result, arrangements for the handling of public relations may be
restricted to the instructional division of the school system.

The amount of money available will naturally have a bearing
upon the question being considered. Schools can do no more than
their funds will permit. Many excellent programs have been crippled
for this reason before they ever had a chance to get under way. Members of school boards are still unwilling to spend money for public
relations in education, yet these same individuals do not hesitate to
make budgetary provisions for this function in their own businesses.

Prevailing attitudes in the community may dictate temporarily
how much organization may be established to carry out the program.
For example, it would not be advisable to set up an office of public
relations in a district where citizens are economy-minded and believe
that the schools are spending entirely too much money, especially if
this meant hiring a full-time director and releasing teachers to assist
in the work of this office. Nor could special services be introduced in
such a district without invoking severe criticism, or illustrated brochures and bulletins be published until a change was effected in the
thinking of the public.

The competency of staff personnel may determine where responsibilities will be placed and what activities will be provided for
in the organization. There would be no point in assigning press
relations to an assistant superintendent merely because of his position, when a teacher with a rich journalistic background might be
released part-time for this work. Likewise, plans for a series of television programs might be carried forward if personnel were available
who know how to write and produce them; otherwise it would be
better to drop the idea until a number could be trained to handle
this medium.

The division of staff responsibilities will have a decided influence
on the plan of organization. Staff responsibilities may be divided according to (1) the publics with whom better relations are wanted,
(2) activities requiring special skills, and (3) a combination of publics
and activities. For instance, the organization would be quite different
if agencies were created to improve relations with pupils and alumni,
parents, employees, the general public, and organized groups in the

community compared with a plan built around interpretative activities by means of printed materials, radio broadcasts, television programs, speakers, motion pictures, press releases, and printed bulletins. Unfortunately, few schools today divide responsibilities according to the publics served but emphasize instead the use of activities requiring special skills. They do not realize that the combination is needed to maintain balance and achieve satisfactory results.

Finally, the nature of the organization may depend upon the underlying philosophy of public relations. This is usually a deciding factor in many situations. For example, take a system in which good public relations is conceived as favorable publicity. Here the superintendent might set up a school-community relations office for presenting highlights of the system through news stories, special events, printed materials, and television programs. At the same time, he might instruct building principals to form teacher committees for supplying news copy and staging special programs, such as open house, exhibits, local observances, and student activities, to impress the public. But if the viewpoint was one of encouraging lay participation in school affairs and asking citizens to help solve educational problems, then provision might be made for lay advisory and study groups in the organizational arrangement, and means might be created for parents to take an increasingly more active part in the everyday life of the individual school.

PLANS OF ORGANIZATION

In general, three plans of organization are used to place responsibility for public relations activities and to facilitate the operation of the program. They may be described as centralized, decentralized, and coordinate plans. Wide variations are found within each type of plan and between them due to the influence of the factors which were discussed in the preceding section.

Centralized Plan

A centralized plan is one in which responsibility for the program is centered almost entirely in the chief administrative officer and his immediate line and staff associates. Several reasons are advanced by those who support this plan of organization. They point out that the superintendent is the person best known to the people of the community, and that they look to him for leadership in matters effecting the welfare of children. He is expected to supply information on the conditions, needs, and practices of the schools. With his associates, he enjoys many contacts with important citizens which enable him to keep his fingers on the pulse of public opinion. As a result, he knows when it is opportune to propose new policies and suggest changes in older ones. Specific assignments can be made and responsibility fixed more easily in the plan. Moreover, the staff is readily available for consultation. The example set by the superintendent and his associates has a wholesome influence on all employees in the system; they show more interest in their own relations with the public.

Thus in a small school system, the superintendent or supervising principal engages in a variety of activities for interpreting the work of the school system and earning the good will of the public. Among others, he may give talks before many groups, join different organizations, participate in community affairs, supply news copy, prepare printed materials, and handle complaints received in the system. He may also consult with teachers on their public relations problems and urge them to improve their relations with pupils, parents, friends, and neighbors.

As a system grows larger and the use of special media is incorporated in the program, he is forced to delegate specific tasks to other people. This requires some plan of organization. It might be a relatively simple plan such as that shown in the accompanying diagram.

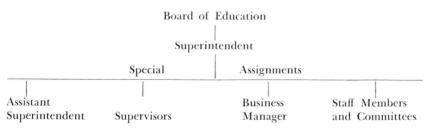

A centralized plan of organization for public relations in a school system of medium size.

The plan would be more complex in a large system if responsibility was distributed rather widely among line and staff officers, and a director of public relations appointed, together with competent teacher assistants, to handle the technical work on some phases of the program. These individuals might be brought together to serve as a planning committee and a coordinating agency for the program. In this instance, the plan of organization might be similar to that presented in the diagram below.

A centralized plan of organization for public relations in a school system of large size.

While the centralized plan of organization is used in the majority of large school systems having planned public relations programs, there are serious weaknesses connected with it. The most serious one grows out of the fact that good public relations can never be achieved solely at the top of the school system. Excellent work may be done by the superintendent and his associates through formal communication media and personal contacts, but this can hardly off-set the destructive influence of poor instruction, low staff morale, and unsatisfactory relations between teachers and pupils, parents, alumni, and other citizens. Another prominent weakness is the failure to involve principals and teachers in the program and to train them to deal with problems which originate in the individual school and can only be solved there.

Decentralized Plan

A decentralized plan is one in which responsibility for the program is centered almost entirely in the building principal and in which the individual school is regarded as the natural unit for public relations. This is by far the most common plan found in school systems today. There is justification for it. As an educational leader, the building principal is in a strong position to foster friendly relations with the school's publics on a neighborhood and sectional basis. He is close to the people and has a more intimate understanding of their needs and interests than do the administrative and supervisory officials at the top of the system. He can work with the instructional and noninstructional staff in establishing need for the program and conduct in-service training through the everyday situations which arise in the school. Excellent media are available for keeping parents informed and educating people in the service area about instructional aims and practices. Through his efforts, the building can become a community center and activities carried on for the improvement of community living.

The plan of organization for public relations in an individual school might be somewhat as follows:

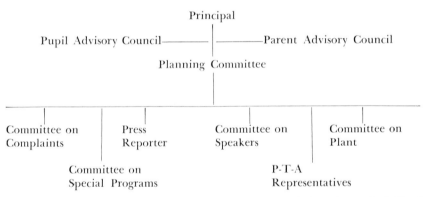

A decentralized plan of organization for public relations in an individual school.

It should be noted that provision is made in this plan for pupil and parent advisement on policy questions that fall within the scope of the principal's authority. The actual planning of the program is done by the planning committee. It includes the principal and representatives chosen by teachers and other staff members. The planning committee is empowered as well to appoint the special committees and to assign specific activities to individuals who are competent enough to handle them. The outstanding feature of this arrangement is the participation of pupils, parents, teachers, and noninstructional staff members.

Although the decentralized plan is excellent in many respects, it is open to criticism in others. It usually means a neglect of public relations opportunities by central administrative officials and a sloughing off of the work they should be doing concurrently with the principal and staff members of the individual school. Without their leadership and direction, some principals are incapable of developing sound programs or they are unwilling to take the initiative. Nor does this plan operate successfully in systems that are shot through with dissension and conflict among staff members and between them and the administration.

Coordinate Plan

A coordinate plan is one in which public relations responsibility of the central administration and that of the building principal and staff are fitted together into a connected and balanced arrangement. Policy and program are developed cooperatively for the system as a whole. The work of one division is planned to complement that of

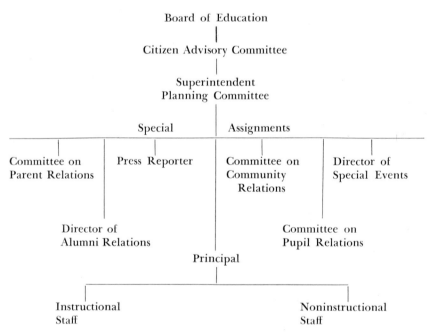

1. **A coordinate plan of organization for public relations in a small school system.**

another, with each undertaking the activities it is best equipped to manage. The use of media requiring technical knowledge and skill is assigned to the central administration, while improvement in relations with pupils, alumni, parents, other citizens, and some organized groups is made a function of the principal and staff of the individual school. The entire enterprise is marked by unity of plan and action.

In a small school system, the plan of organization could be worked out as shown in diagram 1, page 404.

As presented in the diagram, the board of education would consult with a citizen advisory committee on major problems of the school system. The superintendent would be in charge of the pro-

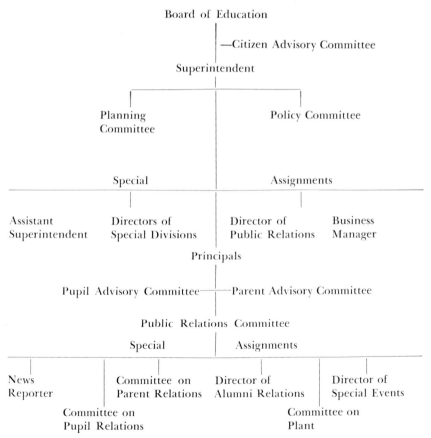

2. **A coordinate plan of organization for public relations in a large school system.**

gram, but the program itself would be developed cooperatively by a planning committee consisting of the superintendent, the building principal or principals, faculty representatives, and representatives of the noninstructional staff. Special assignments would be made by either the supervising principal or the planning committee, depending upon the amount of teamwork in the system. Because of smallness in size, this organization would cover both the central administration and the individual building.

In a large school system, the pattern of organization would, of necessity, be somewhat different. It might take the form shown in diagram 2, page 405.

The principal features provided in both the centralized and decentralized plans of organizations are brought together here. Coordination is effected by the planning and policy committees. They are made up of representatives from all classes of employees. The representatives may be chosen directly from individual schools and divisions of the system, or they may emerge from a line of committees organized at different levels of operation. The problem is that of maintaining balanced representation and still keeping the membership small enough for working efficiency.

RESPONSIBILITIES OF PERSONNEL

No plan of organization will function successfully unless staff members and the members of committees know exactly what they are expected to do and understand the limits of their authority. While detailed assignments may differ between one system and another, the general nature of their responsibilities approximate those described here.

Board of Education

The board of education has important responsibilities in the program of public relations. A primary one is that of adopting a written policy setting forth the social need and value of keeping the people informed and seeking their cooperation in the continuous improvement of schools. Another is to delegate to the chief executive officer and his staff the job of translating the policy into a practical program, yet reserving the right to accept, modify, or reject whatever actions are proposed. A third is to vote funds for financing the program and then to stand fully behind it at all times. A fourth responsibility is to undertake the activities assigned to it as a body and to its members as individuals. And last, to appraise results and make necessary changes in the program.

Superintendent

The responsibilities of the superintendent are leadership and direction of the program by (1) acquainting the board with the social need and value of planned public relations, (2) developing the plans by which the formal policy is translated into action, (3) setting up the working organization and assigning responsibilities to personnel, (4) motivating the staff to participate fully in the program, (5) providing whatever in-service training is necessary, (6) examining school policies and practices for the effect they have on public opinion, (7) performing the activities which are peculiar to his office, (8) serving as advisor to the board of education on questions of public relations policy and procedure, and (9) collecting the data by which the board may judge the effectiveness of the program.

Director of Public Relations

The director of public relations is usually a staff officer who is directly under the superintendent in systems where he is employed. He may have the title of director of public relations, director of school and community relations, director of publicity, director of public information, or coordinator of school-community relations. An inventory of his responsibilities at the present time in a representative sampling of districts shows that his efforts are spent mostly on newspaper publicity, preparation of school publications, production of radio and television programs, and the management of special events. In some instances, he may be asked to make motion pictures and slides, operate a speakers' bureau, represent the superintendent at community group meetings, work with building principals on publicity materials, make surveys of public opinion, or give talks to faculty and parent groups.

These findings suggest a strong tendency to narrow his responsibilities to the preparation and use of special communication media. This is probably due to the fact that public relations programs in larger school systems are concentrated at the top and built around the use of tools in mass communication. This tendency will no doubt change with the growing understanding of school public relations and the organization of programs to include all personnel in the system. In this event, his responsibilities will be to serve as an advisor to the board of education and the superintendent; to plan or help to plan the program; to stimulate, encourage, and instruct personnel in the use of public relations techniques; to supervise the employment of mass communication media; to coordinate the different parts of the program; to conduct research; and, to set up procedures for evaluating the effectiveness of the program.

Administrative Assistants

Assistant superintendents, supervisors, and directors of special departments are included in this category. Besides meeting their daily obligations to interpret the schools through the direct and indirect contacts they have with the public, they may be placed in charge of activities calling for specialized leadership. For example, the assistant superintendent may be made responsible for radio and television programs, the director of research for printed materials, and the head of adult education for special events. Fortunately, there are many competent individuals serving as administrative assistants who are qualified to give specialized leadership or they can acquire the necessary knowledge and skill without too much difficulty.

Principal

The leadership and direction of the program in the individual school are responsibilities of the principal. He carries them out by (1) developing with his staff a program that fits into the frame of the general policy, (2) adapting the program to the needs and conditions of the area served by his school, (3) establishing a plan of organization and assigning responsibilities to personnel, (4) directing the in-service training of staff members, (5) engaging in the activities assigned to him in the program, (6) administering directives from the superintendent and his associates, (7) locating trouble spots and furnishing essential information to the superintendent,

(8) conducting a continuing survey of community attitudes, needs, and opinions, (9) encouraging responsible individuals and groups to make use of the plant and its facilities, (10) taking initiative and cooperating in projects for the improvement of community living, and (11) carrying out recommended procedures for estimating the worth of the program.

Teacher

The teacher is a front-line interpreter of the school system through his daily contacts with members of different publics. In this capacity, his responsibilities are to cooperate in the development of the individual school program; to acquire a thorough knowledge of the school system and be able to discuss it intelligently with others; to do as good a job of teaching as possible; to work constantly for good relations with pupils, parents, and people in the community; to accept and carry out special assignments in the program; to supply information requested by other agents and agencies in the program; to keep his own disagreements with colleagues and prevailing practices strictly within the system; to take an active interest in community life; and to become a student of attitudes and opinions regarding public education.

Noninstructional Personnel

The responsibilities of the noninstructional worker are similar to those of the teacher. He is expected to cooperate in the development of the program; to acquire a knowledge of the schools and be able to interpret them to others; to seek improvement in his relations with different publics; to accept and carry out special assignments; to supply information requested by other agents and agencies in the program; to refrain from criticizing the school before people in the community; and to report what he discovers about the attitudes and opinions of taxpayers toward the system.

IN-SERVICE TRAINING

Provision for in-service training is a part of a good public relations program. Staff members must possess the knowledges and skills required for meeting their responsibilities. Training may be given either through direct instruction or indirectly through a series of devices. The nature of the training will be determined by the past experiences of the staff and the demands of the local program.

Direct Training

The more usual and successful types of direct training are:

1. *Orientation Programs.* These are designed to acquaint the new staff member with the school system and to help him make a satisfactory adjustment. During this training, his attention is directed to the public relations objectives and activities of the school system and the responsibilities he must meet. A staff member who has gone through a good orientation program is better equipped to interpret the schools and to build wholesome relations with the public than one who has not.

2. *In-Service Courses.* These are formal courses taught by competent instructors both from within and from outside the school system. They are used to train personnel for work done in all branches of the system. Courses may be included in radio, television, editing, motion pictures, interviewing, news reporting, opinion polling, and correspondence. They make it possible for interested staff members to receive technical training and qualify themselves to work with special communication media. Other courses of a more generalized nature may also be organized and offered in connection with the public relations program.

3. *Workshops.* The workshop method of training is regarded as an excellent means for increasing staff efficiency. It is built around problems which grow out of daily experiences, or it may be used for planning purposes. Held during the school year, the summer months, or both, the participants meet in small groups with consultants to exchange ideas and to pool their thinking. Groups may be set up to deal with such matters as home visits, open house programs, oral and written expression, relations with parents, lay advisory committees, news reporting, and the like.

4. *Clinics.* This name is sometimes applied to short, intensive training programs for experienced personnel in specialized fields of service. For example, a clinic might be held for teachers who are responsible for gathering and reporting news stories. The purpose

of the clinic might be to review their work and find out how it could be improved; or it might be to propose a new system of reporting and acquaint them with the procedures. The possibilities of clinics for in-service training have scarcely been explored and cultivated in public school systems.

5. *Special Meetings.* From time to time the staff may be called together for special meetings devoted to public relations. Matters of current interest can be taken up with the entire group and points emphasized which are in need of immediate attention. They are more effective for disseminating and imparting important information than written communications. The response to these meetings is favorable when good instructional techniques are employed in the presentation of materials.

6. *Pre-School Conferences.* As the title suggests, they are held before the official opening of school in the fall. Anywhere from three days to two weeks are set aside for the conferences. During this time, the staff can work without interruption on the program for the year. They may be assisted by consultants and resource persons. The results more than justify the time expended.

7. *Study Groups.* Study groups are valuable for the intensive analysis of relationship problems and the compilation of significant information. Participation is on a voluntary basis, but those who take part agree to attend scheduled meetings and remain with their group for the prescribed period of time. The work of analyzing relationships and formulating working hypotheses is done under the direction of a trained leader, and no group deals with more than one problem area. The problem areas may include teacher-pupil relations, teacher-parent relations, administrative-staff relations, relations with community groups, and alumni relations. While this type of study group has not been tried by many systems, those which have tried it are enthusiastic about it.

8. *Faculty Meetings.* Time can be set aside in regular faculty meetings for in-service training in public relations. The agenda should be planned cooperatively by the staff and administration and restricted to topics in which there is a mutual interest. More will be achieved when subject matter is presented with the aid of motion pictures, slides, charts, graphs, printed materials, demonstrations, objects, and panel discussions.

9. *Executive Luncheon Meetings*. Executives need training just as much as other staff members in the school system. This training can be carried on through a series of monthly luncheon meetings. The conference method of discussion, using carefully prepared material, is effective in dealing with problems that need attention and in presenting new ideas for consideration. Not enough has been done to stimulate the growth of executive personnel in school systems generally.

Indirect Training

Indirect training is accomplished through the use of instructive devices. Some of the devices are:

1. *Handbooks*. Two types of handbooks contribute to the training of personnel in service. One supplies information which should be known by staff members in order to discuss the school intelligently with the public. The other outlines the responsibilities of each person in the program and how they should be handled. Both may be revised annually and distributed for ready reference and reading.

2. *House Organs*. These may take the form of a magazine, bulletin, newsletter, or folder. They are prepared for employees of the school system. Published semi-monthly or monthly, they keep readers informed of what is happening in the system and offer many practical suggestions for better public relations. Sometimes they contain a citation column for bestowing recognition on those who have performed outstanding services. An attractive house organ is indispensable in the training program of a large system.

3. *Films and Slides*. Shown occasionally at faculty and other group meetings, they give meaning and reality to the work in public relations. A school system would do well to produce films and slides based on the material in handbooks which are distributed to employees; nothing else will give so much life to this material or stamp it more deeply into their minds. Systems which cannot afford to make their own films and slides may borrow or rent appropriate ones from other systems, commercial agencies, and professional organizations.

4. *Case Studies*. Staff members derive a great deal of benefit

from brief, simple reports of case studies made in the system. Each case study contains a description of a public relations problem and a statement of the methods used for solving it. Not only do these reports help staff members learn how to identify their own problems, but they also show how to go about the task of working them out successfully. They may be published in house organs or printed separately. An edited collection of case studies makes excellent material for an orientation program and for in-service courses.

5. *Bulletin Boards.* Graphic and printed materials can be placed on the bulletin boards in each school and special department of the school system to keep staff members informed and to draw their attention to important ideas and changes in the program.

6. *Exhibits.* Portable exhibits offer excellent opportunities to show visually the need for public relations, how the program is organized, the placement of responsibility, the factors which influence public opinion, topics for news stories, printed communication materials, and similar points of interest. They can be circulated for scheduled viewing in all parts of the system.

7. *External Publications.* Staff members should receive copies of every external publication, including the annual report of the superintendent to the board of education. They should know how the schools are being interpreted to people in the community and the nature of the publications distributed. The information contained in these publications is essential to their own work of telling the school story.

8. *Checklists and Rating Scales.* These devices cause staff members to look at themselves and evaluate their own practices. Used sparingly, they can be valuable aids in the training program.

BUDGETARY PROVISIONS

How much money should a school system spend for public relations personnel, services, and media? Administrators and school board members frequently ask this question. They want to know approximately what their school system will have to pay for a good public relations program. No method has been discovered for calculating this figure, nor is there likely to be one in the future. The cost will naturally vary with the amount of work to be done and the willingness of the system to do it. Therefore, the only practical answer to the question is build the program first and then determine how much money must be appropriated to operate it.

Determining how much money a program will cost is not easy, since much of the activity is interwoven with regular services. However, a number of methods have been advocated for arriving at a cost figure. One is to take a fixed percentage of the total school budget, say one-half of one per cent, and allocate this amount of money for program operation. Another is the so-called "project appropriation" method, whereby the budget is based upon the estimated cost of the projects planned for the year. A third method is followed in systems having a public relations office with a director in charge. The budget is restricted to this office alone and worked out in the same way as the budgets for research, pupil personnel accounting, adult education, and similar departments performing special spervices. Still another method is to make a careful analysis of the program for the year and estimate how much money the board of education must provide. The amount needed can be presented in a separate budget statement or it can be included in the budgets of the several departments and units of the system having responsibilities in the program.

APPRAISING THE PROGRAM

Appraising the program means to judge how effectively it is achieving the purposes for which it was planned. All too frequently the appraisal of school public relations work is based on evidence gathered through casual observations and general impressions, and it is seldom accurate or complete. Unless provision is made for the systematic and periodic appraisal of results, there is no way of knowing what is being accomplished, or justifying the program, and of improving its effectiveness.

Systematic appraisal involves the use of appropriate methods and techniques for collecting and measuring the evidence of results. It involves, further, comparing the findings of one appraisal with those of another and measuring or describing the specific changes and improvements which have taken place. It is only after such changes and improvements have been determined that sound judgments can be reached concerning the worth of the program. These judgments must be consistent with the philosophy underlying school and community relationship activities.

The appraisal of public relations work is somewhat difficult because few reliable methods have been developed for gathering data on outcomes and the direct results are hard to measure. However, much can be done to make typical appraisals more valid, reliable, and objective. Procedures which may be used for this purpose are:

1. *Observations.* Informal appraisals are possible through the careful and unbiased observation of program effects, even though the effects cannot be measured objectively. It becomes evident through observation that a program is producing good results when pupils and parents express more friendly attitudes toward the school, and teachers wish to improve their skill in human relations, manifest a deeper interest in pupil welfare, or take a more active part in community life. It is not difficult to detect favorable changes in the tone of newspaper editorials, letters-to-the-editor, and communications received from taxpayers. Sound guesses may be made about the effectiveness of the program when parents and community leaders are more willing to sit down and to discuss educational problems with school officials. Other opportunities for observing results include the reception accorded to school representatives who appear before civic groups, public reactions to resolutions adopted by the board of education and proposals made by administrators, citizen cooperation on school-community improvement projects, and general remarks by people about the school.

2. *Records.* Various types of records may supply evidence of program effectiveness. A running account of criticisms and complaints which shows both a reduction in number and a narrowing of scope may tell something of the impact of the program. Brief reports written by staff members on a standardized form and telling of significant comments made by people with whom they have talked may give a picture of what is happening. Requests for publications and records of attendance at open affairs and parent-teacher association meetings provide signs of growing interest in the school. The problem-study committees formed during the year and the nature of their activities are evidence that the partnership concept is taking hold. Much can be learned from keeping systematic records of

election returns and the distribution of votes on school proposals submitted to the voters of the district.

3. *Telephone Surveys.* Telephone surveys may be employed to check reader interest in newspaper stories and audience reactions to radio and television programs. A random sample of names is drawn from the telephone directory to make up the list of those who will be called. A brief interview is conducted by telephone and only a few questions are asked. The subscriber may be requested to state whether or not he reads school-news stories in the daily paper and, if so, the kinds of school news he prefers and recent stories he can recall. A similar line of questioning is followed in seeking audience reactions to radio and television programs. Although few school systems have engaged in telephone surveys of this nature, they are the quickest of the survey techniques and their cost is relatively low. They supply useful information in appraising the worth of activities, but not enough to judge attitudes, insights, and understandings of the people interviewed.

4. *The Panel.* The panel technique was described in the chapter dealing with methods for understanding the community. As may be recalled, it consists of a selected jury of laymen who are fairly representative of the population. Interviews are held periodically with individual members of the panel and opinions asked on a scheduled series of questions. An attempt is made to get at the intensity of feelings they express and to note trends in opinions. Commercial interests have employed consumer panels with success in recent years for getting reactions to products and advertising. They have found that for trend studies in opinion, the information supplied by a few panel members is just as reliable as that supplied by a large number of persons. Although there are definite weaknesses in the panel technique—the literature on this subject makes them clear— the advantages are strong enough to off-set them. More use should be made of the panel for collecting evidence of program effectiveness and checking results against those obtained by other methods.

5. *Questionnairies.* Questionnaires are the most widely used method for surveying public opinion and gathering data for judging the worth of the whole program or parts of it. The short questionnaire, in the form of a printed card, may be used when quick re- actions are wanted to some activity or opinion is sought on a par-

ticular problem. This type of questionnaire may be distributed to members of an audience attending a school event, with the request that they fill it out before leaving. It may be inserted in school publications in order to find out if they are read, what features are most appealing, and what the readers think of them. By printing the questions on the back of a stamped, self-addressed postal card, a larger number of readers are willing to reply than if they must address and and stamp the card themselves. When some measure of opinion is wanted at once on a particular problem or issue under consideration, the postal-card type of questionnaire may be sent by mail to a selected list or sample of residents with a request for an immediate reply. Usually a brief statement of urgency for reply brings a satisfactory response.

A more comprehensive type of questionnaire may be administered at regular intervals to staff members and pupils within the school when evidence is wanted on the nature of attitudes and opinions regarding existing policies and practices. Important changes may be discovered and leads disclosed for future planning by making comparative studies of the findings.

The mail questionnaire has been recommended widely as a desirable method of surveying parents and other adults in the community. It consists of a schedule of questions sent by mail to citizens on the survey list. They are asked to fill out the questionnaire and return it by mail at an early date. In some instances, the questionnaire is either published in the local newspaper or else delivered in person to those on the list and the request is made that it be filled out and returned by mail. The cost of preparing and distributing the mail questionnaire is relatively low, and it has the further advantage of permitting the recipient to answer it at his convenience. However, the returns are frequently poor and scarcely representative of the sample to whom it was sent. More satisfactory returns are possible if the questionnaire is delivered and picked up after a reasonable period of time has elapsed. A well-constructed mail questionnaire provides invaluable information in appraising the effectiveness of the program.

6. *Checklists.* Another means of gathering data on the outcomes of the program is the checklist. This instrument may be used for determining how much change has taken place in the attitudes and opinions of the public with reference to a problem or several

problems receiving attention in the public relations program. It consists of a series of multiple-choice questions arranged in a sequential order. The questions are stated as problems, and each is followed by a list of from three to ten possible answers; the informant is asked to choose the answer most nearly representing his viewpoint, opinion, or judgment.

7. *Rating Scales.* Rating scales are somewhat similar in design to checklists. On these the informants are asked to choose from among three to five degrees of opinion or attitude intensity on a series of specific questions. The purpose is that of obtaining a quantitative expression of opinions and attitudes at the levels included in the scale. For example, the question might be asked, "How important do you think it would be for the board of education to establish a research program in the public school system—very important, only fairly important, not important at all?" Or the question might be presented in the form of a series of graded statements with the request that the informant check the one most descriptive of how he feels. Questions may be presented in other forms which are more suitable for the type of inquiry being made.

The construction and interpretation of rating scales which attempt to measure attitude intensity demand expert attention. This work cannot be entrusted to anyone on the staff. It should be assigned only to those who are familiar with social science research methods.

8. *Opinion Polls.* Opinion polls, using direct interviews with a stratified sample of the population, are one of the best methods open to school systems for ascertaining whether or not the views of citizens on selected problems and issues have changed as a result of the program. The nature and amount of change cannot be estimated with reasonable accuracy unless polls are taken at regular intervals and the findings compared. Considerations entering into the building of ballots and the selection and interviewing of the population sample were set forth in a previous chapter.

Chapter Bibliography

1. The School and the Public

Bernays, Edward L., Ed., *The Engineering of Consent*. Norman, Oklahoma: University of Oklahoma Press, 1955. A discussion by eight experts in the field of public relations on how people accept ideas, programs and courses of action. This book is written for public relations in business and industry.

Bogardus, Emory S., *Fundamentals of Social Psychology*, 3rd Ed. New York: D. Appleton-Century Company, 1940. Chapter 30. This chapter describes how public opinion is formed.

Butts, R. Freeman, *A Cultural History of Education*. New York: McGraw-Hill Book Company, Inc., 1947. Chapter 14. A generalized account of the political and social conditions surrounding the establishment of the American public school system.

Callahan, Raymond E., *An Introduction to Education in American Society*. New York: Alfred A. Knopf, 1956. Chapters 3, 6, 7, 10, 12. These chapters deal with the nature of culture, historical background of public education, ideological characteristics of American education, legal foundations, and aims and purposes of education in this country.

Charters, W. W. Jr., "Person-to-Person Influence," *Nation's Schools*, 56:49-52. November, 1955. Shows how face-to-face relations are a powerful determinant of public opinion.

Cocking, Walter D., "Schools Belong to the People," *School Executive*, 171:40. January, 1952. A point of view emphasizing citizen participation in school affairs.

Doob, Leonard W., *Propaganda: Its Psychology and Technique*. New York: Henry Holt and Company, 1935. An interesting and informative discussion of how groups and organizations promote their programs.

Edwards, Newton, and Herman G. Richey, *The School in the American Social Order*. Boston: Houghton Mifflin Company, 1947. Chapters 6-10. An excellent discussion of the forces which influenced the development of the free, tax-supported, public school.

Fetherstone, Thomas C., "Earning Public Appreciation for the Public Schools," *School Board Journal*, 129:27-39. October, 1954. A school board president tells why the people should be kept informed about education in the local district.

Hagman, Harlan L., "Six Major Contemporary Purposes in School Public Relations," *Education*, 69:210-15. December, 1948. A desirable list of objectives for any school public relations program.

Hamlin, Herbert M., *The Public and Its Education*. Danville, Illinois: The Interstate Printers and Publishers, 1955. Chapters 1, 3, 4, 5, 7, 8. Discusses the history of American education and the responsibilities of citizens and educators for schools.

Hill, Guy H., and G. Robert Koopman, *Building Public Confidence in the Schools*. Washington, D.C.: Association for Supervision and Curriculum Development, 1949. "Building Confidence in Public Schools," pp. 8-19. The authors maintain that public confidence in public schools increases when laymen are involved in school affairs.

Jones, James J., "Modern Concepts of Public Relations", *Phi Delta Kappa*, 229-33. March, 1955. Explains the more important viewpoints regarding public relations for public schools.

Knight, Edgar W., *Education in the United States*, 2nd Rev. Ed. Boston: Ginn and Company, 1941. Chapters 6-10. A concise history of events related to education in this country from early colonial times through the struggle for universal public education.

Lasswell, H. D., *Democracy Through Public Opinion*. Menasha, Wisconsin: Banta, 1941. An analysis of the factors which play an important part in the formation of decisions in democratic society.

Meier, Norman C., and Harold W. Saunders, *The Polls and Public Opinion*. New York: Henry Holt and Company, 1949. Chapters 10-14. These chapters deal with determinants of public opinion.

Miller, Carl G., "The Public and the Aims of Public School Education," *Education*, 64:59. September, 1944. A forceful editorial that covers an essential problem in public relations.

Moehlman, Arthur B., *Social Interpretation*. New York: D. Appleton-Century Company, 1938. Chapters 1, 2, 3. Explains the democratic new point of social interpretation.

Odegard, Peter H., *The American Public Mind*. New York: Columbia University Press, 1930. A pioneer volume on the psychology of public opinion.

Owens, Robert G., "Community Control of Public School Policies," *School Board Journal*, 128:51, 106. February, 1954. A convincing series of arguments on why the general control of school policy should be kept in the hands of the people.

Pimlott, J. A. R., *Public Relations and American Democracy*. Princeton, New Jersey: Princeton University Press, 1951. Chapter 9. The author makes a case concerning the social significance of public relations.

Powell, Norman John, *Anatomy of Public Opinion*. Englewood Cliffs, N. J.: Prentice-Hall, Inc., 1951. This book is designed to acquaint the reader with the nature, operation, molding, and influence of public opinion.

Rugg, Harold, and William Withers, *Social Foundations of Education*. Englewood Cliffs, N. J.: Prentice-Hall, Inc., 1955. Chapters 2, 10, 12, 18.

Young, Kimball, *Social Psychology*. New York: F. S. Crofts and Company, Inc., 1944. Chapter 18, pp. 429-42. The nature of public opinion, its place in a democracy, and the psychological factors influencing its formation are discussed.

2.   The Need for Public Relations

Adams, J. Harry, "Keeping Faith with the People," *The Bulletin of the National Association of Secondary School Principals*, 32:24-30. Points out the failure of secondary education to fulfill its role in society.

Brownell, Clifford Lee, Leo Gans, and Tufie Z. Maroon, *Public Relations in Education*. New York: McGraw-Hill Book Company, Inc., 1955. Chapter 4.

Doods, Glenn W., "Does Fiction Libel the Teacher?" *Nation's Schools*, 42:41-43. October, 1948. Lists early works of fiction in which teachers are portrayed unfavorably. Also discusses some modern books which are laudatory of the teaching profession.

Finck, Edgar M., "Facing Criticism Wins Public," *Nation's Schools*, 41:27-28. May, 1948. An illustration of how one school turned public criticism of a program into strong support.

Grinnell, J. Earle, *Interpreting the Public Schools*. New York: McGraw-Hill Book Company, Inc., 1937. Chapter 1. A good discussion of the reasons why schools must keep the public fully informed of their programs and practices.

Griswold, Glenn and Denny Griswold, *Your Public Relations.* New York: Funk and Wagnalls Company, 1948. Chapters 1-2. A good statement of the importance of public relations for business.

Harlow, Rex F., and Marvin M. Black, *Practical Public Relations.* New York: Harper & Brothers, 1947. Chapter 1. Sets forth some factors which gave rise to public relations programs for business and industry.

Hill, George E., "The Teaching Profession and the Public," *School and Society,* Volume 56. November 21, 1942. Analyzes the causes for the poor status of teachers in community life and suggests how it can be improved.

Lundborg, Louis B., *Public Relations in the Local Community.* New York: Harper & Brothers, 1950. Chapters 1-5. Describes the public relations problem of business at the local community level.

Miller, Clyde, *The Process of Persuasion.* New York: Crown Publishers, 1946. This book deals with persuasion methods and practices employed by individuals and groups in their efforts to influence public opinion.

Moehlman, Arthur B., *Social Interpretation.* New York: D. Appleton-Century Company, 1938. Chapter 1, 2. The needs of public relations are pointed up indirectly in the discussion of the social rule of the school.

"National Contests for Schools," *The Bulletin of the National Association of Secondary School Principals,* 34:5-10. October, 1950. Report of a committee recommending policies governing contests together with an approved list of contests.

Smith, Robert A., "Can Business Afford to Neglect Public Education," *Public Relations Journal,* 5:1-7. November, 1949. Makes a plea that business take a stronger interest in public education and help to improve the quality of personnel received from the schools.

Stearns, Harry L., "The Growing Political Reach for the Control of Education," *American School Board Journal,* 118:35-36, 88. May, 1949.

Teacher and Public, Eighth Yearbook, Department of Classroom Teachers. Washington, D.C.: National Education Association, February, 1934. Chapters 1-4.

The Public and the Elementary School, Twenty-Eighth Yearbook, Department of Elementary School Principals. Washington, D.C.: National Education Association, 1949. Pp. 9-14.

Van Zwoll, J. A., "The Need for Public Relations," *The Bulletin of the National Association of Secondary School Principals,* 32:15-23. February, 1948. A philosophical statement concerning the nature of the school and its responsibilities to the community.

Waller, J. Flint, *Outside Demands and Pressures on the Public Schools,* Contributions to Education, No. 542. New York: Bureau of Publications, Teachers College, Columbia University, 1932. Chapter 2. An early study of the types of demands and pressures exerted on schools by outside groups.

Yeager, William A., *School-Community Relations.* New York: The Dryden Press, 1951. Chapters 3, 5, 7. The need for public relations is interwoven with a generalized discussion of the place of the school in society.

3. Understanding the Community

Barnes, Harry E., *Social Institutions.* Englewood Cliffs, N. J.: Prentice-Hall, Inc., 1942. Part I. A thorough treatment of social groups.

Basic Community Survey, Bulletin No. 3014. Lansing, Michigan: State Department of Public Instruction, 1939. A detailed form for use by local schools in determining educational needs and resources of the community. Suggests several items to consider in making a survey.

Stonborough, Thomas H. W., "Fixed Panels in Consumer Research," *Journal of Marketing.* 7:129-38. October, 1942. Valuable for understanding the panel method in opinion measurement.

5. Establishing Basic Concepts

Barr, A. S., William H. Burton, and Leon J. Brueckner, *Supervision*, 2nd Ed. New York: D. Appleton-Century Company, 1938. Chapter 2. The authors give a brief but excellent discussion of the meaning of principles and how they differ from techniques.

Brown, L. H., "Guideposts to Action," *The Bulletin of the National Association of Secondary School Principals*, 32:37-47. February, 1948. A high-school principal describes the public relations policies and program followed in his school.

Campbell, Roald F. and John A. Ramseyer, *The Dynamics of School-Community Relationships*. Englewood Cliffs, N. J.: Allyn and Bacon, Inc., 1955. An excellent treatment of the role of citizens in the work of improving schools and the principles which govern the working together of laymen and educators. Many concrete illustrations are cited.

Commager, Henry Steele, "Our Schools Have Kept Us Free," *Life*, 29:46-47. October, 16, 1950. An excellent statement on what schools have stood for in American life and their problems today.

Educational Policies Commission, *Purposes of Education in American Democracy*. Washington, D.C.: National Education Association, 1938. Helpful in gaining perspective concerning the fundamental purposes of public education.

Godwin, W. R., "A Board Adopts and Prints Its Policies," *American School Board Journal*, 116:22-23, 88. March, 1948. Explains importance of having clearly formulated policies.

Grinnel, J. Erle, *Interpreting the Public Schools*. New York: McGraw-Hill Book Company, Inc., 1937. Chapter 2. A statement of the principles governing a public relations program.

Grinnel, J. E., and Raymond J. Young, *The School and the Community*. New York: The Ronald Press, 1955. Chapter 11. The second section of this chapter enumerates the principles of public relations which underlie good practice.

Hagman, Harlan L., *The Administration of American Public Schools*. New York: McGraw-Hill Book Company, Inc., 1951. Chapters 2-3. Important reading for understanding the functions of public education and the meaning of democratic leadership.

Hulburd, David, *This Happened in Pasadena*. New York: Macmillan Company, 1951. Although the book is slanted in favor of the superintendent who lost his position in this community, it represents a powerful example of the difficulties created in the absence of good public relations.

Moehlman, Arthur B., *School Administration*, 2nd Ed. Boston: Houghton-Mifflin Company, 1951. Chapters 2, 6, 20. This chapter covers the role of education in a democracy, principles of operation, and a generalized discussion of social interpretation as an aspect of school administration.

———, *Social Interpretation*. New York: D. Appleton-Century Company, 1938. Chapters 5-6. The principles of interpretation and the policies on which a program should be based are set forth in these chapters.

Mort, Paul R., *Principles of School Administration*. New York: McGraw-Hill Book Company, Inc., 1946. Chapters 2-4, 13, 14, 15. The purposes of American education as well as certain principles of administration are discussed in some detail.

Public Relations for America's Schools, Twenty-Eighth Yearbook. Washington, D.C.: American Association of School Administrators, 1950. Chapter 1. This chapter enumerates the principles which should govern public relations activities.

Reck, W. Emerson, *Public Relations.* New York: Harper & Brothers, 1946. Chapter 1. This chapter outlines the principles to be followed in a public relations program for colleges and universities.

6. Staff Relations

Alison, David, *Searchlight.* New York: Teachers Center Press, 1951. A story of conflict between staff personnel and the Board of Education and the Superintendent of Schools in New York City, this book is an expose of how bad conditions can become within an educational system. How much is truth and how much is fiction remains for the reader to decide for himself.

Barr, A. S., William H. Burton, and Leo J. Brueckner, *Supervision,* 2nd Ed. New York: D. Appleton-Century Company, Inc., 1947. Chapter 12. Discusses several factors which affect the efficiency of teachers.

Elsbree, Willard A., "A Teacher's Lot Can be a Happy One," *Nation's Schools,* 44:29-30. August, 1944. Points out the necessity of good colleague relationships.

Griswold, Glenn and Denny Griswold, *Your Public Relations.* New York: Funk and Wagnalls, 1948. Chapter 33. A brief discussion of employee relations and suggestions for their improvement.

Moehlman, Arthur B., *Social Interpretation.* New York: D. Appleton-Century Company, 1938. Chapters 8-12. Some problems of staff relations are discussed in these chapters, although they are given over to a description of personnel responsibilities in the public relations program.

Nielander, William A., and Raymond W. Miller, *Public Relations.* New York: The Ronald Press, 1951. Chapter 4. Employee relations in business and industry.

Nylen, Donald, and Leland Bradford, "We Can Work Together," *National Education Association Journal,* 37:436-37. October, 1948. Means of changing human relations in schools are pointed out in this article.

Public Relations For America's Schools, Twenty-Eighth Yearbook. Washington, D.C.: American Association of School Administrators, 1950. Chapters 5-7. The chapters listed deal with the school board, superintendent, and school personnel as agents in a public relations program. They contain suggestions on the improvement of internal relationships.

School Board-Superintendent Relationships, Thirty-Fourth Yearbook. Washington, D.C.: American Association of School Administrators, 1956. Chapter 4. Takes up the factors which influence good relationships between the school board and the superintendent.

Spalding, Willard B., *Changing Concepts in Educational Administration,* Forty-Fifth Yearbook, Part II, National Society for the Study of Education. Chicago: University of Chicago Press, 1946. Chapter 4. "Organizing the Personnel of a Democratic School System. A brief but pertinent discussion of ways to improve schools and relations between people within a school system.

Taba, Hilda, Elizabeth Hall Brady, John T. Robinson, and William E. Vickery, *Diagnosing Human Relations Needs.* Washington, D.C.: American Council on Education, 1951. While this book is intended for use by teachers in diagnosing the needs of children and youth, some of the techniques described could be applied to a study of internal relations among staff personnel.

The Public and the Elementary School, Twenty-Eighth Yearbook, Department of Elementary School Principals. Washington, D.C.: National Education Association,

1949. Chapters 1, 3. A helpful discussion of leadership by the principal and the importance of good teachers in public relations.

Tompkins, Ellsworth, *Keystones of Good Staff Relationships*, Miscellaneous, No. 13, Federal Security Agency, Office of Education. Washington, D.C.: U.S. Government Printing Office. (Pamphlet.) In brief, readable style, with appropriate drawings, twelve "keystones" to good staff relations are described. If followed, they should prove helpful in building staff morale.

Wiles, Kimball, *Supervision for Better Schools*. Englewood Cliffs, N. J.: Prentice-Hall, Inc., 1950. Several chapters in this book are devoted to leadership and practices that produce better relationships among members of the instructional staff.

Yauch, Wilbur A., *Improving Human Relations in School Administration*. New York: Harper & Brothers, 1949. Chapters 11-12. These two chapters provide a pointed discussion of the principal's role in establishing good internal relations. Pertinent information on the whole field of relationships within the school is scattered throughout the remainder of the book.

Yeager, William A., *School-Community Relations*. New York: The Dryden Press, 1951. Chapters 7-8. Some attention is given to internal relations of the board, superintendent, principal, and teachers.

7. Pupils and Alumni Relations

Baxter, Bernice, *Teacher-Pupil Relationships*. New York: The Macmillan Company, 1941. Chapters 1-3, 5. An excellent study of teacher-pupil relationships based upon careful classroom observations.

Calvert, Mellie M., "Remember the Grads," *School Executive*, 63:38-39. May, 1944. Lists several techniques employed by a high school for keeping in contact with former pupils.

Emery, James Newell, "Footprints in Concrete," *School Executive*, 63:36-37. January, 1944. The impressions teachers make on pupils are reviewed in this article.

Fargo, Lucile, *The Library in the School*. Chicago: American Library Association, 1947. A detailed consideration of library administration, with many practical suggestions for making the library an important part of the school.

Fordyce, Wellington G., "Alumni Relations," *The Bulletin* of the National Association of Secondary School Principals, 32:241-45. February, 1948. Stresses the value and means for developing better relations with former high-school pupils.

Gage, Daniel D., "Human Personality and Public Relations," *Public Relations Journal*, 6: 13-14, 18. December, 1950. A somewhat technical discussion of personality and the impressions which one individual makes on another.

Gudridge, Beatrice M., *Person to Person*. Washington, D.C.: National School Public Relations Association, 1956. A practical manual, attractively illustrated, for aiding the classroom teacher in improving relationships with pupils, parents, and members of the community.

Hosking, Elizabeth, "Developing Good Human Relations," *School Executive*, 68:51-52. December, 1948. Tells how a teacher establishes good relationships with pupils.

It Starts in the Classroom, A Public Relations Handbook for Classroom Teachers. Washington, D.C.: National School Public Relations Association, 1951. A practical discussion of many practices which influence relationships with pupils.

Jenkens, David H., and Ronald Lippitt, *Interpersonal Perceptions of Teachers, Students, and Parents*. Washington, D.C.: Division of Adult Education Service, National Education Association, 1951. Chapter 4. Report of a questionnaire study concerning relationships between teachers and pupils and the factors responsible for them.

Lindeman, Winifred B., "The School Librarian," *The Library in General Education*, Forty-Second Yearbook, National Society for the Study of Education. Chicago: University of Chicago Press, 1943. Part II, pp. 141-51. An excellent summary of the functions of the librarian and her relationships with pupils, faculty, and outside agencies.

Lipsy, Jack H., "How Much Homework?" *School Executive*, 75:54-55. October, 1955. The author maintains that too much homework may harm a child's health and the school's public relations.

Mosher, Howard W., "If I were a Teacher I would ..." *Nation's Schools*, 49:55-56. June, 1952. An analysis of replies from several hundred senior high school pupils who completed the statement used in the title of this article.

Olson, Willard C., "Human Relations in the Classroom," *National Education Association Journal*, 36:640-41. December, 1947. Contains many suggestions for improving relationships between teachers and pupils.

Orr, Charles W., "Bus Drivers Carry Good Will," *School Executive*, 75:66-67. September, 1955. The author explains how good public relations are inherent in the work of the school bus driver.

Plutte, William, "Introducing the New School," *School Executive*, 76:68-69. January, 1956. A principal points out what can be done when a new high school is opened to establish good relations with pupils and parents.

Public Relations for Teacher Education. Oneonta, New York: The American Association of Colleges for Teacher Education, 1950. Chapter 12. A short chapter on alumni relations.

Rempel, George A., "How the Custodian Operates as a Public Relations Agent," *Nation's Schools*, 56:96, 98, 100. September, 1955. The importance of the custodian's relations with pupils is discussed as well as his relations with staff personnel.

Robinson, Thomas E., "Growing Bouquets in the Classroom," *The Bulletin* of the National Association of Secondary School Principals, 32:207-13. February, 1948. Several practices detrimental to good relations with pupils and parents are discussed.

Roesch, Winston, "The Pupil in Public School Relations," *School of Education Bulletin*, University of Michigan, 27:65-68. February, 1956. The importance of positive relations with pupils and their influence on parent attitudes and understandings of the school are stressed in this article.

Rummell, Frances V., "What are Good Teachers Like?" *School Life*, 30:4-8. June, 1948. An interesting and worthwhile account of several outstanding teachers and the work they did with pupils.

School-Community Relations, 1947 Yearbook, New Jersey Secondary School Teachers Association. Covers several topics which are pertinent to the development of teacher-pupil relationships.

The Public and the Elementary School, Twenty-Eighth Yearbook, Department of Elementary School Principals. Washington, D.C.: National Education Association, 1947. Chapters 2, 7. Attention is given in these chapters to relationships with pupils and the building of adequate instructional programs.

Witty, Paul A., "The Teacher Who Has Helped Me Most," *National Education Association Journal*, 36:386. May, 1947. A summary of answers contained in several thousand letters pertaining to the traits pupils liked in teachers.

8.   Parent Relations

Action for Curriculum Improvement. Washington, D.C.: Association for Supervision and Curriculum Development, 1951. Chapters 3-4. Treats rather well of the opportunities for parent participation in curriculum and school improvement programs.

Anderson, Vivienne, and Daniel R. Davies, *Patterns of Educational Leadership*, Engle-wood Cliffs, N. J.: Prentice-Hall, Inc., 1956. Chapter 5. Parent participation and parent conferences are discussed in this chapter.

Bacon, Margaret H., "Parents, too, are People," *School Executive*, 76:60-61. February, 1956. A parent expresses her views on how relations could be improved between parents and educators.

Baruch, Dorothy, "Parents and Teachers Work Together," *National Education Associa tion Journal*, 30:259-60. December, 1941. As the title suggests, methods are pointed out for teachers and parents to work together.

Dresden, Katherine W., "Selling the Parents," *School Executive*, 61:32. April, 1942. Discusses printed reports used for contacting and informing parents of school policies.

Gabbard, Hazel F., "Parent Participation in the School Program," *School Life*, 30:23-25. December, 1947. Suggestions for teachers and administrators are given for establish-ing friendly relationships and involving parents in the work of the school.

Grant, Eva H., *Parents and Teachers as Partners*. Chicago: Science Research Associates, Inc., 1952. An excellent manual on ways for increasing cooperation between parents and teachers.

Hightower, H. W., "Progress Reports to Parents of Pupils in Primary Grades," *Nation's Schools*, 49:74-76. April, 1952. A discussion of a new and more comprehensive type of report card.

Jenkins, Leo W., "Our Schools' Iron Curtain," *School Board Journal*, 119:20,79. November, 1949. Emphasis is placed in this article on the difficulties of com-municating with parents because of the language educators employ.

Langdon, Grace, and Irving W. Stout, *Parent-Teacher Interviews*. Englewood Cliffs, N. J.: Prentice-Hall, Inc., 1954. A detailed treatment of techniques for conducting successful interviews with parents.

McIntosh, Martha K., and Martha T. Farnum, "Enlisting Parental Interest and Participa-tion," *National Elementary Principal*, 21:363-69. July, 1942. A good account of how parents may be brought into the school program.

Moehlman, Arthur B., *Social Interpretation*. New York: D. Appleton-Century Company, 1938. Chapter 11. Part of this chapter is given over to parent-teacher relationships and means for strengthening home contacts.

Norby, Theo J., and Albert Grant, "A 'Community-Centered' Report Card," *School Executive*, 75:52-54. October, 1955. A report card shown in this article was worked out jointly by parents and teachers.

Ojeman, Ralph H., and Luella Fatland, "Parents and Teachers as Partners," *National Parent-Teacher*, 40:20-3. September, 1945. Practical illustration are found in this article on how cooperation may be developed between home and school.

Place of Visiting Teacher Service in School Program, Bulletin No. 6. Washington, D.C.: U. S. Office of Education, 1945. Contains many good suggestions concerning the place of the visiting teacher in work with pupils and parents.

Robinson, Thomas E., "Visiting Hours—1 to 3:30 p.m.," *Nation's Schools*, 30:23-24. August, 1942. Describes a system followed successfully in an elementary school for conducting parent-teacher conferences.

Schreiber, Nicholas, "Home Visits That Count," *The Bulletin of the National Associa-tion of Secondary School Principals*, 32:177-79. February, 1948. Contains a number of ideas for undertaking successful home visits by teachers.

Smith, William M., Jr., "Educate For Family Life Adjustment," *Pennsylvania School Journal*, 99:319-20. April, 1951. Tells how pupils, parents, and teacher may plan and work together on a program for family living.

The Public and the Elementary School, Twenty-Eighth Yearbook, Department of Elementary School Principals. Washington, D.C.: National Education Association, 1949. Chapter 4. This chapter contains several illustrations of cooperation between parents and teachers and what each should do to facilitate wholesome relationships.

The School Administrator, Physician, and Nurse in the School Health Program, A report of the National Conference for Cooperation in Health Education. New York: Metropolitan Life Insurance Company, 1942. Sections of this report are valuable in defining the work of health officers and considering their relations with pupils and parents.

"What's All the Fuss About Report Cards?" *Changing Times*, 39-42. November, 1955. An explanation of different types of reporting systems and the reasons for them. Suggests parents take part in report card revision studies.

Yauch, Wilbur A., *How Good is Your School?* New York: Harper & Brothers, 1951. A handbook to help parents evaluate the school. It offers many suggestions for parent participation in educational affairs.

Yeager, William A., *School-Community Relations*. New York: The Dryden Press, 1951. Chapter 8, pp. 155-63. Discusses report cards, home visitations, and parent conferences.

9. Community Relations

Alilunas, Leo J., and William Chazanof, "Teachers Get into the 'Community Swim'," *School Executive*, 75:62-64. September, 1955. This article contains several suggestions for helping the new teacher become active in the life of the community.

Bender, James F., *Make Your Business Letters Make Friends*. New York: McGraw-Hill Book Company, Inc., 1952. Sets forth many suggestions for improving the quality of business letters.

Bortner, Doyle M., "Public Relations Begins in the Principal's Office," *School Executive*, 74:68-70. December, 1954. Shows how the organization and personnel of the school office can improve public relations.

Butterfield, William H., *How to Use Letters in College Public Relations*. New York: Harper & Brothers, 1944. This book could be read profitably by public school administrators.

Canfield, Bertrand R., *Public Relations: Principles and Problems*. Homewood, Illinois: Richard D. Irwin, Incorporated, 1952. Chapters 5-6. The value of community relations is discussed from the viewpoint of a local business.

Crambs, Jean D., "Teachers as a Minority Group," *Journal of Educational Sociology*, 22:400-5. February, 1949. Reports the effects on teachers when they are considered to be different from other people in the community.

Effective Letters. New York: New York Life Insurance Company. A bulletin on letter writing published for employees. Based upon a thorough study of the company's correspondence, it is an outstanding piece of work in this field.

Flesch, Rudolph, *The Art of Readable Writing*. New York: Harper & Brothers, 1949. A book which should be studied thoroughly by school people in preparing written material for public consumption.

Fromuth, Carl L., "Please Be Seated," *The Bulletin of the National Association of Secondary School Principals*, 32:81-88. February, 1948. A realistic explanation of the role of the school secretary in public relations.

Gillen, Paul B., "Training Teachers for Active Participation in Solving Community Problems," *Teachers College Record*, 47:323. February, 1946. An illuminating discussion of the need for training teachers to participate in community affairs,

Harlow, Rex, F., and Marvin A. Black, *Practical Public Relations*. New York: Harper & Brothers, 1947. Chapters 19-20. Shows how business success is tied in with the life of the community.

Jefferson, Joyce Lund, "Teacher Participation in Community Activities and Organizations," *Nation's Schools*, 50:77-79. November, 1952. Points out opportunities and advantages of teacher involvement in community affairs and organizations.

Kindred, Leslie W., "Each Employee an Ambassador," *Nation's Schools*, 42:28-29. October, 1948. Considers means for in-service training in public relations to fit local conditions.

Lundborg, Louis B., *Public Relations in the Local Community*. New York: Harper & Brothers, 1950. Chapters 12-19. An excellent discussion of how business people can participate in community affairs.

Lyons, William J., "What the Community Expects of its Teachers," *School Life*, 30:18-19. November, 1947. Points out what the community expects of teachers, and what teachers expect of the community.

Macomber, F. Glenn, and Albert L. Ayars, "Home Town Becomes a Classroom," *School Executive*, 74:41-44. August, 1955. An excellent example of cooperation between educators and industrialists in studying community resources for instructional uses.

Nielander, William A., and Raymond W. Miller, *Public Relations*. New York: The Ronald Press, 1951. Chapters 19-20. These chapters take up the importance of good contacts, good semantics, telephone usage, and correspondence.

Olsen, Edward G., *School and Community Programs*. Englewood Cliffs, N. J.: Prentice-Hall, Inc., 1949. Contains several chapters on various techniques for teachers and pupils to use community resources.

Public Relations for America's Schools, Twenty-Eighth Yearbook. Washington, D.C.: American Association of School Administrators, 1950. Chapter 7. Emphasizes the need for teachers to take part in community affairs.

School Board-Superintendent Relationships, Thirty-Fourth Yearbook. Washington, D.C.: American Association of School Administrators, 1956. Chapter 8. Opportunities for the individual board member to interpret the school through his community contacts are described.

The Public and the Elementary School, Twenty-Eighth Yearbook, Department of Elementary School Principals. Washington, D.C.: National Education Association, 1949. Chapter 5. Points out the social agencies with which the school should work in meeting the needs of children.

Yeager, William A., *School-Community Relations*. New York: The Dryden Press, 1951. Chapters 13-14. Avenues of cooperating with community agencies and organizations are covered in these chapters.

10. Parent-Teacher Association

Brennan, Katherine A., "Variety in Parent-Teacher Meetings," *National Elementary Principal*, 25:93-94, September, 1945. Five different types of parent-teacher meetings are described.

Brown, Muriel W., *Partners in Education: A Guide to the Study of Home-School Relations*. Washington, D.C.: Association for Childhood Education International, 1950. A pamphlet containing many suggestions for increasing community interest in schools and facilitating cooperation.

Bryan, Roy C., and Mildred Beisel, "Vitalize Your High School PTA," *The Bulletin of the National Association of Secondary School Principals*, 40:139-45. May, 1956. Contains several good suggestions for strengthening the parent-teacher association in secondary schools,

Burgard, Earl H., "The Parent-Teacher Association," *Bulletin of the National Association of Secondary School Principals*, 32:246-54. February, 1948. Considers the activities of parent-teacher groups and their effectiveness for school improvement.

Cline, David L., *An Analysis of Public School Citizens' Committees*. Philadelphia: Temple University, 1956. An unpublished doctoral dissertation. Probably the most complete study of citizens' committees available. Treats of all aspects of their origin and operation.

D'Evelyn, Katherine E., *Individual Parent-Teacher Conferences*. New York: Teachers College, Columbia University, 1946. A manual for teachers on methods of conducting conferences with parents.

Dumas, Enoch, "A Parent-School Relations Program," *National Elementary Principal*, 25:95-101. September, 1945. An excellent account of activities used for bringing about better relations between the home and school.

Gabbard, Hazel F., *Working With Parents*, Bulletin 1948, No. 7, Federal Security Agency, Office of Education. Washington, D.C.: U.S. Government Printing Office, 1949. A number of excellent suggestions are contained in this bulletin.

Grant, Eva H., *Teachers and Parents as Partners*. Chicago: Science Research Associates, Incorporated, 1952. A brief manual containing practical suggestions for improving relations between parents and teachers.

Grinnell, J. W., and Raymond J. Young, *The School and the Community*. New York: The Ronald Press, 1955. Chapter 8. A general discussion of the purposes and practices of the parent-teacher association.

Hymes, James L., Jr., *Effective Home-School Relations*. Englewood Cliffs, N. J.: Prentice-Hall, Inc., 1953. Chapters 3-5, 7. A down-to-earth discussion of means available for improving relations with parent groups.

Lane, Bess B., *Your Part in Your Child's Education*. New York: E. P. Dutton and Company, 1948. An excellent reference for ideas on conducting meetings for parents and activities for groups.

Misner, Paul J., "The Parents' Role in Curriculum Planning," *National Education Association Journal*, 37:156-57. March 19, 1948.

Reeder, Ward G., *An Introduction to Public-School Relations*, Rev. Ed. New York: The Macmillan Company, 1953. Chapter 7. Considers the purposes of parent-teacher organizations, types of information needed by parents, and the program of local associations.

Storen, Helen F., *Laymen Help Plan the Curriculum*. Washington: National Education Association, 1946. Illustrates how citizens have worked with educators to make instructional improvements.

The Parent-Teacher Organization: Its Origins and Development. Chicago: National Congress of Parents and Teachers, 1944. Discusses the parent-teacher movement, its history, principles and program.

The Public and the Elementary School, Twenty-Eighth Yearbook, Department of Elementary School Principals. Washington, D. C.: National Education Association, 1949. Chapter 4. This chapter contains examples of parent-teacher cooperation at the elementary school level.

Yauch, Wilbur, *How Good is Your School?* New York: Harper & Brothers, 1951. Written in an appealing style, this book should be read by parents for the help it provides in understanding the school their children attend.

Yeager, William A., *School-Community Relations*. New York: The Dryden Press, 1951. Chapter 17. A general description of the parent-teacher movement and the organization and program of local associations.

11. Citizen Advisory Committees

"Citizens Committees in Action," *The School Executive*, 171:91-98. January, 1952. A digest of work done by advisory groups in several school systems.

Elzay, Jack, "Are Schools Prepared for Lay Participation?" *American School Board Journal*, 125:27-29, 92. September, 1952. A discussion of some dangers involved in working with advisory groups.

Gaumitz, Walter H., "Improving State School Programs Through Cooperation of Laymen and Educators," *School Life*, 30:15-16. December, 1947. Enumerates successful techniques used at the state level for improving education and discusses some major changes made in school laws.

Giadrone, Angelo, *Lay Advisory Committees*. Washington, D. C.: American Association of School Administrators, 1951. A brief, well-written pamphlet on the principal considerations involved in setting up an advisory committee.

Hamlin, Herbert M., *A Charter for a School-Sponsored System of Citizens' Committees*. Urbana, Illinois: Office of Field Services, College of Education, University of Illinois, 1953. A booklet designed to help educators in organizing citizens' advisory committees. Contains practical information and a proposed policy statement under which committees may be formed.

————, *Citizens Committees in the Public Schools*. Danville, Illinois: The Interstate Printers and Publishers, 1952. A comprehensive and scholarly report on advisory committees. It should be reviewed carefully by school administrators and members of boards of education for the suggestions offered in forming and working with lay groups.

————, *The Public and Its Education*. Danville, Illinois: The Interstate Printers and Publishers, 1955. Chapters 21-23. Methods and techniques of citizen study of and participation in schools are treated in these chapters.

How Can Citizens Help Their Schools? New York: National Citizens' Commission for the Public Schools, 1953. The reasons why schools need help are discussed and specific ways outlined on how the Citizens' Commission can help people in their local communities work for better schools.

How Can We Help Get Better Schools? New York: National Citizens' Commission for the Public Schools. A pamphlet listing questions which people forming citizens' committees should ask about their own schools. It is based on the results of workshops sponsored by the Commission. It is excellent and should be consulted by educators as well as laymen.

How Can We Organize for Better Schools? New York: National Citizens' Commission for the Public Schools, 1953. A handbook for guiding citizens' committees in the work of improving schools.

Hull, J. H., *Lay Advisory Committees to Boards of Education in the United States*. Los Angeles: University of Southern California, 1949. Unpublished doctoral dissertation. Results of a questionnaire study of 44 advisory committees. Summary of the findings available from the California Association of School Administrators, 356 South Oak Knoll, Pasadena, California.

Jones, Howard R., "Is Your Community Ready for A Citizens' Advisory Committee?" University of Michigan, *School of Education Bulletin*, 27:20-23. November, 1955. A discussion of factors that determine a community's readiness to use a citizen committee.

Kindred, Leslie W., "Lay Advisory Commission Puts into Effect the Partnership Between School and Community," *Nation's Schools*, 43:43-44. March, 1949. Summarizes the findings of a study of lay advisory commissions.

"Lay Educational Advisory Committees," *Techniques in School Public Relations,* Vol. 4. Washington, D. C.: National School Public Relations Association, March, 1951. A four-page special service publication of the National School Public Relations Association summarizing information on lay committees.

Moehlman, Arthur B., *Social Interpretation.* New York: D. Appleton-Century Company, 1938. Chapter 18. Though written some time ago, this chapter still contains many helpful suggestions on the organization and program of advisory groups.

Public Action for Powerful Schools, Research Studies, No. 3. New York: Metropolitan School Study Council, 1949. A study of how schools may work with the community to solve educational problems.

Ring, Carlyle C., "Cooperation Solves Jamestown's School Building Problems," *School Board Journal,* 132:47-49. January, 1956. A good example of how citizens can be involved in school problems, and the contribution they make.

Russel, Edward J., "When Recommendations Gather Dust, It's Time for Lay Participation," *Nation's Schools,* 50:35-37. July, 1952. An interesting account of how a lay committee came into existence in a school system, and what was accomplished by it.

"Some Pointers For Citizens' Committees," *School Executive,* 71:66-68. January, 1952. Raises and answers several pertinent questions on the organization and operation of citizen groups.

Stegman, William H., "Citizens Study Salary Policies," *School Executive,* 75:54-56. September, 1955. An example of how community leaders and educators may work together to formulate basic salary policies.

Toy, Henry, Jr., "State Citizen Committees Work for Better Schools," *School Executive,* 70:19-22. February, 1951. Covers the advantages of state citizens' committees and cites examples of work they have done.

Venn, Grant, and Zeno, Katterle, "Let's Clarify the Relationship of Administrator and Citizens' Committee," *Nation's Schools,* 49:51-54. June, 1952. As the title suggests, this article takes up several questions concerning citizens, administrators, and staff members. A strong plea is made for the adoption of policies governing activities of advisory committee.

What Do We Know About Our Schools? New York: National Citizens' Commission for the Public Schools. A penetrating collection of questions people ask about their own schools.

Wyatt, Robert H., "State's School Problems are Studied by Citizens," *Nation's Schools,* 42:50-51. July, 1948. Describes the program in state school studies being carried on in Indiana.

12. Organized Community Groups

Brameld, Theodore, *Minority Problems in the Public Schools.* New York: Harper & Brothers, 1946. A study of policies and practices concerning relationships in seven school systems with members of minority groups.

Brownell, William A., "The Three R's and Today's Schools," *Leadership for American Education,* Official Report, 78th Annual Convention, American Association of School Administrators. Washington, D.C.: American Association of School Administrators, 1952. Pp. 105-17. Analyzes current criticisms regarding the teaching of tool subjects in the elementary school and suggests how these criticisms should be met.

"Earmarks of a 'Front' Organization," *Nation's Schools,* 47:29-30, April, 1951. Helpful in detecting organizations antagonistic to public education.

Education—An Investment in People, Washington, D.C.: Committee on Education, U.S. Chamber of Commerce, 1945. A research report showing the relationship between economic status and the educational level of people in this country. Excellent for refuting claims that public education is an expensive investment.

Education and Industry Cooperate. New York: Hill and Knowlton, Inc. A digest of a study concerning opportunities for closer cooperations between schools and industry.

Education Policies Commission, *Moral and Spiritual Values in the Public Schools*. Washington, D.C.: National Education Association, 1951. A useful volume in answering the critics of secular education.

Elicker, Paul E., "How Good Are Our Schools?" *Collier's* 133:78-83. June 11, 1954. The author answers some of the critics of public education, pointing out that schools today are better than they were in the past.

Gillen, Paul B., "Cooperation Between Industry and Schools," *The Public Relations Journal*, 5:11-15. March, 1949. An appraisal of industry's practices of cooperating with schools and how they should be improved.

Grinnell, J. E., and Raymond J. Young, *The School and the Community*. New York. The Ronald Press, 1955. Chapters 9-10. Relations with religious organizations and recent attacks on public schools are treated in these chapters.

Hulburd, David, *This Happened in Pasadena*. New York: The Macmillan Company, 1951.

Jackson, Merrick T., "Industry and Education," *The Public Relations Journal*, 7:3-4, December, 1951. Points out how cooperation between industry and education may be improved.

Lundborg, Louis B., "Public Relations in the Local Community," *The Public Relations Journal*, 6:3-5, 24-26. February, 1950.

McElroy, "Good Schools Are Up To You," *Woman's Home Companion*, 83:26-28, 30, 73. March, 1956. An intelligent discussion of citizen responsibility for the improvement of schools.

Melby, Ernest O., *American Education Under Fire*. New York: Anti-Defamation League of B'nai B'rith, 1951. Exposes the leading organizations behind attacks on schools, their aims and methods. Also answers their attacks.

Melby, Ernest O., and Morton Puner, eds., *Freedom and Public Education*. New York: F. A. Praeger, 1953. A selection of recent articles that make up a program for answering unfair criticisms of public schools and for improving American education.

Moehlman, Arthur B., *Social Interpretation*. New York: A. Appleton-Century Company, 1938. Chapter 19. Enumerates community groups and explains how they can be used for school support.

Partners in Community Enterprise. New York: American Iron and Steel Institute. A brief well-illustrated pamphlet showing how schools and industry may cooperate.

Public Education in a Dangerous Era, Proceedings of First National Congress, Defense Commission. Washington, D.C.: National Education Association, 1953. An overview of attacks on public education and brief reports of committee discussions. Contains an excellent statement on "Textbooks under Fire."

Reuter, E. Edmund, Jr., *The School Administrator and Subversive Activities*, New York: Bureau of Publications, Teachers College, Columbia University, 1951. Useful in considering administrative means for dealing with loyalty problems of teachers.

Robinson, Donald, "The Lesson Our Schools Don't Teach," *Woman's Home Companion*, 82:40-41, 55-58. October, 1955. The author urges that Communism be studied in schools so that children and youth may know what it promises, how it works, and how to keep from being drawn to it.

Scott, C. Winfield, and Clyde M. Hill, ed., *Public Education Under Criticism.* Englewood Cliffs, N.J.: Prentice-Hall, Inc., 1954. A detailed presentation of criticisms made about schools today. Contains suggestions for meeting attacks and defending public education.

Skaife, Robert A., "Groups Affecting Education" in *Forces Affecting American Education,* 1953 Yearbook. Washington, D. C.: Association for Supervision and Curriculum Development, 1953. Chapter 3. The more prominent anti-school groups are listed, and their programs are described.

————, "The Conflict Continues," *Nation's Schools,* 53:44-49. March, 1954. Brings the attacks on schools up to date and the strategies employed by the attacking groups.

Thayer, V. T., *The Attack Upon the American Secular School.* Boston: The Beacon Press, 1951. Perhaps the best analysis available of motives, methods, and criticisms made by religious organizations against the public schools.

"The Textbook in America," *Saturday Review of Literature,* 35:14-23. April 19, 1952. A series of seven articles written from different viewpoints concerning textbooks and the alleged subversive material some contain.

Van Til, William, "Research Affecting Education" in *Forces Affecting American Education,* 1953 Yearbook. Washington, D.C.: Association for Supervision and Curriculum Development, 1953. Chapter 5. Describes the characteristics of a modern school and the research which supports its quality.

What Education Our Money Buys. Albany: Education Conference Board of New York State, 1943. Although published sometime ago, it is a valuable aid in meeting criticisms on school costs.

Whitman, Howard, "Speak Out, Silent People," *Colliers,* 133:23-28. February 5, 1954. An article showing examples of poor school administration. It creates the impression that these examples are typical of all schools, and gives a distorted view of education which is both unfair and dangerous in its effect on public opinion.

Willett, Henry I., "Public Schools Under Pressure," *The Atlantic Monthly,* 194: 57-62. October, 1954. The common criticisms of schools are considered by the author, and suggestions are made on what should be done to meet them.

Wilson, Sloan, "Public Schools are Better than you Think," *Harper's Magazine,* 211: 29-33. September, 1955. A review of what is wrong with critics of public schools and what is right about the schools.

Yeager, William A., *School-Community Relations.* New York: The Dryden Press, 1951. Chapter 14. A classified list of organized groups found in most communities is presented in this chapter.

13. Educational Associations

Bass, Theodore, "The Teacher Association Discovers Its Public," *The Bulletin* of the National Association of Secondary School Principals, 32:202-06. February, 1948. Relates what one local teachers' association does to interpret its program to the public.

88 Techniques in School Public Relations for Teachers and Administrators. Washington: National School Public Relations Association, February, 1951. (Leaflet.)

It Depends on You. Harrisburg: Pennsylvania State Education Association, October, 1952. A leaflet prepared by the Public Relations Committee of the Association for use by teachers to improve their personal public relations.

Lieberman, Myron, *Education as a Profession*. Englewood Cliffs, N.J.: Prentice-Hall, Inc., 1956. Chapter 9. A discussion of the impact of the occupational relationship between teacher and administrator upon their relationship in educational associations.

"Local Education Associations at Work," *Research Bulletin*, National Education Association, 26:101-40. October, 1948. As suggested in the title this bulletin offers suggestions for local associations in building their programs.

"Localized Public Relations," *New Jersey Educational Review*, 25:154-56. January, 1952. A plan whereby local associations may improve their public relations.

Moehlman, Arthur B., *Social Interpretation*. New York: D. Appleton-Century Company, 1938. Chapters 4, 14. Defines the functions of the teaching profession and how it may best work through organized groups to accomplish its purposes.

"NEA Federal Legislative Policy as Defined in the NEA Platform and 1952 Resolutions," *National Education Association Journal*, 41:479. November, 1952. Indicates the scope of legislative interest taken by the National Education Association.

Public Relations for America's Schools, Twenty-Eighth Yearbook, Washington, D.C.: American Association of School Administrators, 1950.

School-Community Relations. Trenton: New Jersey Secondary-School Teachers Association, 1947. A manual for the instruction of members in public relations.

State Education Associations—Their Organization, Programs, and Staffs in 1947-48. Washington, D.C.: National Education Association. Research Division, 1948. (Mimeographed.) Helpful in getting a picture of what state associations are doing and in appraising their programs.

Summary of Reports of Committees, Commissions, and Council. Washington, D.C.: National Education Association, 1952. A good overview of the work carried on by the National Education Association through its major committees and commissions.

Teacher and Public, Eighth Yearbook. Washington, D.C.: Department of Classroom Teachers, National Education Association, 1934. Describes the role of the National Education Association in interpreting the profession to the public and the part that may be taken in this program by state and local associations.

Why They Teach and Quit. Columbia, Missouri: Missouri State Teachers Association, 1948. A pamphlet outlining, in attractive form, the needs of the teaching profession and the problems that face it. Intended for popular consumption.

14. Student Activities

Boone, W. R., "Student Activities that Count," *The Bulletin* of the National Association of Secondary School Principals. 32:117-23. February, 1948. Analyzes the public relations value of student activities.

Brier, Howard M., "The School Paper is a Public Relations Medium," *School Executive*, 73:84-85. March, 1954. The author illustrates the possibilities of the school paper as an interpretative device.

Chisholm, Leslie L., *The Work of the Modern High School*. New York: The Macmillan Company, 1953. Chapter 15. A general discussion of the background and types of student activities found in secondary schools.

Douglass, Harl R., *Modern Administration of Secondary Schools*. Boston: Ginn and Company, 1954. Chapters 9, 10, 11. A thorough treatment of problems related to the administering of extracurricular activities.

Edmonson, J. B., Joseph Roemer, and Francis L. Bacon, *The Administration of the Modern Secondary School*, 4th Ed. New York: The Macmillan Company, 1953.

Chapters 14, 15. A discussion of factors influencing the organization and administration of student activities, together with a description of the various types.

Grinnell, J. Earle, *Interpreting the Public Schools.* New York: McGraw-Hill Book Company, Inc., 1937. Chapter 11. The author explains how extracurricular activities help to interpret the school.

Hand, Harold C., *How to Conduct the Hidden Tuition Costs Study*, Circular Series A, No. 51, Illinois Secondary School Curriculum Program Bulletin No. 4. Springfield: Superintendent of Public Instruction, 1949. An inventory of the items to look for in determining what pupils must pay to participate in the extracurricular program.

———, *How to Conduct the Participation in Extra-Class Activities Study*, Circular Series A, No. 51, Illinois Secondary School Curriculum Program Bulletin No. 5. Springfield: Superintendent of Public Instruction, 1949. This inventory illustrates the scope of student activities in secondary schools today.

Handbook of the National Junior Honor Society of Secondary Schools. Washington, D.C.: National Association of Secondary School Principals, 1954. Detailed description of the activities of this student organization.

It Starts in the Classroom. Washington, D.C.: National School Public Relations Association, 1951. Pp. 43-50. Tells how relations with parents and the community may be improved through extracurricular activities.

Jacobson, Paul B., ed., *The American Secondary School.* Englewood Cliffs, N. J.: Prentice-Hall, Inc., 1952. Chapter 11. Points out how extracurricular activities may be improved.

Koppenhoefer, H. L., "The Junior Fourth Estate," *The Bulletin* of the National Association of Secondary School Principals, 32:124-131. February, 1948. A brief but excellent discussion of the role of student journalism in school public relations.

Moehlman, Arthur B., *Social Interpretation.* New York: D. Appleton-Century Company, Inc., 1938. Chapter 15, Pp. 300-12. Considers the Public relations value of specific student activities and discusses some of the limitations and dangers of the program.

Nickerson, Madge, and Marion S. Hamlet, "Planning a Graduation program," *The Bulletin of the National Association of Secondary School Principals*, 28:84-95. April 1944. A description of a new-type commencement program and an explanation of how it was developed.

Reavis, William C., and others, *Administering the Elementary School.* Englewood Cliffs, N.J.: Prentice-Hall, Inc., 1953. Chapter 6. This chapter takes up the educational objectives of extra-class activities and describes some which are suitable for the elementary school.

Student Councils Handbook. Washington, D.C.: National Association of Secondary School Principals, 1948. Presents a detailed description of the work done by student councils.

15. School Publications

Blueprint for Action. Washington, D.C.: National Association of Educational Secretaries, 1955. Contains many suggestions of practical worth in preparing a staff handbook.

Dale, Edgar, and Jeanne S. Chall, *A Formula for Predicting Readability.* Columbus, Ohio: Bureau of Educational Research, Ohio State University, 1948. A widely-used readability formula.

Flesch, Rudolf F., *How to Test Readability.* New York: Harper & Brothers, 1951. A popular formula for checking readability and not too difficult to apply.

————, *The Art of Readable Writing*. New York: Harper & Brothers, 1949. Contains many excellent suggestions on factors associated with the readability of written material.

Gray, William S., and Bernice E. Leary, *What Makes a Book Readable?* Chicago: University of Chicago Press, 1935. One of the earlier readability formulas.

Griswold, Glenn and Denny Griswold, eds., *Your Public Relations*. New York: Funk and Wagnalls Company, 1948. Chapter 22. Presents some of the considerations which enter into the production of company or internal publications of business and industry.

Grinnel, J. Earle, *Interpreting the Public Schools*. New York: McGraw-Hill Book Company, Inc., 1937. Chapters 8, 9. Although published sometime ago, these chapters are useful in preparing annual reports and internal publications.

Gunning, Robert, *The Technique of Clear Writing*. New York: McGraw-Hill Book Company, Inc., 1952. The first part of the book contains a readability formula which is practical and easy to apply.

Lorge, Irving, *The Lorge Formula for Estimating Grade Placement of Reading Materials*. New York: Teachers College, Columbia University, 1952. (Mimeographed.) Useful in checking the readability of school publications.

Maurello, S. Ralph, *Commercial Art Techniques*. New York: Tudor Publishing Company, 1952. Discusses and illustrates design, layout, lettering, and other essential points in illustrating publications.

Moehlman, Arthur B., *Social Interpretation*. New York: D. Appleton-Century Company, 1938. Chapter 22. A discussion of purposes, types, editorial methods, and circulation of publications.

Munson, Gorham, ed., *Best Advice on How to Write*. New York: Hermitage House, 1952. Brings together many suggestions for improving the readability of publications.

Nielander, William A., and Raymond W. Miller, *Public Relations*. New York: The Ronald Press, 1951. Chapter 22. Discusses briefly principles and practices underlying the publication of house organs in business and industry.

Print It Right. Washington, D.C.: National School Public Relations Association, 1953. A practical handbook on the preparation of publications.

Petrilli, Thomas, *Photo-Offset Production of School Publications*. Newark, New Jersey: American Graphic, Inc., 1952. A brief manual on copy layout and design for offset printing.

"Planning the Annual Report," *School Executive*, 66:51-62. May, 1947. A section containing articles by superintendents and others on all phases of the annual report.

Rand, M. J., and Lambert W. Baker, "A Small School Can Publish Annual Report," *Nation's Schools*, 52:53-55. September, 1953. A story of how a small, impoverished school district published an annual report.

Reeder, Ward G., *An Introduction to Public-School Relations*, Rev. Ed. New York: The Macmillan Company, 1953. Chapters 5, 6.

Rice, Arthur H., ed., *Today's Techniques*, First Yearbook, School Public Relations Association. Ann Arbor, Michigan: Ann Arbor Press, 1943. Pp. 193-253. These pages cover detailed suggestions, well illustrated, on art work, layout, and printing of school publications.

Sigband, Norman B., "Put Some 'Bang' in Your Annual Report," *School Executive*, 72: 59-61. June, 1953. Steps for preparing an annual report are discussed together with devices for increasing its attractiveness and readability.

Skillin, Marjorie E., and others, *Words into Type*. New York: Appleton-Century-Crofts, Inc., 1948. Helpful in preparing a publication on matters of style, headings, type, and so forth.

Spear, Mary E., *Charting Statistics*. New York: McGraw-Hill Book Company, Inc., 1952. Helpful in selecting various types of charts and graphs for simplifying and presenting statistical data.

Thorndike, Edward L., and Irving Lorge, *The Teacher's Word Book of 30,000 Words*. New York: Teachers College, Columbia University, 1944. A basic word list for checking the readability of vocabulary in school publications.

16. Newspaper Publicity

Ambler, Mary Grace, "School Journalists Keep Community Informed," *Nation's Schools*, 52:64. October, 1953. Describes the system in Abington Township, Pennsylvania, by which pupils participate in gathering, preparing copy for, and reporting school news.

Andrews, Mary G., "Partners in Publicity," *Bulletin* of the National Association of Secondary School Principals, 32:160-70. February, 1948. Contains several practical suggestions for handling school, newspaper publicity.

Benjamin, John P., "Is Your School Message Being Told?" *School Executive*, 72:74-75. September, 1952. Discusses school news which editors of local papers want.

Canfield, Bertrand R., *Public Relations: Principles and Problems*. Homewood, Illinois: Richard D. Irwin, Inc., 1952. Chapter 15. Though written for business organizations, many of the suggestions in this chapter are applicable to schools.

Curtis, Alice Partlow, *Is Your Publicity Showing?* Scranton: International Textbook Company, 1949. A handbook for nonprofessional publicity chairman. Easy to read and attractively illustrated.

Fine, Benjamin, *Educational Publicity*, Rev. Ed. New York: Harper & Brothers, 1951. Chapters 1-9, 13-14, 16, 20. An excellent source of information on educational publicity.

Fine, Benjamin, and Vivienne Anderson, *The School Administrator and the Press*. New London, Connecticut: Arthur C. Croft Publications, 1956. A manual on what school-news stories editors want and how to meet their requirements.

Fry, Harrison G., "The Newspaper Editor Looks at School News," *Bulletin* of the National Association of Secondary School Principals, 32:171-76. February, 1948. Points out how school and press may work together in reporting educational news.

Gaskie, Jack, "Bridging the Gap Between Schools and the Press," *School Executive*, 75:58-59. April, 1956. A newspaper reporter explains how better relations may be developed with the press.

Grinnel, J. Earle, *Interpreting the Public Schools*. New York: McGraw-Hill Book Company, Inc., 1937. Chapters 4, 5. These chapters take up the main points in recognizing, gathering, and reporting school news.

Gross, Neal, *The Schools and the Press*. Cambridge, Massachusetts: New England School Development Council, 1956. A study of the relationships between newspapermen and school administrators in New England. An important document for school administrators interested in better press relations.

Harlow, Rex F., and Marvin M. Black, *Practical Public Relations*. New York: Harper & Brothers, 1947. Chapters 22, 23. Discusses the place of publicity in the public relations program and the importance of the press.

Harral, Steward, *Patterns of Publicity Copy*. Norman: University of Oklahoma Press, 1950. A small book containing many helpful suggestions for persons who handle educational publicity.

Horn, Gunnar, *Public-School Publicity*. New York: Inor Publishing Company, Inc., 1948. Chapters 1-19. A readable series of chapters on how to prepare school news stories.

Let's Go to Press. Washington, D.C.: National School Public Relations Association, 1954. (Pamphlet.) A well-illustrated and written pamphlet outlining ideas and practices for reporting school news.

Moehlman, Arthur B., *Social Interpretation*. New York: D. Appleton-Century Company, 1938. Chapter 21. The viewpoint presented here differs somewhat from that found in other discussions of school, newspaper publicity.

Randolph, Richard W., "Community Press—An Important Medium," *Public Relations Journal*, 7:14-15. November, 1951. Tells how a civic organization makes effective use of newspaper publicity.

Reeder, Ward G., *An Introduction to Public-School Relations*, Rev. Ed. New York: The Macmillan Company, 1953. Chapter 3. A general treatment of the importance and methods of reporting school news.

School Board-Superintendent Relationships, Thirty-Fourth Yearbook. Washington, D.C.: American Association of School Administrators, 1956. Chapter 7. Relations between the superintendent and the local press are covered rather well in this chapter.

The Superintendent, the Board, and the Press. Washington, D.C.: American Association of School Administrators, 1951. (Booklet.) An elemental but practical statement concerning school news and press relations.

Woodman, D. K., "The Birds and Bees of Press Relations," *Nation's Schools*, 57:59-61. April, 1956. A newspaper editor talks directly about the kinds of news from schools that people will read.

17. Audio-Visual Aids

Allen, W. Paul, "Better School Exhibits," *School Board Journal*, 115:22-23. October, 1947. This article presents many practical suggestions for preparing school exhibits.

Brownell, Clifford Lee, Leo Gans, and Tufie Z. Maroon, *Public Relations for Education*. New York: McGraw-Hill Book Company, Inc., 1955. Chapter 12. Takes up types of radio and television programs suitable for school sponsorship.

Callahan, Jennie Waugh, *Television in School, College, and Community*. New York: McGraw-Hill Book Company, Inc., 1953. One of the most helpful books available to school people interested in television. Discusses in detail the establishing of an educational TV station, programming, writing-production techniques, and telecasting techniques for public schools.

Dunham, Franklin, "Radio vs. Television in Schools," *School Life*, 35:115-16. May, 1953. The respective merits of each medium are pointed out in this article.

"Educational TV: A Bargain in Dayton," *Broadcasting, Telecasting*, 48: 52-53. March 7, 1955. Tells how one community undertook educational television on a limited budget.

Griswold, Glenn and Denny Griswold, eds., *Your Public Relations*, New York: Funk and Wagnalls Company, 1948. Chapters 24, 25. Metods of using audio-visual aids in public relations are outlined in these chapters.

Harlow, Rex F., and Marvin M. Black, *Practical Public Relations*. New York: Harper & Brothers, 1947. Chapters 16, 17. These chapters pertain to the use of radio and motion pictures for public relations work.

Haverstick, John, "Tools for Teaching: The 3-D Classroom," The Saturday *Review*, 30:29-33. February 19, 1955. An interesting account of how schools are using audio-visual aids and the trend toward their use in the future.

Henry, Nelson B., ed., *Mass Media and Education*, The 53rd Yearbook, National Society for the Study of Education, Part II. Chicago: University of Chicago Press,

1954. Chapters 4, 5. Chapter 4 deals with the importance of motion pictures in mass media, while chapter 5 takes up the development of broadcasting and its importance in society.

Horn, Gunnar, *Public-School Publicity.* New York: Inor Publishing Company, Inc., 1948. Chapters 23, 24. Relations with radio stations and the broadcasting of school news are treated in these chapters.

Jolly, Fred R., "A Sound Slide Presentation for Plant Visitors," *Public Relations Journal,* 7:19. January, 1951. Tells how one company used sound slides and the subjects covered.

Kieffer, Robert de, and Lee W. Cochran, *Manual of Audio-Visual Techniques,* Englewood Cliffs, N. J.: Prentice-Hall, Inc., 1955. Illustrates and clarifies the use of audio-visual equipment.

King, William H., "New Jersey has learned How Educational TV works," *Nation's Schools,* 53:88, 90, 92. June, 1954. Points out what was learned in developing educational television programs in New Jersey.

Levenson, William B., *Teaching Through Radio.* New York: Farrar & Rinehart, Inc., 1945. Chapters 3, 4, 5, 8, 9. A practical book based on the author's experience with radio in the Cleveland public schools. Contains special chapters on recordings and public relations broadcasting.

Newsom, Carroll V., ed., *A Television Policy for Education,* Parts IV, V. Washington, D.C.: American Council on Education, 1952. A volume reporting the experiences and experiments of educators who have used television. A wide range of topics is covered, including plans for educational TV stations, costs of educational TV stations, programming, and so forth.

Seehafer, E. J., and J. W. Laemmar. *Successful Radio and Television Advertising.* New York: McGraw-Hill Book Company, Inc., 1951. Many helpful suggestions may be secured from this book on the technical side of programming.

Suggested References in Educational Television. Washington, D.C.: Joint Committee on Educational Television, 1954. This bibliography includes books, periodical articles, reports, pamphlets, and surveys dealing with educational television.

This is Educational Television. Washington, D.C.: National Citizens' Committee for Educational Television. A brochure describing the background and implications of educational television. It also tells the story of how educational television stations were developed in four communities.

Waldon, Gloria, "Information Through Film," *Public Relations Journal,* 5:8-12, 30-31. August, 1949. Points out the advantages of films in mass education and the different types of 16 mm films produced today.

Wetter, Allen H., and Martha A. Gable, *Report of Radio-Television Activities,* Philadelphia: The Board of Public Education, 1954. An annual report of radio and television activities conducted by the public schools of Philadelphia. Discusses program planning, properties, special expenses, manuals for teachers, evaluations of programs, workshops, and cooperation with parents.

Williams, Dorothy E., and S. F. W. Morrison, "School Radio Programs—An Adventure in Public Relations," *Nation's Schools,* 54:88-90, 94. September, 1954. An account of how a school tells its story over the air in two, fifteen minute broadcasts a week.

Wittich, Walter A., and Charles Francis Schuller, *Audio-Visual Materials: Their Nature and Use.* New York: Harper & Brothers, 1953. Chapters 10, 11, 13, 14, 15. One of the better textbooks on various audio-visual aids and their uses.

Woodhouse, C. G., "Let Education Speak for Itself," *NEA Journal,* 41:488-89, November, 1952. How radio spot announcements can be prepared and delivered by students.

18. Special Events and Services

Aderhold, O. C., and Joe A. Williams, "Use of the School Plant by Adults of the Community," *School Executive*, 67:49-50. June, 1948. Shows how the school may be used by adults for their own education and recreation.

Adult Education Ideas, "Know Your Population Groups." Washington, D.C.: Federal Security Agency, Office of Education, 1949. (Leaflet.) A brief, but detailed description of how to analyze the educational needs and interests of adults.

Ashby, Lloyd W., "The Cheltenham Adult School," *School Board Journal*, 131:26-27. July, 1955. An adult education program which functions independently of but in cooperation with the school system.

Bliss, Sidney M., "An Essential Step—Publicity and School Building Programs," *School Board Journal*, 118:24-26. January, 1949. Contains detailed instructions on how to win school bond elections.

Bowes, Elmer G., "Welcome to Our Parents' Night," *School Executive*, 75:47-49. November, 1955. A well-arranged program designed to help parents understand the school.

Brownell, Clifford Lee, Leo Gans, and Tufie Z. Maroon, *Public Relations for Education*. New York: McGraw-Hill Book Company, Inc., 1955. Chapter 13. The details of demonstrations and exhibitions are considered in this chapter.

Campbell, Roald F., and John A. Ramseyer, *The Dynamics of School-Community Relationships*. Boston: Allyn and Bacon, Inc., 1955. An excellent discussion of how citizens may take part in the study of their schools. Several illustrations are presented.

Carder, W. H., "Port Townsend Adventure in Good Community Living," *School Board Journal*, 117:23-24, 80. October, 1948. An account of how a recreational activity center was developed for youth.

Day, Bess, "A Career Day as Public Relations," *School Board Journal*, 121:20-22, 96. September, 1950. Points out the value of inviting businessmen to discuss careers with high-school students.

Garber, Lee O., "May a School Board Spend Its Funds to Publicize a Board Election?" *Nation's Schools*, 53:84-85. April, 1954. A significant court case is discussed concerning the authority of school boards to spend public money promoting a district election for building improvements.

Gilson, Goodwin W., "Special Services for the Public," *The Bulletin* of the National Association of Secondary School Principals, 32:214-25. February, 1948. Enumerates several special services schools may perform in the public interest.

Grinnell, J. E., and Raymond J. Young, *The School and the Community*. New York: The Ronald Press, 1955. Chapter 14. A discussion of the nature and value of public exhibits and performances.

Halverson, J. John, "An Adventure in Public Relations," *School Board Journal*, 119:24-25. October, 1949. Tells how community leaders were invited to spend a half-day at the school and what they derived from their visit.

Hiller, Ola B., "Flint's Community Schools," *School Executive*, 75:41-44. November, 1955. An example of how a school system attempted to meet the recreational and social needs of a community.

Holler, Clifford F., "A Successful School Bond Election," *School Board Journal*, 132:32. April, 1956. Explains how the school bond issue was handled.

How Can we Conduct a Winning Campaign? Handbook. New York: Nation Citizens' Commission for the Public Schools, 1955. A practical guide to campaigning for school bond issues.

"Improving Communities," *School Executive*, 71:77-81. March, 1952. A report on community improvements sponsored by schools.

Locke, John F., "The Observance of Special Days," *Techniques*, Volume 3, No. 1. Washington, D.C.: School Public Relations Association, January, 1950. Special days for observances are listed by months and suggestions made for celebrating them.

Miller, Graham R., and Gerald J. Willsea, "Denver Citizens Help Plan Their Schools," *Nation's Schools*, 49:56-60. May, 1952. An example of how citizens may be involved in the planning of new buildings and what their ideas are worth.

Moehlman, Arthur B., *Social Interpretation*. New York: D. Appleton-Century Company, 1938. Chapter 23. A good chapter on the school plant and its public relations value.

Morris, J. E., "This Audio-Visual Department Serves the Community," *Nation's Schools*, 52:72-74. August, 1953. Tells how special audio-visual services are provided for the community by a school system.

Ostrander, Raymond H., "Community Recreation Programs and Their Relation to Schools," *School Executive*, 71:19-22. July, 1952. Treats of the need for recreation and the procedures for developing recreation programs.

Reeder, Ward G., *An Introduction to Public-School Relations*, Rev. Ed. New York: The Macmillan Company, 1953. Chapters 10, 11, 12. Points out the place of the school plant in public relations.

Rich, Kathryn, "In Adult Education, It's Mass Media Tools," *School Executive*, 73:82-83. September, 1953. Describes the use made of radio and television by the Division of Adult Education, Schenectady, New York Public Schools.

Smaage, Leon, "Open House Tells a Story," *School Board Journal*, 132:69-71. March, 1956. An example of how open house for a new school building can aid in acquainting people with the educational program.

Taylor, Ted L., "How to Stage an Effective Parents' Night," *School Executive*, 70:43-45. April, 1951. The elements that enter into a successful open house program are described in this article.

"The Intensive Campaign," *Techniques*, Volume 3, No. 2. Washington, D.C.: School Public Relations Association, April, 1950. A newsletter outlining steps to follow in conducting an intensive campaign for a bond issue.

Wilson, Raymond G., "A Thousand Parents for Open House," *School Activities*, 19:93-94. November, 1947.

Working on the Levy. Seattle: Washington Education Association. Summarizes the findings of a study on why some campaigns succeed and others fail to secure voter approval.

19. Organizing and Administering the Program

Bainbridge, F. W., II, *A Checklist for the Evaluation of Public Relations Programs of Public Secondary Schools*. Auburn, Alabama: School of Education, Alabama Polytechnic Institute. Tries to determine the status of public relations programs through their philosophies and practices.

Campbell, Floy J., "PR and the School System," *The Public Relations Journal*, 8:6-7. March, 1952. An account of how the Oklahoma City Schools use public relations to build public understanding of the educational program.

Canfield, Bertrand R., *Public Relations: Principles and Problems*. Homewood, Illinois: Richard D. Irwin, Inc., 1952. Chapter 2. Organization for business public relations is described as well as the responsibilities of the director.

Fine, Benjamin, *Educational Publicity*. New York: Harper & Brothers, 1951. Chapter 10. This chapter deals with the administration of a public relations office.

Hedlund, Paul A., "Measuring Public Opinion on School Issues," *American School Board Journal*, 116:29-31. April, 1948. Outlines an inexpensive method for measuring public opinion on school issues.

Hickey, John M., "Organizing Effective Public Relations," *The Bulletin* of the National Association of Secondary School Principles, 32:59-72. February, 1948. Presents charts of different types of organization for school public relations.

Kindred, Leslie W., "Each Employee an Ambassador," *Nation's Schools*, 42: 28-29. October, 1948. Points out types of in-service training in public relations.

———, "Planning for Tomorrow," *The Bulletin* of the National Association of Secondary School Principals, 32:305-10. February, 1948. A summary of points to consider in planning a public relations program.

Miller, Delmas J., *An Appraisal Technique for Programs of Public School Relations*. Pittsburg: University of Pittsburg, 1943. Unpublished doctoral dissertation. An instrument for judging public relations activities according to underlying philosophies.

Moehlman, Arthur B., *Social Interpretation*. New York: D. Appleton-Century Company, 1938. Chapters 8-12. Outlines the responsibilities of personnel in the program.

Nielander, William A., and Raymond W. Miller, *Public Relations*. New York: The Ronald Press, 1951. Chapters 27, 29. These chapters describe the work of the public relations director in business organizations and outline the steps in program building.

Parten, Mildred, *Surveys, Polls, and Samples*. New York: Harper & Brothers, 1950. Chapters 2-3. A thorough and practical discussion of how to plan and what methods to use in securing information from the public.

Public Relations for America's Schools, Twenty-Eighth Yearbook, Washington, D.C.: American Association of School Administrators, 1950. Chapter 11. A brief enumeration of techniques for evaluating the program.

Reynolds, Conger, "How We Did It," *The Public Relations Journal*, 7:8-9. June, 1951. Describes a training clinic for advertising and public relations representatives.

"Report on a Study of Public Relations Programs of 55 Food Companies in the United States," *The Public Relations Journal*, 6:7-11. December, 1950. A factual report on various aspects of public relations activities in the companies surveyed.

Seyler, Louise W., *A Rating Scale for School-Home Relationships*. Los Angeles: Board of Education, 1948. A rating scale for use in the elementary school field.

Whittlesey, E. D., "Public Opinion and Public Relations," *The Public Relations Journal*, 5:23-29. July, 1949. Discusses the importance of knowing the climate of public opinion, and explains how it affects good public relations performance.

Wright, J. Handley, "Planning the PR Program," *The Public Relations Journal*, 8:5-6, 12. July, 1952. A general discussion of how business public relations programs are planned.

Index